CHAMELEON HOURS

PHOENIX
POETS

CHAMELEON HOURS

ELISE PARTRIDGE

THE UNIVERSITY OF CHICAGO PRESS
Chicago and London

ELISE PARTRIDGE was born in Philadelphia and educated at
Harvard and Cambridge, where she was a Marshall Scholar,
and at Boston University and the University of British Columbia.
Her poems have appeared in American, Canadian, and Irish
journals, including *Poetry*, the *New Yorker*, the *New Republic*,
the *Southern Review*, *Southwest Review*, *Slate*, the *Fiddlehead*,
the *New Quarterly*, and *Poetry Ireland Review*. Her first book,
Fielder's Choice, was published in 2002. A dual citizen of the
United States and Canada, she has taught literature and writing
at several universities and currently works as an editor and tutor.

The University of Chicago Press, Chicago 60637
The University of Chicago Press, Ltd., London
© 2008 by The University of Chicago
All rights reserved. Published 2008
Printed in the United States of America
17 16 15 14 13 12 11 10 09 08   1 2 3 4 5

ISBN-13: 978-0-226-64791-3 (cloth)
ISBN-13: 978-0-226-64792-0 (paper)
ISBN-10: 0-226-64791-9 (cloth)
ISBN-10: 0-226-64792-7 (paper)

Library of Congress Cataloging-in-Publication Data
    Chameleon hours / Elise Partridge.
        p. cm.
    Poems.
    ISBN-13: 978-0-226-64791-3 (cloth : alk. paper)
    ISBN-10: 0-226-64791-9 (cloth : alk. paper)
    ISBN-13: 978-0-226-64792-0 (pbk. : alk. paper)
    ISBN-10: 0-226-64792-7 (pbk. : alk. paper)
    I. Title.
    PR9199.4.P373C47 2008
    811'.6—dc22   2007033072

♾ The paper used in this publication meets the minimum
requirements of the American National Standard for
Information Sciences—Permanence of Paper for Printed
Library Materials, ANSI Z39.48-1992.

To Steve

verray parfit

Contents

Acknowledgments · *xi*

ONE

Everglades · *3*
Two Scenes from Philadelphia · *4*
Phoenixville Farm · *6*
1959 · *8*
Group Portrait · *9*
The Artists' House · *11*
In the Barn · *13*
Thirteen · *14*
Two Monuments · *15*
First Death · *16*
Miss Peters · *18*
Mia's House · *19*
Supermarket Scanner · *21*
Temp · *23*
For a Father · *25*
Elegy · *26*
The Secret House · *27*
Caught · *29*
One Calvinist's God · *30*
Plague · *31*

TWO

Gnomic Verses from the Anglo-Saxon · 35
Four Lectures by Robert Lowell, 1977 · 36
Sisyphus: The Sequel · 40
Philosophical Arguments · 42
Depends on the Angle · 44
Insights · 45
As I Was Saying · 47
Arcadia · 48
Rural Route · 49
Dislocations · 50
Song: The Messenger · 52
The Book of Steve · 53
August · 58
Buying the Farm · 59

THREE

Cancer Surgery · 63
Prognosis: 50-50 · 64
A Valediction · 65
Room 238: Old Woman and Hummingbird · 67
Chemo Side Effects: Memory · 68
Chemo Side Effects: Vision · 70
Childless · 72
Forty-Eight Years · 73
Granted a Stay · 75
First Days Back at Work · 76
Chameleon Hours · 77
Ways of Going · 78
Farewell Desires · 80

FOUR

    Home Is the Sailor · *83*
    For Jenny · *84*
    The Runt Lily · *85*
    Since I Last Saw You · *86*

FIVE

    World War II Watchtower · *91*
    Crux · *92*
    Pauper, Boston, 1988 · *94*
    Vuillard Interior · *96*
    Where Your Treasure Is · *97*
    US Post Office, December 22 · *98*
    Two Cowboys · *100*
    Ruin · *101*
    Heron, Tampa · *104*
    Tested · *106*
    Epitaph for Diane · *108*
    Edwin Partridge · *109*
    Snail Halfway Across the Road · *110*
    From Feste's Self-Help Book · *112*
    Unknown Artists · *114*
    Phoenix · *116*
    Snapshots of Our Afterlife · *117*
    Small Vessel · *118*

    Notes · *119*

Acknowledgments

I would like to thank the editors of the following American, Canadian, and Irish journals and anthologies in which these poems (or versions of them) have appeared, sometimes with different titles:

AGNI: "Plague" (no. 45)
Books in Canada: "A Valediction," "The Book of Steve"
Boulevard: "Insights"
The Cream City Review: "Ruin"
Descant: "Miss Peters"
Event: "Where Your Treasure Is"
The Fiddlehead: "Granted a Stay" (appeared as "Why Did I Live?"), "August,"
    "Caught," "Chameleon Hours," "Farewell Desires," "Phoenixville Farm,"
    "The Artists' House"
Maisonneuve: "Buying the Farm"
The Malahat Review: "1959"
The New Republic: "Four Lectures by Robert Lowell, 1977" (appeared as "Four
    Lectures by Robert Lowell," 1981)
The New Quarterly: "Childless," "Prognosis: 50-50," "Room 238: Old Woman
    and Hummingbird," "Tested"
The New Yorker: "Chemo Side Effects: Vision," "First Days Back at Work"
Notre Dame Review: "Gnomic Verses from the Anglo-Saxon," "Philosophical
    Arguments"
Poetry: "Rural Route" (appeared as "Burkettville, Maine," December 2000),
    "Pauper, Boston, 1988" (December 2000), "As I Was Saying" (October 2005),
    "World War II Watchtower" (October 2005)
Poetry Ireland Review: "Epitaph for Diane" (appeared as "Elegy"), "Arcadia,"
    "Group Portrait," "In the Barn," "One Calvinist's God"

Poetry Northwest: "Dislocations"

Slate: "Elegy"

The Southern Review: "Edwin Partridge" (appeared as "A Gentle Man"), "Snapshots of Our Afterlife," "The Secret House," "Ways of Going"

Southwest Review: "First Death"

Tar River Poetry: "Everglades"

The Tennessee Review: "For a Father"

TickleAce: "Unknown Artists" (no. 40)

"Two Monuments" first appeared on the Yeats Society of New York website, www.yeatssociety.org.

"The Runt Lily" first appeared on the Parliamentary Poet Laureate website, Canada; thanks to John Steffler.

"Vuillard Interior" first appeared in the anthology *In Fine Form*, edited by Kate Braid and Sandy Shreve (Raincoast, 2005).

"A Valediction," "Caught," "Everglades," "In the Barn," and "Ways of Going" were published in *The Broadview Anthology of Poetry*, 2nd edition, edited by Herbert Rosengarten and Amanda Goldrick-Jones (Broadview, 2008). "Gnomic Verses from the Anglo-Saxon" was published in *The Best of Notre Dame Review: Poems and Stories from Notre Dame Review,* edited by John Matthias and William O'Rourke (Notre Dame University Press, 2008). "A Valediction," "Buying the Farm," "Plague," "Ruin," and "The Book of Steve" were published in *The New Canon: An Anthology of Canadian Poetry*, edited by Carmine Starnino (Signal Editions, Véhicule Press, 2005). "Four Lectures by Robert Lowell, 1977," "One Calvinist's God," "Rural Route," and "Two Scenes from Philadelphia" were published in *The Echoing Years*, edited by John Ennis, Stephanie McKenzie, and Randall Maggs (Waterford Institute of Technology, 2008). "As I Was Saying," 'Buying the Farm," and First Death" were published in *The Anansi Reader*, edited by Lynn Coady (House of Anansi Press, 2007).

I am grateful to Poetry Daily for republishing "Edwin Partridge" (under the title "A Gentle Man"); and to Garrison Keillor for broadcasting "For a Father," "Rural Route," and "Supermarket Scanner" on *The Writer's Almanac*.

The poem used as an epigraph to "Since I Last Saw You" is "Seeing Off Yuan Er on a Mission to Anhsi," by Wang Wei, translated by Red Pine. It is included in *Poems of the Masters: China's Classic Anthology of T'ang and Sung Dynasty Verse* (2003) and reprinted by permission of Copper Canyon Press, www.coppercanyonpress.org. Thanks to Red Pine, Joseph Bednarik, and Copper Canyon.

The following poems from *Fielder's Choice* are used by permission of Signal Editions, Véhicule Press: "1959," "Caught," "Elegy," "For a Father," "Rural Route," "Ways of Going," "Everglades," "Plague," "Two Scenes from Philadelphia," "Phoenixville Farm," "Group Portrait," "The Artists' House," "In the Barn," "The Secret House," "One Calvinist's God," "Gnomic Verses from the Anglo-Saxon," "Four Lectures by Robert Lowell, 1977," "Philosophical Arguments," "Pauper, Boston, 1988," "Supermarket Scanner," "Temp," "Arcadia," "Insights," "Dislocations," "The Book of Steve," "August," "A Valediction," "Two Monuments," "Ruin," "Epitaph for Diane," and "Unknown Artists." Thanks to my editor at Signal Editions, Carmine Starnino.

I am indebted to the Canada Council for the Arts for a grant that assisted me in completing this book; and to the nurses, doctors, and staff at the British Columbia Cancer Agency, who also ensured it could be completed.

I am deeply grateful to the writers, scholars, and editors who offered keen criticism—Ken Babstock, Jeredith Merrin, Barbara Nickel, Christopher Patton, Robyn Sarah, and Patrick Warner; and to the University of Chicago Press—to its anonymous manuscript-readers; to Lindsay Dawson and Rebecca Sullivan; and to my editor there, Randolph Petilos.

Warm thanks to other friends and to family, for interest and insights. For generous help with particular aspects of this book, thanks to Marjorie Townsend Tompkins and Tim Tompkins. For unstinting help with all of it, many thanks to Stephen Partridge. And many thanks to my teacher, Robert Pinsky.

ONE

Everglades

Nothing fled when we walked up to it,
nor did we flinch,
even at the hobnailed gators sunning two-inch fangs,
a licorice-whip snake slipping over our shoes.
The normally secretive clapper-rail
appeared under our boardwalk
glancing this way and that,
casual as a moviegoer hunting for a seat.
Tropical, temperate, each constituency spoke—
the sunburned-looking gumbo-limbo trees
nodded side by side with sedate, northern pines.
Even the darkness gave its blessing
for the moonflower to open under its aegis.
A bird swaying on a coral-bean
sang two notes that might have been "Name me."

Two Scenes from Philadelphia

1. Valley Forge, 1777–1778

Thanksgiving rations, the second year of the war:
a quarter-cup of rice, a dash of vinegar.

Twenty-five barrels of flour; twelve thousand men.
One feasted for two days on a fist-sized pumpkin.

Sentries stood on their hats to warm their feet;
the officers' horses shuddered under needling sleet.

One of three soldiers wintering lost his life.
New Year's morning, a ten-year-old played the fife.

2. *Victorian Interior*

The French windows were swathed with mauve-gray drapes,
ends gathering on plum rugs in velvet folds
reflected in a ten-foot gilt-framed mirror
above the stag crowning the étagère,
black, lacquered cabinets japanned with ivory,
a pinch-stitched mauve petitpoint fireplace screen.
Carved rosettes above brass chandeliers
which Belfast maids kept glinting with their dusters
trapped, in their arabesques, each gram of soot.
Silver brushes etched with swirled initials
lay poised by "hair receivers" on vanities—
crystal jars for collecting straying wisps
to be woven into wreaths or framed in jet.
The door to the master bedroom's marbled bath
was diamonded with ruby stained-glass panes;
on the rosewood desk's ebonized veneer,
Trollope was propped with guides to English dogs.

Phoenixville Farm

for Anne

Each subdivision lawn bore the same shrubs
with minor variations—scraggly, full—
and timid bands of housefinches we glimpsed
through drapes drawn to protect chintz parterres.
Each spring every family on the block
would weed-whack, edge, clip, prune, spray, rototill,
fumigate ants, squash snails. And each fall,
rakes would be dragged jabbing through balding yards,
leaves crammed in plastic bags for Sanitation.
Indoors, forced narcissi sat on sills
by velvet-napped violets; off-white walls wore
oils of red-coated hunters clutching whips.
Guppies flicked bored beside their plastic castles;
bored to anxiety, gerbils quaked in tanks.
We ate peas dribbled from cans, pale canned pear-halves,
sogged blobs of peaches in viscous syrup.
The change of seasons was marked by switching off
or on the central AC's monotone thrum.

At Anne's, nothing was mowed; Queen-Anne's lace
bobbed all over her yard. Buck, her tick-prone hound,
set our agenda, baying us around the farm.
We'd sprawl in wild mustard, withers to withers,
companionable as old cows; breathe deep
skunk-cabbage reek from humming scum-slick ponds
where frogs with hurdlers' thighs zapped gnats and belched.

Hawks tensed above us. We gobbled blackberries
off stabbing vines, smearing our faces purple,
sucked dandelion milk. We warmed wet hands
in the hunter's belly-fur, gouged clean the hoof
that had shattered a rib; watched lambs yank udders;
tried to nurse fledglings, their bodies tufted lumps
of wrinkled dough, each eye a bugging bruise.
A hen might shriek up from a garbage can;
we'd stroke four fresh eggs in a slide of feed.
Burnt-orange flashing in the back field—
a fox, glaring: What are you doing here?
Anne showed us how to scoop a bludgeoning hornet
with one palm from a pane and fling it free,
how baby spiders rappelled down a shed wall.
At dusk the bats that were dangling like berets
from the barn eaves chittered through sycamores;
one moon-white night we chirred around the yard
after a trundling family of raccoons,
the pond throbbing with peepers, *here here here here.*
When parents came next morning to pick us up,
we lay like glossy eggplants in the garden,
white sneakers gobbed with dung. We wanted to hide
like spitbugs in fizzing clots, tuck ourselves in
all winter under a pinecone's sticky eaves.
Some day, some day—we'd each spin sleeping bags,
doze for six weeks, thrust, gnaw, unkink striped wings,
try out our newborn feelers, lurch to Anne's farm,
bathe in dust puddles, lay eggs, and worship weeds.

1959

In the basement:
damp black linoleum, mildewed walls.
But freshly-washed diapers whiten this table.
Clean will reign!
The woman who never raises her voice
launches her whole weight
into scouring a stain.

Her hissing iron
lunges over a scrap of white.
Left, right, left, right,
tight little jabs at the corners
subduing a handkerchief
into a perfect square.
She holds it up like a banner,
aligns it on a stack.
There.
She seizes a crumpled shirttail.

All day,
the spigot weeps, pipes keen;
and, in the dryer's window, arms flail.

Group Portrait

for Marjorie

Great-grandmothers in stern black shoes,
frowning in photos at the beach,
the granddaughter you raised still lives
within your wagging fingers' reach.

One widowed too young, one who mopped
parquet floors as the mayor's maid,
you sailed for the new world by yourselves;
longed for your Belfast families; stayed.

You brought two snapshots of the Causeway;
combs—one silver, two tortoiseshell;
a hard conviction that the pint,
or one cigarette, could lead to Hell.

You taught my mother not to whine,
never to lie. She was to brush her hair
one hundred strokes; act "ladylike";
sit up straight in every chair.

(Only in my mother's dreams
could she shake at you a matted mane,
swing like a gibbon through the woods,
wreck her best shoes in pouring rain.)

I can tell you that the little girl
you cared for never has disobeyed;
she still feels you watching her,
shades under the umbrella's shade;

if she got an urge to throw a plate,
sit down for days, do nothing but cry,
she'd see your bone needles flashing
out of the corner of one eye,

tell over gifts from Providence,
tuck each graying, wispy hair
back into place; start a new task;
make those stooping shoulders square.

The Artists' House

for Ruth K. Fackenthal

Their peeling porch was shaded by bamboo,
a talkative, clacking stand.
The scruffy yard was strewn with cinderblocks—
stages for minstrel flocks
of cardinals, robins, jays.
Under her tire swing, daylilies grew.
We navigated the rhododendron's maze
where Ruth could cup a bumblebee in one hand;
we braided lanyards out of plantain shoots,
watched spiders spinning egg sacs between the beech's roots.

Inside, Ruth's whole family hung on the walls.
In the study Uncle Clint,
unfinished, clutched a glove, a blob of white.
The house wore forest-twilight,
its air tangy with paint.
The upstairs ambled off in crooked halls,
the door to one hung with a crack-faced saint,
the other with a Rauschenberg aquatint.
Ivy crept under one sill across the floor
where swathed old couches sat like longboats hauled ashore.

The kitchen paper revealed, beneath its flaps,
two plaster continents nudging,
a giant with a dozen bulging eyes.
There we boiled green dye,

yellowed a sweatshirt with bark tea,
pinched flour-and-water mixtures into maps:
a lopsided Mount Everest, twin galaxies.
We improvised mobiles—blown eggs and string;
dabbed posterboard with paint-smeared slices of limes;
built masks for Halloween out of paste and shredded *Times*.

On freezer wrap we traced a mushroom's spores;
under the blurry lens
of her junior microscope we squinted at stalks,
eyelashes, slivers of chalk.
Mornings we overheard
her mother humming through her studio door;
sometimes we'd catch a word.
Each day we got out pastels, charcoal, pens
and India inks, in every shade, tone, hue—
boarded the longboats, chose our colors, hummed, and drew.

In the Barn

One morning, on the mud floor of the barn,
we found a snake glittering in the sun—
ten inches patterned like an argyle sock,
black diamonds on gray. Puffing beside his neck

was a red bubble. No—wait—then we saw
he had a frog clamped in his propped jaw.
The bubble was blood. The frog sat elbows-out,
inscrutable, a drowsy magistrate

hearing a plea. His skin was mottled brown,
dark mud splattered on light. His eyes were open,
gold-rimmed, fixed. He blinked; the eyes looked moist.
His neck bulged; the oversized mouth seemed set.

Desperate-eyed, the cows stared up at us,
clinking linked chains, swaying in their stalls.
The snake glanced sideways, but he couldn't budge,
avid, like we were, edging nearer to watch.

At last the frog looked uncomfortable,
as though trying to be dignified. Willful,
the snake was helpless too, frog jamming his jaw.
We ran when a calf started to bawl.

Thirteen

We whacked each other up and
down on seesaws; bashed
a kickball straight into pink lilac.
Waltz-jumped, obedient; in packs swept the rink—
Heidens, hurtling, crouched
into shoot-the-duck.

Shouted out the answers in long division.
Raised twin turreted cities from brown paper.
Feet on handlebars, racing, plummeted
lanes. Hair spiked with burrs all day.
Sockless to choir.

We gawked at forbidden words in the OED,
dared the smoking
breath of a tethered bull.
But almost overnight
shrinking, wary,
we edged like testing cats who clung to a wall—

it was as though we'd bounced, yelling,
up,
and before we bounded off Jen's trampoline
our teams were redivided:
pretty or not.
Earthward, staggering, reaching, reeled, thirteen.

Two Monuments

1. The Tomb of the Unknown Soldier

White marble. Rolled sod.

Black-shod guard: shining shoes
glide up and down red carpet.

The charger's bronze lip curls.

Inside the colonnaded rotunda,
under a Latin diadem,
cases of medals and rosettes.

2. Battlefield

One-room museum:
a letter from an eighteen-year-old, bragging
we'll whup 'em yet!

His dingy, bullet-shredded epaulet.

The wire-rim glasses and dog-eared Bible
of the grandmother who refused to leave her house
when the battle started.
(She died at noon under an exploding shell.)

A grasshopper clinging to a swaying stalk.

A mower roaring over the field.

First Death

for Renée Sicalides

Jean's father died one morning before school
—the first parent we knew to go: a stroke.
She came, red-faced, blank-eyed, to crew that day;
we lugged our racing eight to river's edge.
The honey-varnished hull was balsa-frail—
thrust a heel wrong, you'd splinter through to cold.
We teetered from the slip, clutched inch-wide gunwales,
balancing on one leg like storks; tied in;
brushed past the safety rope, slack as a clothesline,
unraveling by the eager waterfalls.
Jean, who stroked the boat, drove upriver;
all backs coiled with hers, our shoulders strained.
Putt-putting after in a stubby tin launch,
black anorak, black megaphone, our coach.

We shivered under the gloom of a railroad bridge
where kids lobbed chunks of coal at startled boats
and swaying snakes of boxcars, dried-blood red,
rattled away to their obscure horizons.
Two-mile warmup; we slid to rest by the isle,
riding uneasily on the shifting current.
A mallard family bobbed nearby, the male
off on his own, neck-sheen green changeable silk.
What could we say? "Jean—how're you doing?"
Amelia, seven-seat, leaned to pat her arm.
When Karen started a story about her dad,

Irene poked her, brightly changed the subject.
In silence we sat half-listening to the coach—
"Let's try some moves to help you stay together"—
kept glancing at Jean, trying to steady the boat.

One bridge to go; past its black arch, the river,
fast that day, funneled into a froth;
if we weren't careful, we'd ricochet
off squeezing rocks. "Hold water, port!" The cox
yanked the card-size rudder till it nicked the hull.
We were veering, light as a pencil. "Starboard,
pull! Come *on*," Jean cried. "Trying!" yelled Marie.
The boat, a minute-hand, swung stiffly; stuck,
dragging. Dig in, dig in, dig in—*heave*—

at last our bow sat pointing south. Time-trials:
edge to the racecourse starting-line. Blades poised.
"*Partez!*" 38 strokes a minute,
surging, burning, settle, surge, take it up—
"Seat three, you're late. Six, you're late, keep time!"
The cox's clapper clapped like a lone drum,
we skidded with the wind, lost Coach's voice,
churned one blistering power-ten at the end,
then sagging, past the stands. Waves smacked our blades.
The dirty orange finish-line flags flap-flapped.
What could we do for Jean? Nothing. Nothing!
She was the first. "Follow!" the cox was crying,
"Two miles to home! Stay together now,
together!" Our oars left purling circles
that blended, blended; blended; began to fade.

Miss Peters

1900–1967

She strode the parish house in a black cassock—
she'd been allowed to become a deacon.
Occasionally she'd read the day's collect,
her white hair barely visible over the lectern's eagle.
She wrote Canterbury, arguing for priesthood.

"Women can serve the church in so many ways,"
the bishop intoned at a diocesan convention.
She was put in charge of Christian Education.
She chose the angels for the Christmas pageant,
got the Altar Guild reading Sir Thomas Browne.

Now, not far from the Gothic narthex
where she used to straighten, exasperated,
the Youth Choir's robes: "You are a priest forever
after the order of Melchizidek"—
she had it cut into her upright stone.

Mia's House

Summers, the fans would swing their wire faces,
fluttering bureau-scarves—Battenburg laces,

a gilt-edge table runner, pale green linen.
Winters, behind her headboard, she'd hear scrabbling—

squirrels shuffling hoards of nuts. A scratch; pause;
sudden frantic scrapings of delicate claws.

Ivory-cheeked Doulton figures posed in nooks.
Tooled-leather, slipcased, embossed, uncut books;

two marble putti clutching grapes of jade
entwined under a fringed lavender shade.

The former owner's nursery—pink walls, pink floor,
pink-and-white lambs floating across the door—

she used for storing shoes, boxed, in rows,
pink tissue wadded in old spectator toes.

She kept her mansion spotless; lived alone,
flashing slick selves, like mica flakes in stone,

to visitors. She loomed, a French armoire;
skittered, an overlooked dustmouse, behind the bar....

At night the squirrels would jump, hearing her scream.
"Where's Mia?" she shouted in a frequent dream

that vanished under the sofa's claw-and-ball,
rolled like rain off roses flocking the walls.

Supermarket Scanner

Grocery-checkstand
pair of hands:
staring down,
she scans
chocolate bars,
a dozen cans
of "French-style" peas,
jars—mayo, jam . . .
schooled to please
customers shifting
foot to foot—
Good morning, ma'am!
Block of lard,
celery, cola—
barely twenty-one,
no time to scan
—a pack of gum,
debit card—
a human face,
no moment free
to ask the regular
how she is,
the muttering man—
Your Time is Money!
Our checkers' speed
is guaranteed!

Six ears of corn—
worked here three years,
(her mother was
a checker too)
—frozen pound cake—
no better jobs
except the mill.
Powdered milk,
"Improved! NEW!"
puppy kibbles,
large squeeze
bottle of cheese
with coupons
FREE!
carton of Trues,
the plastic sack,
crisp new bills.
Eight customers
watch her arrange
the eggs, the cans,
potato chips
and hand them back.

Temp

For once the bus hadn't been late.
She pressed "Up" at half-past eight,
boarded, stood with averted eyes
as the panelled cage began to rise.
She watched the gleaming silver doors
parting to show identical floors
painted a flat oyster white,
pebble-gray rugs, fluorescent light.
A briefcase and two suits stepped off.
Pinstriped shoulders; stifled cough. . . .
Every week the agency sent
her somewhere new. At Capital/Hente,
she squinted at computer screens,
circling wholesale orders in green.
At Sadwell-Smythe she answered phones
in their blush-pink atrium, alone.
For Prudence Insurance, nine to three,
she tapped in data on an old PC
(hospital stays, rations of pills).
At the gas company she issued bills.
Every week, at each new place,
she'd smile at an adjacent face,
people who might or might not say "hi"
when, going for coffee, they rushed by.
Lunch was a sandwich wrapped in foil,
cans of cola that quietly boiled;

by two she'd swept her desktop clean.
She knew the quirks of copy machines,
she had paced miles and miles
fetching, replacing needed files;
jotted minutes by model ships,
reordered the fat bulldog clips
the VP liked, retrieved his faxes,
proofread printouts on sales taxes. . . .
This building had a penthouse garden
where you could light up. At 3:10
she stepped out between potted trees
and concrete benches. A wan breeze
blew soot her way. Black, gray, dun,
skyscrapers fenced each horizon.
Sparrows pecked at croissant crumbs;
some giant generator thrummed.
3:25, back at her station,
she double-checked the pagination
of reports that had to be couriered
by 4 p.m.; retyped a word;
glanced at her book for tomorrow:
Twelfth Street, tenth floor, D. F. Snow.

For a Father

Remember after work you grabbed our skateboard,
crouched like a surfer, wingtips over the edge;
wheels clacketing down the pocked macadam,
you veered almost straight into the neighbor's hedge?
We ran after you laughing, shouting, Wait!

Or that August night you swept us to the fair?
The tallest person boarding the Ferris wheel,
you rocked our car right when we hit the apex
above the winking midway, to make us squeal.
Next we raced you to the games, shouting, Wait!

At your funeral, relatives and neighbors,
shaking our hands, said, "So young to have died!"
But we've dreamt you're just skating streets away,
striding the fairgrounds toward a wilder ride.
And we're still straggling behind, shouting, *Wait—!*

Elegy

Sixty years I've lived, hardly a cross word said!
(The carpenter found, behind their bed,
a crawl-space where black snakes had bred.)

Each of the Ten Commandments, I kept.
(Broom jabbing, she frantically swept
at filth that flowered while she slept.)

No one can ever say I told lies.
(She faded below her cracking disguise,
fixed as a dead-leaf butterfly's.)

I gave my love to each and all.
(Hoarded in a locked closet down the hall
hatreds muffled by a paisley shawl.)

I never let myself complain.
(Gallons of tears, a wet winter's rain,
whirled at the brim of the churning drain.)

I had the life I wanted to have.
(She stepped unborn into her grave.)

The Secret House

Then is it sin
To rush into the secret house of death
Ere death dare come to us?
— SHAKESPEARE, *Antony and Cleopatra*,
IV.xv.80–82.

Could yours be the Greek Revival façade
glimpsed through this moss-draped avenue of oaks?
The upper-porch balusters are knocked out like teeth,
starlings circle chipped ceiling medallions.
I thought I heard footsteps—
it must have been a deer
startling itself on the old springhouse floor.
At dawn the whole estate was repossessed by fog.

Or maybe it's the farmhouse off the highway
with a roof like a squashed hat,
a stoop defended by blackberry bramble.
Straw juts from the second-floor eaves,
floursack curtains sag in one window.
In the back field I found a tractor, its seat a rusty scoop,
marooned by a barn unshingling itself.

Perhaps you've moved to some spectral subdivision—
buff garage doors, air conditioners exhaling,
TVs exuding polar-cap blues.
I heard one car snuffle off, thought I saw blinds jiggling.
Your house might be any one in the series,
impassive behind its interchangeable mailbox.

I hope that it's the place you've always longed for—
clapboard, ramshackle, gabled,
views of a sapphire chip of bay,
goldfinches tussling in the lilac bush.
A swing sways on your white front porch,
your threadbare sneaks awry below it,
an aria spirals out a side window,
friends are laughing in your exuberant garden.

I hold my breath approaching the door,
wondering if you'll welcome me.
But it's too dark for me to see inside,
and only blackbirds answer my call.

Caught

One wing-tip was stuck to one silk thread.
He ran his six legs through thin air
like a cartoon character,
wrenching
his abdomen to his jerking head.

But the shivering web wouldn't give way.
It had been spun in a couple of hours,
wired casually to a flower.
The fly
writhed above the vetch for half a day.

The spinner was nowhere to be found.
A woodchuck had ripped the web at dawn,
the spider long since skittered on.
He'd start
a new web, elsewhere, once the sun went down.

The glued fly kept flailing. He rubbed his eyes,
kicked himself into a tiny ball,
a trapeze artist, swung loose, fell—
snagged, on
the lowest strand. Twirled; hung, as if surprised.

One Calvinist's God

Your deity was as patient as a heron,
watching and waiting, as if he could stand for a week
without trembling once on those old-man's legs;
then with one jab of his beak

stab you and gulp. Or, a bald eagle, he'd hunch
on a pine snag or barnacled dais of rock,
scowling, scanning the shore for a newborn duck
to scoop from the flock.

Even the hopping robin who tilted one eye
as though listening at blades of grass put you on guard,
in case he should snap you, a thread writhing
from your white-fenced yard.

One midnight, you imagine, you'll be swept up,
a mouse off a toadstool, shrieking into the air;
gathered by ice-pick talons to his tweedy breast,
his yellow-eyed glare.

Plague

Heal-all, yarrow, alum-root,
sweet annie, angelica, hazel shoots;
swinging in foxgloves' purple bells
secrets to make a sick heart well—
at the eastern farm we waded flowers
and herbs renowned for healing power.
Lemon verbena, spearmint beds,
feverfew blooms nodded heads
as I strolled into the waving wood.
Dim, plicking, laundromat-humid;
mosquitoes—motes blown into flight—
almost casually swirling to bite.
Two pinks caught my eye. I bent down.
Caterpillars were going to town
on a faltering stem, bodies slung
underneath like sloths'. The feet clung;
the heads chewed. Four gnashed a meal
under a spray of Solomon's seal
whose white drops quivered. Paired prongs,
the front legs worked like icemen's tongs
curving to stab. Rear-guard pylons,
flat-soled, gray, dutiful cousins,
helped shiver along the elegant back,
blue-and-red pustules edged with black.
Veering into a sunny aisle
—magenta balm, white chamomile—

I saw dozens more, heads like helmets
bobbing over lambs-ears' velvet.
Medicinal ferns were brewed for tea
to soothe sore throats, cure pleurisy —
their two-inch, humping, whiskered lines
writhed over the naturalists' signs.
They sprawled under spindly buds
of red-root, used to strengthen the blood;
a jewelweed's freckled orange scoops
hung by gnawed leaves, spicebushes drooped—
whirling, peering, now I could see
worms glued to boles on every tree.
Plicks I'd thought were rain in my ears
sounded like cuts of tiny shears—
their migrant, hungry, sticking strips
made, as I stood there, saw-toothed rips
in thousands more seedlings. Soon
they'd each find twigs and start to spin;
one moonrise not too far from this,
fresh from a cracking chrysalis,
their tawny, fluttering selves would come
tilting to this wild geranium,
alight on fewer, finer legs
and discharge arsenals of eggs.

TWO

Gnomic Verses from the Anglo-Saxon

adapted and selected

Kings shall rule kingdoms. Winter cold is keenest,
summer sun the most searing,
fall freest with her hand. Fate is almighty.
The old are wisest. Jewels must stand upright
in winking bezels, blades break on helmets,
hawks hunch on the glove, the huffing boar
wander the woods with the ragged wolf.
Truth tells itself always, gold to each man.
Salmon spawn in northernmost streams,
the king in his castle gives his cronies rings;
bears haunt the heath, hastening water
floods the rolling fields of the downs.
Lovers meet in secret, monsters skulk
in the swamp, stars seed the sky.
The troop stands together, a glorious band.
Light lunges at dark, life parries death,
good clashes with evil, the old with the young,
army against army battles for the land;
all of us wait in the Lord's arms
for the decree he ordains, darkly, in secret.
Only God knows where our souls will go.

Four Lectures by
Robert Lowell, 1977

On "Repose of Rivers" by Hart Crane

"What's the plot?
The Mississippi flowing to the sea,
and Crane going from childhood to death.
One of his clearest and his greatest poems,
much quieter than the other we just read.
The river speaks the poem;
the river's washing out to sea
like your own life—the river's doomed,
all childhood memories, washing out to sea
to find repose. The sapphire's the sea,
remorseless, sinister, hard. Angels might
flake sapphire—that might be one of their jobs.
He's taunting you with paradise.
The willows do hold steady sound, and yet
they don't; the sea's fulfillment of a kind,
the end of life. . . . Don't read this just as death-wish;
Crane was unusually full of life."

On "The Yachts" by William Carlos Williams

"This starts as terza rima; here his lines
are much longer than usual. Very few poems
attempt a narrative; you have to do it
plainly, like a sports reporter would.
Is it a satire, against yachts? Or are
they made quite beautiful? What's horrible
about the race, the competition?
(I think he must have watched basketball games.)
The yachts here could be women, thoroughbreds—
anything beautiful trampling over all
it doesn't notice. Beauty's terrible,
expensive, skillful . . . 'arms' . . . they're desperate.
Greeks when they sank a ship mowed the survivors
down, or speared them; the yachts just pass over.
Seems supernatural, doesn't it?
                                        These two
extremes of writing, Williams, Crane—do you
imagine Crane was maddened by this stuff?
He rather liked it, though. Crane could never
describe a yacht, and Williams thought
he was all rhetoric.
                                Two modernists:
Williams was breaking old metrical forms,
and using new material; Crane had read
Rimbaud, brought thunder and obscurity."

On "Out of the Cradle Endlessly Rocking" by Walt Whitman

"Most operatic thing he ever wrote,
a tour de force, probably about something. . . .
What?—I mean personal. Two thrushes, one dies:
imagine someone Whitman was in love with,
lost. The beginning's all one sentence, highly
organized musically, but loose writing,
as Whitman practiced. Tempting to scan; you can't.
The cradle is the sea. It's very odd,
original without one's knowing why.
If you want to say these things, it's falling rhythm.
The ostensible sorrow is the boy
discovering death, desertion. . . . (I'd
be talking through my hat, if I had one on.)
And often rhythmical musical things
aren't good, they're padding for not feeling. What
prevents that here? It's awfully eloquent
wherever you pick it up. 'From such as now
they start the scene revisiting': this has
a tender Pindaric grandeur—I don't know
if you can say that. It's about a child—
that's not a Whitman subject, childhood.
His saddest poem in some ways. Hard to think
that birds meant very much to him. . . ."

On "Goodbye My Fancy" by Walt Whitman

"'Goodbye My Fancy' he intended as
his last poem . . . you're too sick to write your last
poem, when the time comes. Clear and elegant—
except for some of the language, and the meter,
it could be seventeenth-century.
Your eyes water, reading it."

Sisyphus: The Sequel

You pushed it up the hill every day.
Shoved your shoulder against it, sprained
your back.
Finding indentations on its surface,
you dug your fingernails in till they bled.
You invented a device to nudge it

                                           up.

Tried to hire a mercenary to
heave it.

And every day the stone trailed you down.
Some days, bouncing,
it taunted you. Often it pursued
you like a Fury,
a one-rock avalanche.

You begged it for mercy,
sat on it, ate on it, spat on it.
More than once you thought,
                "let it crush me."

But gradually, grudging,
you began to ease it tenderly.
Its freckles you knew like a face's.
Your calling was to take it in your arms.

One dusk you crouched,
bracing yourself
for the bound back down.
A minute passed
as you massaged your calves, hardly noticing.
Five minutes, six—
you hauled yourself over the crest beside it,
laid your palms against it like a physician.
Suspiciously you waited.
                    It didn't move.

Afraid of letting one flare of hope char you,
            you huddled below.
It sat immobile
for hours, a
new-laid egg.

At dawn, you started to laugh.
            Flopped sideways, weak with laughter.

Days later, tapping crisply with a chisel,
you slice a hunk, striped with agony's chevrons.

Philosophical Arguments

You are ushered expeditiously through the average
down immaculate halls of a Roman austerity
till you are guided into the presence of the
Conclusion, enthroned.

Solid samples can be Bauhaus-predictable—
you watch the next *whereas*
being hauled into place like
a prefab hunk of pyramid.

Sophisticals may awe the initiate
like Piranesi *carceri:*
pillared pomp and rhetorical balustrades
flourish upward to no landing.

The spurious quiver, particleboard amalgams,
reproduction façades lit by ersatz lampposts
a challenger could dismantle with a
snort.

But then there are those
with thousands of years of graffiti
looping their colonnades—

discipular additions
dot their grounds like huts,

paragraphs are
balconies;
pages, plazas:

at the courtyard fountain, pilgrims—
the mother at night-school, the seeker, the browser,
the plumber logging on from the Yukon—
cup their hands
and taste.

Depends on the Angle

Woke to find a brown lump
hunched on the curtain rod,
three-inch peeled
gap in the screen—
bat.
       Malevolent blot,
gargoyle
blighting my daisied lace—
       some sleep-of-reason monster
           cruising for changes of scene.

Aimed to whap him out.
At first he tried to squeeze
sideways; then dove
through the glaring room
bleating—
       squeaking—
pleading—
       eave, corner, sill, sill, eave—
       while some red-eyed, ghost-white monster
           shrieked after him. Chucked a broom.

Insights

for Derry Lubell

They arrive unbidden
on nobody's schedule
acorn-size illuminations
plinking into your lap

often incongruous
as if some many-hued wine
variegated the last slurp of pop in your can

anonymously bestowed
as flyers shoved into your chest on the street
cometlike
occasionally they flicker forward in schools

frequently they unscroll themselves
when you're in the middle of something else—
you're gasping as Pavarotti hits a high note from Paris,
a tornado warning flashes across the screen
you're a bear trudging around a campsite
and suddenly you get lucky: a cooler!
or, among the day's usual receipts,
out of the blue, a ticket to agony

the plates of your being tilt
relationships may quiver
like parts of a mobile trembling

into a new suspension
the fine guy-wires
tethering you to your current life
are loosened   tautened

they ping gently like wind chimes
with earlier visitations

sometimes unwelcome in their initial offerings
fended off like malarial mosquitoes
only later do they appear
in their true guise—
the butterfly that applauded on your blistered toe
when you were straining up that mountain

parachutes jerking open
the silken rustle of their sudden knowledge
depositing you in a changing field

As I Was Saying

Blotched undercarpet (no carpet) the hue of lead.
A pilfered coaster
welded to a sill.
Sooty cupboards. One dented
plastic bear rigid with honey.
Nightlong *scritch-scratching*— an anxious mouse
cowering in the crumb pan of his toaster.
The back door bore a Zorro-slash of mustard.

Oh, how sweetly he sang when he wanted
to borrow your money!
While you scurried for work,
he toppled his latest pickups into your bed.

A hundred lists you etched: How I Can Improve.
So what did you think—that was love?
Why didn't you do what I said?

Slit open his mattress, insert two stinking trout,
tip last week's beer over his speakers
and light out.

Arcadia

Everything at your farm was new to me—
nub-wing ducks tipping around a nest;
leaf-hands reaching from a sassafras tree;

and even guinea hens seemed charming there—
shrieking across the yard, dewlaps flapping,
while the shepherd mutt dozed on in his chair.

I learned, that summer, not just to walk by
when hummingbirds backpedaled an instant
catching the sweetness from a flower's eye;

to notice what I'd never have seen
without your love—fields seared for second growth;
a beetle ambling in Thai silk, turquoise-green.

Rural Route

He picked three dozen quarts, starting at dawn;
died suddenly in the garden. "Around one,
he had a stroke—I found him, but he was gone—."
He left a widow, three daughters and six sons.

Two days later, widow and children, at dawn,
picked forty dozen. They ate, washed, dressed;
buried him in the churchyard just after one.
Early the next day, they picked the rest.

Dislocations

During the last hurricane
an iguana
found only on one atoll
was pitched with his comfy palm

and swept bobbing over the Caribbean
to another landfall,
where when he debarked
he discovered he was the only one of his kind.

The monarch aiming for Mexico
winds up in Billings,
this bug that inched into a shipment of tires
at Galveston
is sniffing the Montréal dock with bewildered antennae;

you're a seed snagged
in a cat's whisker,
a pollen-nub
saddlebagged by a bee
that bumbled into an orchid
thinking—it had the right markings—
it was his beloved. . . .

Tipped on the sidewalk
like a tree with its root-ball
swathed in burlap,
your tendrils
tangle so tightly around themselves
they refuse the offerings
of the new soil.

What a surprise
to find
that after all
you're bound to leaf:

if the walls won't stay where they
are, you learn, like Astaire, to flourish across the ceiling;

this starling's heritage
may have been to nibble dropped brioches
in the Tuileries, but
look at her now, making a virtue of necessity
with a bag of cheese curls in the Bronx.

Already you're a hybrid,
you feel your strengths intermingling
like rivers braiding,
you're startled as the young tree
that suddenly keeps finding peaches at the end of its limbs.

Song: The Messenger

*Love dispatched its messenger, who summoned her to
love him.*
— MARIE DE FRANCE, *Eliduc*

No dove trailing Latin-banner
        instructions from her beak—
more an inscribed paddle
        when I was miles up a creek.

Not quite rousing beams
        shot by a midsummer moon—
more a surprise twin-engine
        skidding at me on pontoons.

When the messenger leapt on his bike
        I took your offered hand.
The names of all other suitors
        swirled away like skittering sand.

Down the road I saw our initials
        mowed in a golden field.
A sign at the corner directed,
        unmistakably, "Yield."

It had been one long drought
        or the eye of the hurricane.
I'd parked too long in one spot.
        The meter spelled out your name.

The Book of Steve

1.
Scene from a romance: rambling through a wood,
I almost collide with a giant.
"Are you a creature of good?" You nod.
Together we venture to the next scene.

2.
The cat that followed you home one day—
tentative shadow glimpsed through the screen,
shyly at dusk it would slip from the curb,
ears radaring forward when it caught your tone.

Fifteen years later, each time I appear
you set down bowl after bowl for me.

3.
What would I find, touring your sweet head?
Nooks packed with facts, quartz-glitters of wit,
green terraces orderly thoughts plash down;
knowledges bundled, a forklift memory
to scoop them out. Scenes with cousins; alcoves
cluttered with dumptrucks, bubblegum cards,
papier-mâché models—Saturn, Mars, Earth—
plastic weaponry, a catcher's thumped glove.
Quiet zones like pools we found up the mountain,
truths as plain as a prairie sky.

4.
I moved west to join you with what I could lug
in one stuffed suitcase. Coyotes yowled
from salmonberry clumps, minor alps loomed
at our street's end. Rain pattering on grape,
twinflower, bedstraw, bird's-foot trefoil—
marsh wren swaying in a barely-tethered nest
on our cattail stalk, I clung, bowed, sang.

5.
Minarets shimmying in mauve pools . . .
Jahan, you have nothing on my edifice,
this perfect dwelling I've designed for Steve.
The former tenant, a book-collector,
left basement troves we're still discovering—
eighteen-clause titles, rococo colophons.
Our chimney bricks are precisely aligned
so winds play themes from Mozart concerti.
Self-cleaning gutters, lawn-mowing sheep. . . .
Birds of paradise nest in our eaves.

6.
Driving cross-country, in the prairie center,
I leapt out to capture a sunset blaze
and snapped you instead, poised at our wheel.
How many crumpled maps have I squinted at
on long peregrinations north, south, east?
Let me accompany you everyplace—
glance in your rear-view, you'll catch me winking,
flip down the sunshield, I'll slip to your wrist;
tune the radio above the stations
past static-crackle, then hear me hum.

7.
Pink "Stargazers," white lilies you planted
that spring brocaded the garage's hem;
dabbing in each with affectionate thumbs,
you coaxed up seedlings an eyelash wide.
And that dahlia that tried so hard to bloom!
Translucent fist-bud almost pulsing,
it looked like it would burst, aching green.
The light-ration dwindled, but it leaned, craned
till even the sturdy chestnut trees flared.
Swiveling, basking under your smile,
if I had to go, I would yearn toward you.

8.
Travel memories: thatch, oriels—
we would have been peasants in the Old World,
you monitoring a herd of deer
in a sullen drizzle; evenings I'd have shone
the master's saltcellars, scraped blobs of wax
from a turret sconce. But together we'd have crept
along draughty halls under long-nosed portraits
when the lord was riding, to his library:
mysteries of minuscule; parchment grails.
In the Brueghel painting of the villagefest,
everyone's armwrestling, leapfrogging, whacking a ball;
we hunch on stumps teaching ourselves to read.

9.
Exchanging jokes no one can overhear—
me trailing robes, you flourishing a hat—
we embrace in the parchment initial's ring.
Or, crimson birds with implausible tails,
we go on calling across the margins
over Gothic letters of a *demande d'amour.*

10.

Our particular parliament of fowls:
each year, southering from Siberia,
squawking the whole three thousand miles,
the snow geese glide to Vancouver marsh.
What are they doing so far from home,
skidding amid these alien pumpkins?
Basking in the shallows, they gab and gab,
weary, weary—yet they mate for life.
—No hemlock owls bearing swooping doom,
but paired bald eagles in pine candelabra:
I want that for us, leisure, long views,
sharing through decades one dauntless raft.
—The yellow-headed blackbird, once-a-life vision:
gold vouchsafed on a rusting sedge.

11.

Whenever you look up, there I shall be—
and whenever I look up, there will be you
vowed Gabriel Oak to Miss Everdene.
He sought her when she was lost and foolish—
not for a pen but to set her free.

—I stumble in, shaky on my legs,
I nestle in the crook of your arms.

12.

And I have found Demetrius like a jewel,
Mine own, and not mine own. Yes, you are both,
rare nugget blazing in the general slab,
coveted, safe in my pouch of a heart;
fortuitous prize whose shine I want to share
with others who admire its brilliance too.

Untarnished, rustproof, through fire and ice
your adamant lasts. Glinting on my finger
I wear a hint of you, etched "Courage, Truth, Love."

13.
Café of wobbling tables, coffeemaker lamps,
choice of paperbacks comfortably slumped,
students gnawing pens on scraped velvet chairs.
The nearby pawnshop is stacked with striped Frisbees,
tie-dyes are fluttering by the Seed 'N' Feed.
Chocolate cake, two forks; folksinger twanging—
here I can almost pretend we're twenty,
we've just escaped home, we've got enough verve
to light city blocks. All these years with you!
A sense of infinite possibility
flares before me as you touch my hand.

14.
Let's age together like old-growth trees,
our knobby elbows sueded with moss,
draped over each other in a tipsy embrace,
staggering after our thousandth waltz.
We'll toast each year with another ring,
welcome hawks like finials to balding heights.

When the end comes, shall we crash to earth
comic and good-natured about it
as the bridal couple in the video
toppling as they tango the town-hall floor?
Thudding to the ferns, we'll sleep like spoons again,
looped with huckleberry, frogs booming at our feet,
nurse-logs to saplings bowering a new age.

August

Late August night,
I'm dozing in bed—

crickets sturdily cheeping—
elm nodding its head—

suddenly, *flare!*
glaring swath—

star, plummeting—
singed path.

If only some giant
had tossed that huge ball

through galaxy air—
if it hadn't fallen

and snuffed itself out
blazing along its arc,

but lay safe, nestled
in a glove in the dark

(a fireproof mitt:
clouds, congealed)—

the fielder pivoting
at the edge of the field. . . .

Buying the Farm

Crossing over—
will we be standing at a dory's prow,
clouds cooperating grandly in the background,
profiles like captains charting the Passage,
new moon, ice floes, capes?

Pass away
like an unlucky dynasty
or a craze for snuff bottles,
our lives no thicker than a snowflake?

A little folding of the hands to sleep—
straw hat tipped over my nose,
I'm dozing to the lilac's inquisitive wrens;
you, your spade flung aside,
sprawl, just starting to snore.

It's curtains for us,
clasping hands behind the dusty, still-swaying swag—
at last these doublets can come off,
the swipes of rouge and sideburns, then we'll stroll
to greet the flashing city with our true faces.

Let's *sleep with the fish*
—yellow tangs flocking like suns,
eels with Sid Caesar eyes
easing into a Romanesque coral-arch.

It's the end of the line,
the train nudges its way to the platform's edge,
we're the only two in the graffiti-swirled car
soft-shoeing down the gum-gobbed aisle.

And yes, let's *buy the farm* —
the loft's tucked full of hay,
the combines are waiting,
here is your morning basket of fresh eggs.

THREE

Cancer Surgery

Squeak squeak . . .
        where?
middle-of-the-night

fenced by steel rails,
tethered to a pouch

        light
        knifes under the door

    squeak   GLARE

            the nurse's shoes

Dark again.
Red digits blink: morphine drip.
Chest a gauzy snowpatch, itchy with tape.
A silver balloon sways on the updraft—
messenger from some festivity
too far to imagine, ocean-trench creature
bobbing dopily
where goggle-eyed fish ghost by.

How did I land here,
shot down like a migrating bird
who had other latitudes in mind?

Prognosis: 50-50

—To ride as hard at life
as that ten-year-old girl
galloping flat-out over the prairie!

Because that's how hard death
is thundering at you,
his knuckles white
on the black pommel;
too late you'll see
the east gate has been shut,
spurs glitter
on his needle-toed boots.

A Valediction

Thump on the roof.
The owl again?
Rising short shrieks—
mouse? rat?
I counted ten.

Terrified yelps
squeezed by a talon.
To have that be
your final say!
And the last vision

looming feathers,
diving beak.
Clutched, wriggling,
squeaking—
speak!

What was he crying—
"Mother, help me"?
"Eli, Eli,
have mercy on me"?
"I am not ready"?

Neck snapped, dangling;
a moment: taken.
Hamlet wouldn't
kill Claudius, so.
Too small a ration.

Foraging, scrabbling,
snatched; plea.
Hunching wings,
wad of bones
spat by the tree.

Room 238: Old Woman and Hummingbird

Wrung,
stiffened
like a dried dishcloth;
wrenched
sideways
in the wheelchair,
fingers hooked
as if to grip
        a ledge
            that keeps slipping
                    her grasp—
                        she peers:
                                ruby sheen
                    iridescent green
                                        vibrates
                                            bloom to bloom.

Chemo Side Effects: Memory

Where is the word I want?

Groping
in the thicket,
about to pinch the
dangling
berry, my fingerpads
close on
air.

I can hear it
scrabbling like a squirrel
on the oak's far side.

Word, please send over this black stretch of ocean
your singular flare,
blaze
your topaz in the mind's blank.

I could always pull the gift
from the lucky-dip barrel,
scoop the right jewel
from my dragon's trove. . . .

Now I flail,
the wrong item creaks up
on the mental dumbwaiter,

No use—
it's turning
out of sight,
a bicycle down a
Venetian alley—
I clatter after, only to find
gondolas bobbing in sunny silence,
a pigeon mumbling something
I just can't catch.

Chemo Side Effects: Vision

Gnats in dervish clouds,
indistinguishable, words fizzle.

Or keep fading in and
out of focus—
tiny climbers screened
in cheesecloth mist, sliding
along the oblong glacier.

Serifs ascending, descending,
I want to recognize all of you
even when you're a dozen to the pinhead—
f's fiddlehead fern,
hydrofoil dot balancing
on i's pilaster,
the diminutive compartments of a's, e's, p's,
beer-bellied cousins d and b.

But they clump,
a jumble of type
after the printer's apprentice upends
the basket. Impenetrable
as a playground clique,
schools of black fish foggily quivering
on silty beds. . . .

Eyes that have brought me so many words,
are you too dim for the world to keep courting?
Days, lay out your wares in the honking bazaar!

So many small things I still want to see:
sheen of my nephew's corner eyelash,
snowflake circuitry, fleas' thighs,
nebulae flocking in my husband's iris,
the peaks and valleys of each mustard seed.

Childless

Helixes snapped like crepe-paper streamers,
our DNA ladder
sways with frayed ends, an idle last rung.
No filaments spiraling us to the future;

no second-movement piccolo takes up our themes.
Tick and a tock, mere antiphons—
will our Möbius affections
start to grate?

Always each other's most favored nation,
this tiny economy will someday cease.
Two small figures at the end of a pier,
we watch other ships assume the horizons.

Your blue eyes in a rounder mien,
that three-generations' compounded patience
that makes your stalwart pulse andante—
how I wanted that seeded, perennial.

Minor characters from a serial novel,
we turn out of sight down a boulevard
hand in hand, at the end of Book Three.

Forty-Eight Years

Lilac scent, April,
six A.M. wrens.
Jimmy next door coughing as usual.

     Silence;
      sirens.
Ambulance idling.
A white van edges in.

Baggy black suit, black tie,
the coroner's driver
jokes with a boy
mowing the next lawn.

The door creaks back;
Jimmy's wife first.
Two red-faced men maneuver
a vinyl sack.
She stares at the van
as it turns down the lane.

A day later, at my door:
"I've locked myself out of the kitchen!
That's where he died, you know.
They worked on him an hour.
I cradled his head in my hands,

I said, 'Jimmy? Jimmy?'
We were married forty-eight years."

Thanksgiving:
I bring her flowers when I come for tea.
A tin tray with Big Ben still sits near the set—
"That's where we ate."
Shag rug flattening like matted fur;
skeins at a loss in a knitting bag.

Granted a Stay

Was there a midnight call from a magistrate's office—
gold-fringed flag, sleek pens, curt "Let her go"?
—The vulture-clique flapped off, the hearse
glided its unctuous self back to the garage.

Perhaps distracted by a good steak
and a surge of bonhomie,
the deputy himself decided, what the heck,
not today—the guillotine needs disinfecting.

Maybe, like a peering satellite, St. Jude
happened to glimpse my candle sinking in a narthex.
Blood oranges tossed to Buddha's halcyon lap,
prayers nestled by warm stones in Jerusalem's wall. . . .

I couldn't bear to crush the spiders' egg sacs,
hard-spun orbs about to float their chances.
Perhaps their eight-eyed god unplastered me
from the terminal web?

Striding from my prison in loose clothes,
nape still slick from the rasping maw—
who will be my companions on this bus?
I board with a gratis ticket to unknown towns.

First Days Back at Work

If I can pannier
a pinhead's worth of pollen
back to the desk—

If like the emperor penguin
I could lay
one egg,
warm its delicate
surprises on
my toes—

Such nimble kneaders, my fingers
used to be.
Will the loaf still rise?

I strain
like an old tug
hauling copses of logs.

Chameleon Hours

for my brother Tim

The horror: to be shunted
like a caboose rusting at a siding,
or parked expensively
like a summering mink.

Absurd, the concrete-rooted flagpole
flapping identical colors year after year,
the 5,000-pound safe dumb,
its luggish tumblers locked.

—To appear tripled each spring
at a new garden's edge!
Better a burger-wrapper
tumbleweeding down Broadway

than a dignified boxwood
sheared to the same oblong
June after June.
Oh, grant me more chameleon hours,

weeks restless as magma—
make me a virtuoso of
upheaval, uncatchable
as mercury's silver beads. . . .

Ways of Going

for Steve

Will it be like paragliding—
gossamer takeoff, seedlike drifting down
into a sunlit, unexpected grove?

Or ski-jumping—headlong soaring,
ski-tips piercing clouds,
crystal revelations astonishing my goggles?

Maybe I'll exit with the nonchalance
of a ten-year-old skateboarder,
wheels' down-the-hill my bravura farewell.

Or shimmy into the afterworld,
salsa dancer on a flatbed truck—
maracas coda, bangles flashing
as the parade lurches around the corner.

With sudden relief: a tortoise that had scrabbled
over a stony beach, flippers slipping and flailing,
splashes home in a graceful slide.

Skittery flicker of a glare-weary lizard
startled into the sheltering wings of a leaf,

rusting freighter with a brimming hold
shimmering onto a crimson edge. . . .

Sad rower pushed from shore,
I'll disappear like circles summoned
by an oar's dip.

However I burn through to the next atmosphere,
let your dear face be the last thing I see.

Farewell Desires

To unwind yourself like Houdini
from desires' pinioning buckles,
to bob away, an untethered dory
from a golden shore.

To be tumbled by whim
bloom to bloom to bloom,
not snapped by stubborn longing
into carnivorous sepals.

Throw out the devil of hoarding,
his bower-bird piracy
and magpie curios.
Let my green wants

be maple seeds
twirling into a ditch, my wishes
crackers flung over the transom
to battling gulls.

Goddess of discards,
let me be a waterfall
pouring a heedless mile,
stride barefoot over the drawbridge
to the plain road.

FOUR

Home Is the Sailor

Gabriele Helms, 1967–2004

The redwing blackbirds' epaulets

kept flashing

tiny threats;

tilting
keel

(no time, no time

for farewell)

channel bell-buoys *chiming-chime;*

spinnaker puffing

chiming "time"—

some hooded captain grabbed the wheel.

For Jenny

1973–2002

Not just the roses—
but sugar-water glazing the gouged rink;
swallow's nest—dun, nubbly mud;
clothesline dishcloth shimmying in a breeze;
soap-bubbles pearling a breakfast sink.

The Runt Lily

Rhonda Maretic, 1962–2004

While its Stargazer cousins shot up,
doubling weekly until
their heavy buds, like beaks,
bobbed and jabbed at the woodshed's sill,
this stubby one
struggled through choking bindweed
sideways—craning,
lunging as far as it could toward sun.

One sullen dusk, gales slashed.
Next day I found
the stalk slumping,
curled leaves awry, smudged brown
under raindrop loads,
two pale buds swinging, doused.
At the stem's base
officious sowbugs, armored, twitching, flowed.

Finally eked out one flower.
Streaked flamingo-and-white,
pulsing
by the spiky apple even past twilight—
all July
crowded by brassy dandelions
it tilted—
a quivering face, elated, at blank sky.

Since I Last Saw You

Morning rain dampens the dust in Weiching
new willow catkins turn an inn green
drink one more cup of wine my friend
west of Yang Pass there's no one you know
——WANG WEI

One month
Why couldn't you stay for another cup? Another?
The fiddleheads have opened, their edges brown.
Fuzz from the catkins zigzags on a stream.
When you get to the pass, clutch my gift tighter.

Two months
A crab bobs deeper into weedy black,
fat claw jutting like a pirate's knife.
I can still hear the lapping of your boatman's oars.
The moon-road's quavering, I can't follow.

Three months
That crane was waiting in the marsh for you.
I can't keep listening to the broken-throated cries—
yours or his?—as he carried you away.

Six months
Dreaming, I ran to a scholars' pavilion
where I thought I'd glimpsed you. When I spoke
it folded like a fairground tent after dusk.

Eight months
Over bridges woven of magpie feathers
some voyagers cross to the unknown world.
Was the black-and-white warm on your bare feet?

Ten months
Bighorn-nimble, you scale Immortals' mountains.
I think I see your clambering speck
appear and vanish behind banners of mist.

One year
Let's sit down for another cup of wine
under the peach, by new fiddlehead ferns.
The wind will scatter the catkins in your arms,
and I can hold you one more day in mine.

FIVE

World War II Watchtower

Squat concrete turret
furnished with gray pebbles
white-splatted by gulls.
Damp, fusty crests of sand;
bolts the size of a palm, rusted.

View: gold-spangled ocean, buoy-bells
ting-tinging.
Toylike twin-engines trail
ads for lotion.
Tourists dowse for coins, sift pink cockleshells.

After a day swinging horseshoe crabs—
tideline helmets—
the boys grab dinner: doughnuts, cigarettes,
whiffs of paint-thinner—
then crouch in these rough walls
and test their echoes.

Lost boys, don't bivouac here.
Gauge your luck, in the lighthouse-glare,
and go:

your open eyes aren't freckled with Omaha sand;
you're not the great-uncle bobbing at Juno.

Crux

Upside down like a child
clinging to the monkey bars,
a bloated mosquito dangled
from a web's crystal threads.
Bewitched with glue, he swayed,
game slung on a pole—
then, as if to argue,
jabbed his bayonet head
skyward; twitched; hurled himself
backward yanking, heaving
to loosen four legs, flung
two out like a Rockette—
wings whirred, blurring, flailing,
he jerked, flipped right, squeezed,
but his lunging ditchwater inch
could barely shiver the net.

Self-possessed, idling, calm,
riding out every quiver,
the spider perched at the rim.
What should the witness do?
Should I, like God, swoop down,
with capable hands arrange
some culpable mercy?
Or not intervene (like Him)?
Would I be stealing, too,
if I sliced the legal strands
(the pest was writhing again)
row on inevitable row?
Her abdomen's ample bulb
was flecked domestic brown.
Perhaps she needed the meal
(the mosquito, desperate, flexed
and sprang—up-down, up-down)
to lay a quotient of eggs.

Rain slashed the web at dusk.
One wisp kept floating,
festooned with severed legs
and half a rainbowed wing.

Pauper, Boston, 1988

The landlady got no reply
that April day when she stopped by,
rapping on the grimy steel door
—Washington Way, Apartment 4,

"senior housing"—gray concrete,
sixteen storeys, honking street,
scabbed dumpster hulking just outside.
Security came. The tenant had died

approximately three days before,
according to the coroner.
Housing notified his VA,
and the funeral home, Francis Shea,

who did city cases for set fees.
Management changed the lock and keys;
Maintenance was dispatched to clear
the rooms where he had lived five years.

(No one knew the man's history—
he'd said he had no family
that could be traced; that he used to box;
worked in a factory gluing clocks;

had breakdowns, landed on the street.
A cop had noticed his swollen feet
month after month, and finally called
someone in Housing at City Hall.)

It took a day to get the place clean.
At the end they'd filled thirteen
trashcan liners; then they tossed his bed,
scattering armfuls of moldy bread

to curious pigeons. The Veterans
sank a flag by his prepaid stone.
The City paid the last of his rent;
Housing recycled his documents.

Vuillard Interior

Against brown walls, the servant bends
over the coverlet she mends—
brown hair, brown flocking, a dun hand
under the lamp, the servant bends
over the coverlet she mends
draped across her broad brown skirts;
knotting, nodding, the servant blends
into the coverlet she mends.

Where Your Treasure Is

Where your treasure is, there will your heart be also.

Who am I?

1.
Plastic-scent interior,
AM babble.
Oil, oil.

2.
With my black eye, I see, I see
nothing; I transmit
hours of celebrities.

3.
Vaulted, I hoard twelve sheaves of stock,
a wolf's-head brooch
with ten black pearls,
a pair of ruby-crusted clocks.

4.
My heart is in this spiny heel,
my sole studded with gold nails.

US Post Office, December 22

Midnight; I slosh through the lot
fumbling bills. Sleet's pelting sideways.
Whack snow from fleece gloves, grope the box,
scan Christmas cards. Rustling—a sneeze—
whirling, I glimpse brown fatigues
crumpled by the "Wanted" display.
Supersize cup; trainers splitting;
slashed ski-coat—grease blotching green;
red knuckles clutch tattered knees.

I try not to stare. Her nook
overflows with dented white scraps—
Priority boxes, cancelled
(my catalogues: *"Finest Ash Sleds!"*);
mattress, bunched white plastic bags.
Hair straggles from her Rangers cap.
"Last Chance Markdowns! Holiday Joy!"
Hot chocolate steams for Santa; Labs
sprawl on their monogrammed beds.

I edge close; lean. "Are you all right?"
She shrinks toward the salt-stained floor
like a baby rabbit I brushed once
trembling in a barn's webbed gloom
near shark-jawed mowers, bright scythes.
A minute. I inch toward the door.
She lowers her head. In the lot
my husband's car, idling, sputters.
Can our shelter not spare any room?

Or did she decide not to go?
She'll hunch and toss, waiting for day,
beneath the eagle's blue claws.
Then—out of sight, out of mind?
The poster of the Christmas stamp
shows refugees nestling in hay,
an unwanted baby receiving
gold vessels from three bending kings.
Even the cattle look kind.

Two Cowboys

He yanked the child along,
six years old? dressed like him—
ebony snakeskin boots
scuttling through blaring cabs;
black bolos fluttering;
hats bobbing, black rolled brims.

Were they running late for a wake?
The father scowled. His nose
was gnarled, a boxer's; blond
ponytail fraying, slicked.
The boy tried to keep pace—
skittered along on scuffed toes,

lurched off a curb. The man
swore, quickening his stride.
Oh not to be left behind
when all you clutch is one hand!
Was the boy saddlebag freight
flung on for aching rides?

At the light, he glanced toward me.
Brown colt-eyes, wary, full.
Let him be dashing from shifts
at the fair's Wild West tent.
Let me not find him years on
tossed, broken by bulls.

Ruin

Boulevards with planted medians,
hotels like perfume boxes
strewn over the landscape,
a pink mall looming by a lagoon—

the tourists set out for jungle
on a new road
laid like electrical tape
through the trees.

Cola trucks veered past,
their bottles jumping.
Chickens turning circles
in muddy yards,

cul-de-sac,
lake,
white pigs snuffling
in a ditch—

the group bought tickets
at a shed
shading packets of film
on a styrofoam cooler.

Birdsong tinging,
bright beads of water—
they plunged under
branches swagged

with Spanish moss—
ancient rains
that had caught and frayed—
posed by a stela,

fumbled deeper—
"There!" "I saw it first!"
Two hundred feet high,
white stone sown with green.

They clambered up.
From the pyramid's top
all they could see
was slash-horizon,

green pelt bunching
on the land's back.
The guidebook said
towns thousands of years old

lay clenched underneath.
—Down again, at the cola stand:
a sad-eyed monkey
scampered the length

of his twine leash,
dropped to his haunches.
Long, elegant fingers,
a baby's nails—

someone offered a sip
from her bottle of water.
He tilted it, took a swig.
Her piece of egg he threw in the dirt.

On their way back
they snapped a jaguar
crouching to keep its balance
in the bed of a pickup.

Heron, Tampa

Beyond green plastic chairs
in white hibiscus, sturdy as a stake.
Unwillingly on show
for tourists' disposable flash.
Deliberating, preens. Stares
down her beak's spike at the pool's
blinding turquoise, teens on spring break
shrieking. Cannonball *splash*.

At dusk they scatter; she stalks,
hurricane-gray, over putting-green sod,
crest ruffling in hot wind.
Near her, wrapper-jabbing gulls
stop squabbling; a begging duck
backs off. She fixes the lake
as if she'd like to stab
that speedboat's whomping hull,

scoop bulging rings of oil,
bruise-purple, green, slithering from the pier.
Palms waggle restless heads;
lightning-jolts probe through reddening sky.
Jetskis rev, the lake's edge boils.
She hops up on a chaise
still heaped with crumpled towels.
One breaking cry—

swiveling, she glares at rows
of lawn-serviced shrubs and cockle-doorbells,
lanterns knobbing locked gates
daubed matching sea-green blues,
domino miles of condos.
Ask us now: who owns this?
Not me, me, me, not me.
Sentinel, help us choose.

Tested

Again he's starting across.
Perhaps a minuscule crack
in the prisoner's-yard of the sill
somehow escaped his glare
on his first surveying rounds.
Inching doggedly east,
he pivots; scrabbles back.

Clamshells bulk in his path.
Scrambling over a rim,
he noses, arrowing, higher;
six precise gold feet
tap tinnily on each ridge.
Wheeling at the bumpy summit,
deftly he inquires, grim.

No exit there. Edging down,
resumes his obsessive lane.
At the sill's end he halts;
strokes, with exacting legs,
each antenna's feather
as if caressing two whips.
Swiveling toward the pane,

suddenly he rises up,
hovering, trying to gauge
how hard to ram; launches
himself at the glass, *thud-*
thud, thud, bashes, jabbing,
bounces, lunges, fumbles,
slides with a BZZZZZT of rage

sideways on its icelike slick,
clinks upside down on a tin.
Buzzing, indignant, flips
himself; quivering, probes
the label's blackberries
with a doctor's questing touch.
No—just papery twins.

Face up along the sill,
crisping, three blue-black flies.
He trudges past them; stops;
strokes his antennae, now
weary, a man running
fingers through thinning hair.
Maybe he's closing his eyes,

at wit's end—for a second.
I have to serve the hive.
Rice-paper wings blur;
tiny chopper, deliberate,
he levitates; vibrates; aims
his diamond head at the dazzle
and drives, drives, drives.

Epitaph for Diane

Diane Jarvis Hunter

She thrust herself at life, a honeybee
thorax-deep in each quivering corolla;
flew pollen-spangled each day back to the hive—

willing, too, to go with what might happen,
like seeds of roadside grass on Fortune's scarf
ferried to be sown elsewhere, and grow new.

Edwin Partridge

1923–2005

Barely nineteen, volunteered for the war.
On a sweaty Pacific island
monitored radar,
hearing pilots rumble off
into black;

silently noted
which friends didn't come back.
One August dawn,
only wind-rattled palms.
He was grateful just to sail home.

Later, with wife and sons, he'd scan the sky
for blips of green—
hummingbirds swooping to his feeder.
Each dusk, for them,
he'd daub it clean.

A grin and a nod meant "Good."
Always the right word, or none.
He read to his sons, dried dishes,
cleared neighbors' drives,
hewed their wood.

At eighty, quavering hands;
teetering on each threshold.
Tenderly he'd loop
his wife's last dahlias with string
so they could stand.

Snail Halfway Across the Road

You haul your burdens tipped high—
that notched, dinged brown shell
a body shop–hopeless car—
lugging, a Brueghel peasant,
a kindling-scrounger's cord:
one stuck pine needle, awry.

There's not a second to stall
as you glide, scrunch, glide;
your scalloped jelly-foot
ripples, ripples, grips. You lean
toward the yellow line,
a swimmer arcing for wall,

heaving your tilting load
past a black-diamond lariat—
snake squashed to a figure-8
(a crow jabs the baked tail),
his slanting saffron swiftness
punished for seeking the road.

Sets of oblivious treads
bear down, bear down, bear down.
Jaunty on a labouring back
you inch your history forward.
Bowsprit-antennae plunge, rise;
safety's ten lifetimes ahead.

From Feste's Self-Help Book

Childhood

You came into this world trailing clouds all right,
        they just happened to be big black ones.
In the castle you drank from a poisoned goblet
        and were changed into something even bears cringe at.
When you awake baling-wired in thorns,
viceroys around you cobwebbed to their steins,
moth-eaten ermines, a muttering king—
                what choice do you have?
Rapell down the turret with your cap and bells.

Adolescence

Handed a baton in a bad-luck relay,
you've overshot the cliff and are pinwheeling down,
flailing in time to that whistling-wind keening
that lets viewers know you will soon be compressed
under a subsequent sequence of rocks.
            Squashed into pleats a centimeter wide?
Stride till you're 3-D again.

Adulthood

You're staggering through a dark wood,
soundtrack a fugue.
> Remember wrens risk a hand for a single seed,
> orchids can sprout from duff alone.

Executive Summary

How many can you feed from your sourdough lumps?
> Each morning, braid a loaf. Give them away.

Unknown Artists

1.
In the picture snapped at the festival,
she's standing, fifth row, twenty-fourth from left,
her face partly hidden by someone's fedora.

2.
She bourréed, stage left to right, in *The Nutcracker*.

3.
He daubed a cow's haunch into a master's Nativity.

4.
For an August *Figaro*, she lobbed her notes
with the chorus's into a pink-swirled sky.

5.
The viola part she played at her quartet's recital
was carried home that night, by a couple whistling.

6.
His winged saint, like a nuthatch inching down a pillar
(fourteenth century, "from the workshop of")
survived in one corner of a dim museum
open twice weekly at the curator's discretion.

7.

The red scalloped tails of the kissing birds
she'd inked on the baptismal scrip
for that Mennonite child, April 1810,
were admired again when a grizzled farmer,
rummaging in his great-uncle's cabinet,
unrolled them, presented them to the county seat.

8.

One poem he wrote was glanced at by a student
riffling through a book, looking for something else,
in the clammy stacks of her college library;
like a purple lupine by a hiker's dusty boot,
it pleased her and refreshed her, before she trudged on.

Phoenix

Wakes
to a whiff of stale fireplace,
ash flour-fine on her lids.

Flashes
on feather-tips blazing,
scorched-grass reek,
eye-searing embers.

Fireweed rising. . . .

Lurches to her feet,
sooty pinions cramped,
blistered leg still tender.

What conflagration?

Shake out your wings.

Snapshots of Our Afterlife

Light for traveling as cherry petals,
       we make the transition in
       impulsive gusts.

Or thread our way
behind a wandering doe—
       a god of crossroads, avuncular, nods.

Islands erupting over thousands of years
       crown in mid-ocean.
       Two petrels land.

Parallel beams piercing lint nebulae,
       jaunty twin lasers, we blaze
       past Pluto.

Crickets trading comments
               beneath a joint stone.

Small Vessel

A miniature boat found in a medieval hoard in Derry, Northern Ireland

Like a gold-plated half avocado
with a hatpin mast,
bean-sprout rudder,
oars slender as dragonfly torsos.

How fragile, our contraptions;
uninsurable storms!

What sail
could we use?
A petal?

I trust in your arms.

Notes

Dedication: "He was a verray parfit, gentil knyght"—Geoffrey Chaucer, General Prologue, *The Canterbury Tales.*

"Thirteen": "Heidens"—Eric Heiden, Olympic speed-skating champion.

"Miss Peters": "You are a priest forever/after the order of Melchizidek"—Psalms 110:4; Hebrews 5:6, 6:20, 7:17, 21.

"Four Lectures by Robert Lowell, 1977": As a student in classes taught by Robert Lowell (1917–1977), I took detailed notes on his remarks about nineteenth- and twentieth-century writers. When in a poetry seminar a few years later I was asked to write a dramatic monologue, I put some of Lowell's words into verse.

"Philosophical Arguments": Giovanni Battista Piranesi (1720–1778)—Italian designer, etcher, engraver, and architect, who published in 1749–1750 a series of prints, "Invenzioni capric di carceri," depicting fantastical prisons.

"Depends on the Angle": "sleep-of-reason monster"—"The Sleep of Reason Produces Monsters" is the title of an etching by Francisco de Goya, depicting bats and owls flapping around a sleeper's head.

"Song: The Messenger": "Love dispatched its messenger, who summoned her to love him"—from *Eliduc,* in *The Lais of Marie de France,* translated by Glyn S. Burgess and Keith Busby (Penguin, 1999). Marie de France, who flourished in the late twelfth century, is the earliest known French woman poet.

"The Book of Steve":

1. "Are you a creature of good?"—adapted from Chrétien de Troyes, *Yvain*, in *Arthurian Romances*, translated by William W. Kibler (Penguin, 1981). In this romance, someone wandering through a forest meets a giant and asks him this question.

5. Shah Jahan—the builder of the Taj Mahal.

10. *Demande d'amour*—This term is used for questions sometimes posed in medieval courtly literature, intended to provoke a discussion from the audience listening to the narrative being read aloud.

11. "Whenever you look up, there I shall be. . . ."—Thomas Hardy, *Far From the Madding Crowd*. This is what Farmer Gabriel Oak says to Bathsheba Everdene when he first proposes to her.

12. "And I have found Demetrius like a jewel. . . ."—William Shakespeare, *A Midsummer Night's Dream*, IV.i.191–92.

"Since I Last Saw You": The poem used as an epigraph is "Seeing Off Yuan Er on a Mission to Anhsi," by Wang Wei, translated by Red Pine, from *Poems of the Masters: China's Classic Anthology of T'ang and Sung Dynasty Verse* (Copper Canyon Press, 2003). The Chinese word for "willow" is a homophone of another word meaning "Stay behind." Thus the Chinese gave friends willow catkins as parting mementos.

"Where Your Treasure Is": "Where your treasure is, there will your heart be also"—Matthew 6:21; Luke 12:34.

NMR	Nordic Resistance Movement
NPD	National Democratic Party of Germany
ONP	One Nation Party
PEGIDA	Patriotic Europeans Against the Islamization of the Occident
PiS	Law and Justice
PVV	Party for Freedom
REP	The Republicans
RN	National Rally
RSS	National Volunteer Organization
SD	Sweden Democrats
SNS	Slovak National Party
SRP	Socialist Reich Party
SVP	Swiss People's Party
UKIP	United Kingdom Independence Party
VB	Flemish Bloc/Flemish Interest
XA	Golden Dawn

Abbreviations

AfD	Alternative for Germany
ANS/NA	Action Front of National Socialists/ National Activists
APF	Alliance for Peace and Freedom
B&H	Blood & Honour
BJP	Indian People's Party
DF	Danish People's Party
EAF	European Alliance for Freedom
EDL	English Defence League
EKRE	Conservative People's Party of Estonia
ENF	Europe of Nations and Freedom
ESM	European Social Movement
FN	National Front (France)
FPÖ	Austrian Freedom Party
FvD	Forum for Democracy
GRECE	Research and Study Group for European Civilization
KKK	Ku Klux Klan
LN	Northern League
LPR	League of Polish Families
L'SNS	Kotleba – People's Party Our Slovakia
MHP	Nationalist Action Party
MSI	Italian Social Movement
NF	National Front (UK)

an earlier draft of the gender chapter and helped me reshape and rethink it. My fantastic graduate student Jakub Wondreys did vital research assistance for the book and helped me construct the chronology and the glossary. He also read through the full manuscript and provided me with helpful comments. I thank him for all his work and cannot wait to repay it, by editing his dissertation. Finally, a shout out to my friend and publisher Craig Fowlie, who made time in his extremely busy schedule to provide me with great feedback on the full manuscript, despite the fact that it is published by a competitor. Perhaps he is right after all: Scousers are special.

I have written several books before, some purely academic, some mostly non-academic. In most cases, I acted quite quickly on the initial idea, but it then took me a (very) long time to turn it into a book. This book is the exact opposite. I have been brooding over this idea for more than a decade, returning to it each time I was asked for a recommendation for a relatively short, non-academic book after giving a public lecture. But once I approached Polity with the idea, the book almost wrote itself – if I could find time for it in between family, lectures, meetings, teaching, and travel. I want to thank the three anonymous referees for their constructive and encouraging reviews and my editors at Polity, Louise Knight and Sophie Wright, for their quick and hands-on editing style. It confirmed my long-held feeling that Polity is indeed the perfect publisher for this book.

After the Caliphate

For my girls, Fiona and Maya

After the Caliphate

The Islamic State and the Future of the Terrorist Diaspora

Colin P. Clarke

polity

First published in 2019 by Polity Press
Reprinted:2019 (twice)

Polity Press
65 Bridge Street
Cambridge CB2 1UR, UK

Polity Press
101 Station Landing
Suite 300
Medford, MA 02155, USA

ISBN-13: 978-1-5095-3387-9
ISBN-13: 978-1-5095-3388-6 (pb)

A catalogue record for this book is available from the British Library.

Library of Congress Cataloging-in-Publication Data
Names: Clarke, Colin P., author.
Title: After the Caliphate : the Islamic State & the future of the terrorist diaspora / Colin P. Clarke.
Description: Medford, MA : Polity Press, [2019] | Includes bibliographical references and index.
Identifiers: LCCN 2018044631 (print) | LCCN 2018046064 (ebook) | ISBN 9781509533893 (Epub) | ISBN 9781509533879 (hardback) | ISBN 9781509533886 (pbk.)
Subjects: LCSH: IS (Organization) | Terrorism--Religious aspects--Islam. | Terrorism--Prevention.
Classification: LCC HV6433.I722 (ebook) | LCC HV6433.I722 C624 2019 (print) | DDC 363.325--dc23
LC record available at https://lccn.loc.gov/2018044631

Typeset in 10 on 16.5 Utopia Std by
Servis Filmsetting Ltd, Stockport, Cheshire
Printed and bound in the United States by LSC Communications

For further information on Polity, visit our website: politybooks.com

Contents

Acknowledgments   vi

Foreword by Ali H. Soufan   ix

Introduction   1

1   The Long Road to the Caliphate   10

2   The Inner Workings of the Islamic State   39

3   The Coming Terrorist Diaspora   69

4   From "Remain and Expand" to Survive and Persist   105

5   After the Caliphate: Preventing the Islamic State's Return   134

Notes   160

Index   211

Acknowledgments

I am grateful to many people for contributing to this study and for their enduring support, without which this effort would not have been possible. I owe so much to the University of Pittsburgh's Graduate School of Public and International Affairs (GSPIA), especially to Phil Williams, who is both a mentor and a friend. At the RAND Corporation, I would like to thank my friends and colleagues Chad Serena, Christopher Paul, Patrick Johnston, Brian Michael Jenkins, Seth Jones, Andy Liepman, and Howard Shatz, among others, for intellectually stimulating conversations over the years. Also, special thanks are due to Valerie Nelson, who helped me with the dozens of op-eds that originally motivated me to write this book. Her help, but more importantly her sense of humor and wit, were indispensable to me while I was writing. At Carnegie Mellon University, I thank Kiron Skinner and my wonderful colleagues, as well as my students, with whom I've spent countless hours speaking about the subjects covered in this book.

At Polity, I would like to offer the sincerest thanks to Louise Knight, Nekane Tanaka Galdos, and their team. Polity was such a well-organized group and Louise's sense of humor helped push me through. Her patience, encouragement, and kindness brightened many of my days.

I would like to acknowledge the many named and unnamed scholars and practitioners who took time away from their busy schedules

to avail me of their expertise and knowledge in this area, whether in interviews or in conversations about this subject which helped shape my thinking, including Graeme Wood, Daniel Byman, John Horgan, Bruce Hoffman, J. M. Berger, Haroro Ingram, Aaron Zelin, Daveed Gartenstein-Ross, Michael Kenney, Martha Crenshaw, Elisabeth Kendall, Fred Wehrey, Mia Bloom, Derek Henry Flood, Zack Gold, Zachary Abuza, Jason Warner, Craig Whiteside, Amir Jadoon, Hassan Hassan, Amar Amarasingam, Charlie Winter, Rukmini Callimachi, Brian Fishman, Assaf Moghadam, Tom Joscelyn, Robin Simcox, Pieter Van Ostaeyen, Louis Klareves, Jean-Marc Oppenheim, Mary Beth Altier, and Sam Mullins.

I am so thankful to Ali Soufan and my colleagues at The Soufan Center in New York City. I read about Ali and his heroism when I was a graduate student and have always admired him, even before I knew him. Especially given the topic discussed in this book, which can be dark at times, I think this world needs more heroes, and Ali is one of mine. Moreover, sometimes people you idolize from afar let you down once you meet them in person, but not Ali. For all of his success, he's an even better person, so it's surreal that I now have the opportunity to work alongside him.

Many thanks to Alastair Reed, Renske van der Veer, Bart Schuurman, Christophe Paulussen, Jos Kosters, and my colleagues at The International Centre for Counter-Terrorism – The Hague (ICCT); Michael Noonan and my colleagues at the Foreign Policy Research Institute (FPRI) in Philadelphia; and Seamus Hughes and his team at the Program on Extremism at George Washington University.

Most importantly, I would like to thank my family and friends, who mean everything to me. I've been blessed to have a tight-knit group of friends and we've done an admirable job of keeping in touch over the many years. It's amazing to watch how our lives have changed

as we each raise families of our own. None of this would be possible without my parents, Phil and Maureen, who instilled in me the value of hard work, not by spelling it out explicitly, but by quietly setting the example. I love you guys. Thanks go to my brother Ryan and my sister Katie, who are my siblings but, more importantly, my friends. Lastly, I would like to thank my wife Colleen, an amazing partner and mother and the rock of our family. Her smile alone is enough to get me through my toughest days. Without her help, this book would certainly not have been possible.

Any and all mistakes contained here within are the sole responsibility of the author.

Foreword

Ali H. Soufan

Almost 18 years ago, the United States was attacked by al-Qaeda, a Salafi-jihadist terrorist organization of around 400 members, based primarily in Afghanistan and led by Osama bin Laden. The United States responded swiftly, and, along with its allies and partners, defeated that version of al-Qaeda. Today, however, a new jihadist threat has emerged around the world. It consists of many different organizations that have successfully embedded themselves in local conflicts, making them incredibly difficult to target.

In *After the Caliphate*, terrorism scholar Colin P. Clarke traces the evolution of the global jihadist movement from its earliest days all the way up to and through the collapse of the caliphate. In my career as an FBI Special Agent, I experienced firsthand the depth of commitment of some of al-Qaeda's most committed ideologues. Clarke's book goes a long way toward capturing the essence of what made al-Qaeda, and then the Islamic State (IS), so unique – an unwavering commitment to reinstating the rule of the caliphate through any means necessary. Over time, the leadership of the global jihadist movement has changed hands, from Osama bin Laden to Abu Musab al-Zarqawi to Abu Bakr al-Baghdadi. What will the future of the movement look like? Will Hamza bin Laden, Osama's son, re-emerge to lead al-Qaeda in its next chapter as the group seeks to reclaim the leadership of aspiring jihadists from Europe to the Middle East and beyond? Or will the movement

splinter and fracture, leading to a decentralized and dispersed cluster of groups and lone actors tenuously linked by ideology and common cause?

During his bloody reign, the Jordanian al-Zarqawi planted the seeds for the rise of IS, exporting his draconian vision throughout the broader region. Other jihadist ideologues, including Abu Musab al-Suri, contributed significantly to the call to establish a caliphate, something al-Qaeda was never able to achieve but that IS ultimately did. Bloodshed plays into the jihadis' overall game-plan, which has always been about exploiting chaos and weaponizing sectarianism. There is a common factor linking the franchise groups and affiliates of both IS and al-Qaeda. That factor is the narrative of bin Ladenism. We must dedicate ourselves to destroying that narrative and only when we do so will we finally defeat them. But the threat is far from static and has in fact mutated from an organization that attacked the United States on September 11, 2001 into what it is today – a dystopian ideology. Bullets don't kill narratives, messages, thoughts, or beliefs. What we need is a new strategy that moves away from the myopic obsession with tactical gains and ad-hoc counterterrorism responses. Indeed, it is the legacy of our tactic-driven response to 9/11 that has facilitated the growth of bin Ladenism far beyond what Osama bin Laden could have ever imagined.

The United States in particular, and the West in general, have failed to adequately understand the worldview and belief system underpinning the global jihadist movement. In the words of Olivier Roy, a world-renowned scholar of Islam, the threat posed by IS is not about the radicalization of Islam, but, rather, about the Islamization of radicalism. Groups like al-Qaeda and IS have successfully mobilized the grievances of Muslims, especially young Muslim men, who are seeking to take control of their own destinies to provide meaning to

what they see as an otherwise meaningless existence, characterized by mediocrity, isolation, tedium, and a perception of discrimination and an overall lack of opportunities to succeed in mainstream society. The global jihadist movement has filled this void by propagating a narrative that highlights the action, excitement, and camaraderie of joining the caliphate. IS excelled at tailoring its messages to myriad demographics and lowering the barriers to entry for those not well steeped in Islamic theology, culture, or practice.

Following the events of the Arab Spring, bin Laden ordered al-Qaeda to begin focusing more on issues directly related to the grassroots and local levels. The Iraq war was a primary motivation for many jihadists nearly a decade prior, when the US invasion of Iraq helped breathe new life into the ideology and narrative espoused by al-Qaeda. But the Arab Spring refocused the movement, or at least al-Qaeda, on rebuilding its network and planting the seed for future generations. Bruce Hoffman has called this deliberate strategy "quietly and patiently rebuilding." The global jihadist movement endures by taking advantage of chaos in failed states and ungoverned territories. At a more granular level, al-Qaeda has used the past few years to refocus its effort, allowing IS to suffer the brunt of the West's counterterrorism efforts while its members ingratiate themselves in parochial conflicts in Yemen, Mali, and the Philippines.

What primarily brings together jihadists in the contemporary era is no longer the shared experience of training camps, although that is one factor, but rather something far more tangible – a commitment to the jihadist narrative and the ideas and beliefs that drive the recruitment of new members and the regeneration of this global network of terrorists. If we ever hope to bring an end to the so-called Global War on Terror, it is essential to find political solutions to the conflicts in weak states where jihadist groups seek refuge and safe haven. Only by diminishing

the environment that fuels radicalism and terrorism can the international community begin to make sustainable and lasting progress. This means looking beyond purely military solutions and working to ensure that those regions most beset by bin Ladenism have a vested interest in working together toward an improved future.

The cancer of bin Ladenism has metastasized across the Middle East and North Africa and beyond. The split between IS and al-Qaeda was part ideological, but also a difference between and among personalities. IS has changed from a terrorist group to a proto-state and is now reverting back to a clandestine guerrilla organization focused on subversion and the selective application of violence. Now that the caliphate has been crushed, Clarke's book is critical in helping us understand what might happen next. From the deserts of North Africa to the jungles of Southeast Asia, *After the Caliphate* is a groundbreaking work of scholarship that fills a critical void in the contemporary literature on terrorism studies and should prove a useful guide to scholars and practitioners alike.

Introduction

"Soon after buying her, the fighter brought the teenage girl a round box containing four strips of pills, one of them colored red."[1] This is a line from a story by Rukmini Callimachi of *The New York Times* from March 12, 2016. Re-read that line again, and let it sink in. The sentence describes a jihadist terrorist from the Islamic State (IS) who purchased a teenage girl, from the Yazidi religious minority in Iraq, at the equivalent of a slave auction and was forcing her to consume birth-control pills to ensure that, no matter how many times he savagely raped her, his captive would not become pregnant. This situation played itself out throughout parts of territory in Iraq and Syria under the control of IS, which declared itself a caliphate and set out to build what terrorism expert Martha Crenshaw calls a "counter-state" using any and all means necessary, including rape, murder, and torture.[2]

The brutality was not merely limited to sexual slavery. There were also beheadings and crucifixions. Some IS captives were burned alive, while others were locked in a cage and submerged in water until they drowned. Many of these actions were recorded and posted online by the group itself, to promote a level of anomic violence that would come to shape and in many ways define its brand. Just a few years ago, horrified onlookers must have wondered how we arrived at a place where a terrorist organization could conquer and control territory, systematically eliminate its rivals, and intimidate

the international community from action to halt this blatant display of barbarism.

By mid-2018, the physical caliphate had all but been destroyed, its fighters killed, captured, and chased from their erstwhile strongholds in Raqqa and Mosul. But, as Graeme Wood points out, the caliphate was more than just a territory or a proto-state – it was, and indeed still is, "a phenomenon in both physical and mental space."[3] IS as an idea, as an ideology, and as a worldview is far from over. The group will eventually seek to relocate to another country and establish new franchise and affiliate groups. The purpose of this book is to analyze what happens next with the Islamic State and to determine whether or not, and to what extent, it will manage to adapt and regroup after the physical fall of the caliphate. What form will its relationship with al-Qaeda take? How might its tactics and strategy change in the future? This book will attempt to answer these questions and more, while taking stock of IS – its roots, its evolution, and its monumental setbacks – to provide some insights into what the road ahead could look like.

In many respects, the establishment of the caliphate was an anomaly. Historically, the global jihadist movement has been largely decentralized, consistently inconsistent in its ability to marshal the resources and groundswell of support necessary to achieve anything close to what IS did when it established the caliphate with a headquarters in Raqqa. From bin Laden to Khalid Sheikh Mohammed, the global jihadist movement has had its share of charismatic personalities. But for the past four decades, it rarely constituted anything close to a monolithic movement operating with a common purpose and core agenda.

The future of the movement is therefore likely to resemble its past – with peripatetic and divided groups of militants dispersing to new battlefields, from North Africa to Southeast Asia, where they will join

existing civil wars, establish safe havens and sanctuaries, and seek ways of conducting spectacular attacks in the West that inspire new followers and motivate existing supporters. In this fragmented and atomized form, IS could become even more dangerous and challenging for counterterrorism forces, as its splinter groups threaten renewed and heightened violence throughout the globe. Even if foreign fighters return home in much smaller numbers than initially expected, the next five-year period could very well be characterized by a spike in attacks.

At its peak from 2014 to 2016, the caliphate briefly represented the apex of the global jihadist movement – the closest thing it has ever had to a lasting presence. But with the caliphate in ruins, it will revert to decentralized and dispersed clusters of groups and lone individuals or self-starter groups, tenuously linked by ideology and common cause, although, as history has shown, over time parochial interests tend to trump the movement's globally focused veneer.[4] In order to understand how we got to where we are today and what lies ahead, it is critical to look back to the roots of IS – both how and what it learned from its predecessors, and how it differs from other milieus within the global jihadist universe.

The opening chapter takes us from the beginnings of the global Salafi-jihadist movement following the Soviet invasion of Afghanistan in 1979 and traces its evolution through the next three decades, leading up to the events of September 11, 2001. Initially dubbed the "Arab Afghans," fighters from the Middle East, North Africa, and elsewhere flocked to Afghanistan to help repel the Soviet Red Army following Moscow's hasty invasion. These militants moved on following the Afghan conflict to form the core of al-Qaeda, growing the organization in Sudan before branching out to fight in places like Somalia, Bosnia, Algeria, and Chechnya during the 1990s. Differences over objectives and ideology led to numerous splits within the movement, as fighters

dispersed from al-Qaeda to join existing militant groups through-out the globe, although due to the trappings of globalization, many were able to remain linked to the core organization from perches in Southeast Asia, Europe, and elsewhere.

After the US invasion of Afghanistan in 2001 and an unrelent-ing drone campaign, al-Qaeda scattered and established franchise operations in Yemen (al-Qaeda in the Arabian Peninsula, AQAP), North Africa (al-Qaeda in the Islamic Maghreb, AQIM), and Iraq (al-Qaeda in Iraq, AQI), while also maintaining ties with groups in parts of Africa (al-Shabaab) and Asia (Abu Sayyaf Group and Jemmah Islamiyah). Core al-Qaeda in Afghanistan and Pakistan was largely decimated, but several of the franchise groups flourished during this period, including AQAP and AQI, the latter of which was led by the spiritual godfather of IS, the Jordanian Abu Musab al-Zarqawi. Over time, AQI would morph into the Islamic State in Iraq (ISI) in the mid-2000s, a name which the group would keep until early 2013 when it changed officially to IS, following its falling-out with al-Qaeda. The detailed history of the movement described in this first chapter is critical because one potential future alternative in the post-caliphate environment is a return to the franchising model that al-Qaeda pio-neered following the onslaught against its core organization based in South Asia.

The book then moves to explore the genesis of the Islamic State and the structural factors and variables that contributed to its rise, includ-ing rampant sectarianism in Iraq and the political vacuum caused by the Syrian civil war. A close look at IS infrastructure, decision-making apparatus, and its approach to building the caliphate shows how each informed the group's approach to conquering new territory and implementing the pillars of a sovereign state, while also developing a unique ability to recruit foreign fighters. This analysis is accompanied

4

by a strategic snapshot of IS's ideology, its long-term objectives, and a discussion of the group's capacity to plan and conduct attacks (operational capabilities) and to maintain itself as a cohesive entity (organizational capabilities). In particular, it is these organizational capabilities which will play a substantial role in determining the future of the organization, helping it transition smoothly from a territorially based insurgent organization to an underground, clandestine terrorist group. Its network-like qualities, affiliate franchise groups, and social media expertise contribute to its protean structure and ability to survive.

The Islamic State is a pioneering terrorist group in several ways, from its ability to raise and spend money to its multi-tiered approach to conducting terrorist attacks (inspired vs. directed). IS's use of social media and encryption to direct terrorist attacks overseas sets it apart from any terrorist groups of the past. As evidenced by the Paris November 2015 attacks and the Brussels March 2016 attacks, at its peak, IS sustained the ability to strike into the heart of Europe. The second chapter examines various aspects of the group's financing and its tactics, including how IS operates on the battlefield, from vehicle-borne improvised explosive devices (VBIEDs) to ambushes and hit-and-run attacks. This extends to IS's exhortation for its followers to conduct attacks in the West, including a synopsis of so-called vehicular terrorism, a tactic pioneered by IS that has emerged as a new trend in terrorism directed against the West.

Chapter 3 offers a rigorous evaluation of the Islamic State's future, based – in part – on the current trends we are witnessing. This includes a deeper discussion of the so-called free-agent jihadists or roving militants who will seek to travel to active conflict zones to link up with existing terrorist and insurgent groups, acting as a force multiplier. For most of its surviving fighters, the war is not over – many of these

militants will almost certainly move on to new battlefields to continue waging jihad. As *New Yorker* columnist and Middle East expert Robin Wright recently commented, "hundreds of jihadis are believed to be searching for new battlefields or refuge in Muslim countries."[5] The mobilization of jihadists in Iraq and Syria dwarfs similar phenomena that helped define civil wars and insurgencies in Afghanistan, Bosnia, Algeria, and Chechnya. This is an especially ominous observation since the foreign fighter networks formed during those conflicts went on to form the core of al-Qaeda.

Wherever IS fighters fleeing Iraq and Syria congregate next, it will most probably be in a weak state plagued by persistent civil conflict, sectarian tensions, and an inability of the government to maintain a monopoly on the use of force within its borders. There are several potential candidates for the next IS headquarters, including North Africa (Libya, the Sinai Peninsula in Egypt), Central Asia (Afghanistan, the Caucasus), Southeast Asia (the Philippines, Indonesia), or destinations within the Middle East, possibly including Yemen. What these destinations have in common are weak security services, existing or recent sectarian conflict, and a population considered fertile for and receptive to the Islamic State's propaganda. Moreover, recent IS propaganda has demonstrated an interest in expanding beyond already-existing affiliates, to include insinuating its fighters and garnering new recruits in countries like Myanmar, India, and the Democratic Republic of Congo (DRC).

The penultimate chapter focuses on "core IS" in Iraq and Syria and how it will seek to transition from an insurgent organization to a terrorist group. Three years after IS captured major cities and towns throughout Iraq and Syria, the anti-IS coalition has made significant progress in countering the group and retaking territory. Nevertheless, predictions of the group's ultimate demise are premature. Rather

than an end to the group, what we are witnessing is more accurately a transition from an insurgent organization with a fixed headquarters to a clandestine terrorist network dispersed throughout the region and globe. The differences matter, as counterterrorism and counterinsurgency are two completely different strategies. Insurgent organizations hold and seize territory, can exercise sovereignty over a population, operate in the open as armed units, and can engage in mass mobilization, while terrorists conduct attacks with members operating in small cells – they rarely hold territory, and if they do it tends to be for a short period of time. At the time of this writing, IS leadership is more fractured, flimsy, and sporadic than at any point to date, but its intelligence service, the Emni, remains intact and is working to exploit missteps by the Islamic State's adversaries, including the Kurds, the Assad regime, and the Iraqi government, especially to the extent that these actors reinforce already-existing sectarian issues in the region.

One major inflection point is IS's ongoing competition with al-Qaeda and whether this will result in IS seeking rapprochement with the latter group or, on the contrary, intensifying its current rivalry as a way to differentiate itself and "outbid" its erstwhile collaborator. IS and al-Qaeda are competing for influence throughout the globe: in Afghanistan, Yemen, Libya, Saudi Arabia, Tunisia, Mali, Sinai, South and Southeast Asia, Syria/Iraq, Iran, the Caucasus, and Africa. As IS fighters disperse following the collapse of the caliphate, some have speculated that these fighters will reinforce existing *wilayats*, or provinces, but the collapse could have a deleterious effect upon the IS brand and thus lead to an ascendant al-Qaeda in places we might expect to see IS reinforced. Current and aspiring jihadists may view the al-Qaeda–IS relationship and competition through a zero-sum lens; the two groups "play off each other's successes and failures."[6] In some theatres, the two groups may engage in a process of

outbidding, ramping up violence in the near term to prove dedication and capability. The question of "preference divergence," wherein franchises face the dilemma of investing in local interests versus diverting resources toward global objectives, now seems more relevant than at any previous point in the conflict.

What is being done to counter IS and its returnees, including the hardcore fighters and mercenaries who will remain in the region, is the focus of the final chapter. This includes finances, logistics, and support for existing militant structures throughout the region and beyond. What are the policy implications of dealing with returning foreign fighters? What can and should states do to help deal with this immense challenge? Finally, how will the counterterrorism strategy pursued by the West affect the various trajectories of the splintered IS elements?

Answering these and other questions, this chapter engages with the myriad public policy issues concomitant with returnees and the decision of how best to reintegrate these people into society, or whether to deal with them in a more punitive manner. Entire families that at one time willingly departed Europe to join the Islamic State are now trickling back home, posing significant challenges to European authorities. Not all returnees should be viewed the same, as some will be willing to reintegrate, others will be reluctant to, and still others may be incapable of doing so, traumatized by the horrors of what they witnessed (and in some cases participated in) during the conflicts in Iraq and Syria.

While causing a terrorist organization to break apart might seem like a positive outcome – indeed, this is one of the primary objectives of most counterterrorism campaigns – it often causes the emergence of new, and in some cases more violent, splinter organizations (indeed, we could already be witnessing this in parts of the Sinai Peninsula in

Egypt). Dismantling and destroying IS and similar organizations are worthy strategic goals, but policymakers must also be prepared to limit the effectiveness of splinter groups as they emerge in the aftermath of a successful campaign against the parent group. The coalition fighting IS must continue to pursue a multipronged strategy. On the one hand, splinter cells must be aggressively targeted through capture-and-kill operations to prevent further metastasizing. On the other, this approach cannot be pursued in isolation; rather, it must be coupled with efforts to promote good governance and reduce corruption in fragile states while building the partner capacity of security forces in the most affected countries.

Countering IS has become a global priority. Yet there still exists nothing close to an international consensus on what must be done to prevent a future mobilization of jihadists motivated by a desire to establish a caliphate by any and all means necessary, with death and destruction paramount to this quest. The Global Coalition to Defeat ISIS consisted of five specific lines of effort, including: providing military support to partners fighting IS; impeding the worldwide flow of foreign fighters; stopping the financing and funding of its organization; addressing humanitarian crises in the region; and exposing the true and odious nature of this barbaric group determined to enslave its enemies and conquer its neighbors. The international community has vowed "never again," but can it keep that pledge? What makes this time different? This book offers some possible responses to the threat posed by a resurgent, post-caliphate IS. But first, let's go back to the beginning – to 1979 – and the events that triggered the modern era of the global jihadist movement and everything it epitomizes.

1

The Long Road to the Caliphate

Osama bin Laden was killed on May 2, 2011, following a United States Special Operations Forces raid on his compound in Abbottabad, Pakistan. His death marked a major turning point in the US-led Global War on Terror, closing a chapter that had begun nearly a decade earlier on September 11, 2001. But the significance of bin Laden to the global jihadist movement goes back much further, and can be traced back to Afghanistan in late 1979, following the Soviet invasion of that country and the subsequent defense of the territory by Afghans and foreign fighters from throughout the Islamic world.[1] The earliest known attempt to organize foreign fighters, many of them from Arab countries, was through the establishment of al-Qaeda,[2] or "the Base," at a meeting in Peshawar, Pakistan, in 1988. Al-Qaeda itself was the outgrowth of an organization called Maktab al-Khidamat (MAK), established by a Palestinian named Abdullah Azzam.

The organization's early efforts focused on recruiting Arab fighters to join the resistance in Afghanistan, where the so-called mujahedin, or holy warriors, were fighting to expel Soviet troops from the country.[3] At this point in al-Qaeda's nascent history, the goal of establishing a caliphate was more of an abstraction than anything. The immediate necessity was merely embryonic survival. Early members of MAK, which was initially founded in 1984, included Azzam, bin Laden, and the Algerian Abdullah Anas. In the mid-1980s, bin Laden met

10

and joined forces with Ayman al-Zawahiri, the current leader of core al-Qaeda. Zawahiri eventually merged key members of his group, Egyptian Islamic Jihad (EIJ), with al-Qaeda, once it emerged as its own entity in the late 1980s, at which point MAK had become more focused on humanitarian efforts rather than actual fighting.[4]

Al-Qaeda has continued to evolve over the years. Now entering its third decade, al-Qaeda is many things – terrorist organization, global jihadist network, brand and franchise group for Salafi-jihadists throughout the world. But beyond al-Qaeda, the global jihadist movement is a collection of groups and personalities – it is far from the unitary actor so often portrayed in the media. This trope actually plays into the hands of the jihadists, distorting the magnitude of the threat and making the movement seem omnipotent, when in reality it suffers from many of the same shortcomings, vulnerabilities, principal–agent and collective action challenges as other transnational non-state actors. The establishment of the caliphate has been a unifying, if not quixotic, rallying point for jihadists. But it's been more of a battle cry, or an ideal, than an actual realization. That is, until IS was able to establish one that spanned the deserts of Syria and major cities in Iraq.

To many, Osama bin Laden and al-Qaeda represented the threat posed by jihadists to the West. But as witnessed by the emergence of the IS, the threat is, and in fact always has been, much broader than al-Qaeda. So while the killing of bin Laden was both a symbolic and tactical achievement against al-Qaeda and its allies, from a strategic standpoint, the battle continues. Even in the immediate aftermath of bin Laden's death, few serious commentators believed that his demise in any way signaled the end of the global jihadist movement. Accordingly, remarking on the event, reputed terrorism expert Brian Michael Jenkins soberly noted, "the death of bin Laden does not end

al-Qaeda's global terrorist campaign."[5] Nor did it foreshadow an end to the global jihadist movement that al-Qaeda helped to spawn.

Al-Qaeda has always been a central node – indeed, *the* central node – in the constellation of jihadist entities throughout the globe. But the movement is much bigger than one man, more complex than one organization. This book takes as its starting point the global jihadist movement as it coalesced during the Soviet–Afghan War, and the 1980s as its logical beginning. The movement as a whole remains the unit of analysis throughout this research. To even begin to understand what the global jihadist movement is, there are several critical questions this chapter will seek to answer:

- *What are the origins of the global jihadist movement and how has it evolved over time?*
- *What is the ideology underpinning and motivating this movement?*
- *What are the goals and objectives of the movement?*
- *What strategy is the movement pursuing to achieve its goals?*
- *How is the movement structured to execute this strategy?*

Evolution over Time

"The global jihadist movement" is a rather broad term encompassing groups, organizations, and individuals, as well as hinting at a specific worldview motivated by the ideology of Salafi-jihad, which advocates a raised awareness among Muslims to reclaim their faith and use violence, when necessary, to restore Islam to its proper status as a beacon of religious, political, military, economic, and cultural guidance.[6] There is no universally accepted definition of what constitutes

the global jihadist movement or how to measure its evolution over time, which provides scholars with a real challenge in terms of analysis.

This all leads to the difficulty of attempting to study the movement as a singular and consistent unit of analysis. Even al-Qaeda, certainly a more discrete entity, poses "a common analytic problem" in terms of "defining just what the group is."[7] It is part of the reason why, even years after the 9/11 attacks, prominent terrorism scholars still openly posited the question, "what is the current Al Qaeda? An organization? A movement? An ideology?"[8] To ascertain a more fundamental understanding of al-Qaeda and the global jihadist movement it helped create, it might make sense to start with the death of its leader, an event that left millions worldwide hopeful that the scourge of Salafi-jihadist terrorism would die along with the man who was, for more than a decade, the world's most sought-after man.

Al-Qaeda, perhaps correctly, is frequently analyzed as the nucleus of the global jihadist movement, conceptualized as four distinct – though not mutually exclusive – dimensions: al-Qaeda Central; al-Qaeda Affiliates and Associates; al-Qaeda Locals; and the al-Qaeda Network. Al-Qaeda Central is essentially the core of the original al-Qaeda and is comprised of the group's initial leadership, including Ayman al-Zawahiri, and is based in Pakistan. Al-Qaeda Affiliates and Associates are made up of "formally established" terrorist groups that have worked closely with al-Qaeda over the years, including the Libyan Islamic Fighting Group (LIFG), the Islamic Movement of Uzbekistan (IMU), and Jemmah Islamiyah in Indonesia. Al-Qaeda Locals are "amorphous groups of Al Qaeda adherents" with "a previous connection of some kind" to al-Qaeda, no matter how tenuous. Finally, the al-Qaeda Network consists of homegrown Islamic radicals scattered throughout the globe with no connection whatsoever with al-Qaeda

or any other terrorist group, but who are prepared to conduct an attack in solidarity with the ideology of Salafi-jihad.[9]

Daniel Byman's analysis largely overlaps with Hoffman's, but instead collapses the second and third categories together, which he labels as "formal Al Qaeda affiliates or other groups that have varied relationships with the core but cooperate at least to some extent."[10] But the most satisfying analysis of the global jihadist movement is by Seth Jones, who also largely agrees with both Hoffman and Byman, but who more clearly draws a distinction between "affiliated Al Qaeda groups" and "other Salafi-jihadist groups." The former are groups that became formal branches of al-Qaeda by having their emirs swear *bay'at* – loyalty – to core al-Qaeda's leaders, which is then either officially accepted or rejected.[11] At one time, al-Qaeda affiliates included al-Qaeda in the Arabian Peninsula (AQAP), al-Qaeda in the Islamic Maghreb (AQIM), al-Shabaab in Somalia, al-Qaeda in Iraq (AQI), and Jabhat al-Nusra (JN) in Syria. More recent developments regarding the latter two groups will be discussed in more detail in forthcoming chapters. Groups that are more appropriately labeled as "other Salafi-jihadist groups" include Ansar al-Sharia Libya, the East Turkestan Islamic Movement, and Imarat Kavkaz in the Caucasus.[12] Byman refers to similar groups, namely those that might receive training from a franchise group, as Ansar Dine in Mali did from AQIM, as "affiliates, once-removed," something akin to a jihadi distant cousin.[13]

Ideological Underpinnings

It would be wholly inaccurate to attempt to portray a monolithic ideology shared by the global jihadist movement. But, writ large, the ideology of Salafi-jihadism is the overarching banner under which

most of the world's violent Sunni jihadists unite. This ideology is a specific strand of militant Sunni Islamism and can be defined as groups that stress the need to return to the "pure" Islam practiced by the Salaf, or pious ancestors, and those believing that violent jihad is a personal religious duty.[14] Many trace the origins of this line of thought back to Ibn Taymiyyah, an Islamic philosopher who advocated and participated in jihad against the Crusaders and the Mongols in the late thirteenth century.[15] Still others list the most prominent influences for modern-day jihadists as the Muslim Brotherhood, or Sayyid Qutb, an Egyptian Islamist whose views had a tremendous impact upon leading al-Qaeda ideologues, including Ayman al-Zawahiri, who credited Qutb with being "the spark that ignited the Islamic revolution against the enemies of Islam at home and abroad."[16]

But Azzam found the Brothers' worldview to be slightly parochial and instead agitated for a different ideology, one based on a "territorial view of Islam" focused on the necessity of driving infidels from Muslim lands.[17] In 1984, Azzam authored a *fatwa* titled *In Defence of Muslim Lands*, which provided the ideological underpinnings of modern-day jihad, laying out the justifications for and the differences between offensive and defensive jihad.[18] Interestingly, IS focused far more on seizing, holding, and governing territory than al-Qaeda ever did.

In many ways, the dominant ideology espoused by groups like al-Qaeda, the Islamic State, and others reflects the notion that violent jihad is the only path to defending the Islamic world. As part of its brand, al-Qaeda considered itself to be *the* vanguard of Muslims everywhere – the worldwide Islamic community, or *ummah*. In declaring jihad on America, bin Laden argued that the West, and in particular the United States, was overtly hostile to Islam and the only way to respond to this aggression was with extreme force and violence – the only language that America understands. The Salafi-jihadi ideology

15

believes in an inextricable link between the United States and Israel, commonly referred to as the Crusader–Zionist alliance, a theme also referenced in speeches by hardline Islamist groups from Lebanon to Palestine. In his speeches, bin Laden exhorted his followers to fight back and defend Islam from the United States, which has unleashed against Muslims "an ocean of oppression, injustice, slaughter and plunder."[19] Therefore, the next logical step is jihad. In essence, the core of the Salafi-jihadist ideology is individual jihad fused with collective revenge.[20]

From an intellectual standpoint, jihadi totalitarian ideology is a closed system, but it also allows for disagreements over strategy, tactics, and other critical issues.[21] In short, interpretation is not as draconian as some scholars make it out to be and debate is tolerated. Analysis of al-Qaeda's internal documents reveals a group at ease with allowing for internal disagreement and debate amongst its members and the leadership.[22] One well-known ideological divide in the broader jihadist universe dates back to the early 1980s and is between those who desire to strike "the far enemy" and those whose interests are more locally focused, preferring to target what they perceive as apostate regimes throughout the Muslim world. In any case, al-Qaeda followed a dual strategy which allowed it to pursue both objectives simultaneously.[23] But this strategic incongruence is reflected in the global jihadist movement's multifaceted nature. It is a network of networks rather than a single, coherent entity.

Primarily, and almost exclusively, the bulk of guidance on contemporary insurgency is manufactured by Salafist ideologues. Individuals like Ayman al-Zawahiri, Abu Musab al-Suri, Anwar al-Awlaki, and Abu Yahya al-Libi served among al-Qaeda's most prominent voices, proffering advice on strategy, operations, and tactics (in addition to a host of other issues including diet, grooming, and marriage).[24] These modern-day insurgency theorists were highly adept at propagating

the narrative that the Muslim *ummah* is being oppressed and only through force would this oppression cease, allowing Muslims to regain their dignity and honor. And even though it has since been crushed, the establishment of the caliphate was intended to be positive affirmation that an Islamic State could be a viable entity in the contemporary era of international relations.

Goals and Objectives

What are the goals and objectives of the global jihadist movement – or, in other words, what is the movement's *raison d'être,* or reason for being? At some point, attacking the West, and the United States more specifically, ultimately superseded other goals as the primary motivation of the global jihadist movement, led by al-Qaeda. Indeed, this motivation to kill Americans on US soil became "so obsessive that it impelled the group to seek out ways to achieve this task," driving innovation in tactics, techniques, and procedures.[25] Other correlated objectives included taking over territory and developing physical sanctuaries and safe havens from which to operate, with the longer-term objective of declaring "emirates" in these territories.[26]

Some would argue that, when looking at the data on where jihadists have successfully attacked, the United States falls further down the list of al-Qaeda's primary targets. The same factors that make Europe so vulnerable to the threat posed by terrorists, and especially by foreign fighters (geography; the number of citizens who traveled to Iraq or Syria; lack of counterterrorism capabilities, including screening, watch-listing, and whole-of-government programs; poor continent-wide information-sharing and intelligence and law-enforcement coordination; and the relationship between Muslim communities

and host-nation governments) present favorably for the United States. As former Director of the National Counterterrorism Center (NCTC), Nicholas Rasmussen acknowledged in Congressional testimony, compared to European counterparts, US ports of entry are under far less strain from migration, and US law enforcement agencies are not nearly as overtaxed by the sheer numbers of terrorist plots and potential suspects.[27] The greater threat to the US homeland specifically comes from individual and small autonomous cells, which are hard to detect, radicalized online, and capable of executing low-level attacks. Put simply, the data indicate that the far greater threat emanates from individuals who are already in the United States. As Brian Michael Jenkins has observed in his empirical study on the origins of America's jihadists, "American jihadists are made in the United States, not imported. Of the 178 jihadist planners and perpetrators, 86 were U.S-born citizens. The other were naturalized U.S. citizens (46) or legal permanent residents (23) – in other words, people who had long residencies in the United States before arrest."[28]

As captured in the title of this book, establishing an Islamic caliphate has long been a goal central to the movement. Perhaps one of the biggest misconceptions surrounding the differences between al-Qaeda and the Islamic State is that the latter favored establishing a caliphate while the former did not, which is inaccurate. Both organizations believe in establishing a caliphate, but they each see this happening along different timelines. For al-Qaeda, the establishment of a global caliphate, part of the "Definitive Victory" phase of its seven-stage plan, would occur no earlier than the 2020-2 timeframe, the final stage in al-Qaeda's "Twenty-year plan."[29] Al-Qaeda's goals changed over time, as the group's leadership recognized that its initial focus on a caliphate stretching from historic "Al-Andalus" to Southeast Asia first required laying the groundwork by gaining legitimacy at the local

level. The manner in which al-Qaeda has pursued this goal has led it to intervene in numerous civil wars. In fact, terrorist groups do not cause civil wars, but emerge from them, since "wars are perhaps the richest soil for seeding and growing violent groups of all stripes."[30]

And while many have remarked that the Islamic State has eclipsed al-Qaeda as the pre-eminent and most successful terrorist group in the contemporary era, it is important to take note of one of al-Qaeda's overarching goals – to advance the global jihadist movement "as a whole," even if it is not al-Qaeda leading the movement, a goal which "it has made considerable strides toward" even as it has been hampered. Indeed, the byproducts of al-Qaeda's success include the proliferation of foreign fighters, the destabilization of regimes where jihadists maintain a presence, and the cultivation of anti-Western sentiment amongst pockets of the Muslim world, especially in Europe.[31] Al-Qaeda's actions have helped contribute to a self-sustaining network of jihadists and, even as "Al Qaeda declines, the broader movement it fostered remains robust, with other causes and organizations capitalizing on the ideology and networks that the group promulgated."[32]

It also remains paramount to remember the fundamentals upon which the global jihadist movement resides – namely, the pursuit of jihad. Even as al-Qaeda's goals have shifted and evolved over time, its original goal remains the most important to the movement as a whole – to "promote jihad awareness" and "prepare and equip" jihadist cadres in order to develop "a unified international Jihad movement."[33] Accordingly, as spelled out in al-Qaeda's Constitutional Charter, all other goals are subsidiary to jihad: "An Islamic Group, its only mission is to Jihad, because Jihad is one of the basic purposes for which al-Qaeda personnel come together. In addition, they perform other Islamic duties if possible. Jihad will take precedence over other duties in case of interference."[34]

On the recruitment front, the core demographic of the move-ment remains disenfranchised, disillusioned, marginalized youth that are vulnerable to radicalization and the message of violent reli-gious extremism. The Islamic State has dipped into this same pool to populate its ranks, with perhaps more of an emphasis on enlisting Westerners with criminal backgrounds, especially in Europe, where terrorists and criminals now recruit from the same milieu.[35] Even well before the Islamic State was credited with inspiring lone wolf attacks in its name, al-Qaeda had always urged potential followers to conduct "DIY terrorism," or do-it-yourself attacks against soft targets in the West.[36] As the name suggests, lone wolves can be non-affiliated jihad-ists who simply share the same worldview and accept core tenets of a similar ideology while acting independently of any specific organiza-tion. Recruiting in diaspora communities is another favored method of encouraging supporters to launch attacks.[37] Jihadist groups have been particularly successful in rallying European-born Muslims and converts to their cause and, in the past decade, there have been plots and attacks throughout Western Europe, including several spectacular attacks in European capitals such as London, Paris, Madrid, and Berlin.

Strategic Decision-making

Al-Qaeda's leadership is tasked with making decisions that will both help to grow the organization and get it closer to achieving its primary objectives. In part, al-Qaeda relied on spectacular attacks as part of its global strategy. Throughout the 2000s, al-Qaeda's leadership believed that external operations against the West would help it achieve its goals of "integration, unity, growth, and gaining strategic leadership in the militant milieu" and therefore required its franchises to attack Western

interests.[38] These attacks were designed to achieve several interrelated objectives simultaneously, including garnering widespread attention for the global jihadist cause, bringing Muslims under the banner of al-Qaeda as a vanguard movement, and driving the United States from Muslim lands, as occurred in Lebanon in 1983 and again in Somalia in the early 1990s.[39] Spectacular attacks like 9/11 were designed to invite overreaction. As Assaf Moghadam astutely notes, "wounded and humiliated governments subjected to such surprise attacks are more likely to opt for harsh and risky responses against the perpetrators, thereby running the risk of drawing the two sides into an escalating, often protracted confrontation that is costly in both human and economic terms."[40]

Another strategic objective and deliberate part of al-Qaeda's plan is to forge unity among "foreign militants" in the broader jihadist universe, as smaller groups begin to perceive al-Qaeda as the "strong horse" and unite behind it.[41] Al-Qaeda has also demonstrated a knack for pragmatism when operating in the midst of other countries' civil wars. In Yemen, Iraq, Mali, and Somalia, jihadists have functioned in an almost parasitic manner. After infiltrating the ranks of local rebel groups, militants parrot their grievances and champion parochial objectives. Al-Qaeda ingratiates its fighters within extant networks of insurgents fighting against what they deem to be oppressive regimes. This ramps up proselytization efforts and introduces a narrative that mixes local issues with that of the global jihad.[42] There exists a constant tension over striking the proper balance between local and global objectives: "Civil war, domestic and transnational terrorism, and the involvement of foreign fighters have been essential components of jihadist strategy since the 1980s."[43]

Through its participation in conflicts throughout the globe, al-Qaeda has fostered relationships and sustained alliances with other

militant organizations and has been far more effective on this front than most terrorist groups historically.[44] Moreover, as al-Qaeda scholar Barak Mendelsohn declares in his book on the expansion of al-Qaeda's franchises, "Following a carefully planned strategy is particularly important for an actor with ambitious territorial aspirations that require navigating an intricate environment encompassing multiple fronts."[45] The group has expanded beyond its base in South Asia to encompass wide swaths of Africa and the Middle East. It has ensured longevity by devolving power to its local franchises.[46] The continued expansion of al-Qaeda is part of a multi-pronged strategy that also includes "bleeding wars" of attrition in Afghanistan and Iraq, as well as building an infrastructure of supporters in the West, especially in Europe.[47]

Throughout the group's evolution, its leadership has continued to play a major role in its longevity. The Amir is the overall leader of al-Qaeda and is tasked with a broad array of responsibilities, including planning on multiple levels (operational, strategic, tactical, logistical, and organizational), approving annual plans and budgets, and, just like any corporate chief executive officer, serving as the face of the organization.[48] As the founder of al-Qaeda and leader of the organization until his death at the hands of US Special Forces in May 2011, there is still debate over exactly how important bin Laden was to the movement.[49] Though bin Laden fancied himself part "lecturer-businessman" / part "activist theologian," his leadership style has been described as "soft-mannered, long-winded, project-oriented, media conscious."[50] On the other hand, his former deputy and now overall Amir of core al-Qaeda, Ayman al-Zawahiri, has been described as "a formidable figure," a "committed revolutionary," who is simultaneously "pious, bitter, and determined," and since its early days had been "the real power behind Al Qaeda."[51]

Organizational Structure

Since it would be a mistake to analyze the global jihadist movement as a monolithic entity, there is no single unified organizational structure, per se. However, scholars and analysts have discerned how groups like al-Qaeda and the Islamic State have chosen to structure their organizations, so analyzing those groups is useful in gaining a greater understanding of the infrastructure. In many ways, al-Qaeda has always been "more an idea or a concept than an organization" and "an amorphous movement tenuously held together by a loosely networked transnational constituency rather than a monolithic, international terrorist organization with either a defined or identifiable command and control apparatus."[52] In terms of its organizational structure, al-Qaeda has always been something of a paradox, "tightly supervised at the top but very loosely spread at the bottom."[53] At its peak, the group maintained an indelible or semi-permanent presence in 76 countries, "including those without discernable Muslim communities, but which were suitable for procurement, e.g. Japan, Bulgaria, Slovakia."[54]

Al-Qaeda is best described as a networked transnational constituency which, especially since the attacks of September 11, 2001, has shown itself to be a nimble, flexible, and adaptive entity, even as it has been reduced considerably by the constant barrage of American counterterrorism efforts worldwide. After all, "[f]or more than a decade, it has withstood arguably the greatest international onslaught directed against a terrorist organization in history."[55] As an organization, al-Qaeda was not averse to taking risks. Accordingly, its organizational style encouraged the adoption of innovative terrorist techniques, such as those devised by individuals outside of the group's organizational boundaries, including "independent terrorist

entrepreneurs" like Khalid Sheikh Mohammed, the so-called "master-mind" of the 9/11 attacks.[56]

As Rohan Gunaratna remarked in his landmark work on al-Qaeda, part of what makes the organization so unique is its "mobility and capacity for regeneration."[57] Within the broader jihadi universe, al-Qaeda existed as a central node and maintained connections, link-ages, and alliances with a diverse array of groups, including the Afghan Taliban, Chechen rebel groups, Abu Sayyaf Group (ASG) in the Philippines, and the IMU.[58] In many ways, Afghanistan, despite its geographic location outside of the Middle East and North Africa, has served as one of the, if not the, most critical hubs in the global jihad over the past four decades. It is a place that militants have continually returned to, even after other conflicts have drawn them away.

Still, there is no such thing as a permanent headquarters for the global jihadist movement. Whether in Khartoum or in Kandahar, jihad-ists are opportunistic by nature and, like a trickling stream, will always find their way to the lowest point, or the area most beyond the reach of formal governments and standing armies. After the Soviet occupation of Afghanistan drew down, Pakistan began pressuring foreign fighters to leave the region. Many jihadists fled abroad to Yemen, Sudan, and Jordan. Bin Laden was still providing support to members of EIJ, a sig-nificant contingent of whose fighters remained behind in Afghanistan and Pakistan. Another large group of EIJ fighters relocated along with Zawahiri to Sudan, where they hatched a plot to assassinate Egyptian leader Hosni Mubarak during an official state visit. The assassination attempt failed, but the plot highlighted further tension between bin Laden's focus on the "far enemy" and Zawahiri's continued obsession with Egypt and apostate regimes within the Middle East and North Africa.

The core of what had become al-Qaeda also traveled with bin Laden

from Afghanistan to Sudan, which the Saudi militant viewed as having serious potential as his group's next logistical headquarters.[59] Initially, bin Laden's concerns shifted to supporting jihadists in Yemen in their battle against the Communists, although he also allegedly provided support to militants in the Philippines, Algeria, Jordan, Eritrea, Pakistan, Bosnia, Tajikistan, Lebanon, Libya, Chechnya, Somalia, and Egypt during this time.[60] After the 1995 Dayton Accords ended the Bosnian conflict, some foreign fighters made their way to Sudan, while many other battle-hardened jihadis returned to Afghanistan, bringing back newfound expertise and tradecraft which they would teach to their militant brethren in al-Qaeda training camps, where Egyptians, Chechens, Uzbeks, and Palestinians honed their skills. In terms of geopolitics, failed states usually make for poor neighbors, but can serve as welcome hosts to non-state actors, including transnational terrorist groups and violent insurgencies. Al-Qaeda's Afghan sanctuary ebbed and flowed for two decades in the lead-up to 9/11, providing somewhat hospitable terrain for the militants, while affording them with access to other jihadists.

While it started as a single, monolithic entity, al-Qaeda today is a decentralized, networked, transnational terrorist organization. Al-Qaeda also needs a healthy budget to maintain its rather substantial structural costs, in addition to the costs of conducting operations. This includes money for subsistence living for its members (as well as for those who have families), communications, travel expenses, media and propaganda, and the provision of social services to selected constituents in an effort to buoy its popular support.[61] As groups grow more networked, it can be more challenging to retain their cohesiveness. Maintaining lines of communication, agreeing on shared goals and objectives, and remaining relevant in the increasingly crowded universe of global jihad are time-consuming and expensive undertakings,

especially when law enforcement and intelligence services around the world are seeking to combat this network wherever it pulses.

One of the core missions of a terrorist organization's bureaucracy is to fulfill a human resources function, to include recruiting new members. Despite the image conjured when envisioning a dark network dispersed throughout dozens of countries worldwide and forced to communicate covertly, al-Qaeda remained a highly bureaucratic organization throughout most of the 1990s and 2000s. In the lead-up to the attacks of September 11, 2001, al-Qaeda could accurately be characterized as a "unitary organization" with many of the characteristics of a "lumbering bureaucracy."[62] In al-Qaeda's training camps in Afghanistan, recruits were required to take a written exam and sign a contract before acceptance into the group. The contract detailed the moral responsibilities of would-be al-Qaeda members, as well as the stipulations of remuneration, including marital and family allowances, vacation time, and reimbursements for expenses incurred.[63] The group's organizational structure included the following components, in addition to the top leadership: the Secretary, the Command Council, the Military Committee, the Documentations Unit, the Political Committee, the Media Committee, the Administrative and Financial Committee, the Security Committee, and the Religious Committee.[64]

Campaigns and Operations

So what has the global jihadist movement looked like in action? That is, where has the movement launched attacks, conducted operations, and waged campaigns of violence to achieve its goals? Following the end of the war against the Soviets, many jihadists fled Afghanistan to join new conflicts, linking up with militants in other countries where

civil wars raged. According to Fawaz Gerges, "Bin Laden tapped into a rising generation of mujahideen . . . radicalized by the Afghan war and the persecution of Muslim communities in Bosnia, Chechnya, and elsewhere."[65] Indeed, veterans of the conflicts in Afghanistan, Bosnia, and Chechnya formed the core of al-Qaeda, which was cementing its reputation as the most capable entity within the broader global jihadist movement.

Bosnia

In the early 1990s, during the brutal wars that characterized the disintegration of the Federal Republic of Yugoslavia, some areas of the Balkans featured battles that had Bosnian Muslims fighting for survival against Bosnian Serbs, who were Orthodox Christian. The plight of Bosnian Muslims led to an organized call for foreign fighters to travel to Bosnia to help, as many jihadists did, initially under the guise of a variety of charities and humanitarian services. The projected numbers vary widely, but most reliable estimates suggest that between 3,000 and 4,000 foreign fighters actually fought in Bosnia, many of whom were veterans of the war in Afghanistan, hailing from the United States, Turkey, Jordan, Iran, Syria, and elsewhere.[66]

In April 1992, Sheikh Abu Abdel Aziz Barbaros established the El Mudžahid Battalion and worked to recruit fellow jihadists to join al-Qaeda-linked militants in Bosnia.[67] Unsurprisingly, a significant effort was made to recruit volunteers from Western Europe, given the proximity to the conflict.[68] The call to jihad was endorsed by influential clerics throughout the Middle East, especially as the Serbian military ramped up its campaign of ethnic cleansing. Islamic charities, including Al-Kifah and the Benevolence International Foundation (BIF), led by bin Laden associate Enaam Arnaout, siphoned off funds to support

the jihadists. When the conflict in Bosnia ended in 1995 with the signing of the Dayton Accords, hundreds of foreign fighters left Bosnia and headed elsewhere to fight, including many who went to Chechnya.[69]

Chechnya

Throughout the 1990s, Russia fought two wars against rebels in Chechnya seeking to secede and declare independence. Initially, the rebels' guiding ideology was secular-nationalist in nature, but soon morphed to Islamist-inspired after the arrival of jihadist foreign fighters in the mid-1990s. Jihadists slowly built a presence toward the end of the first Chechen war (1994–6) and factored significantly into several prominent battles against Russian soldiers.[70] Many of these foreign fighters were veterans of previous conflicts, including the Soviet–Afghan War, Tajikistan, and Bosnia.[71] Among these fighters were Sheikh Ali Fathi al-Shisani, a Jordanian-Chechen, and Ibn al-Khattab.[72] Khattab was a Saudi militant responsible for establishing training camps and indoctrinating Chechen fighters with Saudi-imported Wahhabism, not the traditional Sufism more common to Chechens, which is more moderate.[73] Khattab provided money and ideological inspiration, but also brought tangible fighting skills, leading an ambush on a Russian convoy in the mountains at Yaryshmardy in April 1996 that killed nearly 100 soldiers.[74] In addition to their ability to raise funds, jihadist foreign fighters in the Chechen theatre were especially valued for their fighting and organizational skills.[75]

There was a point in time when Chechnya was extremely important to al-Qaeda and the global jihadist movement. In 1996, al-Zawahiri was arrested trying to travel there, and spent six months in a prison in Dagestan.[76] In his book *Knights Under the Prophet's Banner*, he argued that Chechnya could become a "strategic lynchpin" for the jihadist

movement with the territory forming part of a "mujahid Islamic belt" across the region, connecting to Pakistan in the east and Turkey and Iran in the south.[77] The continuity between conflicts was also important, as fighters exchanged new skills which helped enhance the global jihadist movement's ability to influence conflicts it inserted itself into anywhere, unconstrained by geography: "These conflicts were further linked by a common group of fighters who gained credibility and combat experience ultimately culminating in improved military effectiveness."[78]

Franchise Groups and Affiliates

The other important development affecting the global jihadist movement was the ebb and flow of al-Qaeda and its dispersion following the US-led invasion of Afghanistan in 2001. The same thing is currently happening with the Islamic State, as it seeks to expand in Afghanistan, the Sinai Peninsula, and Southeast Asia, to name just a few places. Accordingly, the key to understanding what comes next with the Islamic State's collapse is looking back at how al-Qaeda devolved. The group's expansion has been described as a goal in and of itself as well as part of the organization's strategy to survive and penetrate new territories.

Throughout the early to mid-2000s, al-Qaeda expanded to Saudi Arabia (2003), Iraq (2004), Algeria (2006), and Yemen (2007). It formed franchises in Somalia (2010), Syria (2012), and an affiliation in South Asia through al-Qaeda in the Indian Subcontinent (2014). Al-Qaeda's expansion occurred in two specific ways – either implementing "in-house" expansion through establishing an affiliate group on its own, as it did in Saudi Arabia and Yemen, or merging with existing jihadist

groups in exchange for an official pledge of allegiance from the group to al-Qaeda. This model was on display in Iraq, with Abu Musab al-Zarqawi's group, Tawhid wal Jihad; in Algeria, with the Salafist Group for Preaching and Combat (GSPC); and in Somalia, with al-Shabaab.[79]

There are pros and cons to establishing affiliates. On the positive side, franchise groups made al-Qaeda seem ubiquitous, as AQI, AQAP, AQIM, and al-Shabaab conducted attacks in al-Qaeda's name. The method of franchising also offers "strategic reach" and allows the group to ingratiate itself into new theatres. But there are many negative aspects, too, including that an affiliate can damage the brand through its actions, as AQI did with its relentless sectarian attacks against Iraqi Shiites. Affiliates can also exploit the brand name and enjoy its benefits without doing much in return to advance the core group's mission, something Daniel Byman calls "shirking."[80] Moreover, enlisting affiliates led to a change in the strategic direction of core al-Qaeda, which had to spend more time attempting to manage the franchise groups, and in some cases "make concessions to address the narrow concerns of local groups joining its global banner."[81] Will IS face the same predicament? Or will its offshoots secure even more autonomy as the core of the group is crushed and its command-and-control capabilities systematically dismantled?

Saudi Arabia

In the spring of 2003, bin Laden stood up al-Qaeda's first franchise group, al-Qaeda in the Arabian Peninsula (the group initially referred to itself as "the mujahideen in the Arabian Peninsula") using al-Qaeda's own fighters as an example of "an in-house creation."[82] Although al-Qaeda operatives in Saudi Arabia were able to launch some successful attacks, including the Riyadh compound bombings

in 2003, the militants were systematically wiped out by Saudi internal security services. For a counterterrorism force that many outside observers were probably skeptical of, "the results were impressive: many on the most wanted lists were either captured or killed in shootouts across the kingdom."[83]

The other major reason why the al-Qaeda venture in Saudi Arabia failed was due to the much greater attraction of traveling to Iraq, where aspiring jihadists could engage with and kill American soldiers. The war in Iraq, therefore, was a much higher priority for Saudi jihadists. "To potential recruits and donors, there was no doubt paramilitary warfare in Iraq represented a politically more legitimate and theologically less controversial enterprise than bombings in the streets of Riyadh," according to Thomas Hegghammer.[84] In sum, "the decision to introduce a Saudi branch proved disastrous" for al-Qaeda, although its franchise in Iraq would enjoy far more success – at least initially, before succumbing to problems resulting from its rampant sectarian agenda later on.[85]

Iraq

Al-Qaeda's Iraq franchise was its first affiliate resulting from a merger, in which Abu Musab al-Zarqawi's Jama'at al-Tawhid wal-Jihad (TWJ) and al-Qaeda joined forces. Both groups had their own motives for the merger. For al-Qaeda, the group's leadership felt compelled to expand into Iraq after the US invasion, lest it risk being marginalized at a time when jihadists were flocking to the country to fight American soldiers. Al-Qaeda lacked a domestic infrastructure in Iraq, and so had to partner with another jihadist outfit already established in the area. For Zarqawi and TWJ, the move to merge with al-Qaeda to form AQI was a pragmatic decision to gain access to core al-Qaeda's deep-pocketed

donors throughout the Gulf, as well as to adopt a brand that would help attract foreign fighters.

Saudi militants in AQI provided the most money of any foreign contingent to the group, and also accounted for nearly three-quarters of all AQI's suicide bombers at the height of the insurgency in 2006 and 2007.[86] The most common nationalities of foreign fighters who traveled to fight in Iraq were, in order, Saudi, Libyan, and Syrian.[87] Moreover, since TWJ was composed primarily of militants from Jordan, Syria, Lebanon and the Palestinian territories, AQI had a significant non-Iraqi core from its inception.[88]

From the start, there were tensions between AQI's Iraqi members and foreigners.[89] These tensions extended to the leadership, including the Jordanian-born Zarqawi, who himself was constantly at odds with core al-Qaeda's leadership on a number of issues – above all, his penchant for targeting Shiites.[90] The insubordination of AQI would be a harbinger of the future, foreshadowing the rise of IS.[91] As Fishman notes, "Zarqawi and Al Qaeda were allies of convenience rather than genuine partners."[92] Zarqawi never fell in line with core al-Qaeda's agenda and consistently clashed with bin Laden and Zawahiri, successfully maintaining his autonomy and ignoring the leadership's repeated pleas to focus on the Americans rather than the Shia.

The egregious sectarianism of AQI was more than just a theological dispute – core al-Qaeda recalled what happened in Algeria, after the population turned against the Armed Islamic Group (GIA), a Salafi-jihadist group that resorted to killing fellow Muslims and even targeting neutrals who did not provide overt support to its agenda. Indeed, there was another connection between AQI and Algeria, since, amongst its foreign members, Zarqawi's group boasted many militants from the Maghreb who would help core al-Qaeda establish links with the GSPC to form al-Qaeda in the Islamic Maghreb, or AQIM.[93]

Algeria

Al-Qaeda's Algerian franchise, like AQI in Iraq, resulted from a merger and was not an organic al-Qaeda "startup." Al-Qaeda allied with the GSPC in an effort to expand its brand and its operations throughout North Africa. As with its other affiliates, there was consistent pressure from core al-Qaeda for AQIM to expand its purview to focus more on the global jihad, as opposed to purely localized objectives. Its most high-profile attack against a Western target occurred within Algeria, against the Tigantourine gas facility in In Amenas.[94] And while AQIM did conduct attacks outside of Algeria, including in Niger, Mali, and Mauritania, it never developed into the global threat core al-Qaeda had hoped it would.[95] By 2013, nearly 90 percent of AQIM activity took place within Algeria, and 80 percent of its attacks were directed against state security forces.[96] It was never able to escalate beyond this, more likely due to a lack of capability than a lack of will or desire.

Al-Qaeda was similarly disappointed by its inability to capitalize upon GSPC's European connections, especially in France, where Zawahiri and others believed they could tap into Muslim anger over that country's controversial headscarf ban.[97] GSPC also had connections in Germany, Spain, and the United Kingdom.[98] Camille Tawil, a journalist and long-time al-Qaeda watcher, speculates that the group was hoping to use GSPC's European linkages to pull off an attack similar to the 2004 Madrid train bombings.[99] This is yet another area where IS has proven to have bested al-Qaeda, evidenced by its deadly reach into Europe and its ability to direct, inspire, or launch attacks in Belgium, France, Spain, Germany, the UK, and elsewhere.

The decision to join with al-Qaeda was a far more pragmatic one for Algerian jihadists. GSPC was a failing group, so by adopting the al-Qaeda brand it hoped to bring in a fresh influx of recruits from

throughout the region.[100] Moreover, leaders like Abdelmalek Droukdal had a somewhat personal reason for seeking the affiliation, as he believed it would enhance his own standing within the organization, as well as making AQIM appear to be more dangerous than it might have been otherwise.[101] Joining al-Qaeda was not popular with everyone in GSPC – rather than join AQIM, many jihadists accepted the government's amnesty, which could be one of the reasons why Algeria has been less affected by the wave of jihadist violence that swept across the region with a renewed ferocity after the emergence of IS.

Even though it never launched major attacks in the West, AQIM did pioneer innovative methods, including an intense focus on propaganda and "media jihad."[102] There was also a clear indication of tactics shared through training, as after 2007 AQIM began utilizing improvised explosive devices and coordinated suicide bombings.[103] Above all else, AQIM is perhaps best known for its ability to finance its organization through crime, especially kidnapping.[104] Al-Qaeda's North African affiliate grew so successful at funding its organization through criminal activities that it was able to begin sending money back to core al-Qaeda in something akin to a mafia soldier kicking a "tax" up to the *capo*, in a sign of respect. Ideologically, core al-Qaeda and AQIM held largely the same views, which helped attenuate unnecessary friction between the groups. Still, even with an ideological affinity, core al-Qaeda desperately needed one of its franchises to develop the capability to launch a spectacular attack in the West. Its next franchise group in Yemen would evolve to fill this role.

Yemen

Al-Qaeda's Yemen franchise occurred as an in-house expansion, with the establishment of "The al-Qaeda Organization of Jihad in the South

of the Arabian Peninsula," which became "The al-Qaeda Organization in the Land of Yemen" and eventually gave way to al-Qaeda in the Arabian Peninsula (AQAP) when al-Qaeda's Saudi and Yemeni networks merged in early 2009.[105] In 2013, AQAP leader Nasir al-Wuhayshi was elevated to the position of al-Qaeda's general manager by its leader, Ayman al-Zawahiri, a nod to the importance of AQAP amongst the orbit of al-Qaeda affiliates. Accordingly, AQAP used its leaders' ties to core al-Qaeda leadership as a recruiting pitch to persuade aspiring jihadists to join its ranks.

Of all the affiliates, AQAP emerged to become the most operationally capable. When core al-Qaeda went years without being able to pull off a spectacular attack against the West, AQAP managed several "near misses" against US airliners, including the notorious underwear bomber plot and another plot against cargo planes with explosive-laden printer cartridges onboard. AQAP was considered such a high-level threat that former CIA Director David Petraeus once referred to the group's master bombmaker, Ibrahim Hassan al-Asiri, as "the world's most dangerous man."[106] Al-Asiri was killed in a drone strike in Yemen in August 2018.

Another important success by AQAP has been the continued evolution of jihadist propaganda and media outreach.[107] A major part of this success was due to the emergence of American-born radical cleric Anwar al-Awlaki, who before his death had developed a global following among jihadists, especially those from the West who were drawn to his cult of personality, including Nidal Hasan, a US Army psychiatrist who communicated with Awlaki through email for over a year before going on a shooting rampage at Fort Hood, Texas, in November 2009, where he killed 13 people.[108] Awlaki's influence continues to live on today on the Internet, years after his death.[109]

AQAP was also the most adept of all the franchises at effectively

balancing local versus global objectives.[110] "AQAP has been far more sensitive to local grievances and tribal identities, in part because al-Qaeda has learned and transmitted lessons about respecting nationalism to its affiliate," notes Byman.[111] In Yemen, jihadists have maintained good relations with the local tribes and been flexible with the imposition of sharia, jettisoning the more draconian rules more common to the Islamic State. Yet, even while focusing on issues most pressing to Yemeni tribesmen, AQAP still managed to play a role in the Charlie Hebdo attacks in Paris, France, in January 2015.[112] The group also maintains an increasingly close relationship with Al-Shabaab in Somalia and has served before as an interlocutor between other franchises, including Shabaab, AQIM, and JN.[113]

Somalia

Harakat al-Shabaab al-Mujahidiin (a.k.a. Shabaab, or "The Youth") is a radical fundamentalist faction that split off from the Islamic Courts Union (ICU) in Somalia, which itself was the outgrowth of al-Itihaad al-Islamiya (AIAI).[114] Many of al-Shabaab's founders fought in Afghanistan during the anti-Soviet jihad in the 1980s.[115] When the United States deployed to Somalia in the early 1990s to provide humanitarian assistance, bin Laden used this event as an opportunity to position al-Qaeda militants in East Africa, a move that would facilitate al-Qaeda's bombing of the US embassies in Nairobi, Kenya, and Dar es Salaam, Tanzania, several years later, in 1998.[116] Al-Shabaab formally coalesced around 2005, when a network of Afghan veterans of Somali origin, ex-AIAI militants, and al-Qaeda remnants throughout the Horn of Africa joined forces.[117]

  Approximately a year after its founding, al-Shabaab was able to network and recruit among Somali clans to grow its organization follow

ing Ethiopia's invasion of Somalia in late 2006.[118] The Ethiopian incursion breathed new life into what was at the time a rather fledgling organization, although one imbued with an experienced jihadist pedigree. The fighting between Shabaab and Ethiopian forces became known as the "dirty war," with both sides eschewing previously recognized norms regarding the use of violence. Shabaab introduced suicide bombing to Somalia for the first time, while the Ethiopians responded by using white phosphorous bombs to clear out entire neighborhoods.[119] Atrocities committed by Ethiopian forces led to the mobilization of foreign fighters, including members of the Somali diaspora living in the United States, as more than 40 Americans traveled to Somalia to join al-Shabaab.[120]

Even though many foreign fighters were motivated by Somali nationalism, defending Somalis from Christian Ethiopia also dovetailed with al-Qaeda's narrative. In 2010, al-Qaeda and Shabaab formally merged, as the Somali terror group's leader Ahmed Godane declared his group's intention to operate with a more "global mindset."[121] Al-Qaeda had considered Somalia as a place to seek safe haven back in the early 1990s, but decided against it due to terrain considered inhospitable for a terrorist group as well as issues related to the country's complex clan dynamics.[122] Furthermore, al-Qaeda was cognizant of the population's hostility toward non-Somalis, and the austere Salafist interpretation of Islam is far from universally accepted throughout the country. And even while al-Qaeda initially decided against seeking sanctuary in Somalia, it *has* proved to be a hotbed for terrorism and insurgency, largely as a result of its status as a collapsed state and near-constant anarchy, which has led to a power vacuum that violent non-state actors have filled.

Al-Shabaab has not demonstrated a proclivity to attack the West, but the group has conducted several high-profile attacks outside of Somalia, including the Kampala bombings in July 2010 in Uganda,

the Westgate Mall Attack in Nairobi, Kenya, in September 2013, and an attack at a university in Garissa, Kenya, in April 2015. These attacks could foreshadow Shabaab's development into a force throughout the region and not one strictly resigned to Somalia.[123] Fighting against a range of adversaries, including the African Union Mission in Somalia (AMISOM), forces from the Transitional Federal Government (TFG), and the Kenyan military, the group's control of territory has ebbed and flowed since 2011, with the loss of territory (especially coastal territory) significantly impacting Shabaab's ability to raise money. Nevertheless, the group has consistently demonstrated resilience in the face of adversity, successfully transitioning "from an insurgent group that controlled territory to a terrorist group that commits indiscriminate attacks on civilians and combatants alike."[124] Attacks on civilians have been accompanied by criticism from core al-Qaeda leadership, which is perhaps one reason Shabaab did not claim the deadly car-bomb attack in Mogadishu in October 2017 that led to over 300 casualties.[125]

The evolution of the global jihadist movement transformed al-Qaeda, long the movement's primary bulwark, into a decentralized network of terrorist groups operating in Yemen, Iraq, Algeria, Somalia, and elsewhere. It is crucial to understand how this evolution – perhaps what some might consider a devolution – occurred, in order to judge whether or not IS could follow a similar path. As of late July 2018, the counter-IS fight was winding down in northeastern Syria as the Islamic State's territory was reduced to less than 1 percent of what is was at its peak, mostly centered around the Hajin pocket and other towns and villages in the Central Euphrates River valley. Nevertheless, the group was estimated to still have between 20,000 and 30,000 fighters just in Iraq and Syria. And the Islamic State's ideology is still viable as a means of conveying specific grievances to young Muslims while also offering an attractive worldview that frames things in terms of "us" versus "them."

2

The Inner Workings of the Islamic State

Al-Qaeda may have birthed several highly capable offshoots, but the transition of one of those off shoots – al-Qaeda in Iraq (AQI) – into the Islamic State was not a linear one. It involved bloody confrontations between erstwhile allies within the jihadist movement, and a lasting cleavage that has led to continued fighting and division between IS and al-Qaeda to the current day. Understanding this split is key to understanding IS, its inner workings, and its motivations.

Following the tumult brought forth by the Arab Spring, Syria descended into civil war. To al-Qaeda leadership, Syria was the opportunity the group was looking for to reassert itself on the world stage and once again become a relevant player in the heart of the Middle East. Al-Qaeda expanded into Syria in January 2012 with the establishment of Jabhat al-Nusra (JN), led by a Syrian AQI (now Islamic State of Iraq (ISI)) fighter, Abu Muhammad al-Joulani. Core al-Qaeda sought to uphold the chimera of deniability in its relationship with its nascent Syrian branch. In April 2013, the ISI declared JN its subsidiary, although Joulani scoffed at this arrangement and instead declared his loyalty to Zawahiri and core al-Qaeda. Core al-Qaeda's inability to control its affiliates had not only damaged its brand, but had now led to the emergence of what would become its most significant rival.[1] The fall-out resulted in ISI's expansion into Syria and its subsequent rebranding as the Islamic State (IS). Moreover, when the

fissure occurred, the majority of foreign fighters in Nusra's ranks left the group to join IS.[2] Zawahiri publicly denounced the split between the groups in February 2014. No matter, the stage was set for the rise of IS.

In order to properly understand the rise and fall of IS, it is crucial to have a firm grasp of the group's capabilities – both how it is able to plan and conduct attacks (operational capabilities) and also how the group maintains itself as a cohesive entity (organizational capabilities). IS is a pioneering terrorist group in several ways, from its ability to raise and spend money to its multi-tiered approach to conducting terrorist attacks. IS's use of social media and encrypted apps to direct terrorist attacks overseas sets it apart from any terrorist groups of the past. As evidenced by the Paris November 2015 attacks and the Brussels March 2016 attacks, at its peak IS sustained the ability to strike into the heart of Europe while simultaneously managing a proto-state spanning Iraq and Syria.

Operational Capabilities

The Islamic State's ability to plan and execute attacks, against both conventional and unconventional forces on the battlefield, as well as abroad in Western cities, makes it a relatively unique organization in terms of its operational capabilities. Its fighters have mastered a diverse array of tactics, from VBIEDs to ambushes and hit-and-run attacks. Moreover, the leadership's exhortation for its followers to conduct attacks abroad, including so-called vehicular terrorism or ramming attacks, is a tactic pioneered by IS that has emerged as a new trend in terrorist attacks directed at the West. To remain relevant, as IS loses its last remaining territory in Iraq and Syria, it may

seek to rely on launching spectacular terrorist attacks in the West to maintain morale and burnish the group's brand. This section will discuss the group's operational capabilities, which include financing, weapons, intelligence, the ability to maintain a safe haven, and training.

Financing

At the height of its territorial control in 2015, the Islamic State generated more than $6 billion – the equivalent of the gross domestic product of Liechtenstein.[3] While IS's territorial control has declined, it still retains financial power; IS's surviving leadership is alleged to have smuggled as much as $400 million out of Iraq and Syria and used it to invest in legitimate businesses – hotels, hospitals, farms, and car dealerships – throughout the region, including in Turkey, where some militants have also reportedly made large purchases of gold.[4] IS's financial holdings and funding model have made it the wealthiest insurgent group in history, and its diversified funding portfolio and ability to raise money through criminal activities provide it with an opportunity to survive and even make a comeback in Iraq and Syria over the next several years.[5]

Following its obstreperous rise to global infamy in 2014, IS was enshrined in media-fueled hyperbole. While, much of the time, the superlatives were misplaced, one area in which they were unquestionably warranted was in regard to its finances. Indeed, the war chest it amassed in 2014 and 2015 easily made it the richest terrorist organization in the contemporary era.[6] IS is different from previous terrorist groups because the territory it controlled provided extremely lucrative resources, such as oil, and a renewable funding source in the form of a taxable population. As former Assistant Secretary for Terrorist

Financing at the Department of the Treasury Daniel Glaser has noted, IS generated its wealth from three primary sources: oil and gas, which generated about $500 million in 2015, primarily through internal sales; taxation and extortion, which garnered approximately $360 million in 2015; and the 2014 looting of Mosul, during which IS stole about $500 million from bank vaults [7]

To put IS financing in perspective, it is useful to consider not only IS's similarities to other groups but its differences as well. Indeed, there are far more differences than similarities, as IS is unique in the scale and scope of its financing activities. Like many other terrorist groups in the contemporary era, IS relies on a range of criminal activities, including – but not limited to – extortion, kidnapping for ransom, robbery and theft, and antiquities smuggling. IS may also have been involved with narcotics trafficking.[8] There is little evidence to suggest that foreign donations from nation-states have also been a significant funding source for IS, although wealthy individuals from the Gulf have been accused of financing terrorists in Syria.[9]

In addition to funding its organization from the bottom up, through petty criminality, IS also relied on a top-down funding structure from a range of sources associated with its control of territory. As mentioned in the introduction, IS is unique in recent history as one of the few terrorist groups to generate most of its funding from the territory it held – revenue amassed from taxation and extortion, the sale of oil and various oil-related products, looting, confiscation of property and cash, and fines levied against the population by the religious police for a litany of offenses.[10] IS's reputation as incorruptible – a defining characteristic inherited from its predecessors AQI and ISI – helped boost popular support.[11]

Most concerning, however, is that IS continues to make money from

oil to this day, despite the drastic reduction in its territorial holdings. In late June 2018, four members of IS's Oil and Gas Network were killed during Coalition operations in the central Euphrates River Valley in Syria.[12] According to a United Nations Security Council report from the summer of 2018, IS has regained control of oil fields in northeastern Syria and continues to extract oil, both for its own use, and also for sale to locals.[13] So while significant progress has been made in combating IS's ability to raise money through oil, this revenue source has yet to be completely eradicated and probably never will be. Even when IS's predecessors did not control large swaths of territory in Iraq from 2006 to 2009, they were similarly able to raise substantial sums of money from oil, including by extorting local and regional distribution networks.

One of the core difficulties in degrading IS's considerable material wealth was that much of what it amassed was collected in and through the territory over which it presided. Indeed, as much as 80 percent of its fortune was acquired by mimicking one of the central functions of modern nation-states – that is, collecting taxes and tariffs from the local population.[14] In this sense, IS was unique in the recent history of insurgency. It was entrepreneurial and, to a large extent, self-sufficient.[15] As an upshot of this (and notwithstanding much spurious media coverage), there is scant evidence to suggest that foreign donations were ever a significant source of funding for it.[16] As the organization evolves in years to come, these revenue streams will probably change; indeed, external funding from sympathetic state and non-state donors could one day comprise a much larger proportion of its coffers.[17]

The war against IS has vividly shown the intractability of counter-terrorism financing. Sanctions, one of the principal traditional tools

for this area of policy, were demonstrably insufficient, and even the impact of the Counter-IS Coalition's targeted, intelligence-led strikes on oil operations and cash storage sites in Iraq and Syria in 2015 proved to be impermanent. To cripple its material wealth, a combination of civilian and military measures was required, with global backing. Every potential facet of IS revenue had to be considered for targeting or sanctioning, and the most difficult areas to obstruct – taxation and extortion – became long-term targets for post-conflict stabilization.

As the organization continues to be degraded, its primary sources of revenue will change and its leadership may seek to secure external funding from sympathetic donors throughout the Arab and Islamic world, or nation-states in the Middle East that view IS as a potentially useful proxy in the region's ongoing internecine conflict. Still, this remains a remote possibility for two reasons. First, IS has demonstrated such an extreme sectarian agenda that its egregious behavior is beyond the pale even for states that normally sponsor terrorist groups. Second, the counter-threat finance measures devised and implemented by the international community, in partnership with private-sector entities including major banks, has made it extremely difficult for terrorist groups to take advantage of the licit financial sector to store, transfer, or launder illicit revenues.

Weapons

During its peak, IS could be considered one of the most well-funded terrorist groups in history, and, also, one of the most well-equipped.[18] The Islamic State managed to acquire an impressive arsenal of weapons to equip the army of its proto-state. IS fighters trained with small arms, but also learned how to use heavy-caliber weapons that

could be used in more conventional-style skirmishes. Its fighters proved innovative, demonstrating the skill and alacrity to modify a range of weapons systems. The group displayed a remarkable ingenuity in training new recruits, adept at onboarding both battle-hardened jihadists with experience in previous fronts, and newly arrived Europeans with little or no knowledge of military tactics. Its fighters' willingness to die in suicide attacks was unprecedented in terms of overall numbers, lending credence to the saying that quantity can have a quality all of its own. Some scholars have argued that IS's ability to wage conventional warfare was so advanced that the organization of its military capabilities bore resemblance to the warfighting functions of the United States military in terms of combined arms concepts and command and control.[19]

Unlike many terrorist and insurgent groups that operated during the Cold War, IS was not forced to rely upon external states to provide it with weaponry. Instead, its fighters forcibly looted hundreds of millions of dollars' worth of weapons and equipment from Iraqi and Syrian military installations.[20] IS maintained a diversified source of weapons, including those acquired from other insurgents in Syria who defected to the Islamic State; weapons purchased from other insurgents who received them from foreign donors; weapons captured from defeated adversaries; and weapons bought from or traded for with corrupt members of the security forces in Syria and Iraq.[21] The group even managed to wrangle sophisticated anti-aircraft weaponry such as the Chinese-made FN-6, which was provided to Syrian rebels who were ultimately overrun by IS fighters.[22] Nearly 90 percent of the weapons and ammunition acquired by IS originated in China, Russia, and Eastern Europe.[23] Unlike in some conflicts where much of the weaponry on the battlefield is old or antiquated, the lion's share of IS's weaponry, and especially the ammunition it was using, was

predominantly found to have been delivered to the region since the Syrian conflict began in 2011.[24]

IS was not the prototypical insurgent group – it was equipped more like a conventional military. Armored vehicles were purchased on the black market or scavenged from the Iraqi security forces which had retreated from the battlefield [25] The use of "technicals," which are pick-up trucks modified with machine guns or anti-aircraft weaponry, provides the militants freedom of movement and much-needed mobility. IS fighters have used artillery and RPGs in Syria while also making use of Humvees and T-55 tanks captured from the Iraqi security forces.[26] Other types of weapons include M79 anti-tank rockets made in the former Yugoslavia, American-made M16 and M14 rifles, as well as assorted small arms and ammunition.[27] Many of the weapons and equipment that IS militants fought with were initially distributed to the Iraqi Army to provide it with both a qualitative and quantitative edge over its adversaries.[28] In October 2014, US planes dropped weapons intended for Kurdish fighters in Kobani, but instead ended up in IS-controlled territory and were ultimately commandeered by the militants.[29]

In terms of tactics, IS demonstrated interest and skill in experimenting with new technologies and elevated the use of suicide attacks to a new level. Between December 2015 and November 2016, IS conducted an astounding 923 suicide operations in Iraq and Syria alone.[30] Many of these attacks involved the use of VBIEDs. IS was able to record its attacks and then distribute the footage as propaganda.[31] This also set IS apart from other groups, including al-Qaeda and Hezbollah, both of which engaged in similar kinds of propaganda distribution, but never achieved the same scope or scale as IS did with its battlefield footage. Throughout the conflict there were reports of IS fighters using drones in a number of different ways, from surveillance and reconnaissance to actual attacks involving grenades and explosives.[32] And in keeping with

the findings of Truls Hallberg Tønnessen, the primary strength of IS is not necessarily the acquisition and use of advanced technology, but the improvised use of less advanced and easily accessible technology to great (and lethal) effect.[33]

Intelligence

For the Islamic State, its intelligence capabilities served a dual purpose, having both internal and external objectives. Internally, IS sought to purge all potential spies and suspected collaborators. Externally, its intelligence service was used to attack its opponents, both within the region and farther abroad. Ominously, the intelligence skills IS fighters learned in Iraq and Syria could serve them well if they seek to return to their countries of origin or third-party countries to mount attacks. If IS is able to reconstitute its organization in the future, even in a far more limited form, its residual intelligence capabilities will probably be a major reason why.

IS relies on subversion and clandestine operations to execute attacks in both Syria and Iraq, including suicide bombings, assassinations, and other guerilla-style tactics, extending to offensive raids on critical military targets, such as Syrian Army bases. During the earliest stages of the conflict, in response to US airstrikes, IS fighters worked to stress the importance of operational security to fellow fighters, imploring them to assume a "covert posture submerged within the population," don masks that covered their faces, and even eschew any identifying information while operating in public.[34] In many ways, IS's intelligence service was one of its fundamental drivers of battlefield success and organizational cohesion. Soon after assuming leadership of the group, Baghdadi relied on IS's internal security apparatus to purge the organization of suspected informants.[35] When new recruits arrived

from abroad, especially from Western countries, they were screened and vetted by IS fighters through a series of interviews, during which personal information was obtained and cross checked, passports were examined and donations were accepted.[36] IS maintained impeccable records of who was joining the organization in an effort to weed out spies and exact revenge on those who defected.

For IS, counterintelligence was a top priority. A captured IS computer even revealed a downloaded copy of the US Army and Marine Corps Counterinsurgency Field Manual (FM) 3-24, which the group presumably studied to better understand US operating procedures.[37] Intelligence agencies and security services in Western countries, particularly in Europe, remain highly concerned that sleeper cells of fighters will arrive back in their home countries with newly acquired skills in how to conduct surveillance, how to avoid detection, and how to build a clandestine network.[38] Those returning in order to plan an attack will do so surreptitiously, and many could seek to return to the illicit networks they belonged to before departing for Syria.[39]

The IS intelligence apparatus, also sometimes referred to as "Emni" (Arabic for "trust," "security," and "safety"), fulfills a wide range of internal security and external intelligence services, to include everything from rooting out informers to planning external attacks across the globe, including the Paris November 2015 and Brussels March 2016 attacks.[40] Former Baathists from Saddam Hussein's secret police played an instrumental role in helping to organize the Emni.[41] Some have compared the Emni to East Germany's Stasi, a brutal domestic intelligence agency that spied on citizens and foreigners alike.[42] Emni members successfully penetrated government institutions in Iraq, as well as various agencies within adversary forces, such as Kurdish intelligence, and within the ranks of Al-Nusra.[43] The Emni holds a special place within IS and, according to Rukmini Callimachi, is

afforded "carte blanche to recruit and reroute operatives from all parts of the organization – from new arrivals to seasoned battlefield fighters, and from the group's special forces and its elite commando units."[44]

Before IS sought to expand into new territory, its intelligence operatives were sent to collect information on the existing political and ideological make-up of the area. Once IS actually moved into the territory, those individuals already identified as potentially resistant to the group would be rounded up and executed.[45] Such a sophisticated strategy should give pause to anyone who believes IS would be unable to once again infiltrate areas that have recently been reclaimed by Iraqi or Syrian forces, respectively. IS has also allegedly sent militants abroad to Turkey, Europe, and elsewhere as forward deployed assets, to be used as sleeper cells at some undetermined point in the future. As Bruce Hoffman notes, the Islamic State's "investment of operational personnel ensures that IS will retain an effective international terrorist strike capability in Europe irrespective of its battlefield reverses in Syria and Iraq."[46]

Sanctuary, Safe Haven, and Operational Space

As the world learned on September 11, 2001, when violent terrorist groups are allowed to persist unfettered in safe havens and sanctuary, they can develop the capability to plot and execute spectacular attacks. Without Raqqa as a headquarters, it remains debatable whether or not IS would have been able to plan an attack as sophisticated and coordinated as that launched in Paris, France, in November 2015. Sanctuary and control of territory – operational space – enable financing, which in turn helps facilitate the process of state building. As IS built its state, this in turn increased its legitimacy as an entity able to provide law and

order and other basic trappings of a state, further attracting foreign fighters and their families to travel to the territory. The caliphate was becoming a reality.

Since the late 1990s, Sunni violent extremism has become a major threat to global stability and it now has more groups, members, and safe havens than at any other point in history.[47] And more so than any other insurgent group in recent memory, the Islamic State was able to hold and actually control vast swaths of territory across two sovereign countries. At its peak, the Islamic State controlled more than 100,000 km² of territory containing more than 11 million people, mostly in Iraq and Syria.[48] It maintained its de-facto headquarters in Raqqa, Syria, and its primary base of operations in Iraq was in Mosul. Throughout the course of the conflict, IS occupied parts of Idlib and Aleppo provinces, where training camps were established. At various points, in Aleppo, the group controlled the Jarabulus crossing to the west and the Tal Abayd crossing to the east, critical chokepoints that regulated the flow of men, money, and *matériel* coming into Syria from Turkey.[49] Losing the physical caliphate may tarnish its brand in the eyes of some, but the fact that it was able to successfully establish a caliphate in the first place will remain a viable propaganda tool for the group in recruiting new members and lifting the morale of the global jihadist movement as a whole. As Aaron Zelin remarked:

The most important take away is that it happened. No longer do individuals or jihadis have to point to a historical idealized past of the original Rashidun Caliphate. Rather, they can point to two to five years ago and that it was here and it was doing well from their perspective. As a result, it is about a lived nostalgia rather than just a pure utopian fantasy whether you agree or disagree with how well things actually were under IS rule. It's all about

how jihadis, supporters, and fence-sitters think of the experience. Many believe that if their enemies didn't attack them it would have been successful.[50]

IS enjoyed safe haven in Syria largely unmolested for long enough to allow it to really hold territory that it could use to train, produce media, and begin implementing the foundational elements of its caliphate. There is a direct connection between controlling territory and earning money. Consider that, for long stretches of time during this conflict, IS was earning well over $1 million per day from the sale of oil and oil-related products.[51] Furthermore, IS checkpoints throughout the territory it controlled provided the militants with multiple opportunities to "tax" those attempting to pass through. IS was so brazen in some parts of the territory it controlled that it allowed municipal workers and civil servants to remain in their jobs, including some city mayors and other top local officeholders who were allowed to keep their posts, provided they acknowledged the legitimacy of IS's rule.[52] Accordingly, the control of territory meant the control of resources, including oil, wheat, water, and ancient artifacts, all of which were sold to further expand IS's financial portfolio.

Sunni disenfranchisement in both Iraq and Syria contributed to the Islamic State's ability to establish sanctuary in those countries.[53] Even after IS has been largely vanquished in Iraq and remains severely attenuated in Syria, poor or non-existent governance remains a major concern in both of those countries. These areas remain a concern because IS has been able to orchestrate attacks when under immense siege from the Coalition, taking advantage of ever-smaller swaths of territory that the group can still utilize as a safe haven to plan, plot, and incite from.[54] The US intelligence community remains extremely concerned about IS developing an "alternate safe haven," that is,

another area outside of Iraq and Syria where its remaining fighters are able to congregate en masse to establish a robust presence and begin reconstituting.[55] Safe havens are spaces that are not simply ungoverned, but alternatively governed – they are governed by insurgents or terrorist groups who may seek to ally with or tolerate an IS presence in places like Libya, Afghanistan, Egypt's Sinai Peninsula, or throughout isolated archipelagos in Southeast Asia. Herein lie some of the dangers inherent in splintering, especially when certain regions already possess the militant infrastructure to allow splinter movements to flourish by providing a ready-made environment for terrorism and insurgency.

Training

By the summer of 2014, IS had already established logistical hubs for resupply, a functioning operational headquarters, training camps, and other vital infrastructure throughout Syria. Training for IS recruits, especially foreign fighters, was multi-purpose, at once designed to build a militant's practical skills, but also to "imbue him with a sense of solidarity with a larger cause."[56] After being properly vetted, new recruits would spend several weeks undergoing both religious and military training, tailored to align with their assigned role within the organization. Highly skilled recruits were selected to receive further training on more sophisticated weapons.[57] IS selected certain operatives for its "special forces program," which involved ten levels of training.[58] IS is far from the Navy SEALs, but a dedicated special forces program is a lot more than most insurgent groups are capable of achieving, with the exception of groups like Hezbollah, which is in a class of its own in many ways (and benefits from the largesse of Iran).

From 2012 to 2015, well over 100 jihadist training camps were identified in Syria and Iraq, used not only by IS but also by Nusra and a range of other violent militant groups.[59] A major part of what happens in IS training camps is religious instruction and ideological indoctrination.[60] As Graeme Wood has noted, "the religion preached by its most ardent followers derives from coherent and even learned interpretations of Islam."[61] Perhaps interestingly, it seems that many IS recruits were in need of strict lessons in how to interpret the Islamic State's austere view of Salafism – after all, only a mere 5 percent of incoming recruits were judged to have an "advanced" knowledge of Islam, while 70 percent were described as having only a "basic" grasp of the religion.[62] Even with a simplistic interpretation of religion, it was clearly still a significant motivating factor for recruits to join IS.[63]

IS also trains young children in their "Cubs of the Caliphate" camps, where children as young as 5 years old are indoctrinated in the group's ideology and taught how to kill.[64] Horgan et al. have described the six stages of child socialization to IS, including seduction, selection, and subjugation, among other disturbing aspects of the process.[65] In Syria, this has included an aggressive campaign targeting "youth, especially boys, to override parents' authority, create new power structures in society, and propagate [IS's] ideology."[66] The head of Germany's domestic intelligence agency has warned that the return of children "brainwashed" by the Islamic State poses a "massive danger" to his country in the near term and well into the future.[67] A captured French jihadist claimed that IS "made concrete plans" to send children (mostly Syrians) to Europe to conduct attacks against Western targets, but would only do so once the kids reach adolescence so that facial recognition software would not be as effective.[68]

Organizational Capabilities

IS's organizational structure may help it transition smoothly from a territorially based insurgent organization to an underground, clandestine terrorist group. Its network-like qualities and affiliate franchise groups contribute to its protean structure and ability to survive. Another important element to analyze is how IS went about building its state and the manner in which it constructed a bureaucracy to help it operate more effectively.[69] It even required recruits to fill out highly detailed "onboarding" documents which asked for name, address, phone number, and detailed information about the network that recruited them, a measure ostensibly implemented to enhance operational security.

This section also examines the "virtual caliphate" – that is, IS's ability to survive online through its use of information operations and social-media savvy. Even before Raqqa fell, the IS media machine kicked into high gear, working assiduously to dispel any notion of defeat as merely temporary and crafting a narrative of redemption, vengeance, and a future return to the glory days of the caliphate. The truth is that the establishment of the caliphate is a once-in-a-lifetime event and a feat unlikely to be repeated anytime soon. But IS will still attempt to use it as "proof of concept" in the future, demonstrating that it could be accomplished as a way of attempting to unify jihadists around its brand and core ethos.

Recruitment

In addition to recruiting within the region, IS was able to successfully recruit thousands of European Muslims to join its ranks. There were a significant number of Westerners counted among IS's ranks,

including fighters from the United States, the United Kingdom, Australia, Scandinavia, and many European countries. There was also an outsized contingent of jihadist fighters from Trinidad and Tobago.[70] Why were so many young men and women from the outskirts of London, Paris, and Brussels so enamored with an ultra-violent, atavistic terrorist organization that sought to take the world back to the seventh century? This is the subject of ongoing debate between two French scholars of Islam, Gilles Kepel and Olivier Roy, concerning the topic of radicalization. What can explain so many French citizens going on to join IS? Why has France been among the most targeted countries in the West by jihadists? Kepel lays the blame squarely with religious extremism, while Roy argues that European jihadists who traveled to the caliphate and participated in gruesome actions are merely nihilists using Islam as a pretext to carry out sociopathic fantasies.[71]

According to Rik Coolsaet, "joining IS is merely a shift to another form of deviant behavior, next to membership of street gangs, rioting, drug trafficking and juvenile delinquency."[72] A 2012 report by the European Parliament titled "Europe's Crime–Terror Nexus: Links Between Terrorist and Organised Crime Groups in the European Union" noted the prevalence with which jihadist attacks involved links to criminality, including drug trafficking.[73] In some sense, a background in the criminal underworld left behind for militant Islam can play into the appeal of what has been called "jihadi cool," which blends "traditional notions of honor and virility, but also a strong undercurrent of oppositional, postmodern cool."[74] Thomas Hegghammer has referred to elements of this trend as "the soft power of militant jihad," while observing that "In Europe, radicals sometimes wear a combination of sneakers, a Middle Eastern or Pakistani gown and a combat jacket on top. It's a style that perhaps reflects their urban roots, Muslim identity and militant sympathies."[75]

IS's predecessor, AQI, was led by a criminal-cum-jihadist named Abu Musab al-Zarqawi, whose background included street gangs and prison time for sexual assault.[76] Indeed, IS seems to attract many jihadists with a similar profile, including the main link between the Paris November 2015 attacks and the Brussels March 2016 bombings, Salah Abdeslam, known for his penchant for drinking, smoking, and gambling, rather than his piety. Abdeslam was a regular patron (and brother of the manager) of a Molenbeek bar named Café del Beguines, a place known for drug dealing and other illicit activity and closed down after "compromising public security and tranquility."[77] Abdeslam was the only surviving member of the group of terrorists that formed the core of the French–Belgian nexus.[78] He has been back and forth to court, and his refusal to cooperate with authorities has made him something of a cult hero to aspiring jihadists, even cited as the inspiration for a March 2018 attack at a French supermarket.[79]

Molenbeek came under intense scrutiny following the Paris and Brussels attacks. It is a gritty neighborhood of Brussels where a "hybrid subculture of crime, violence, and jihadi activism has taken root."[80] It symbolizes the epicenter of the crime–terror nexus. It has a history with Islamic radicals and their networks, and is plagued by high levels of unemployment, and when compared with the rest of Belgian society its residents suffer from severe educational disparities, a disproportionately high involvement in the prison system, and isolation from wider Belgian society. Matthew Levitt described Molenbeek as "like another world, another culture, festering in the heart of the West."[81] In fact, Molenbeek was so insular that it was not particularly strange that a charismatic imam named Khalid Zerkani (a.k.a. "Papa Noel") with deep hatred for the West encouraged young Belgian men with ancestral roots in Morocco and other majority-Muslim countries to commit acts of criminality in order to finance jihad.[82]

Besides Abdeslam, several other notorious IS terrorists had criminal backgrounds, including the leader of the Paris attacks, fellow Belgian Abdelhamid Abaaoud. Others include Ahmed Coulibaly, a key figure in the Charlie Hebdo attacks; Mohamed Lahouaiej Bouhlel, the terrorist who killed 84 people by driving a truck through a crowd on Bastille Day in Nice, France; and Anis Amri, the Tunisian jihadist responsible for ramming a truck into a Berlin Christmas market.

Leadership

As has been well documented by now, the leadership core of the Islamic State congealed in Camp Bucca. Many of its top leaders have been eliminated – although, at the time of this writing, the so-called Caliph is still alive, on the run, and in hiding. With most of the original leadership gone, the chances increase that remaining fighters will splinter off and be absorbed by new groups elsewhere, even as "core IS" inevitably attempts to reconstitute itself back in parts of Iraq and Syria. The splintering of the group will lead to further decentralization and a situation in which there is a decreased threat from any one major jihadist group, but an increased threat from dozens of smaller outfits, some of which may eventually grow to become more lethal than the group from which they were originally derived.

IS is led by Abu Bakr al-Baghdadi, an Iraqi also known as Ibrahim Awad Ibrahim al-Badry, born in Samarra in 1971.[83] Captured by US forces near Fallujah in 2004, al-Baghdadi spent years at Camp Bucca, a detention facility where he is thought to have grown even further radicalized and anti-American, while also broadening his network among aggrieved Iraqi Sunni Arabs, including many from Anbar and Nineveh provinces.[84]Along with other Islamic State leaders – including Abu Muslim al-Turkmani, Abu Louay, and Abu Kassem – Baghdadi

used his time as a networking opportunity to meet and organize with jihadists, ex-Baathists, and violent criminals.[85] Upon their release, they formed the core of what evolved into the Islamic State, after Baghdadi helped engineer the defection of al-Qaeda in Iraq from the broader al-Qaeda orbit.[86] Baghdadi obtained a doctorate in Quranic studies, for which he studied the theology of Islam's central text, from Saddam University in Baghdad. This education allowed him to burnish religious credentials that other jihadist leaders have never been able to claim, including al-Qaeda leaders Osama bin Laden and Ayman al-Zawahiri. The legitimacy afforded by his religious education was one of several factors – along with familial lineage traced back to the Prophet – that cleared Baghdadi's way to declare himself Caliph, or ruler of all Muslims, in a historic speech at the Grand Mosque in Mosul in June 2014.[87]

While the group's leadership cadre did include some prominent foreign fighters, such as a Chechen named Omar al-Shishani,[88] there were also former Baath party military and intelligence officers that held high-ranking positions during Saddam Hussein's regime, including Abu Ali al-Anbari and Abu Muslim al-Turkmani.[89] Two other former regime-loyalists-turned-IS-members were Fadel al-Hayali and Adnan al-Sweidawi, both of whom served as military officers and Baath party insiders.[90] Indeed, IS maintained a leadership council, a cabinet, and had ties to local leaders. The leadership council helped deal with religious issues and doctrine, but also apparently made decisions about executions. The cabinet maintained oversight on finance, security, media, prisoners, and recruitment, while local leaders were comprised of roughly a dozen deputies spread between Iraq and Syria.[91] IS operates in a more decentralized fashion than al-Qaeda ever did, with operations carried out by a network of regional commanders who each maintained responsibility for subordinates, who

had their own autonomy, but were also able to collaborate and coordinate with the regional commanders on a variety of tactical issues.[92]

Before being killed in a US airstrike in August 2016, Baghdadi's deputy was Abu Muhammad al-Adnani, a Syrian jihadist who fought against US forces in Iraq and was captured in 2005. Like Baghdadi, Adnani was detained in Camp Bucca for a period of time. He would go on to become the terrorist group's chief spokesman, tasked with directing its media campaign and information operations.[93] In June 2014, al-Adnani was the first member of IS to officially declare a caliphate in Iraq and Syria. He was designated as a terrorist by the US Department of State in August 2014, and a $5 million bounty was subsequently placed on his head. Al-Adnani's legacy continues to live on through audio recordings. In the most notorious of these, a nine-minute audio recording titled "Die in Your Rage" from September 2014, he implores Muslims in Western nations to carry out lone-wolf attacks. In addition to serving as spokesman, al-Adnani headed IS's previously aforementioned *Emni,* or external operations unit, which was responsible for planning attacks outside of IS territory. Al-Adnani is thought to have had a hand in planning some of the most spectacular attacks ever conducted by the group, including the Paris November 2015 and the Brussels March 2016 attacks.[94]

Ideology

Just as salient as the military skills taught in IS's training camps was the religious instruction and indoctrination of IS recruits and members, including young children. The next generation of youngsters has already been brainwashed, force-fed a highly sectarian and *takfirist* worldview. The Islamic State has proven to be the most austere of all Salafi-jihadist groups, even eclipsing al-Qaeda in its austere

interpretation of *sharia* law. As IS seeks to expand abroad following the collapse of its caliphate, it will probably need to do what al-Qaeda has successfully done to co-exist in certain locales – that is, tailoring its ideology (and tempering it where necessary) to fall more closely in line with local attitudes, as AQAP has done in Yemen and as its various iterations have attempted to do in Syria.

The brand of Islam practiced by the Islamic State has been described, perhaps most accurately, as "untamed Wahhabism" that views the killing of those deemed unbelievers as a necessity to furthering its mission of purifying the community of the faithful.[95] The group's ideology, defined by an extremely narrow interpretation of *sharia* on social and criminal issues, explains its use of beheading as a way of murdering its victims, who have included several Westerners, Christian and Yazidi religious minorities, Shiite Muslims (considered apostates), Kurds, Alawites, and even other Sunni Muslims whom IS deems worthy of elimination. It has been labeled "the most elaborate and militant jihad polity in modern history."[96]

After it seized Mosul in June 2014, IS publicized a "city charter" that called for the amputation of thieves' hands, mandatory prayers, the banning of all drugs and alcohol, and the desecration of shrines and graves considered to be polytheistic.[97] The group's adherence to such an austere, unforgiving brand of Islam is reminiscent of AQI's split with core al-Qaeda, and once again al-Qaeda senior leadership, including Ayman al-Zawahiri, viewed the group's extreme violence as ultimately counterproductive.[98] The public split with al-Qaeda has seemingly forced jihadists to choose sides,[99] although, in an interesting twist, some IS fighters probably get some of their ideological guidance on building an Islamic State from "The Management of Savagery," a manifesto penned by one of core al-Qaeda's main ideologues, Abu Bakr Naji.[100] Its ideology has been described as "aggressive" and

"expansionist" with no recognition of modern-day political borders.[101] To be sure, IS regards state boundaries as "artificial creations of colonial powers designed to divide the Muslim world."[102] The fact that IS has announced the establishment of an Islamic state is proof in the eyes of many Muslims worldwide that Baghdadi will be able to resurrect the caliphate.[103]

For IS, the future is one in which a caliphate stretches across the globe. Indeed, the state-building project undertaken by IS was one in which Baghdadi saw his organization "taking a first step toward erasing the artificial boundaries imposed by colonial powers to divide Muslims."[104] The Islamic State's ideology is "an extremist reading of Islamic scripture" and one which espouses "sharply anti-Shiite sectarian views and harsh application of Islamic law."[105] IS's ideology promotes a worldview that essentially "classifies and excommunicates fellow Muslims."[106] That most IS recruits have a poor understanding of Islam is a benefit to recruiters, who in some ways prefer recruits with an unsophisticated command of their religion, as it makes them more malleable and less likely to question those who seek to indoctrinate them.[107] Furthermore, IS and its ideology will persist for generations. While the physical caliphate has been destroyed, the fact that it was established will help fuel the duration of the ideology well into the future.[108]

Human Resources and Bureaucracy

In the post-9/11 era, it became fashionable to talk about how terrorist organizations like al-Qaeda were "networked," assuming a transnational posture that showed scant resemblance to the vertically structured, top-down ethno-nationalist terrorist groups of the 1980s. But in fact, al-Qaeda, and the Islamic State after it, were both highly bureaucratic in nature, even though both groups maintained a global

presence. And even though IS was extremely brutal in doling out punishment to those who "broke the rules," its leadership was also aware of the importance of providing services to the constituency it claimed to represent. During the midst of civil war, internecine violence, and widespread sectarian strife, IS provided predictability, however draconian. Its vast governance network, spearheaded by the *hisbah,* or religious police, dispensed swift justice for a wide range of offenses, but Syrians, Iraqis, and those foreigners who emigrated to the caliphate understood what they needed to do and how they needed to live in order to stay alive. This imbued IS with a sense of political legitimacy that few terrorist groups ever manage to acquire.

All told, IS attracted approximately 43,000 fighters from more than 120 countries.[109] The conflict in Syria has attracted more Westerners than any other conflict in the modern era, including the 1979–89 anti-Soviet jihad.[110] The number of foreign fighters arriving to join the Islamic State finally tailed off in September 2016, dropping from approximately 2,000 recruits crossing the Turkish–Syrian border each month, to only 50.[111] A vast majority of those fighters hailed from the Middle East, North Africa, and other regions typically associated with global jihad, such as the Caucasus and Central Asia. Besides foreign fighters and militants from Saudi Arabia, Tunisia, Lebanon, and Jordan, IS was comprised of thousands of Iraqis and Syrians.[112] After the initial US invasion of Iraq in 2003, a radical Salafi cleric from Aleppo named Abu al-Qaqaa became the primary point of contact for Syrian recruits who were eager to join AQI under the leadership of Zarqawi.[113] The group has also won recruits following large-scale prison breaks throughout Iraq, replenishing its ranks with hardened jihadists, violent sociopaths, and career criminals.[114] Moreover, the group deliberately recruited extremely young fighters, including many teenagers, while others were even younger.[115]

Included in the panoply of individuals recruited by IS were children as young as 6 years old, some of whom were trained to become suicide bombers.[116]

In line with IS's declared goal of establishing an Islamic caliphate, the group has devoted a robust portion of its funding to the nascent stages of state building. In August 2014, IS began paying municipal salaries, provided public works, maintained electricity, trash, and sewage services, offered health care and education to its supporters, and even attempted to enforce parking laws and regulations in areas it controlled or claimed to control.[117] In these areas, it also ensured the availability of basic necessities such as gas and food.[118] In Mosul, IS held a "fun day" for kids, distributed gifts and food during Eid al-Fitr, held Quran recitation competitions, started bus services, and opened schools. More so in Iraq than in Syria, IS has been aware of dealing with the local population in Sunni-predominant towns, villages, and cities.[119] An analysis of al-Qaeda in Iraq reveals that that group, too, was a bureaucratic and hierarchical organization that tried to keep an ironclad grip on the money it earned from a series of rackets.[120] So, it should come as little surprise that its progeny is as well.

IS may be wealthy, especially when compared to other terrorist groups, but it also maintains a vast human resources-type network to deal with medical expenses for fighters (and their families), legal support, safe houses, and administrative expenses (e.g., utilities) in the areas under its control and other logistical requirements of clandestine organizations.[121] It has consistently compelled mid-level bureaucrats and technocrats to remain in their positions in order to ensure continuity.[122] IS's use of former Assad-regime loyalists displayed a pragmatism that was vital to the success it had in holding on to territory it captured.[123]

In areas it controlled, IS went to work building its state, which

included all the facets of a normal local government, from police cars and ambulances to traffic cops at intersections; it even opened a complaints desk, for civilians to voice their concerns, and nursing homes, for elderly relatives of jihadists and their extended families.[124] The provision of public services became an important component of constructing the state. IS sent out its members to repair potholes, administer post offices, distribute food to those in need, and even began a campaign to vaccinate its subjects against polio.[125] IS also had a Consumer Protection Authority office.[126] As Graeme Wood notes, "The Islamic State, like any other government, had to administer its territory and population, and was busy building bureaucracies for taxation, health, education, and other official functions."[127] In the areas in Syria under its control, IS set up an electricity office that monitored electricity-use levels, installed new power lines, and instructed workshops on how to repair damaged ones.[128] In Libya, the IS state-building apparatus established an "Office of General Services" to ensure that businesses were officially registered so taxes could be collected.[129]

A census was conducted in Mosul, where citizens were counted and catalogued according to occupation. Business owners' names were recorded in ledgers, along with their religion and sect.[130] Its administration, bureaucracy, and governance structures have been described as "very sophisticated" and "capable of enduring for years."[131] The Islamic State's bureaucratic apparatus required recruits to complete paperwork that listed their prior education, employment experience, interests, and skills. This information was used to scout talented members and identify jobs that would best suit the capabilities of these individuals.[132] IS members created rules and regulations that governed "everything from fishing and dress codes to the sale of counterfeit brands and university admission systems."[133]

Media, Public Relations, and Propaganda

IS has displayed an adroit understanding of its media, and used it in a way no other terrorist group had done in recent memory. IS has relied on a sophisticated approach to media, especially social media, in spreading its message, sowing terror and fear, recruiting new members, and countering Western efforts to shape the narrative.[134] Perhaps most impressive has been the speed with which IS is able to produce its media campaigns, responding in real-time (by "live tweeting") to events as they unfold on the ground. This mode of communication has been described as a "swarmcast" for its interconnected, dispersed, and resilient form.[135]

IS dedicated attention and resources to spreading its message and diffusing its propaganda, exemplified by its pervasive use of social media, including active Twitter campaigns in each of the provinces where it operates and promotes its activities and the battles it fights.[136] As one commentator noted, "Gulf state fundamentalists, battle-hardened Chechens, and middle-class Londoners were all drawn into IS by its powerful messaging and the promise to, in a twist on an old phrase, be the evil you want to see in the world."[137] IS propaganda was directed at terrorizing foreign populations while also admonishing the group's followers to act, as evidenced by the rash of attacks in the West over the past several years, to include increasingly low-cost, opportunistic attacks using vehicles to ram pedestrians. Through a deliberate process of recruiting members with a background in production, editing, and graphic design, IS constructed the most elaborate media apparatus of any terrorist organization to date – a legacy that will assuredly be carried forth by the global jihadi movement as it plans its next move.[138]

The group has been successful at conducting information warfare for several reasons. First, information power-related personnel

are accorded high levels of prestige or are otherwise well rewarded. Second, the caliphate narrative is incredibly effective, both for unifying their operations and messages, and for providing a compelling frame for those operations for their supporters and potential supporters. Third, the group's major themes are cleanly grouped and tightly focused, which makes message discipline easy. The themes are also germane to several important and diversified sub-narratives that are specifically targeted to different audiences.

To date, IS has taken advantage of social media to disseminate its message and ideology far beyond what al-Qaeda was ever able to achieve.[139] Despite the attention afforded to the Islamic State's execution videos, the group actually produces much more material, and on a broader range of topics, than what gets reported in the mainstream media.[140] Of all the messages propagated by IS, the establishment and implementation of the "caliphate" is a unique selling point, as it retains historical and religious resonance for the broader Muslim *ummah* and harkens back to a point in history when Islam experienced its Golden Age.[141] IS attempts to communicate the core narrative that its caliphate is a triumphant, model society to all of its potential recruits.[142] IS is more capable than al-Qaeda ever was and continues to grow as an organization and an ideology.[143] Many fear that the legacy of IS will live on through its media/propaganda, calling for the nostalgia of the caliphate.[144]

IS did use social media to broadcast the beheading of several Westerners it had kidnapped, but it also used Twitter, Instagram, YouTube, and Facebook to show its humanitarian efforts, including fighters handing out ice-cream cones to children, in an attempt to appeal to its constituents. It has even developed its own video game modeled after *Grand Theft Auto*.[145] IS has produced several popular series such as *Knights of Martyrdom* and *Risen Alive*, which emphasize

the camaraderie of jihad by showing militants fighting together on the battlefield.[146] *Dabiq* is IS's magazine, which is an English-language production used to help lure more recruits.[147] The magazine is multi-faceted, reporting battlefield statistics but also laying out a thoroughly detailed religious explanation for its actions, especially its attempt to establish an Islamic caliphate in Syria and Iraq.[148]

Just like other millennials, the concept of "oversharing" extends to terrorists as well. The use of multiple media platforms has served as a cache of open source intelligence (OSINT) for intelligence and law enforcement authorities attempting to track, monitor, and combat IS.[149] Simply from monitoring jihadists' use of social media, Western authorities have been able to gain insight into foreign fighters traveling to Syria and Iraq to fight with the group, as well as to map the rift that developed and eventually led to a split between IS and Jabhat al-Nusra.[150]

Even though IS militants communicate openly on some social media forums, its media wing remains incredibly agile. When its accounts on Twitter and other sites are shuttered, new accounts appear almost immediately. It relies on services like JustPaste.it to distribute battle summaries, SoundCloud for the release of audio reports, Instagram to share photos, and WhatsApp to swap graphics and videos.[151] Other commonly used apps include Ask.fm, PalTalk, kik, and Tumblr.[152] The Islamic State dedicates a significant portion of its resources to media and propaganda.[153] Fawaz Gerges estimates that IS allocated one-third of its annual budget to a combination of propaganda and governance.[154]

The Islamic State's slogan is "Baqiya wa Tatamaddad" - "Remaining and Expanding." Rather than living under apostate regimes in the Middle East or morally bankrupt societies in Western nations, Muslims who join IS can enjoy an ideal Islamic community, and those

who resist this call will be vanquished. This vision is furthered by videos that focus on the caliphate as a benevolent state committed to public works and Islamic welfare.[155] IS propaganda is meticulously tailored to different target groups it seeks to recruit, from criminals and gangsters to technically minded professionals.[156] Its members understand their audience better than the West does and it has been able to position itself as a group with countercultural appeal – so-called "jihadi cool."[157]

IS has a legion of "fanboys" who disseminate the group's propaganda.[158] "IS's social media success can be attributed to a relatively small group of hyperactive users, numbering between 500 and 2,000 accounts, which tweet in concentrated bursts of high volume."[159] Between June and October 2015, Twitter suspended or removed the accounts of over 125,000 IS sympathizers or members.[160] A RAND Corporation report from August 2016 noted that, if Twitter continued its campaign of account suspensions, this harassment could force IS supporters to lose valuable time reacquiring followers and could ultimately push some to use social media channels that are far less public and accessible than Twitter.[161] Once technology companies like Twitter and Facebook began policing their sites more aggressively, jihadists migrated to other platforms to communicate, including Telegram, which IS fighters used both to recruit and to plan terrorist attacks.[162]

3

The Coming Terrorist Diaspora

For many of the Islamic State's surviving fighters, the loss of Iraq and Syria may merely signal a temporary pause in the fight.[1] A significant percentage of militants will almost certainly seek out new battlefields to continue waging jihad.[2] The caliphate has indeed collapsed and the organization has splintered. Accordingly, to speak of IS as a monolith going forward might not make much sense. While IS may be a singular brand, it encompasses a wide swath of jihadists with similar but not necessarily identical objectives. There will continue to be, well into the foreseeable future, a medium-intensity yet highly capable insurgency, based along the Euphrates River Valley with tentacles stretching throughout parts of eastern Syria and northern and western Iraq. There will also be IS's international footprint, its provinces abroad, which will ebb and flow in operational tempo while also maintaining varying degrees of linkages to areas of the former caliphate.

In early February 2018, the United States began downsizing its military footprint in Iraq, shifting personnel and resources to other hotspots around the globe, including Afghanistan. As of April 2018, President Trump publicly called for the withdrawal of US troops from Syria, with the White House Press Secretary Sarah Huckabee-Sanders announcing: "[T]he military mission to eradicate IS in Syria is coming to a rapid end, with IS almost being completely destroyed."[3] But, as

recent history has proven time and again over the past decade and a half, a violent Sunni jihadist group, whether it calls itself IS or rebrands under another banner, will reconstitute in parts of Iraq and Syria to challenge existing governance structures while planning new attacks and organizing into a formidable fighting force.

IS Affiliates Abroad

Just as al-Qaeda did before it, the Islamic State has spun off a constellation of franchise groups and affiliates around the globe, each of which has the potential to grow into a formidable terrorist organization in its own right. As of late 2018, the United States Department of State had designated IS franchise groups in Indonesia, the North Caucasus, Afghanistan, Algeria, Libya, the Sinai (as well as mainland Egypt), Somalia, Tunisia, the Philippines, Bangladesh, the Greater Sahara, and West Africa. This section will focus on the three most pernicious IS satellites, located in the Sinai, Afghanistan, and Libya, respectively, while also analyzing some of the other areas where IS affiliates have demonstrated serious potential to evolve into more dangereuos long-term threats. But to understand the scale of this threat, it is essential to have a comprehensive understanding of the nature of these groups, which, while IS-affiliated, may differ significantly across several important measures.

Table 3.1 assesses these franchise groups in order to determine what type of group the IS affiliate should be characterized as. There is a growing body of scholarship that differentiates between terrorism, insurgency, and guerrilla warfare, and an in-depth analysis of these differences is beyond the scope of this book.[4] This table looks at the size of the group, its primary targets, organizational structure,

Table 3.1 Analysis of IS affiliates

Affiliate	Size	Primary Targets	Structure	Strategy	Territorial Control	Reach	Typology
Afghanistan	500–1,000	Civilians Insurgents	Decentralized	Punishment	Geographically divided	Regional	Insurgents
Libya	500–800	Security forces	Hybrid	Guerrilla	Small pockets Contested	Transnational	Terrorists
Philippines	750	Civilians Security forces	Hybrid	Guerrilla	Dispersed Localized	Regional	Guerrillas
Sinai	500–750	Civilians Security forces	Decentralized	Punishment Guerilla	Shifting Ungoverned	Local	Guerillas
West Africa	3,500	Civilians	Hybrid	Punishment	Large swaths	Regional	Insurgents
Yemen	100–250	Security forces	Decentralized	Guerrilla	Small pockets	Local	Insurgents

strategy,[5] extent of territorial control, and reach (defined as area of operations). The final column of the table classifies each affiliate according to typology. In other words, whether the group most closely resembles a terrorist organization, insurgent group, or guerrilla army. Indeed, just as insurgency and terrorism are not the same, the objectives of counterinsurgency and counterterrorism are different, too. Nuanced approaches to fighting adaptive adversaries require a different mix of tools – military, police, diplomatic, economic – to effectively counter the protean campaign of violence waged by IS affiliate groups.

Sinai Peninsula

The vast, ungoverned territory of Egypt's Sinai Peninsula has long been home to smugglers, terrorists, and an array of other non-state actors and it has once again become attractive territory to radicals and extremists.[6] With its fluctuating number of fighters, decentralized structure, and hybrid strategy of attacking both security forces and Egyptian civilians, the IS branch in the Sinai could most aptly be described as a guerrilla movement that relies on terrorist tactics, including raids, ambushes, and bombings, to keep the government from extending reach into the Sinai in any meaningful way. The Sinai has long been considered one of the world's most lawless areas, due in part to geography and a Bedouin culture that is nomadic and fiercely anti-authoritarian.

Egypt experienced a spike in violence following the ouster of Mohammed Morsi, a Muslim Brotherhood leader voted into office following Arab Spring protests.[7] The Sinai already has a dedicated IS franchise group that continues to gather momentum, particularly in the face of the ineptitude of Egyptian security forces. Signs of a merger

between Egyptian groups and IS became apparent as early as 2014, when elements of Ansar Bait al-Maqdis (ABM) pledged allegiance to IS and made efforts to establish connections with IS fighters in Libya.[8] This connection could very well grow in the future, with money and weapons being exchanged between IS militants in Libya and Egypt.[9] The Sinai was critical terrain for the militants and became, in effect, "both a haven and a crossing point for smuggling fighters, weapons and illicit goods" between Egypt and the Maghreb.[10]

Throughout the Sinai, IS-affiliated militants pursue a hybrid strategy of attacking both Egyptian security forces and civilian non-combatants, the latter part of the strategy introducing a highly sectarian dimension to the conflict. IS fighters in the Sinai regularly clash with Egyptian security forces and have launched attacks over the past several years in which hundreds of Egyptian troops have been killed.[11] IS's Sinai affiliate has also demonstrated its penchant for conducting spectacular attacks, evidenced by the downing of Metrojet Flight 9268, when an IS bomb killed all 224 people onboard an airliner destined for St Petersburg, Russia. The group is also responsible for attacking Coptic Christian churches and firing rockets into Israel.

Weak Security Forces

Despite having a formidable conventional military, at least by regional standards, Egypt has struggled mightily to contain the growing insurgency in the Sinai. There are serious concerns that the Egyptian military's failure to adequately combat IS's Sinai affiliate could lead the group to eventually develop into a highly capable franchise group, similar to the evolution of al-Qaeda in the Arabian Peninsula (AQAP), al-Qaeda's Yemeni affiliate. Many argue that the Sisi government's

approach to counterinsurgency is myopic, leading the population of the Sinai to support the militants.[12] This provides an opening for jihadists, as the government has little-to-no presence, economic conditions are dire, and local Bedouins have long operated with autonomy. In response to the growing anarchy in the Sinai, Israel has waged a covert air campaign over the past two years, relying on a mix of unmarked drones, jets, and helicopters to target militants; in what clearly marks a new development in the relationship between Cairo and Tel Aviv, these operations have all been launched with the tacit approval of Egypt's top military leadership, signaling how desperate Sisi is for help in containing the threat.[13] IS's Sinai-based affiliate has demonstrated the capability to wage a prolonged insurgency replete with terrorist tactics and guerrilla-style attacks against the security forces, thus increasing the possibility of a lingering low-intensity conflict that could plague ineffectually governed parts of Egypt for years.

Ungoverned Territory

The operational tempo of terrorist attacks seems to have increased in intensity from 2015 to 2018, while the insurgency itself is morphing and spreading into different territories within Egypt. By the spring of 2016, IS in the Sinai had moved into parts of the Western Desert, Upper Egypt, and Greater Cairo.[14] Repeated offensives by the Egyptian military to dislodge IS militants in the northern part of the Sinai have so far been unsuccessful.[15] The jihadists' reach and influence remains localized to the Sinai and other areas within the country, but has the potential to spread beyond Egypt's borders and grow into a regional threat. As evidence, IS's Sinai affiliate has broadened its targets, recently declaring war on the Palestinian militant group Hamas, sparking fears that IS could attempt to move into Gaza, bringing its fighters even closer

to the Israeli border.[16] Now that ties between IS in the Sinai Hamas have been severed, the threat to Israel has been reduced, although not totally eliminated.[17] Israel's concerns are warranted, as the Sinai has traditionally been an anarchic region and one which is geographically ideal for violent Salafists, given its proximity to Israel.[18]

Sectarianism

Well before the Arab Spring, Egypt suffered from periodic spasms of religious and political violence, and has long been fertile soil for religious extremism, evidenced by the domestic terrorist campaigns waged by groups like Egyptian Islamic Jihad and Gama'a al-Islamiyyah. But the recent wave of attacks has assumed an even more virulent sectarian character and the tactics used by jihadist groups in the Sinai include roadside IEDs, suicide bombings, and assassinations.[19] Put simply, because of its geography, history, and cultural significance, Egypt is too valuable for jihadists to ignore.[20]

Egypt's Coptic Christian population has borne the brunt of these attacks, essentially under assault by Salafi-jihadists for much of the past two years. In April 2017, terrorists waged a week-long campaign of attacks against Christians, including bombings on Palm Sunday in Alexandria and Tanta,[21] and another shooting at a monastery one week later.[22] Toward the end of December 2017, 11 were killed in an attack on a Coptic Church near Cairo.[23] And it is not just Christians who are under attack. In November 2017, in what has been recorded as Egypt's deadliest terror incident to date, over 300 Sufi Muslims were killed in an attack on their mosque in the Sinai.[24]

Afghanistan and Pakistan (AFPAK)

IS has been operating in Afghanistan since approximately 2014 under the auspices of the Islamic State in Khorasan Province (ISKP). Through a series of coordinated and highly lethal attacks targeting Afghanistan's minority Shiite community, IS has established itself as one of the most poignant drivers of instability in that country, further intensifying the sectarian element of the conflict in Afghanistan.[25] ISKP has also frequently battled with the Taliban, especially in Nangarhar and Zabul provinces between 2015 and 2017, and the organization split in the summer of 2017, with one faction declaring loyalty to a former Lashkar-e-Taiba commander and the other, comprised mostly of Central Asians, coalescing behind an ex-Islamic Movement of Uzbekistan (IMU) leader.[26] The Central Asian faction dominates territory in northern Afghanistan while the Pakistani-led faction is more active in southern and eastern Afghanistan, closer to the Pakistani border.[27]

Although ISKP has clashed with Taliban fighters and launched attacks against the Afghan government and military – in January 2018, the group killed 11 soldiers at the Kabul military academy – it is most widely known for its brutal and unrelenting attacks against Afghan civilians and non-combatants, including the non-governmental organization Save the Children.[28] Attacks against civilians form part of ISKP's approach to insurgency, which follows a strategy of punishment. The essence of this approach is deliberately targeting non-combatants, either to provoke a government overreaction or to demonstrate to the civilian population that the security forces are weak and the state illegitimate. A July 2016 attack on Hazaras organizing a protest march in Kabul killed over 80 civilians and wounded another 250 people. Then, in late October 2017, the group orchestrated

a wave of suicide bombings directed at Shiite targets, including several mosques, which killed more than 100 and wounded another 200.[29]

IS has also attacked hospitals, hotels, and military installations, and has launched attacks in both Afghanistan and Pakistan and appears to be gaining ground in the latter, especially in Balochistan.[30] An October 2016 attack on a police training college in Quetta resulted in more than 60 dead and another 120 wounded, most of them cadets. Although IS claimed this attack, there was some speculation that the attack was actually committed by another militant group, Lashkar-e-Jhangvi (LEJ), and that IS "outsourced" the attack to LEJ.[31]

Violent Competition

Although its presence in Afghanistan initially surfaced in 2014, ISKP became an official IS affiliate in January 2015, starting with a group of defectors from the Pakistani Taliban, or Tehrik-i-Taliban Pakistan (TTP). The Pakistani militants helped IS to establish a foothold across the border in Afghanistan, in the southeastern districts of Nangarhar province.[32] The organization was then reinforced by approximately 200 IS militants from the core group in Iraq and Syria, who traveled to Afghanistan to bolster the nascent affiliate.[33] Soon after it was established, it sought to actively recruit and absorb disaffected Taliban fighters into its ranks.[34] By 2018, ISKP had grown into a formidable threat, continuing to absorb new fighters, including further defections from the Afghan Taliban and returning foreign fighters fleeing Iraq and Syria.[35] The spike in violence, worrying even by Afghan standards, could signal violent competition between ISKP and the Afghan Taliban, evidence of a process of outbidding wherein terrorist organizations engage in escalating violent competition to prove which group is the most dedicated and likely to prevail.[36]

Infrastructure for Jihad

Afghanistan is a country wracked by violence dating back decades, and, accordingly, already has an established infrastructure for jihad, making it an attractive place for terrorists and terrorist groups to relocate. By late 2015, ISKP fighters had already taken over territory in Nangarhar, Farah, and Helmand provinces.[37] Moreover, ISKP is just 1 of over 20 militant groups operating in the region.[38] It is difficult to estimate how many fighters ISKP has under arms, although US military officials have claimed that over 1,600 IS-linked militants have already been killed, though nobody quite knows how many fighters remain.[39] At the end of December 2017, Russian officials pegged the number at about 10,000 and growing.[40] More conservative estimates place the number somewhere around 700 active fighters, while other experts assert that the number is unknowable, yet probably falls somewhere between 500 and 1,000.[41]

Precisely accounting for the number of fighters in specific groups is always fraught with risk, although what most analysts can agree upon is that new recruits are flocking to Afghanistan regularly. ISKP frequently receives an influx of new recruits from those who leave the IMU.[42] The British government has voiced concerns that citizens from the UK have made their way from Iraq and Syria to join up with IS in Afghanistan.[43] The Iranian government has made it known that they are preparing for ISKP to receive an influx of fighters now that the caliphate has crumbled in Iraq and Syria.[44]

Persistent American Presence

Because Afghanistan has had a persistent American military presence for the past 17 years, it stands to reason that jihadists will continue to

be attracted to this theatre for the opportunity to engage in combat with US troops. The situation is mutually reinforcing. As ISKP continues to gain strength, the United States feels pressured to become more involved, so as not to repeat the mistakes of Iraq in 2011, when a precipitous withdrawal from that country helped fuel the rise of IS there.[45] Indeed, the presence of IS is one of the reasons President Trump, at the urging of Secretary of Defense James Mattis, ultimately decided to keep US troops in the country. In April 2017, in a display of brute force, the United States dropped the "Mother of All Bombs," killing scores of insurgent fighters, yet the threat remains constant from an array of Afghan and foreign jihadists.[46]

Libya

Of all the IS satellites, Libya just may have the potential to be *the* most dangerous safe haven for the group in the near future. The territory is awash in weapons, there is no recognized government to speak of, and it serves as a focal point and crossroads for jihadists of all stripes, located across the Mediterranean Sea from Europe. Two deadly terrorist attacks in Europe have been tied back to Libya already. The danger emanating from this country is more than about just IS; it's the combination of potential threats coalescing to make Libya into the kind of safe haven that Afghanistan was in the decade prior to September 11, 2001.

Failed State

The 2011 intervention left Libya with dueling governments – one recognized by the United States and the international community, the other aligned with General Haftar. In the chaos, Libya also became

a safe haven for the Islamic State.[47] The situation in Libya has been described, quite accurately, as one "marred by a prolonged period of political fragmentation, violent conflict, and economic dislocation."[48] "Libya has the most potential to replicate the Islamic State's model in Mesopotamia if things go right for it," according to North Africa expert Aaron Zelin.[49] The anarchy in Libya is now the fourth-largest foreign fighter mobilization in recent history, behind the ongoing civil war in Syria, the Afghan jihad of the 1980s, and the 2003 Iraq war.[50]

One troubling scenario that could boost IS's Libyan branch is the absorption of former al-Qaeda in the Islamic Maghreb (AQIM) fighters as that group continues to decline.[51] Libyan jihadists are believed to be planning attacks on the country's "Oil Crescent" and there is evidence to suggest regional cooperation between IS-affiliated militants in Libya and networks of associates in Morocco, Algeria, and Tunisia.[52]

All In for IS?

IS was well positioned to take advantage of the chaos that engulfed Libya in the immediate aftermath of the post-Qaddafi era, capitalizing upon decades of hatred for the long-time Libyan dictator. Early on, some of its members formed the Islamic Youth Shura Council.[53] Soon thereafter, its Libyan affiliate began building its network by poaching jihadists from existing groups, including Ansar al-Sharia.[54] Around 2012, the Katibat al-Battar al-Libiyah brigade (KBL), a notorious group of Libyan foreign fighters, had been active in both Syria and Iraq and brought important capabilities and expertise to the fledgling IS presence in the country.[55] By November 2014, IS accepted the Libyan start-up as an official *wilayat,* or franchise, with Libyan jihadists returning home from fighting abroad.[56] Several hundred jihadists returned to Libya, declared allegiance to IS, and set up shop in Derna.[57]

The Libyan branch has ebbed and flowed over time, expanding its physical and media presence by early 2015.[58] By the end of 2015, its fighters had assumed control over large sections of Sirte and, by the following summer, IS militants were attempting to consolidate control of territory near Misrata.[59] By early 2016, there were around 1,500 IS fighters in Sirte, but, following a bloody seven-month battle, IS was cleared from its stronghold by the end of the year, forced to withdraw from territory it once completely dominated.[60] The group has managed to maintain an on-again, off-again presence in Bengazhi, which has been plagued by violence for years.[61] IS is now once again attempting to re-establish itself as a legitimate governing entity in pockets of Libya, and Salafists have slowly been assuming control of critical internal security functions. Over time, the goal of IS is to gradually marginalize opposition to its rule and impose a semblance of order that has been elusive since NATO forces deposed Qaddafi nearly a decade ago.[62]

Hub for External Operations

In Libya, where as recently as late 2017 IS boasted approximately 6,500 fighters, the group has carved out space roughly 100 miles southeast of its former base of operations in Sirte.[63] Its members have successfully connected with existing jihadist networks as they began building an infrastructure in Sirte.[64] In addition, IS maintains training and operational bases throughout the central and southern parts of the country.[65] In a sign of Libya's growing importance as a hub for external operations, US bombers conducted airstrikes against IS training camps in Libya in late September 2017, killing dozens of jihadists linked to the Islamic State.[66]

To date, IS's Libyan affiliate has been tied to two major external operations, successfully tallying attacks on European soil, including

the deadly Manchester concert bombing in May 2017 and the Berlin Christmas market attack in December 2016. The group has also launched devastating regional attacks, in Bardo and Sousse, Tunisia, respectively, with links back to Libya.[67] The country remains in a state of constant conflict and anarchy, awash in weapons, with various jihadists fighting, switching sides, and occasionally cooperating. Most alarming, the Islamic State maintains specialized entities in Libya, including the "Desert Brigade" and the "Office of Borders and Immigration," which is responsible for external operations, logistics, and recruitment.[68]

Other Locations

The collapse of the caliphate has major significance for Iraq and Syria, the two states where IS once maintained its sanctuary, but also for countries where fleeing foreign fighters might go next. The preceding section discusses IS hubs in the Sinai, Afghanistan, and Libya, but there are other potential hotspots of interest throughout the globe, several of which will be detailed below.

Turkey

At the top of this list should be Turkey, a logical landing spot for many IS militants based purely on geography, located directly north of and contiguous to both Iraq and Syria. IS activity in Turkey is clustered around major cities along the border with Syria (probably due to proximity, travel routes, and population density) and the majority of IS-linked attacks have a connection back to the core group in Iraq and Syria.[69] In early February 2018, "thousands" of IS fighters apparently

fled Iraq and Syria while a substantial number "have gone into hiding in countries like Turkey."[70] These revelations are nothing new. Journalist and renowned IS expert Rukmini Callimachi's interview with a former IS fighter from Germany revealed that IS deliberately dispatched hundreds of its fighters to Turkey.[71] In the aftermath of IS's deadly attack on Istanbul's Reina nightclub in the early hours of January 1, 2017 – an attack which killed 39 and wounded 71 – it was revealed that IS had established robust cells operating throughout the country.[72]

Turkey could serve as a logistics hub to plot future attacks and, unlike many other terrorist sanctuaries such as Afghanistan, Libya, or Somalia, Turkey is *not* a failed state. This is important because militants have easier and more reliable access to communications, transportation, and financial networks. There is also the possibility that a spectacular attack could be engineered from Turkish soil, as one nearly was with the improvised explosive device airmailed from Turkey to Australia in August 2017.[73] Over the past decade, Turkey has slowly developed into a country with dense pockets of support for Salafi-jihadist groups, including IS and al-Qaeda, which have used it as a base to mobilize support for their operations.[74] Still, the Turkish military and internal security forces are well trained and highly capable, making it less likely that IS will be able to escalate its campaign beyond the level of low-intensity conflict. In any case, Turkey is more attractive as a logistical hub for planning and acquiring the resources necessary to plot and conduct terrorist attacks in either Europe or the Middle East.

Yemen

The IS presence in Yemen has ebbed and flowed over the past several years, although AQAP remains the dominant militant group in the

country, even as both entities come under intense assault by an array of counterterrorism forces. By late 2016, IS in Yemen was mainly confined to the Qayfa front in al-Bayda' and was estimated to have approximately 100 fighters, although the US Department of Defense acknowledged that IS increased its presence from 2017 to 2018, with militants taking advantage of a power vacuum due to that country's ongoing civil war.[75] American airstrikes targeted IS training camps in al-Bayda' in mid-October 2017, killing scores of fighters in this collapsed state flanking Saudi Arabia's southern border.[76] The Trump administration has moved Yemen higher on the United States' list of counterterrorism priorities, as American policymakers and military officials are increasingly concerned that IS fighters fleeing Iraq and Syria will head to the southern parts of the country. In fact, in May 2018, IS for the first time issued instructions for its fighters to travel to the group's stronghold in al-Bayda'.[77]

Still, it is no certainty that IS will find sanctuary in Yemen, a country dominated by al-Qaeda in the Arabian Peninsula in the Sunni heartland of its remote tribal areas.[78] Indeed, the growth of the Islamic State and its announcement of expansion into Yemen in November 2014 helped AQAP by allowing the latter to contrast its style to the comparatively excessive and brutal methods of IS. AQAP specifically announced that, unlike IS, its fighters would never target "mosques, markets and crowded places," ensuring it would earn some degree of legitimacy among Yemen's civilian population.[79] And, despite a relentless onslaught from US airpower and American-backed forces, AQAP remains a major threat in Yemen and, compared to IS, is the far more powerful of the two groups, especially in the hinterlands of Shabwa and Abyan provinces.[80]

Even as IS has successfully staged coordinated, guerilla-style attacks throughout Yemen, the main driver of instability continues

to be the ongoing proxy war between Iran, supporting the Houthi rebels, and Saudi Arabia, which, along with the United Arab Emirates, has been waging an unrelenting air war in Yemen, leading to further instability and various humanitarian crises.[81] But if Yemen receives an influx of foreign fighters from Iraq and Syria, IS could certainly grow into a more odious threat. There is already a fairly robust network of militant Salafist groups active throughout the country.[82] Yemen could prove to be a country where al-Qaeda retains its position as the dominant jihadist group and successfully consolidates the disparate cells and small groups of militants under its aegis – or, at least, influence – and that, over time, the majority of IS fighters may eventually gravitate to AQAP both to seek its protection and also to join forces merely to survive.[83] As of mid-2018, IS was struggling to recruit locally among tribes where they are fighting, since the focus of locals is mainly on battling the Houthis and not necessarily declaring loyalty to the Islamic State. Nevertheless, the battle fronts are prime recruiting grounds, so it seems inevitable that IS will continue to maintain at least a steady, low-level presence in Yemen for the foreseeable future.[84]

South Asia

When attempting to answer the question of where the Islamic State might reconstitute next, part of the answer may lie in an area where IS's remaining leadership feels the group *must* expand to remain relevant. An analogous situation unfolded with al-Qaeda in 2003 following the US invasion of Iraq. Al-Qaeda strategists felt that the group would be marginalized within global jihadist circles if it failed to establish a franchise group in a Muslim country "under siege" from non-Muslims. In a similar way, the Rohingya crisis in Myanmar – where a Muslim minority is being oppressed by a Buddhist majority – could serve as

a motivating factor for the Islamic State to expand throughout South and Southeast Asia.[85] In January 2018, Malaysian authorities arrested two IS-linked Indonesian citizens who were allegedly planning to kill Buddhist monks in retaliation for the treatment of Rohingya Muslims in Myanmar.[86] Similarly, Akayed Ullah, the Bangladeshi immigrant who detonated a pipe bomb in the New York City subway in December 2017, was said to have visited a Rohingya refugee camp just before returning to the United States and detonating his explosives.[87]

As the Islamic State and al-Qaeda continue to compete for new recruits and territory, the international community should be on high alert for a new IS franchise breaking ground in virgin territory.[88] Yet even if this occurs, it will probably do so not as a result of a centrally directed, command-and-control-driven approach to expanding, but rather from local conditions favorable to a revolutionary movement that offers the promise of upending the status quo in a province, country, or region experiencing high levels of political and/or religious strife and where it is the norm, not the exception, to solve problems through the use of political violence, rather than negotiation or power sharing. In other words, we should look at this global network not as the direct result of a corporate strategy, but rather as an opportunistic, even parasitic, entity. According to this theory, the ideal territory for expansion is a fragile state plagued by persistent civil conflict and sectarian tensions, and with a population considered fertile for and receptive to the Islamic State's propaganda.[89] Myanmar is one such country, even though there are already indications that al-Qaeda in the Indian subcontinent has begun working with local jihadist groups on the ground there.

A new franchise group in Myanmar would allow IS to gain many of the benefits of affiliation by furthering its strategic reach, leveraging local expertise, spreading innovation, and increasing the group's

legitimacy in a part of the world where until now it has lacked a significant presence. There are currently several important impediments to Myanmar developing into the next jihadist hub, especially a lack of logistical infrastructure that includes weapons, safe houses, and a robust network of travel facilitators.[90] That dynamic could change over the next few years with a sustained effort and assistance from returning foreign fighters and existing IS operatives in the broader region, including Bangladesh – making the country a ripe target for IS expansion.[91]

Another South Asian hotspot with a growing IS presence is Bangladesh, a nation with a history of Islamic militancy but long overshadowed by Pakistan. The Islamic State has launched dozens of attacks in Bangladesh against an array of targets, from aid workers to Catholic priests. The most notorious attack came against the Holey Artisan Bakery in Bangladesh's diplomatic quarter in July 2016, when attackers pledging allegiance to IS killed 29 people using bombs, machetes, and small arms.[92] Bangladesh may ultimately prove to be a future battleground between IS and al-Qaeda, with the latter acting through its franchise group al-Qaeda in the Indian Subcontinent, or AQIS.[93] Since 2013, hundreds of Bangladeshis have perished in terrorist violence throughout the country, mostly at the hands of AQIS militants.[94]

Another potential post-caliphate growth area for the Islamic State is the disputed Kashmir territory fought over between India and Pakistan, which could prove to be fertile ground for an IS affiliate. Even though several prominent jihadist groups are already active in the region, including Hizb-ul-Mujahideen (HM), Lashkar-e-Taiba (LeT), and Jaish-e-Mohammed (JeM), IS could seek to entrench its operatives in a conflict with great symbolic and religious significance for Muslims worldwide.[95] Moreover, because Kashmir is considered such a sacred

cause to Pakistan, a growing IS presence in any future conflict in this territory might also earn the group external support from Pakistan's Inter-Services Intelligence (ISI) agency, which has a long history of providing various forms of both active and passive support to a bevy of jihadist groups.[96]

Southeast Asia

Throughout Southeast Asia, entrenched rivalries, repeated splintering of terrorist organizations, and infighting between factions of jihadi groups have limited their reach in the recent past. But there is a rich history of Islamic militancy in Southeast Asia, from the al-Qaeda-linked Jemmah Islamiyah and Abu Sayyaf Group, to older groups like the Moro Islamic Liberation Front (MILF). Geography is also a critical factor. In some ways, it facilitates terrorism and insurgency, since the islands, peninsulas, and archipelagos that dot the region are particularly difficult to govern. But in other ways, geography is a blessing for authorities in the sense that the Philippines and Indonesia are difficult to reach from the battlefields in Syria and Iraq and are dispersed across a vast distance, making it challenging for jihadists to concentrate or mass forces in any one area.

This is an important variable to consider, especially because Indonesia is the world's most populous Muslim nation and one which has struggled to keep a lid on extremism and radicalization. Jihadist violence in Jakarta and other parts of Indonesia has ebbed and flowed over the past several years.[97] It has included suicide attacks against police and even a suicide attack conducted against churches by a family that had returned from Syria.[98] Indonesia's counterterrorism chief has warned of sleeper cells in every province of the country.[99] The main effect of the collapse of the caliphate in the Middle East has been

to reenergize, "expand and transform local extremist movements" throughout the region.[100]

Yet, even despite the distance, fighters from Southeast Asia are making successful return trips to their countries of origin. As of December 2017, 30 fighters from the Philippines had returned there from Syria and Iraq.[101] In an attempt to expand in Indonesia, IS has pursued an aggressive campaign of recruitment and propaganda dissemination.[102] The lines of communications stretch across battlefields, with Southeast Asian fighters in Syria communicating with militants back home in Indonesia and the Philippines to help recruit fighters and coordinate movement into Marawi.[103] Katibah Nusantara, the Southeast Asian wing of IS, was formed by Malay- and Indonesian-speaking fighters in Syria.[104] In Southeast Asia, the lure of establishing links with the Islamic State is driven by local dynamics, but has had a galvanizing "effect of a general revival of *jihadi* fervor," especially in Indonesia.[105] There have been numerous reported cases of radicalization amongst guest workers and so-called "migrant maids" from the region being radicalized by IS propaganda.[106]

In many ways, the Philippines could prove to be an appealing destination for IS fighters to relocate and establish a home base.[107] The geography of the country – the Philippines is an archipelago consisting of more than 7,600 islands – makes counterinsurgency and maritime security difficult for the Filipino government. Moreover, the presence of longstanding insurgent groups that already embrace a radical Islamist agenda could allow IS to gain a foothold as it works to champion local grievances. It helps that Muslim insurgents in the area often clash with Christian militias, providing IS the sectarian angle it has been able to successfully exploit elsewhere, including in Afghanistan, Egypt, and Yemen.[108]

It was recently discovered that core IS in Iraq and Syria sent nearly

$2 million to militants in the Philippines to help the group wage the battle for the city of Marawi.[109] Southeast Asia has long been a hotbed of Islamic extremism and violence. It is also worth noting that jihadist militants linked to Abu Sayyaf and other groups operating in the region have demonstrated a remarkable ability to self-fund their organizations without the need for donations from external sources, relying instead on various criminal activities, including robbery, illicit smuggling, and kidnapping for ransom.

Neighboring Indonesia, for example – home to the world's most populous Muslim country – was one of several bases of key al-Qaeda leaders before the 9/11 attacks, and more recently has seen an uptick of arrests related to terrorist plots by Islamic extremists.[110] Still, the nucleus of jihadists actively fighting in – and possibly returning to – the Philippines and other Southeast Asian countries is relatively small compared to other countries in other regions, such as North Africa, in both absolute and relative terms. Nonetheless, as core IS unravels, the region is likely to continue to become increasingly useful to the group as a safety valve outside of the Middle East.

The Combating Terrorism Center at West Point's report on Islamic State activity in Southeast Asia reached several interesting conclusions, noting that IS relies on local militant groups to adopt its brand; in the Philippines specifically, the most common target of terrorists was the military, and small arms were used in most attacks; and an estimated 45 percent of IS attacks and plots in the region had both "financial and communication ties to Southeast Asian Islamic State operatives in Syria where group members sought to enable and guide attacks remotely."[111] A lack of cooperation between intelligence and militaries, including maritime forces, further complicates the issue of counterterrorism.[112]

The situation in Southeast Asia exemplifies some of the challenges

in defining what exactly constitutes an IS fighter, and thus an IS affiliate. Some militants have declared allegiance to IS and others have been semi-recognized by IS central, meaning that IS media will claim credit for their attacks. In other cases, IS fighters in the region receive some material support, but does that constitute an ongoing relationship, or are these isolated incidents of support? Core IS recognized Isnilon Hapilon as its chief representative in Southeast Asia, but most of the fighters he commanded seem to have been killed in Marawi, as were a significant portion of the Maute group, although these groups are slowly reforming. Lastly, what are we to make of the Abu Sayyaf Group fighters in Sulu and Jolo, who never declared their loyalty to IS and were outside of the command-and-control network of Hapilon? Many experts consider ASG more akin to a network of gangs rather than an actual organization with an identifiable chain of command. Fighters might fly the black flag of IS for intimidation purposes or invoke the IS name when seeking to negotiate higher ransom payments for kidnapping victims.[113]

Russia and Central Asia

Of all the potential future jihadist hotspots, Central Asia could be the most unassuming and least-hyped region as a future home of returning foreign fighters seeking to make another run at the caliphate. According to the Soufan Group, the former Soviet Republic is host to the highest overall number of foreign fighters. There is a long history of jihadist mobilization throughout Russia, and, throughout Central Asia more broadly. The latter has spawned groups like the Islamic Movement of Uzbekistan, initially formed in opposition to Uzbek strongman Islam Karimov in the 1990s, although its fighters would soon go on to forge strong links with al-Qaeda and other elements

of the global jihadist movement. Militants from the Ferghana Valley fought together in Tajikistan's civil war from 1992 to 1997, gaining experience and growing their networks.[114]

Central Asia is a region where the rule of law is weak, levels of corruption are high, and poverty, extremism, and radicalization are endemic.[115] Indeed, a study by the Royal United Services Institute (RUSI) geared toward understanding the variables that contribute to radicalization among Central Asian labor migrants working in Russia found that there is some evidence of structural factors leading to marginalization, exclusion, and alienation of Kyrgyz, Tajik, and Uzbek laborers in Russia, although the authors of the report stopped short of establishing causal links leading to radicalization.[116] Even without a causal link, however, some scholars have concluded that the working and living conditions for Central Asian labor migrants working in Russia were so miserable that many who radicalized and traveled to Syria and the Levant "expect that they are on a 'one way journey,' some to martyrdom but most for a completely new life, and do not plan to return."[117]

There are direct connections between countries from the Former Soviet Union (FSU) and the Middle East. Turkey has been a popular destination for Muslims from Central Asia, but Ankara has grown wary after attacks by members of the Central Asian global diaspora, particularly ethnic Uzbeks, in Istanbul, St. Petersburg, Stockholm, and New York City.[118] The result could lead Turkey, or other countries in the region, to deport former foreign fighters to third-party countries, as Turkey did with 16 IS fighters it deported to Malaysia in August 2017, in what terrorism expert Kim Cragin has dubbed "foreign fighter 'hot potato.'"[119]

Even Kazakhstan, a country of approximately 18 million where 70 percent of the population identifies as Muslim, and one which has traditionally been immune from the type of jihadist violence experienced

by its smaller, poorer neighbors, has suffered from several terrorist attacks over the past few years.[120] Authoritarian leaders across the region have used the threat of IS-influenced terrorist attacks as a tool to crack down further on dissent, as leaders in Kyrgyzstan have done.[121] During the Soviet era, religion was suppressed, pushing radicals to the margins and forcing them to remain well organized in order to survive. In addition to the IMU, several other jihadist groups operate throughout Central Asia, including Hizb ut-Tahrir al-Islam (Party of Islamic Liberation, HuT), the Jamaat of Central Asian Mujahidin, and the Uyghur Islamic Party of Eastern Turkestan (now known as the Turkestan Islamic Party, or TIP) separatist group, which has been extremely active in the Syria jihad.[122]

Toward the end of 2017, Russia overtook Saudi Arabia and Tunisia for the dubious distinction of being the largest exporter of IS fighters.[123] One factor that could play a key role facing Russia in the future is the struggle for supremacy between jihadist groups in the Caucasus. A competition for recruits and resources is intensifying between the two dominant jihadist entities, fostering decentralization of the insurgency.[124] And, despite the falling-out and subsequent competition for recruits and resources between the al-Qaeda-linked Caucasus Emirate and the IS-linked Wilayat Qawqaz, one issue with the potential to unite these feuding Sunni factions is a shared antipathy for the Russian government, especially as Putin continues to support the Shiite axis of Iran, the Assad government, and Lebanese Hezbollah against Sunnis in the Syrian civil war.[125]

In recent years, many high-ranking jihadists have switched allegiance from the Caucasus Emirate to Wilayat Qawqaz. The Islamic State, in their eyes, is the most legitimate force espousing the austere brand of Salafism popular among jihadists, particularly the younger generation.[126] The split between the two groups centers around which

93

faction can demonstrate a stronger resolve to fight the adversary – in this case, the Russian state and security services.

In the past, Islamic militants have launched many high-profile attacks on Russian soil, including ones specifically targeting transportation infrastructure – suicide bombings in the Moscow Metro in 2004 and 2010, an explosion that derailed the Moscow – St. Petersburg express railroad in 2007, and suicide attacks at the Domodedovo Airport in 2011, a bus in the city of Volgograd in 2013, and in the St. Petersburg metro in 2017. For the most part, Putin responded to these attacks by sending Russian security services into jihadist enclaves such as Dagestan and Chechnya. Rhetorically, Putin and the Russian propaganda machine capitalize upon these attacks by portraying all Kremlin enemies, both foreign and domestic, as part of a vast terrorist conspiracy.

If returnees were to go back to Russia in large numbers, they would face a draconian security force unconstrained by human rights or laws regulating the use of force. Nevertheless, these returnees would come back to territories like Chechnya, Dagestan, and Ingushetia – areas with an existing jihadist infrastructure and the ability to occasionally launch attacks into Moscow and other urban areas of the Russian homeland.

Sub-Saharan Africa

As evidenced by al-Qaeda's attacks on American embassies in Kenya and Tanzania in 1998, there have long been connections between Salafi-jihadists and certain parts of East Africa, but, in the main, Africa more broadly never registered especially high on the list of attractive destinations for radical jihadists. That is no longer the case. The growing threat of the global jihadist movement now extends deep

into Africa, beyond North Africa and into vast pockets of territory pockmarking the Sahel, the Lake Chad Basin, the Greater Sahara, and throughout East Africa, stretching from the Horn of Africa south all the way to Tanzania and Mozambique.[127] And while al-Qaeda was once the premier jihadist group on the continent, myriad splits and fissures have led to a dizzying array and patchwork of militant groups with fluctuating alliances and loyalties.[128] With the establishment of the United States African Command, or AFRICOM, in 2007, the US military has significantly ramped up operations in Somalia, Kenya, Niger, and elsewhere.[129]

The two primary jihadist groups, al-Qaeda and IS, are locked in a battle for recruits, financing, and territory. As of late April 2018, the al-Qaeda affiliate al-Shabaab in Somalia claimed to command between 4,000 and 6,000 jihadists. Al-Qaeda's Mali affiliate, the Group for Support of Islam and Muslims (JNIM), boasts approximately 800 fighters, while Boko Haram, an AQIM affiliate,[130] fields an estimated 1,500 fighters. On the other side of the ledger, IS in West Africa (a splinter group of Boko Haram) numbers around 3,500, while IS in the Greater Sahara, operating between Mali and Niger, is one of the smallest offshoots, with 450 active fighters.[131] IS maintains a footprint in Somalia as well, although its capabilities pale in comparison to those of al-Shabaab.[132] IS in Somalia is a breakaway faction of al-Shabaab, as is a smaller splinter group, Islamic State in Somalia, Kenya, Tanzania, and Uganda.[133] A range of other jihadist groups are also active on the continent, including Ansar Dine, al-Mourabitoun, and Ansaru.[134]

Accompanying the proliferation in jihadist groups and splinters and offshoots has been a sharp spike in attacks.[135] AQIM remains a potent force in parts of North and West Africa, launching over 100 attacks in the region in 2016 alone, including several high-profile attacks in places like Ivory Coast and Burkina Faso, previously

unscathed by the type of attacks that frequently inflicted other nations in West Africa, including Nigeria.[136] According to a report by the Foundation of Defense for Democracies, "Between January 2007 and December 2011, jihadists conducted 132 successful, thwarted, or failed attacks against Western interests in Africa. This figure nearly tripled to 358 attacks between January 2012 and October 2017."[137]

East Africa

The Horn of Africa has long served as a cradle for militant jihad. Since the early 1990s, there has been a reputed al-Qaeda presence throughout the region. The 1998 embassy attacks in Kenya and Tanzania proved how widespread and entrenched al-Qaeda's infrastructure throughout East Africa had grown. The current manifestation of the threat, al-Shabaab, has withstood an onslaught from the US-backed African Union Mission in Somalia (AMISOM) peacekeeping forces and an array of other external military forces, from Kenya to Ethiopia. Al-Shabaab has repeatedly suffered defections from its organization, although it hasn't appeared to slow the group down in the least.[138] The organization has repeatedly demonstrated a remarkable ability to regenerate itself.[139] More recently, in an attempt to present an enlightened image and demonstrate to the local civilian population that it has its best interests in mind, al-Shabaab banned the use of plastic bags, a coup for environmental advocates but not likely to curb the group's appetite for suicide bombings and assassinations.[140]

And although the Islamic State is desperately seeking to establish a foothold in Somalia, al-Shabaab has staved off the challenge due to its unmatched capacity for violence, its ability to govern, and its propaganda and media efforts.[141] The numbers of people killed in al-Shabaab attacks is astronomical. Between September 2006 and October 2017,

al-Shabaab deployed at least 216 suicide attackers who carried out a total of 155 suicide bombing attacks, killing at least 595 and possibly as many as 2,218 people.[142] Despite the egregious violence, the group has managed to present itself as a viable governing alternative to the current Somali government, exploiting the grievances of the population and working to minimize corruption.[143] Finally, its cooperation with both transnational jihadist groups like AQAP and local expertise have fostered innovation and improvement in the capacity to construct highly lethal IEDs.[144]

Because of such a robust al-Qaeda presence in the Horn of Africa, IS is unlikely to rely on the region as a hub for its operations. Unlike Boko Haram, al-Shabaab has at present been relatively successful at denying IS space to operate and minimizing the number of recruits who have defected to the IS-affiliate. West Africa, on the other hand, has been far more inviting to the Islamic State, even as it continues to compete with other regional terrorist groups like al-Qaeda in the Islamic Maghreb.[145]

West Africa

On the other side of the continent from the Horn of Africa, West Africa has also traditionally been a bastion of al-Qaeda support, although IS has been gaining ground since the end of 2017. Since 2013, a spate of highly lethal attacks has targeted foreigners throughout the region, including in Algeria, Mali, Burkina Faso, and Ivory Coast.[146] The increase in the sophistication of attacks in West Africa appears to be the result of the transfer of tacit knowledge between skilled jihadists from IS and al-Qaeda and local African militants. Indeed, the explosives, types of mines, shells, and weapons being used all indicate an advanced level of expertise compared to previous years.[147]

Al-Qaeda has successfully tapped into new markets, breaking ground in parts of the region previously unaffected by terrorism, such as northern sections of Burkina Faso, where local militants mix with transnational jihadists.[148] Burkina Faso has been greatly impacted by spillover violence originating across the border in neighboring Mali, where JNIM has battled the French military in its quest to control territory and establish *sharia* governance.[149] Al-Qaeda has had a major impact on the deadliest terrorist organization in the region, Boko Haram, from the beginning, helping the group launch its terror campaign in 2009, while urging its leadership to adopt and introduce suicide bombing as a tactic in 2011.[150]

Still, even though al-Qaeda has a longer history of operating throughout West Africa, the Islamic State is mounting an aggressive campaign to supplant its rival and establish its own strategic reach. IS is indeed preparing for a long-term presence throughout West Africa, and the behavior of the Islamic State in West Africa (ISWA) in Nigeria and Niger looks eerily similar to how the Islamic State built its state in Iraq and Syria, providing governance for locals in exchange for the ability to levy taxes on the local economy.[151] According to AFRICOM officials, ISWA is considered to be a longer-term strategic threat compared to Boko Haram, which is viewed as more parochial and Nigeria-focused.[152]

Now that a fissure has cleaved Boko Haram in two, the future of militant jihad in West Africa may hinge on which group – IS or al-Qaeda – is able to network with groups already present on the continent, and which is able to provide a more attractive alternative to fighters returning home from the Middle East. Even before overt signs of a split, there were hints that IS and Boko Haram were cooperating. In April 2016, a convoy of Islamic State fighters in Libya delivered a shipment of weapons, mostly small arms, machine guns,

and rifles, to Boko Haram militants near the Chadian border.[153] To date, there is evidence that jihadists fleeing the caliphate have sought out Africa specifically, traveling to northeast Nigeria and parts of Libya.[154]

Europe

There is no real concern that IS would ever attempt to establish a caliphate in Europe, but given that over 4,000 European citizens traveled abroad to join jihadist groups in Iraq and Syria, it is critical to examine both the impact upon the continent, and also the role that Europe will probably play in the immediate aftermath of the collapse of the caliphate. According to some estimates, approximately 30 percent of European foreign fighters have returned home to their respective countries, while another 14 percent have been confirmed dead.[155] This means that Europe faces overlapping challenges of dealing with those who have already returned, preparing for those who still might return, and figuring out how to prevent this entire phenomenon from repeating itself in a few years, if another caliphate is declared in Libya, Afghanistan, or elsewhere.

The foreign fighter phenomenon in Europe reinforces the global nature of conflict in 2019 – what happens in Mosul has consequences in Molenbeek. In the three-year period between June 2014 and June 2017, there were 32 jihadist attacks in Europe alone: 17 in France, 6 in Germany, 4 in the United Kingdom, 3 in Belgium, 1 in Denmark, and 1 in Sweden.[156] Between June 2017 and June 2018, there were another dozen attacks, including 6 more in France, 2 in the UK, and 1 each in Belgium, Germany, Finland, and Spain.

France

Without question, France has been disproportionately affected by the cascading consequences of the civil war in Syria and the rise and fall of the Islamic State. Nearly 900 French citizens relocated to Iraq and Syria, although close to 200 have died in combat.[157] France has suffered devastating terrorist attacks on its own soil, more than 20 in the past 4 years alone, including the November 2015 Paris attacks which resulted in the death of 130 civilians and the Nice truck attack that killed 86 more. Some scholars have traced France's problem with jihadism back to French political culture, noting the aggressively secular nature of Francophone countries. This militant secularism, when combined with high rates of unemployment and urbanization, could be a uniquely influential factor in why so many French citizens join the jihad.[158]

While Muslims make up 4.9 percent of the overall population in Europe, in France the percentage is 8.8 percent.[159] Its prisons have become veritable breeding grounds for Islamic radicalization, a troubling trend throughout the continent more broadly, but one particularly acute for a country where crime and terror frequently overlap, and one to which an untold number of foreign fighters (and their families) may continue to return home.[160] More than half of the 20,000 suspects on France's so-called "S-List" (S standing for "state security") are thought to have links to jihadist groups, a staggering figure.[161] Young children who were part of the caliphate and lost their parents in the fighting are now returning to France, including to their home neighborhoods like Saint-Denis, where they are being placed with foster families or community centers for orphans.[162] But these neighborhoods remain incubators of jihadism, with extremely high levels of crime and unemployment, presenting serious concerns that these children – some of whom witnessed horrific atrocities in the Middle

East – could be recruited by radical Islamists intent on conducting attacks within France in the name of the Islamic State.[163]

Germany

Germany has also been a major source of foreign fighters and has suffered several high-profile attacks on its soil, the most devastating of which was carried out by Anis Amri, a Tunisian jihadist with links to IS in Libya. In this attack, 11 people were killed and another 55 wounded, when Amri drove a truck through a crowded Christmas market in Berlin in December 2016.[164] Nearly half of the 900 Germans who traveled abroad to fight with jihadist groups in Iraq and Syria had contact with extremist mosques in the country.[165] In response, Germany has moved to ban Islamist groups believed to be responsible for radicalizing citizens and encouraging them to travel abroad to fight with IS and other militant groups.[166]

Germany has experienced a major surge in the overall number of terrorism-related prosecutions in recent years, with over 900 cases filed in 2017 alone.[167] In a media interview, the head of Germany's Office for the Protection of the Constitution, Hans-Georg Masasen, warned of the dangers posed by "kindergarten jihadists" and women and children who were "brainwashed" by IS and intent on returning home to Germany.[168] Without question, the arrival of over 1 million migrants in the past few years, many of them Muslims, has placed a strain on the German government to dial down tensions between ethnic Germans and newly arrived asylum seekers from the Middle East, Africa, and South Asia. There are legitimate concerns that an influx of Muslims will lead to a rise in right-wing groups throughout Germany, including groups like PEGIDA, or Patriotic Europeans Against the Islamization of the West.

United Kingdom

The United Kingdom has a lengthy history with terrorism, and more recently with Islamic terrorism, following the London bombings of July 7, 2005, when several militants linked to al-Qaeda conducted suicide attacks against tube trains and a bus, killing 52 and injuring another 784 people. And while the UK remained mostly immune from terrorism directed and inspired by IS initially, there were several deadly attacks conducted over the span of a few short months in 2017, including a combined knife and vehicle attack on Westminster Bridge and Parliament in March; a suicide bombing in Manchester that killed 22 people outside of a concert in May; and another combined knife and vehicle attack at London Bridge and Borough Market in June.[169] Three months later, in September, a terrorist bombing at the Parsons Green Underground station wounded 30 people, though none were killed.

Britons were among the most prominent members of the Islamic State, including Mohammed Emwazi (a.k.a. "Jihadi John"), an IS executioner, and Junaid Hussain, perhaps IS's most well-known "virtual entrepreneur."[170] Organizations like al-Muhajiroun, a banned Islamist network once led by convicted terrorist Anjem Choudry, also recruited and encouraged British Muslims to travel to and fight in Iraq and Syria.[171] Moreover, networks like al-Muhajiroun and Sharia4Belgium had spent years – or in the case of the former, decades – laying the groundwork for and building the infrastructure that was in place by the time of IS's caliphate declaration in 2014.[172] Speaking in late 2017, Gilles de Kerchove, the European Union's counterterrorism coordinator, commented that approximately 25,000 British citizens are possibly Islamic radicals, with around 3,000 considered to be "a direct threat" by British intelligence agencies.[173] In one particularly chilling case, a British IS supporter named Umar Haque attempted to recruit young

children at a private Islamic school in London, some as young as 11 years old, and to teach them to launch terrorist attacks across the capital.[174]

Belgium

For a small and somewhat ordinary European country, Belgium has figured prominently in jihadist terrorism, with the greatest number of foreign fighters per capita of any country in the West.[175] There have been several terrorist attacks in Belgium linked to IS, including the March 2016 attacks in Brussels at the airport and Maalbeek metro station, which killed 32 people.[176] Several high-profile IS fighters were Belgians, including the charismatic jihadist Abdelhamid Abaaoud, the ringleader of the Paris November 2015 attacks.[177] Belgium was also home to militants such as Fouad Belkacem, the one-time leader of Sharia4Belgium, and Khalid Zerkani, a veteran of al-Qaeda training camps who recruited young Belgians and sent them to fight in Iraq and Syria.[178] Of the nearly 70 Belgians identified as fighting in Syria, almost all were members of Sharia4Belgium, which was particularly active in Antwerp, but elsewhere as well.[179]

Immediately after the Paris and Brussels attacks, a section of Brussels named Molenbeek came under intense scrutiny as a locus of jihad inexorably linked to terrorism. This municipality, right in the heart of Belgium's capital, was a place where 80 percent of the population was of Moroccan origin.[180] Compared to the rest of Belgium, its residents were poor, young, and suffered from high unemployment and crime rates.[181] According to a story in *Politico*, of more than 1,600 organizations registered in Molenbeek, more than 100 had links with crime, and an additional 51 were linked to terrorism.[182] In many ways, however, the Brussels attacks marked a turning point for Belgium's

long-criticized security services. Once considered inept and aloof, the Belgian security services have made significant progress improving their counterterrorism capabilities. As Renard and Coolsaet point out, the most important change has been a "broader policy shift from a narrow counterterrorism approach solely based on law enforcement and intelligence gathering towards a more comprehensive approach that combines repression and enhanced prevention."[183]

This chapter focuses on Europe not because it has the prospect of turning into the next IS state-building project, but rather because the continent's citizens helped build the caliphate. Talk of "no-go" zones has been overhyped, but there have been neighborhoods that became notorious as radicalization hubs, including parts of major European cities like Paris, Brussels, London, and Barcelona. So there is no chance that IS, or whatever terrorist entity follows it, will seriously attempt to make Europe into a jihadist sanctuary. However, the same countries discussed above that supplied recruits to IS could end up doing so again, this time with its younger generation, if the Islamic State is able to successfully regenerate itself. The most likely place for this to happen could be back where it all began, in Iraq and Syria.

4

From "Remain and Expand" to Survive and Persist

While it has become fashionable to defy conventional wisdom and to proffer the final demise of IS, few serious analysts argue that the Islamic State has been defeated once and for all. Many believe that the group will rise again, most probably right back in Iraq, or perhaps more likely Syria, where it is currently reverting to its previous form as a "mobile, brutal Sunni Arab insurgent organization."[1] The future of IS in the Middle East is of a group that will hunker down, husbanding its resources and going to ground, laying the foundation for a long-simmering insurgency while it bides time. IS and its followers view the establishment of the caliphate as a watershed moment in history – this is *the* defining moment for contemporary Islam, the Salafi-jihadists' "Khomeini moment," which indicates a historical achievement that will reverberate well beyond the present day. And, moving forward, the remaining sinew of the organization will stop at nothing to return to this glory.

The defining characteristics of IS in the future are those of an organization that is well prepared, able to adapt and evolve, and poised to take advantage of any missteps by the governments in Syria and Iraq, as well as continued ineptitude and weak capacity of the security forces operating throughout the region.[2]

Preparation

There is no doubt that IS has prepared for the long haul in the valleys and gullies along the Euphrates River. Its fighters have stockpiled arms, fuel, water, and food in trenches.[3] Because IS controlled such large swaths of territory across Iraq and Syria – at its peak, the group occupied an area the size of Britain with 12 million under its sway – it was able to enjoy unmolested freedom of movement to prepare for the next phase of the conflict.[4] Militants pre-positioned large quantities of cash, which they buried under sand berms and hoarded weapons, ammunition, and bomb-making materials in pre-fabricated tunnels throughout parts of northern Iraq.[5] After declaring the caliphate in 2014, IS leadership recognized that it would inevitably return to these areas to re-instigate guerilla warfare.[6] The Iraqi security forces have reclaimed Mosul and ejected IS from the majority of its Iraqi strong-holds, but they have done so with the backing of the US military and its Coalition allies. But for the Islamic State, this is a generational struggle, and its remaining leadership probably believes that the United States will ultimately withdraw, and the sectarian strife that has defined post-Saddam Iraq will return with a vengeance, pushing Sunni Arabs back into the Islamic State's embrace.

It comes as little surprise that IS would prepare for the next phase of its lifecycle, because it has been following a similar pattern of behavior since its inception, dating back to the mid-2000s when IS was known as al-Qaeda in Iraq, led by the Jordanian terror chieftain Abu Musab al-Zarqawi.[7] Many of the Islamic State's surviving fighters are thought to be holed up, hiding in isolated terrain, such as desert or mountainous regions, and among civilian populations in Iraq, Syria, and Turkey.[8] As Hassan Hassan has pointed out in his research, as part of a "calculated strategy," the Islamic State's remaining fighters

deliberately "melted away" in the border region between Iraq and Syria divided by the Euphrates River.[9] They live to fight another day, while mimicking the strategies of subversion and sabotage perfected by other Maoist-style insurgencies throughout recent history.

Adaptation

Above all else, it is critical to understand that the Islamic State is a learning organization. This is one of the key precepts of its success. In preparation for previous times of uncertainty, it has been revealed that the group has widely read Abu Bakr Naji's *The Management of Savagery*, a jihadi gospel of sorts for waging an unrelenting campaign of insurgency and violence against the enemies of Islam.[10] It is thus important to note that, while IS has indeed lost most of its territory, it still boasts a committed cadre of operatives, including members of its elite intelligence unit, the Emni, and militants with administrative and bureaucratic experience – what IS experts Benjamin Bahney and Patrick Johnston have dubbed "the glue of the IS organization from top to bottom."[11] These organizational skills are indispensable to the group's ability to survive, serving as "muscle memory" for how to galvanize fighters and marshal the resources necessary if the caliphate is ever to be restored.

Even in early 2018, there were already clear signs that IS had regrouped. In the Hamreen Mountains, in northern Iraq, a group of between 500 and 1,100 IS fighters calling themselves "the White Flags" reconstituted, coordinating attacks on local security services.[12] Throughout Kirkuk, IS fighters constructed fake checkpoints to ambush Iraqi security forces operating in the area. They also set out to destroy oil tankers and target Shiite civilians making religious pilgrimages.[13] In

Kirkuk and elsewhere, including Diayala and Salahaddin, IS sleeper cells helped organize what Hassan Hassan has called "rasd," roughly equivalent to scoping, or reconnaissance, of these areas to determine how best to operate before reorganizing small formations of fighters.[14] And despite the onslaught of US bombing raids, pockets of militants remain holed up in Hajin, north of Abu Kamal, and Dashisha, on the outskirts of Deir ez-Zor.[15]

Besides recapturing physical territory in the areas where it formerly governed, the Islamic State will continue to perpetuate the "virtual caliphate," tailoring messages to Western audiences that elicit sympathy while urging revenge (this subject will be covered in depth in chapter 5).[16] By inciting Muslims to commit acts of terror in its name, IS remains relevant by keeping its brand in the news cycle, ensuring its ability to recruit new members, including younger generations of Muslims who may revere the generation that came before them and was able to successfully establish a true Islamic caliphate. Again, al-Suri's ideas, promulgated during the late 1990s, have proved to be much more salient for how things have evolved into the modern era of terrorist attacks by al-Qaeda and IS, as well as by their affiliates. The trend of "do it yourself" terrorism carried out by inspired jihadists with no direct links to any established group is a major concern for the future evolution of terrorism. Joining a group is now considered less important than committing an act in the name of bin Laden, or, more recently, Baghdadi. Zawahiri is far less charismatic than bin Laden was, which partly accounts for his limited ability to inspire the kind of widespread growth of the movement al-Suri had envisioned. Still, as evidenced by their releasing media within a week of each other in late August 2018, both Zawahiri and Baghdadi remain focused on exhorting their followers to launch attacks against the West, with the IS leader urging "the supporters of the Caliphate" to conduct attacks

using guns, knives, or bombs in the West.[17] But the path forward is anything but linear. The current situation in Syria is one of a highly fractious and atomized jihadist landscape.[18] Now, perhaps more than at any other point in the conflict, IS is vulnerable to having its fighters absorbed by al-Qaeda, which is a reverse of the process that began in 2014, when IS was consistently convincing large segments of al-Qaeda-related groups to join the Islamic State.[19] Al-Qaeda has even begun using "re-radicalisation" programs, complete with courses based on a "sharia-bureau approved curriculum of jihad" to indoctrinate fighters joining its organization after having recently been IS members.[20]

Opportunism

Even though the Islamic State has changed, the structural factors throughout the Middle East which facilitated its rise have not. In some instances, they have worsened. Civil wars, jihadist ideology fueled by sectarianism, a dearth of regime legitimacy, economic weakness, and external intervention by states still largely define regional politics.[21] In his book *Waging Insurgent Warfare*, Seth Jones details the three most important factors in increasing the probability of an insurgency: local grievances, weak governance, and greed – all three of which are apparent in Iraq and Syria.[22] Not only are these factors important in *starting* an insurgency, but also they factor into the duration of an insurgency. IS has been particularly adroit at capitalizing upon the grievances – both real and perceived – of Sunni Arabs in Iraq and Syria, and will be actively looking for the next opportunity to further exacerbate latent and existing ethnic and religious strife in local communities. There is also the potential that IS could seek to co-opt Sunni tribes in the

region, as it has done before, especially in 2014–15, through a combination of money and coercion.[23]

Throughout parts of Hawija district in Iraq, Islamic State fighters return to their former strongholds in the dark of night, sometimes to threaten villagers, other times to exact revenge by assassinating their enemies.[24] In Syria, IS fighters continue to inhabit ever smaller chunks of territory due west of the Syrian–Iraqi border, while also demonstrating the ability to launch sporadic attacks in some of the suburbs around Syria's capital, Damascus. IS is constantly searching for new pipelines of recruitment and its ideology remains popular among residents of Palestinian refugee camps, in concert with the Khalid bin al-Walid Army.[25] There is a real sense that if the Islamic State's former urban strongholds, including areas like Tal Afar and Qaim, are not quickly addressed with a robust and comprehensive stabilization and reconstruction plan, they will soon fall back under the sway of those advocating violent extremism.[26] In addition to these areas, others considered "high-risk" include western Mosul, Hawija and its surrounding environs, and a swath of territory along the Tigris River from Baiji to Sharga.[27] Given the Iraq government's poor track record of assuaging Sunni grievances, few are sanguine that Baghdad will muster the political will to pacify the populations of Ramadi, Tikrit, Samarra, and Fallujah, cities that comprised a considerable portion of violence in the so-called Sunni Triangle.

As other rivalries flare up in Syria, the fight against IS is taking a back seat. Indeed, the Syrian Democratic Forces, backed by the United States, are focused on fighting elements of the Assad regime, while Turkey is focused on countering the People's Protection Units (YPG) and SDF in northern Syria. This all takes away from the fight against the Islamic State, which has used the respite to begin connecting cells and supply lines across Syria.[28] The Assad regime has done remarkably

little to combat IS, instead preferring to focus on other anti-regime elements around Homs, Hama, and Aleppo. Indeed, many fleeing IS fighters appeared to be able to move with impunity through territory nominally controlled by the Assad regime, which was either unwilling or unable to prevent their freedom of movement.[29]

The post-conflict reconstruction challenges in Iraq, particularly in places like Mosul, are immense. As RAND researchers Shelly Culbertson and Linda Robinson highlight in their work, another wave of violence could easily devastate Iraq "in a matter of months" if stabilization activities are insufficient and underfunded.[30] In neighboring Syria, although post-conflict reconstruction seems years away at this point, if and when eastern portions of the country begin to be rebuilt, IS will probably rely on its Syrian members to infiltrate security and governance structures.[31] IS knows these cities, towns, and villages and the local populations that still live there. Even though the territory it once controlled has now been largely usurped, when it was attempting to govern, IS did so quite effectively, providing its subjects with security, justice, and a clear, if draconian, set of rules by which to live.[32]

Strategy

At its apex, the Islamic State's strategy could perhaps best be summarized through its oft-repeated slogan, *"Baqiya wa Tatamaddad,"* or "Remaining and Expanding."[33] But with the loss of the caliphate, IS, and the global jihadist movement writ large, is in flux once again. And since the movement is far from a monolith, it is difficult to conceptualize an overarching strategy, per se, although it has become clear that both IS and al-Qaeda are actively seeking to remain in areas where they are currently strong, while also opportunistically dispersing fighters

and resources to new areas where they can refortify, and expand once again, with the ultimate goal of controlling large swaths of territory and people. IS is known for many things – its penchant for violence, its ability to raise funds, and its sophisticated propaganda apparatus – but perhaps its greatest strength, and the one characteristic that will help it survive, is its oft-overlooked willingness to evolve and change in response to conditions on the ground. Its surviving leadership remains extremely aware of the need to balance strategic considerations and encourage strategic learning via doctrine.[34]

The global jihadist movement's most prolific strategists believe in the objective of establishing a caliphate, even while they disagree over the strategy to achieve this goal, as well as the timeline.[35] There is already compelling evidence that the movement is invoking the nostalgia of the caliphate to begin framing its future strategy.[36] Raqqa has been recaptured, but the Islamic State proved to its followers – and to the world – that, despite the enormous odds against such a proposition, it is possible to construct a jihadi proto-state capable of both governing and defending its borders. Granted, that state has now been conquered, but the fact that it could be established in the first place is the narrative that IS will cling to in its future propaganda. Moreover, it will highlight that this state could only be realized by the will of God, and that the reason it no longer exists is due to the actions of the infidels and Crusaders, evoking images of an eternal battle between good and evil, believers and non-believers, faithful Muslims and everyone else. As Craig Whiteside argues:

To fuel the information campaigns of the next three decades, much like yesterday's jihadists look back to Qutb and Azzam, IS and its rivals (including al-Qaeda) will use the caliphate idea and the understanding of the importance of local control and

governance as proof positive of how to advance this political goal in the future. No one can ever tell them it is impossible anymore.[37]

The ongoing split between IS and al-Qaeda has not prevented the former from relying on the strategic guidance provided by notable figures from the latter, including jihadist strategists such as Abu Musab al-Suri, Abu Bakr Naji, and Anwar al-Awlaki.[38] Overall, despite current fissures in the movement, its leaders and followers have far more in common than they may recognize. As Daniel Byman has argued, "If jihadists disagree on fundamental outcomes, then any unity of purpose or organization will be much harder to achieve. If the question is simply one of priorities, then changes in circumstances can bring different factions together in the name of expediency."[39] In the past, opposition to apostate regimes and Western imperialists has proven to be an attractive elixir in this regard. By slightly reframing its narrative and modifying its tactics, the global jihadist movement could seek to unite its own warring factions.

Sardonically, it may be the Coalition's destruction of the caliphate that helps the movement refine its overall strategy. IS proved that building a state could be done successfully, albeit temporarily, while al-Qaeda would suggest that the caliphate collapsed because its declaration was premature, and the focus should instead be on gradualism and educating the global *ummah*.[40] In recent years, al-Qaeda's strategy has morphed from one focused obsessively on attacking the West to one defined by a desire to win the support of local populations in the areas it operates in.[41] A troubling scenario is one in which the erstwhile strategies of IS and al-Qaeda successfully merge into a singular, coherent approach for the global jihadist movement more broadly – one defined by cultivating local support on a truly global level, while

aggressively attacking nation-states and groups it deems as enemies, infidels, and adversaries.

Tactics

At the heart of the movement's future strategic direction will be the tactics adopted to achieve its objectives along the way. Along the same lines as the jihadists' approach to strategy, both IS and al-Qaeda offer unique refinements and approaches to tactical innovation that, if combined and harnessed in concert, could prove to have a devastating and destabilizing effect in various theatres throughout the globe.[42] Moreover, as commercial off-the-shelf technologies become ubiquitous and easier to acquire, it would come as little surprise if jihadist groups were to exploit advances in unmanned aerial systems, artificial intelligence (AI), and 3-D printing to close the gap between their capabilities and those of advanced militaries. Indeed, as Daveed Gartenstein-Ross has noted, "for jihadist organizations, the ability to innovate is a necessity, not a luxury."[43]

The Islamic State's unique contribution to tactical evolution has been impressive. IS has pioneered the use of the virtual planner model for external operations.[44] This innovation allows terrorists in one location to direct attacks in another part of the world with only an Internet connection and reliable encryption.[45] In many cases, jihadists are able to leverage local criminal networks that act as facilitators to help acquire the logistics and resources necessary for an attack.[46] Even as Western nations have devoted substantial resources to countering this threat, savvy tacticians within the global jihadist movement will continue to rely on encrypted online messaging applications to identify local recruits and provide them with directions and technical expertise to attack

targets, a development that poses a formidable threat to countries with less than adequate military, intelligence, and law enforcement capabilities.[47] The devastating Paris November 2015 attacks could serve as the model operation from the terrorists' point of view.[48]

The other more recent tactic to take note of is al-Qaeda's focus on "winning hearts and minds" as a method of securing and cementing its legitimacy among local constituencies.[49] Al-Qaeda has repeatedly demonstrated a pragmatic approach to operating in amidst civil wars, as evidenced by its actions in Syria, Yemen, and Mali.[50] If the global jihadist movement recognizes the importance of popular support and subsequently tones down its sectarian rhetoric, it remains entirely possible that Salafi groups could emerge as more preferable alternatives than the weak and corrupt regimes holding office throughout large swaths of the Muslim world.

Ongoing Debates in Jihadi Ideology

Sunni jihadism is a "social movement family with its general foundation in Sunni theology, more specifically in the concept and practice of Jihad, and to some extent in the specific doctrine of Salafism."[51] As Cole Bunzel points out, while IS and al-Qaeda are the "principal organizational expressions" of the jihadi movement, jihadism is both an ideology and a "highly developed system of thought deeply-rooted in certain aspects of the Islamic tradition," and, as such, the sum of the movement itself is far greater than its individual parts.[52] The split between IS and al-Qaeda is occurring amidst a wider disagreement permeating the ranks of some of the leading jihadist ideologues. The infighting is nothing new. There have been many well-publicized spats in the past between jihadist leaders. What used to be hashed

out through long and highly esoteric handwritten letters exchanged between ideologues has now devolved into social media feuds playing out in the public domain in chat rooms on the Internet. Rik Coolsaet commented on the continued rift between the two groups, noting that "a small but strident camp of hardliners consider Daesh's official ideology insufficiently radical and are pushing for an even more extremist stance that would exclude all possible cooperation with other jihadist groups, including al Qaeda."[53]

The debate centers on several themes in particular – takfirism, *tatarrus*, *sharia* law, and when to declare a caliphate – but is also reflected in both organizational and operational differences between the global jihadist movement's two heavyweights. The subject which has led to the most caustic debate has been over who can claim to be a proper, devout, and righteous Muslim. IS has taken takfirism, or the practice of declaring other Muslims to be non-believers due to their supposed apostasy or heresy, to new extremes.[54] Yet, ultimately, its leadership eventually recognized that this practice might be counterproductive, especially as the group is losing territory and needs to rejuvenate its ranks with an influx of new recruits. In September 2017, IS religious leadership appeared to soften its stance on this matter, issuing a revocation of an earlier religious edict that broadened the scope of takfirism.[55] Still, the debate continued to rage, with the ideological rift mostly centered on whether those who remain reticent to excommunicate apostates and unbelievers should themselves be excommunicated.[56] Some of the Islamic State's hard-core ideologues view the group's commitment to takfir as even more important than prayer and other fundamental components of Salafism.[57] Apparently, there is even a hardcore group of IS militants, which Tore Hamming refers to as "the extremist wing of the Islamic State," that sees Baghdadi as "soft," leading to further fragmentation of the group.[58]

Another thread within this debate is over the concept of *tatarrus*, or whom and what constitute legitimate targets for jihadists' violence. "Al Qaeda has tried to learn its lesson from this and compared to 15 years ago, the group is far more discerning in its targeting, while the same cannot be said about IS. The differing approaches have been described as 'winning hearts and minds' (al-Qaeda) versus 'crushing necks and spines' (IS)."[59] This shift is reflected in the styles and organizational structures of the two groups. To succeed, al-Qaeda believes that the support of the population is crucial, part of its Maoist-style insurgent approach, while IS's focoist-style approach views violence as instrumental and redeeming.[60]

Even before the Arab Spring, as early as 2010, bin Laden was advocating for a change in al-Qaeda's approach, calling for "an advisory reading and development of our entire policy."[61] In September 2013 Zawahiri authored "General Guidelines for Jihad," which called for a more restrained approach, one consistent with a population-centric strategy.[62] This extends to how harshly to implement *sharia* law, especially taking into consideration local and tribal mores and customs. And for those jihadists arguing that al-Qaeda has lost its way, the move to be more accommodating toward civilian populations is perfectly in line, and in fact synchronized, with its strategy of garnering lasting and widespread popular support before it declares a caliphate of its own, which has always been part of al-Qaeda's long-term strategy.

The IS–Al-Qaeda Dispute

The fall-out from the split between IS and al-Qaeda has led to a competition viewed by both sides as zero sum in nature, where progress by one of these groups signaled a loss for the other. One of the primary

drivers of such a heated competition is that, in many ways, the ideology and objectives of the group are so similar. The Islamic State reverted to extreme levels of violence as one method of differentiating itself from its rivals, including al-Qaeda. Both groups are attempting to recruit from the same milieus and influence similar constituencies. The main differences are that IS sought to create a caliphate on a timeline considered premature by al-Qaeda, and IS pursued a far more sectarian agenda in attempting to achieve this objective. Whether and how these differences are ever resolved will have a major impact on the future of the movement writ large.

The split itself occurred at the leadership levels of these groups, so one of the most interesting questions is: to what extent do foot soldiers and mid-level commanders really care, in actuality, about the previous infighting and strategic disputes? For some of the fighters at these levels, there is an obvious parallel to conflicts between street gangs, where members like the Bloods and Crips "fly their colors" – or represent their gangs by wearing their distinctive colors – and continuously disparage their adversaries by posting "dis videos" online, mocking and threatening rivals.[63] The bitterness and divisiveness of the feud has played out on social media, with leaders on each side hurling vituperation and casting opprobrium on the other as "bad Muslims." The initial castigation came from al-Qaeda's leader Zawahiri himself, who fulminated against IS for being deviant from the al-Qaeda methodology.

The truth is, as outlined in chapter 1's discussion of al-Qaeda in Iraq, that the relationship was doomed from the start. The group that would eventually become IS has always been something of a rogue element, formed and led by Zarqawi, who fought hard to preserve the independence of his affiliate. Even after pledging his loyalty to bin Laden and assuming the al-Qaeda moniker, Zarqawi still ignored directions from al-Qaeda's core leadership and narrowly pursued his own sectarian

agenda in hopes of igniting a Sunni–Shia civil war, first within Iraq, and then throughout the wider Islamic world. One of al-Qaeda's first steps to present itself as more evenhanded was denouncing blatant sectarianism and working to convince AQI to jettison sectarianism as a guiding principle. When, in July 2005, Zawahiri penned a letter to the leader of AQI chastising him for his group's wanton slaughter of Shiites, the former stressed the overall negative impact these actions were having on the al-Qaeda brand and urged him to eschew targeting other Muslims. When Zarqáwi disregarded Zawahiri's advice, he cemented AQI's reputation as a ruthless organization where violence was almost an end in and of itself.

So while the initial rift began deepening in Iraq in the mid-2000s, it developed into an internecine struggle during the early years of the Syrian civil war. Following the fall-out, al-Qaeda has worked assiduously to reestablish itself as a major factor in the Levant; to accomplish this, it has been forced to overcome several significant setbacks related to its organizational unity and coherence.[64] Al-Qaeda's initial presence in Syria was through an affiliation with Jabhat al-Nusra, the Islamic State in Iraq's erstwhile Syria branch. In mid-2016, Nusra rebranded itself as Jabhat Fateh al-Sham and later merged with other terrorist splinter groups to form Hay'at Tahrir al-Sham (HTS), a jihadist umbrella organization, which put even more distance between itself and al-Qaeda. As of mid-2018, al-Qaeda had no formal affiliate in Syria but still commanded the loyalty of several high-profile militants. Some al-Qaeda loyalists announced the formation of yet another new group, Tanzim Hurras al-Din, or the Religious Guardians' Organization, in 2018. While HTS remains focused on events in Syria, Tanzim Hurras al-Din is headed by al-Qaeda veterans who may seek to use Syria as a base to launch high-profile terrorist attacks against the West.[65] This posture is a departure from al-Qaeda's recent focus on grassroots

appeal in Syria and, if it comes to fruition, it will probably have significant ramifications for the group's return to its former glory. Another important angle is that there are several Jordanian jihadi veterans among Tanzim Hurras al-Din's leadership cadre who were close to Zarqawi and, as such, there is both historical and ideological affinity with IS, which increases the probability that Hurras might successfully poach IS members and bring them into the al-Qaeda fold.[66]

The rebranding process for al-Qaeda in Syria was undertaken partly out of necessity, but it was also strategic in nature. From a pragmatic standpoint, the rebrandings have served to put some distance between al-Qaeda and a host of imitators and rivals. This could be an effort by the group to learn from past mistakes, when the leadership's reluctance to publicly disavow Zarqawi traded short-term gains for long-term losses and eventually contributed to the split, an event that seemed like an existential threat to al-Qaeda throughout 2014. The strategic part of the rebranding is no different from a company's use of public relations and marketing to refashion its image – al-Qaeda now seeks to present itself as the "moderate alternative" to the Islamic State.[67] The IS brand was represented by the caliphate and the group's reliance on anomic violence, while al-Qaeda sought to position itself as an organization more adept at strategic planning and with more attractive prospects for enduring success in the future.[68]

Although the rebranding is considered a feint by many counterterrorism scholars, it just might have worked to recast al-Qaeda's image within Syria.[69] And so, even while the emergence of IS at one point threatened the existence of al-Qaeda, it also presented the latter with an opportunity. Al-Qaeda's calculated decision to distance itself from its former satellite organization was an effort to portray itself as a legitimate, capable, and independent force in the ongoing Syrian civil war. Another objective was to prove that the militants were dedicated

to helping Syrians prevail in their struggle.[70] Finally, it would give core al-Qaeda a modicum of plausible deniability as it paves the way for its erstwhile allies to gain eligibility for military aid from a collection of external nations.[71]

Now that the Islamic State has lost its caliphate, al-Qaeda may be the only group viewed as militarily capable of challenging the Assad regime's grip on power, although, as of early 2019, that seems like a long shot. Al-Qaeda could certainly prove to be the longer-term threat to stability in Syria, primarily due to its grassroots support and local appeal. Unlike the Islamic State, al-Qaeda is perceived as an entity willing to work with the population and possessing the resources necessary to provide at least some of the trappings of governance. In the long term, al-Qaeda could resemble Lebanese Hezbollah – a violent non-state actor that has solidified political legitimacy while still retaining its ability to wage large-scale acts of terrorism and political violence.[72]

Depending on where it operates, al-Qaeda has shifted between protector, predator, and parasite, labels which are not mutually exclusive. In both Yemen and Mali, its members demonstrate a remarkable knack for pragmatism when operating in the midst of brutal civil wars. After infiltrating local rebel groups, al-Qaeda fighters parrot their grievances and champion parochial objectives. After ingratiating its fighters, al-Qaeda then ramps up proselytization efforts and introduces a narrative defined by a mixture of local and global themes. Unlike the Islamic State, al-Qaeda is willing to work with other groups, as it has been doing in Syria, where it typically puts locals in charge of units, battalions, and other military formations, lending a sense of local legitimacy to its face in the country. Moreover, al-Qaeda has displayed a penchant for cooperation beyond immediate conflict zones, as evidenced by on-again, off-again tactical cooperation with Iran.

One of the most debated issues within the global jihadist movement is the so-called "near versus far debate" about which enemies the militants should concentrate the bulk of their efforts fighting – local apostate regimes or Western countries, especially the United States, but increasingly also the United Kingdom, France, and Australia. Al-Qaeda in Syria has managed to boost its brand through the provision of local services, including water and electricity, while also working to support local bakeries and control market prices of basic foodstuffs. Its leadership publicly announced that it will refrain from attacking the West, at least temporarily, in order to avoid Western counterterrorism reprisals, while simultaneously conserving its resources to concentrate on overthrowing the Assad regime, by far the top priority of Syrian Sunnis.

Al-Qaeda's Syrian leadership also recognizes that it is infinitely more successful when it focuses on local issues instead of a more amorphous and contested struggle with the West. These tensions seem to be at least partly to blame for the continued fracturing and splintering of al-Qaeda in Syria and its multiple iterations and offshoots. The debate over whether to focus locally or to revert back to a relentless quest to conduct spectacular attacks in the West could lead to a long-term and enduring fissure within the global jihadist movement. With the movement already divided by the al-Qaeda – IS split, this issue, similar to the decision on when to attempt to establish the caliphate, is a core ideological debate that is unlikely to be settled anytime soon.

For all of al-Qaeda's attempts at moderation, IS has behaved in an entirely opposite manner, as it pursued an uncompromising strategy of sectarianism, barbarity, and conquest. IS fully embraced sectarianism, seemingly making the killing of Shiites its *raison d'être*. And while al-Qaeda's propaganda might still be peppered with derogatory references to Shiites, in general it favors a much more measured

approach than IS. The groups are different in many ways, some subtle and others not. For example, rather than working with local groups, IS consistently acted as a conquering army, routing local militant leaders rather than working alongside them. In addition, locals were taxed, extorted, and closely policed by IS religious patrols to ensure strict adherence to *sharia* law.

IS's approach to warfare was reflected in its fighting style, whereby the group relied on conventional means of warfare, including artillery and tanks, in combination with some asymmetric tactics. When IS assumed control of a certain swath of territory, it often installed foreigners (Chechens, Tunisians, and Uzbeks) in command of the area. But its success came with a price. The more territory IS took over and the more brazen its displays of military might, the more likely the Coalition could no longer ignore its actions. The result was that, compared to other Salafi-jihadist groups operating in Syria, IS bore the brunt of Western counterterrorism operations, a development that suited al-Qaeda just fine.[73] The relentless stream of IS propaganda directed at the West – particularly the gruesome videos of beheadings, burnings, and crucifixions – left the Coalition with little choice but to set its sights on the caliphate.[74] The success IS experienced in building its proto-state elevated it to the top priority for the Coalition. Accordingly, al-Qaeda in Syria was given breathing room to patiently rebuild its credibility and political legitimacy among locals.[75] Gartenstein-Ross has described this as a "strategy of deliberate yet low-key growth."[76]

The future of al-Qaeda and IS will be largely defined by the competition between the two. There is little debate that, beginning around 2014, IS could successfully lay claim to be the undisputed leader of the global jihadist movement. Once its caliphate collapsed, that began to change, and its current decline may be accompanied by al-Qaeda's rise back to preeminence. There are clear signs that al-Qaeda has modified

its tactics to take advantage of what it sees as a unique opportunity. In Syria's Idlib province, al-Qaeda successfully cultivated grassroots support and by mid-2017 was beginning to accept former IS fighters into its ranks, a development most would have thought unthinkable just a year or two earlier. Al-Qaeda's leadership realizes that its response to the Arab Spring was sclerotic and is now making amends, focusing its resources and energy on the concerns most salient to Sunnis, a strategy that has helped the group spread its roots throughout northwestern Syria. It has also used this strategy successfully throughout parts of Yemen, where it operates under various front organizations, branches of Ansar Sharia, and other Salafi groups.[77]

Al-Qaeda's more balanced and predictable approach to governing is geared toward winning the popular support of civilian populations. Life under the Islamic State, even for its own loyal subjects, was enforced by draconian religious interpretations and subsequent enforcement of punishments for those who were not fastidious and completely obedient. Al-Qaeda was far less stringent and could be indifferent to perceived offenses that would draw harsh rebuke from the Islamic State. The year 2018 marked the 30-year anniversary of al-Qaeda's founding and it is clear that the group has evolved, adapted, and learned over time. Its ability to establish widespread political legitimacy through a refurbished image could propel the group through well into its fourth decade.

This shift over time by al-Qaeda to a more tolerant organization was in part a result of Zawahiri's leadership. For all of the criticism he endures for lacking charisma, a critique most jihadist scholars find unassailable, Zawahiri does give al-Qaeda the benefit of continuity and a historical appreciation for what has traditionally worked and what has failed in the jihadists' ongoing struggle against their adversaries. With his direction, the group has made course corrections based

on trial and error and actively sought to amend previous errors in doctrine and strategy.

Al-Qaeda in Syria has gone to great lengths to protect its image by rebranding its affiliate several times already. Bilaad al-Shaam, or the Land of the Levantine People, is highly coveted by multiple groups within the global jihadist movement for religious and geographical reasons. Zawahiri sees Syria as an opportunity to demonstrate relevance, juxtapose al-Qaeda to the Islamic State, and position his group as the more capable and pragmatic entity and, thus, the group worth siding with as the competition continues.

Perhaps the most interesting change in al-Qaeda's behavior since the death of bin Laden is that the group no longer seems obsessed with striking the West and, indeed, according to Bruce Hoffman, in 2015 Zawahiri issued strict orders to Mohammed al-Jolani not to use Syria as a launching pad to attack the West.[78] There are several possible reasons for this decision, including that al-Qaeda's infrastructure in Europe was not nearly as robust as that of the Islamic State, and thus any attack was pobably going to pale in comparison to what IS had already achieved.

Another, more nefarious possibility is that Zawahiri is merely playing the "long game" while strategically concealing al-Qaeda's Khorasan Group assets as IS is further attenuated. Again, this might be changing with the continued splintering of groups in Syria and the emergence of Tanzim Hurras al-Din. At least in terms of capability, if not intent, discerning a group's organizational structure could provide clues to its reach and ability to conduct external attacks. Do groups adopt a more decentralized structure to conduct external attacks, or are attacks outside of the group's main territory a byproduct of a flatter structure? Relatedly, it is possible that too much structure is assigned to jihadist groups by those attempting to analyze them. Al-Qaeda and

IS, in addition to their respective affiliates, may in reality be far less monolithic than scholars and analysts believe.

The Future Is the Past

There are three distinct possibilities for the future of the al-Qaeda–IS relationship: status quo, outbidding, and rapprochement, each of which will be described in detail below. Suffice to say that whatever form this relationship assumes moving forward, it will be shaped just as much by decisions undertaken by the groups and their leadership cadre as it will by exogenous factors, which include actions pursued by nation-states, and probably by broader geopolitical phenomena, as evidenced by previous changes ushered in by events like the Arab Spring.

Status Quo

A continuation of the status quo would see the two groups remain at odds in something of an uneasy co-existence, operating in similar locales and attempting to recruit new members from the same pool of people, while also competing for access to weapons, financing, and territory. This scenario features continued clashes and frequent spats of violence where the dispute gets kinetic, but still remains confined to low-intensity conflict marked by assassinations, defections, and online verbal disputes and harassment. In the Middle East and other areas where the global jihadist movement predominates, one particular cliché still has currency – *the enemy of my enemy is my friend*. After all, as described in other parts of this analysis, these groups have more commonalities than they have differences.

Outbidding

Another possibility for al-Qaeda–IS relations in the future is the prospect that the two groups ramp up the competition by engaging in escalatory attacks against each other (as well as against security forces) in a process known as outbidding, wherein violent non-state groups rely on extreme violence to persuade potential acolytes that their terrorist or insurgent organization has a stronger resolve to fight the adversary.[79] This situation has played out historically before, in Sri Lanka, Northern Ireland, Lebanon, and the Palestinian territories. It could once again become a defining feature of the conflicts in Syria, Afghanistan, Libya, and West Africa, where the competition between al-Qaeda and IS leads to a spike in suicide bombings, IEDs, and armed attacks. As part of this scenario, in areas where both groups maintain a presence, the result is a violent struggle to exert dominance and command the loyalty of the population by demonstrating superior military prowess vis-à-vis their rivals.

Rapprochement

The possibility of rapprochement between al-Qaeda and IS seems unlikely given the current state of affairs between the groups, but it should not be wholly jettisoned as a possibility. It may take a few years, but a marriage of convenience in which tactical cooperation becomes a necessity is an entirely realistic scenario.[80] The result of enervated enmity would lead to decreased violence between the groups and act as a force multiplier for Salafi-jihadism, vastly increasing the threat of more spectacular-style attacks around the globe.[81] By working together and pooling the resources of the two groups, the newly formed (or reformed) organization would be enhanced by

tacit knowledge transfer of sophisticated bomb-making methods, and shared tactics, techniques, and procedures for improved operations security.

For this to happen, there would probably need to be progress on mitigating some of the previously discussed disputes between the two groups and a recognition that ideological differences should not limit operational capabilities. Where this becomes most concerning is if the groups reunite and dedicate a significant portion of their efforts to attacking the West; it is not difficult to imagine a blitzkrieg-style propaganda offensive highlighting the merger while simultaneously imploring jihadists to launch attacks worldwide. To be sure, there are serious obstacles to these groups reuniting, but stranger things have happened. Al-Qaeda seemingly overcame the Sunni–Shia divide by cooperating with Iran, especially once the group's leadership realized it could benefit from tactical cooperation with the mullahs in Tehran.[82] So, in the end, if each group recognized the net benefits of a partnership, a working relationship in the future is not entirely out of the question.

Several top terrorism scholars have voiced skepticism regarding future rapprochement, especially since al-Qaeda and IS are engaged competitively on two different levels – ideologically and militarily. Hassan Hassan, IS expert and co-author of *ISIS: Inside the Army of Terror*, is a fervent believer that no long-term merger will be possible, remarking, "Even if the two organizations find it operationally expedient to work together, their overall strategies and visions cannot be bridged. Each views the other's strategy as ineffective."[83]

Nevertheless, a major event like the death of Baghdadi could prompt change and, relatedly, the split is most pronounced at the leadership level. Among the lower ranks, there is more fluidity between groups, so there could be room for future collaboration and

cooperation between al-Qaeda and IS "pools."[84] Bruce Hoffman agrees that the death of Baghdadi could lead to a voluntary amalgamation of the remaining IS fighters with al-Qaeda, or a bid from al-Qaeda (or its acolytes) to undertake a hostile takeover of the surviving IS remnants. Further, since the leaders in charge of IS's external operations and intelligence operations are former Ba'athists – and both pragmatists and survivors – there is a chance that they might ally themselves to whomever and whichever group offered the best prospects for survival and continuing the fight.[85]

What Happens Next?

The three possible futures for al-Qaeda and IS laid out above could each contribute in a different way toward a broader overview of the groups' relative strengths and weaknesses. The section below outlines four distinct potential contexts, beyond whether or not the two groups ever overcome their differences. These contextual scenarios assess the

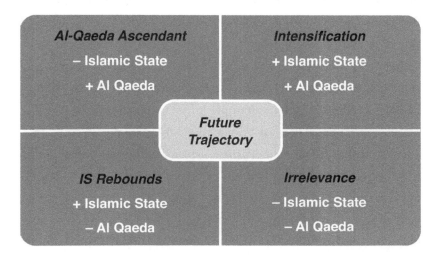

relative strength and weakness of each group and suggest a myriad of factors that might result from the outcome. It should be noted that in each of the scenarios described below, the groups remain as separate entities, but that does not entirely rule out on-again, off-again cooperation in specific regions at various times, although the cooperation does not signal anything close to reunification.

Intensification

In this scenario, both al-Qaeda and IS are at increased strength. This could result from any number of real-world developments, including a retrenched Western posture in the Middle East, North Africa, and South Asia. This scenario would see an expansion of the current wave of religious terrorism and could breathe new life into the global jihadist movement as a whole. Over the past two decades, there have been several times when analysts have predicted the demise of the movement – namely, almost immediately after the United States declared its Global War on Terror; once again following the death of Osama bin Laden; and more recently, following the recapture of the Islamic State's strongholds in Mosul and Raqqa and the destruction of its state-building project. But, rather than view the end of the caliphate as the beginning of the end of the movement, some see its establishment in the first place as proof of life, given the destructive energy it produced, luring legions of Muslims from around the world to make *hijrah* (emigration) to its state. Both al-Qaeda and IS could take advantage of exogenous shocks to the system, including another global financial crisis, which, in a world of finite resources, would directly impact nation-states' ability to counter these groups. Predatory insurgent organizations feast on the carcasses of states where civil wars have ravaged institutions and bureaucracies, the official organs of state

power projection and legitimacy. Jihadist groups flourish in regions of the world characterized by state failure, lack of good governance, inability to establish widespread rule of law, weak security services, and high levels of corruption.

Irrelevance

Another possible future of the global jihadist movement is retrenchment, dissipation, and a move toward increasing irrelevance. In response to the establishment of the caliphate, there was a pendulum swing back in the other direction, as states moved to harden borders, information sharing and cooperation between intelligence services increased, and advances in technology favored counterterrorism forces. The use of biometrics and the integration of artificial intelligence into the targeting process could help Western militaries be both more effective and discerning in their hunt for terrorist leaders hiding in austere terrain. Another facet of this future potentiality is that the narrative crafted by the Islamic State and similar groups could fail to resonate with future generations and be exposed as bankrupt and contradictory. This scenario is embodied by a shift in the threat landscape where dangers posed by terrorist groups persist, but the gravest concerns to international security are manifested in nation-states and great power rivalries, not non-state actors. Furthermore, the threat of major combat between well-equipped nation-states could make proxy conflict less likely, as states seek to avoid escalatory actions that could lead to war.

Al-Qaeda Ascendant

A scenario in which al-Qaeda is ascendant and the Islamic State falters could result from an increase in external support to the former and increasing isolation of the latter. The percolating conflict between Sunni and Shia powers, represented by the bitter feud between Saudi Arabia and Iran, respectively, could lead some Sunni powers to become more tolerant of al-Qaeda and even sponsor it as a proxy force. Al-Qaeda would be well positioned to receive this type of support since it has worked diligently to refashion its image as a more moderate entity since the Arab Spring. IS is still considered too extreme and has never received external support, even from some of the more hardline boosters of Salafism throughout the Gulf. If al-Qaeda gets involved in certain conflicts that are both seminal and highly symbolic, such as Kashmir, it could further burnish its image as the real vanguard of Islamist rebels committed to defending Muslims. Further, if al-Qaeda focuses its resources on striking the West, and is able to do so success-fully, this may provide the momentum necessary to supplant IS as the leader of the global jihadist movement, and even poach IS fighters, as it has done already in parts of the Middle East and Africa.[86]

IS Rebounds

This scenario predicts the demise of al-Qaeda while the Islamic State rebounds and flourishes, in a replay of the situation during the period from 2014 to 2016. During this time, IS was ascendant and al-Qaeda was caught flat-footed, failing to anticipate the events surrounding the Arab Spring and then responding in a sclerotic manner, as other groups took advantage of the power vacuum to promote their own agendas and ideologies. Ultimately, al-Qaeda benefitted from the chaos that

resulted from the Arab Spring, but continued success is far from a *fait accompli.*[87] There is no doubt that IS will indeed reconstitute itself and will almost certainly do so in Iraq and Syria, in addition to other potential locations. But the question is: to what extent does IS rebound and can it rise like a phoenix from the ashes to reclaim its past glory? It remains doubtful that the international community, having once been so negligent, could look away yet again as the group attempted to rebuild a state. The memories of past atrocities are still too fresh. But, most of all, for the countries most affected by the rise of IS – those in the region and others in the West where foreign terrorist fighters and their families are now attempting to return home – the terror and instability conjured by the Islamic State is still quite palpable. In fact, the pivotal time period that could engender this scenario was the 2017–18 timeframe, a time when the caliphate was decimated and al-Qaeda's strategy to quietly and patiently rebuild took shape. The result could be that al-Qaeda temporarily rises above IS as the target most concerning to Western counterterrorism forces, which once again attack al-Qaeda wherever it coalesces, elevating IS simply by default, as its fighters seek to "quietly and patiently rebuild" in their own right.

5

After the Caliphate: Preventing the Islamic State's Return

Whether it is al-Qaeda or IS, or a rejuvenated hybrid entity with off-shoots pockmarking the globe, how can the global jihadist movement be defeated once and for all? The track record for preventing another mass mobilization of jihadists in the future is not promising. Despite the fact that the West has been concerned with foreign fighters and their return for nearly three decades, there has been little tangible progress on crafting policy responses to dealing with the threat. Whether in the immediate aftermath of the end of the Soviet–Afghan war in the late 1980s, Bosnia and Chechnya in the 1990s, Iraq in the 2000s, or Syria in 2014, when it comes to preventing a worldwide flow of foreign fighters, the West always seems to be starting from scratch. As of 2018, there were an estimated 230,000 Salafi-jihadists worldwide, accounting for a 247 percent increase from 2001 to 2018. This means that the so-called Global War on Terror has failed to reduce the number of terrorists worldwide and, despite the massive resources dedicated by the West toward this mission, there are now more jihadist groups active than at any point since 1980.[1] A defining moment for this movement was the establishment of the caliphate.

But even as the jihadists' state-building project in Syria and Iraq begins to fade from recent memory, there is no time to lose in preparing to prevent the next attempt at building a caliphate, whether the destination is Sirte, Libya, or Nangarhar province in Afghanistan. Despite

an intensified scrutiny on establishing robust counter-measures, there is still no unified policy in terms of preventing citizens from traveling abroad to join terrorist groups, or widescale agreement among states with respect to important issues such as citizenship deprivation, prosecution and length of sentences, punitive versus rehabilitative measures, or best practices and lessons learned regarding prison radicalization, recidivism, and deradicalization and disengagement initiatives. The patchwork of policies and widescale disparities in resources to enact these policies increase the likelihood of a future foreign terrorist fighter mobilization, even if it is not quite on the scale of IS's recent attempt to establish a caliphate.

The question now becomes, in the immediate aftermath of the caliphate's destruction: how will the international community ensure that it never returns? This will require a comprehensive response that is both carrot and stick. Returning foreign terrorist fighters, and in some cases their families, will need to be dealt with, while the campaign to counter IS on multiple levels – national, regional, and global – must simultaneously remain on the offensive to prevent splinter groups from reconstituting and to deny the group any opportunity to revive the *joie de vivre* it once inspired in tens of thousands of supporters, many of whom traveled to the Middle East to help build and defend the caliphate.

The physical manifestation of IS's state-building project has been crushed, but by no means has the ideology motivating tens of thousands of people to risk their lives defending the caliphate been weakened. If anything, the two-year period during which IS governed its own proto-state offered its followers proof of the concept that the establishment of a caliphate is more than just a jihadi talking point. Rather, it is an attainable goal worthy of dedicating one's life to. The sole reason for its destruction, the propaganda reminds IS adherents,

is the Crusader–Zionist axis led by Western nations, especially the United States. Baghdadi proclaimed in an audiotape that was released in August 2018 that the United States "boasted of its so-called victory in expelling the state from cities and countryside in Iraq and Syria, but the land of Allah is wide and the tides of war change."[2] So, while the West breathes a collective sigh of relief that IS has been ousted from Raqqa and Mosul and nearly 70,000 IS fighters have been killed, the group's leader is confidently appealing to its supporters to remain loyal, patient, and steadfast until the moment is ripe for a revival.

Well before the collapse of the Islamic State's caliphate, countries around the world were concerned about a flood of returning foreign fighters. And while the numbers have been far lower than expected, for myriad reasons, the challenge of dealing with returnees is no less complex.[3] Preventing the return of the Islamic State is going to require a mixture of preventive and punitive measures, including discerning the proper way to deal with returnees, but also defending against future threats related to IS's core capabilities – social media and propaganda, financing, and the ability to harness new technologies to recruit and radicalize a fresh generation of followers.

There is little consensus in the West as to the best way to counter the threat. Moreover, with finite resources and a fleeting attention span, national governments must balance the threat posed by terrorism with a litany of other challenges, from climate change to energy insecurity. The global jihadist movement, while a major threat to international security, is merely one of many threats. Finally, some policymakers and military officials may conclude that the mission is complete. After all, the Islamic State's caliphate has been unquestionably destroyed. But in many ways, the challenges associated with the *aftermath* of the caliphate will be even more difficult to solve than the physical caliphate itself, which at least provided a clear target for the international

community to focus on and work against. The exodus of fighters from Iraq and Syria seems poised to reset the cycle once more, the same cycle that has been repeating itself since the fateful days of the Soviet-Afghan War, when Osama bin Laden and his group of "Afghan Arabs" spread throughout the globe and planted the seeds for what would grow into the global jihadist movement and all of its manifestations.

Dealing with Returnees

The prospect of returning foreign fighters and their families has understandably occupied much time and energy in policy and law-enforcement circles.[4] These fighters may attempt to return to their countries of origin, whether close to the battlefields of Syria and Iraq, or farther afield to Europe, Asia, and North America. Those states equipped with more robust national screening mechanisms, law enforcement, and intelligence structures stand a better chance of stopping the fighters at their border, blunting the impact of these returnees. But not all Western security services are created equal. Further complicating the issue is the inability to even agree on the definition of who constitutes a foreign fighter in the first place.[5] Moreover, the category of returnees is not nearly as homogeneous as it may seem. Just as foreign fighters who traveled to the Middle East left for different reasons and fought with different groups, those who return will do so for varying reasons as well.

The first subgroup of returnees might be labeled the "disillusioned." These individuals went to Syria looking for utopia, adventure, and a pure expression of religious identity, but instead found something much different.[6] Local Syrians did not respect them and, in many cases, viewed them as "adventure seekers," naïve about the harsh realities of

what constituted on-the-ground truth in the ruins of Syria's civil war. Some foreign fighters were lured to the caliphate through guilt – IS propaganda targeted to Western Muslims repeatedly admonished them for remaining in their safe and comfortable environs in Europe, North America, and Australia, while their fellow Muslims were wantonly slaughtered by the Assad regime. After arriving in the caliphate, these individuals struggled with food, financing, and the tribulations of war. Upon returning to the West, they could mentor other radicalized youth. These fighters may require psychological treatment in addition to prison time.

The second subgroup could be labeled the "disengaged, but not disillusioned." Just as there are many reasons why militants go to fight, there are many reasons why they leave a conflict – marriage, battle fatigue, desire to be with family.[7] So they may have left, voluntarily, but remain committed to jihadism and the core tenets of Salafi-jihadism. Accordingly, individuals might grow disillusioned with IS as an organization, but not with jihad as a whole. These are among the most dangerous returnees who may be living back in their countries of origin. They might be on the authorities' watch-list, but as we have seen time and again, terrorist attacks are committed with regularity by so-called "known wolves," or individuals already on the radar of law enforcement and security services for their connections to extremist circles and ideology.

The third subgroup could be called the "operational" returnees. These are returning fighters who attempt to resuscitate dormant networks or create new ones, recruit members, or conduct home-grown-style attacks. They are likely to be pre-positioned and likely to attempt an attack under the command and control of IS remnants in the Middle East.[8] These individuals are the most dangerous and deadly.[9] The November 2015 Paris attacks are perhaps the clearest

example; they were conducted by foreign fighters, who were trained in Syria and dispatched to France.[10] Operational returnees are of even more concern if one believes that hundreds of operatives have already been deployed to Europe, with hundreds more hiding out on Europe's doorstep in Turkey.[11] Turkey in particular remains an attractive staging ground for returning foreign fighters, given its proximity to the battlefield and the presence of pre-existing support networks.[12]

The fourth and final subgroup are those individuals captured on the battlefield and returned to their countries of origin against their will. This is a group that will require close assessment to determine which, if any, crimes have been committed, and whether or not there is ample evidence to move forward with a prosecution. Accordingly, many states have been unable to secure criminal convictions for returning foreign terrorist fighters, and even those who have been jailed ultimately received shorter prison sentences than many prosecutors would have hoped for.[13] As outlined in a report by the Radicalisation Awareness Network (RAN), there are three primary scenarios in these cases: prosecution; non-prosecution/resocialization (what I refer to as rehabilitation and reintegration); and dealing with children.[14] Each of these scenarios will be explored in more detail below.

Prosecution

Prosecuting foreign fighters who have returned is difficult on a number of levels. There are challenges regarding gathering admissible evidence that can be used in court, and even when prosecutions are secured, the length of prison sentences can be short. Further, there are warranted concerns about foreign fighters potentially radicalizing other prisoners, although special accommodations are now made to separate hardcore jihadists from the general inmate population in

most prisons. But an unknowable question is: when these individuals serve their sentences and are released back into society, what kind of threat might they present?

In late May 2018, on the very same day he was released from jail, a Belgian jihadist went on a killing spree in the city of Liège.[15] It is almost certain that we are likely to see similar incidents playing out in the future. The resources required to track, monitor, and surveil individuals suspected of radicalization are immense and the mission itself seems somewhat unrealistic. European authorities lament that their already finite resources have been stretched thin by the sheer volume of potential suspects who need to be identified and tracked. The US-led coalition has scrutinized captured computers, documents, and cellphones to put together a global profile of IS members and sympathizers, a list with approximately 19,000 names on it that has been shared with Interpol.[16] The challenge is immense and the security forces will need more manpower simply to monitor and surveil these suspects, to say nothing of conducting investigations and pursuing prosecutions.

There are also widely different scenarios for a returning foreign fighter, their spouses or partners, and any children involved, some of whom may have no paperwork after being born in the caliphate. In turn, there are also myriad categories of prosecution, including prosecuting terrorist crimes within the territory of the so-called caliphate in Iraq and Syria, and raising the issue of how *foreign* national courts can prosecute terrorist crimes that have been committed in Syria and Iraq. There are also attempts to prosecute fighters taking place in Syria, through a combination of the Assad regime's judicial system and ad-hoc courts administered by non-state actors like the Kurds and other militia groups.

There are approximately 3,000 suspected members of IS awaiting trial in Iraq.[17] It is estimated that more than 100 of them are

Europeans.[18] Prosecuting terrorist crimes within the territory of the so-called caliphate in Syria and Iraq is a contentious issue. Under customary international law, Iraq has the legal obligation to prosecute war crimes that have been conducted on its territory, or to extradite those who have committed them. The situation in Syria is far more complex. As international law expert Tanya Mehra has described in detail, in Syria, "the judicial system has become a patchwork of 'ordinary' and 'special' courts that have jurisdiction."[19] Depending on their location within the territory of Syria, courts are run either by the Assad regime – which, after years of slaughtering its own people and using chemical weapons against civilians, lacks political legitimacy amongst most Syrians – or by armed groups scattered throughout the country, including the Syrian Democratic Forces, or SDF.[20] The SDF currently holds hundreds of IS prisoners. Moreover, as the SDF and other Kurdish groups are still actively engaged in fighting, including against Turkish forces on Syria's northern border, there are fears that the fighting will distract from their responsibility to guard IS fighters being held prisoner, increasing the chances for prisoner escapes.[21]

There is also the issue of how courts in states in the West can prosecute terrorist crimes that have been committed by its citizens while they were living under the caliphate. There have already been convictions of this kind in Canada, the United Kingdom, Belgium, Norway, and the Netherlands, with fighters prosecuted for crimes including attempted travel to Syria, recruitment, planning of an attack, and "terroristic murder."[22] Further, it is entirely conceivable that, in some instances, crimes committed in Syria and Iraq by European nationals could qualify as war crimes or crimes against humanity.

Dealing with the issue of prosecuting cases of terrorism is fraught with challenges. Many states lack well-developed jurisdictional infrastructures, and the capacity of their judiciaries, national courts, and

other institutions could be severely under-resourced. These courts struggle to prosecute the cases they have and can be overwhelmed easily by having to handle just a small cluster of additional cases. Complex cases can be lengthy and time-consuming, while also depleting finite resources necessary for other criminal justice issues. There are also a number of unique circumstances facing courts in Western countries in prosecuting those citizens who have made it back home, as well as from the massive influx of Iraqi and Syrian migrants into Europe, some of whom might be victims, witnesses, or perpetrators of various crimes, to include terrorism.

So far, at least, it appears that many Western countries do not want to deal with their citizens who have been apprehended on the battlefield and are now being held in the Middle East.[23] But if these individuals are left to be prosecuted in Syria or Iraq, there are legitimate concerns that their prosecutions will certainly not meet fair-trial standards and could be politicized. A dearth of adequate funding for specialized war units or chambers needed to deal with these types of crimes means that these trials could be hasty, resulting in false convictions or what some perceive to be overly draconian sentences in proportion to the specific crime committed.[24]

The issue of whether or not to accept citizens who want to return home after leaving their countries of origin to help establish the caliphate crisscrosses legal, moral, and ethical seams. The governments of European countries are opposed to the death penalty, so leaving citizens of their country in Iraq and Syria is a dilemma, given concerns about the likelihood of receiving a fair trial. The case of a French woman named Emilie Konig is an archetypical example. After leaving France to live under the caliphate, Konig was captured during the war against IS and is now being held in the Kurdish region of Syria. The Kurds administer justice in this region, but, under international

law, the territory is still part of Syria.[25] Understandably, many French citizens are wary of having individuals like Konig return to the country. The issue of how to deal with potential returnees has become a political lightning rod in many Western countries. In the meantime, many wives and children of IS fighters remain in limbo, as thousands languish in detainee camps throughout northern Syria while decisions on their fates are postponed.[26]

The United Kingdom is one of many European nations facing a tremendous strain on its resources, as more than 80 prisoners convicted of terror offenses between 2007 and 2016 were due to be released in 2018.[27] Its nationwide program to prevent radicalization and violent extremism, known as PREVENT, has been widely criticized for being ineffective and lacking a proper assessment and evaluation methodology. One case plaguing the UK is that of two members of the so-called "Beatles," British-born IS members known for their barbarism, which included the torture and murder of several Western captives.[28] There are serious jurisdictional issues in this case and much hand-wringing over who should prosecute these militants. The UK insists it does not want them back on British soil, while the United States is pressing London to bring the men to trial. If Britain doesn't prosecute them, they could ultimately end up at the notorious US prison at Guantánamo Bay, Cuba.[29] American policy is ambiguous, partly by design, but partly due to incoherence. The resulting inertia might afford policymakers and military officials with more time to figure out what to do with the captured terrorists.[30] Still, the dearth of strategy and seeming lack of urgency has attracted pointed criticism from a number of human rights groups.

Above all else, the most serious challenge to prosecuting foreign terrorist fighters remains the issue of evidence. To be useful, the evidence gathered to prosecute cases of terrorism must be able to pass

muster in a legitimate court of law and it remains extremely dangerous to travel to a war-ravaged country to investigate and collect evidence. Some non-governmental organizations are on the ground in Iraq and Syria and have slightly changed the landscape by their presence alone.[31] Internet-based evidence is also a new element to consider, although with the phenomenon of spoofing, "deep fakes," and other forms of digital manipulation, many courts will understandably be wary of evidence generated via social or other online media.

Cross-border legal cooperation is a major hurdle as well, and not all courts are in agreement about the utility of, or ethical considerations surrounding, secret, restricted, or classified information and its use in court.[32] The other methods of documenting terrorism-related crimes are International Commissions of Inquiry and various resolutions passed by the United Nations Security Council (UNSC), including UNSCR 2379, which established an Investigative Team to support domestic efforts to collect, preserve, and store evidence, in Iraq, of acts committed by IS that may amount to war crimes, crimes against humanity, and genocide. There has also been a case in the United States – and there remains the possibility for similar cases in other Western countries – in which evidence taken from the battlefield was used successfully in court to prosecute individuals for crimes related to the support of terrorism.[33]

Rehabilitation/Reintegration

There are other options besides incarcerating returnees and, indeed, in many cases, this is the desirable approach, especially where the individual has not committed violent acts and demonstrates no propensity to do so in the future, although assessing this possibility is a precarious undertaking. Now that Western governments have made it clear

that terrorism prevention, deradicalization, and countering violent extremism, especially among the youth, are among their top priorities, something of a cottage industry has emerged, with a long line of NGOs and other entities proclaiming to have the "silver bullet" to solve radicalization. The hard truth is that most programs do not work and even those that have shown promise often have difficulty demonstrating a correlation between the design of the program and its range of outcomes, to say nothing of establishing something like a causal link.

The United States Institute for Peace (USIP) has identified several promising themes across first-generation deradicalization programs implemented in the Middle East and South Asia. First, the intervention would address the affective – that is, a focus on social factors including emotional support, a sense of community, and social obligation. Second, it would target the pragmatic, or logistical factors, such as financial stability, education, vocational training, and other skill acquisition. And third, it would focus on the ideological bonds underpinning the thought processes and value system of the individual. [34]

There are widely different approaches both across and within regions. In Saudi Arabia, there has been an interesting evolution over time. At first, Saudi rehabilitation and reintegration programs focused almost exclusively on the ideological and psychological component, sending individuals to deradicalization sessions with imams and counselors, while also providing financial incentives to disengage from militancy. The recidivism rates from these programs were quite high and, to their credit, the Saudis shifted their approach. Reintegration programs now focus more on the returnees' families and do more to assist with rebuilding relationships between the individual and their family, society, and country.[35] By and large, however, one of the biggest differences between deradicalization programs in Europe and those in Muslim-majority countries is that the latter are almost always

government-run and mandatory, which in turn calls into question their legitimacy and effectiveness, especially if the intent is to measure individuals' willingness to voluntarily turn away from jihad.[36]

France is a country with nearly 20,000 people considered to be at risk of radicalization by government authorities. In prison, the risk of radicalization is acute, because imprisoned jihadists may proselytize and recruit, an issue France has dedicated much time and attention to, but still struggles with. In prisons, case managers will meet with Islamists to discuss the contradictions in their ideologies, offering individual psychological treatment and meetings with case workers and chaplains.[37] But a parliamentary commission in France published a report noting that deradicalization programs in that country, especially those that existed outside of the penal system, "were hastily conceived and in some cases marred by severe deficiencies."[38] In Vilvoorde, Belgium, authorities responded to large numbers of youth leaving for Syria by implementing an intensive early-intervention program which built upon government engagement with communities and families to identify youth who may be at risk of radicalization.[39] The program in Denmark has come under fire for being too liberal and forgiving in its treatment of returnees. The program in Aarhaus is often lambasted by its critics as an example of appeasement and a fear of confronting the problem of militant Islam in a secular, European society. At the national level, Denmark seeks to arrest and prosecute returning foreign fighters with a proven involvement in terrorism, but others are assisted in gaining access to employment, housing, education, and psychological counseling.[40]

Programs designed to counter violent extremism and reintegrate "at-risk individuals" have been roundly lambasted as ineffective, and in some cases worse – counterproductive. There are numerous examples of failed programs, with shortcomings ranging from an

inability to measure outcomes to actual spikes in violence following some interventions, as witnessed in Kandahar, Afghanistan, following a program featuring cash transfers as a development assistance tool.[41] Some practitioners lament that efforts to counter extremism should be organic and powered by grassroots initiatives.[42] Others insist that current efforts are futile because it will probably be years before we know which programs work best and why. Measurement, evaluation, and assessment in this area are notoriously difficult for social scientists, and the scores of self-proclaimed "deradicalization experts" who have cropped up with countering violent extremism (CVE) programs for sale amount to little more than modern-day snake-oil salesmen. This is not to dismiss some of the extremely important and necessary work being done, but rather to issue a rebuke to junk science and a suggestion to governments that progress in this area will be slow and probably characterized by setbacks and false positives.

Even after years of commissioned studies, carefully planned interventions, and generously sponsored government initiatives, there is still no "tried and true" method for deradicalization, reintegration, or countering violent extremism. It remains difficult to know what works and whether or not these programs are effective. There is a lack of reliable data on outcomes from rehabilitation programs and no uniform approach, which makes it impossible to conduct rigorous comparative analyses. Still, despite the problems plaguing these efforts, it is imperative that the international community keep trying to make progress. Moreover, there is a growing corpus of lessons learned that could inform the debate. One of the major findings from a global multi-year series of workshops on foreign terrorist fighters (FTFs) found that the international community would be well served by focusing on capacity-building efforts geared toward comprehensive community engagement and preventative measures.[43] This requires

a whole-of-government approach and robust engagement with civil society, as well as public–private partnerships that might be focused on employment, education, or job training.

Generation Jihad: Born into the Caliphate

Among the many traumas of the Syrian civil war and spreading sectarian violence that characterizes large segments of the Middle East, the issue of children in the caliphate is perhaps the most egregious. What these children saw, and indeed what some of them were coerced to do, is impossible for most human beings to conceptualize. Some children witnessed killings, beheadings, and brutal atrocities, while others actually participated in these heinous acts. Many were brainwashed, indoctrinated with the virulent screed of sectarian hatred. As a result, most of these youngsters will never be the same – what will they grow up to be like as teenagers and adults? What impact could they have on neighbors and classmates at school? Court documents from proceedings in the UK have showed that children as young as 2 years old who have been exposed to IS indoctrination have demonstrated a fascination with guns and beheadings.[44]

IS pursued a deliberate and calculated strategy of targeting children and young teens, especially males, in order to "create new power structures in society," spread its ideology to young recruits, and sow the seeds for the next generation of future jihadists. The physical territory of the caliphate is gone, but its core messages, ideas, and narrative have already been implanted in countless numbers of young Muslims.[45] The Islamic State ran schools for children, where textbooks indoctrinated the pupils by focusing on a select few themes considered most important by IS leadership: encouraging violence, driving an apocalyptic narrative, establishing a purist "Islamic" state, and labeling it a caliphate.[46] The

last part is especially crucial for the future of the Islamic State, as young children were brainwashed with the notion that what IS had achieved – and indeed what these children, their families, and neighbors helped to build and were an integral part of – was an achievement of historic proportions, a caliphate "based on prophetic methodology" that was the first and only *true* Salafi-jihadi state, an embodiment of political and religious authority for Muslims everywhere.

Future IS propaganda will seek to harness the legacy of its European fighters killed in battle, thus directly impacting the younger generation of children in marginalized neighborhoods, towns, and cities throughout Europe, from Malmo to Marseille. There are thousands of youngsters scattered across the continent who lost older siblings whom they probably looked up to. These deceased young men are now eligible to be lionized as IS martyrs in the heavily immigrant enclaves where they grew up, much in the same way that fallen Hamas militants are worshipped in Gaza, Tamil fighters were celebrated in Jaffna, or Irish Republican Army "volunteers" were revered in West Belfast. IS will deploy nostalgia in similar ways to how they have used it in the past and present – as a multidimensional propaganda tool. The "nostalgia narrative" will not only be deployed at a transnational level, through its central media units, and at the provincial level, through its provincial media units, but also at highly localized and even individual levels through on-the-ground networks.[47]

Yet the issue of dealing with the children of the caliphate is not as simple as some would like to pretend. These young people are *both* victims and perpetrators, a fact which cannot and should not be ignored. There is a growing body of evidence of atrocities committed by children associated with IS. In one instance, a 13-year-old British citizen executed a Kurdish prisoner. In another, a 7-year-old boy appears in a video holding a severed head. And the horrors are not merely relegated

to the battlefield in Iraq and Syria. Europe has witnessed numerous cases where teens and pre-teens have been implicated in terrorist plots – a 13-year-old in the suburbs of Paris; a 12-year-old German Iraqi in Ludwigshafen, western Germany; and the United Kingdom has identified over 2,000 adolescents under 15 years old as "possible extremists."[48]

It is important not to look at the problem of "non-adults" as one singular cohort. Some children were more directly associated with violence than others, while certain groups of children were specifically groomed and recruited to form the future backbone of this group. A study by the International Centre for Counter-Terrorism – The Hague (ICCT) recommends dividing children into two distinct groups. Young children (aged 0 to 9) who were born in the caliphate or brought to IS-controlled territory at an extremely young age should be viewed and treated primarily as victims. All told, approximately 730 children were born in the caliphate to parents from elsewhere.[49] But older children should be scrutinized more closely. For the latter group, it will be critical to assess what level of indoctrination was involved, whether or not these children received training (and, if so, what kind and at what level), and, perhaps most importantly, their potential involvement in violent activities.[50]

Endgame for IS or New Beginnings?

Even though the main objective of the Coalition to Defeat IS was targeting and effectively defeating it, the degradation of a terrorist organization can lead to organizational fractures or splintering.[51] While causing IS to break apart might seem like a positive outcome, it is a double-edged sword in the truest sense, clichés aside. The fracturing

of the Islamic State could lead to the emergence of new, and in some cases more violent and operationally capable, splinter organizations.[52] In Sub-Saharan Africa, Salafi-jihadism is spreading and countries with no prior experience of this threat have now been suffering from a spate of attacks. In the DRC and Mozambique, new groups have emerged, some using the Shabaab brand name even though there are no formal links with the Somali terrorist group.[53] So the threat is not just from off-shoots of the two primary Salafi-jihadist groups – IS and al-Qaeda – but also from *their* offshoots, compounding the challenge and presenting a nightmare scenario in which franchises eventually have enough clout to spawn derivative terrorist organizations in diverse locales, including in countries with little to no prior history of jihadism.

Dismantling IS is a necessary strategic objective, but policymakers, government officials, and military leaders must also be prepared to deal with splinter groups as they emerge in the aftermath of what seems to be a relatively successful campaign against the parent group. With IS, these splinters could form their own, new organization, or be absorbed into existing franchise groups or affiliates from North Africa to Southeast Asia.

As discussed earlier in this book, the Islamic State – a splinter of al-Qaeda in Iraq or AQI, which itself was previously a splinter of al-Qaeda – is one of many terrorist groups that resulted from the successful fracturing of a pre-existing group.[54] It seems rather ominous that some of the most lethal and durable terrorist groups can trace their origins back to a splinter movement. The Liberation Tigers of Tamil Eelam (LTTE) coalesced between the late 1970s and early 1980s from a cacophony of Tamil rebel groups. Hezbollah, too, grew into the formidable politico-military force it remains today after its modest beginnings as a cast-off of the Afwaj al-Muqawama al-Lubnaniya (AMAL), formed in the early 1980s with help from Iran, supposedly in response to Israel's invasion

of southern Lebanon. Other prominent splinter groups have flourished at various points in Algeria, Thailand, and Northern Ireland.

Splinter groups are often only slight variations of the original groups, with minor differences in ideology, but more significant discrepancies over strategy, tactics, and the utility of violence, some of the main points of contention discussed in the section on the IS-al-Qaeda dispute. That some of these groups were more savage than their predecessors is an unfortunate outcome of effective counterterrorism campaigns, which inevitably produce second- and third-order effects. Again, the Islamic State is instructive in this regard, as its emergence, consolidation of power, and declaration of a caliphate in the heart of the Middle East posed a far greater threat than al-Qaeda in Iraq ever did. IS generated significant income flows from a variety of sources, controlled swaths of territory on at least two continents, and could deploy operatives into Europe to conduct spectacular attacks in the West. It is certainly possible that if Islamic State is degraded to the point it is no longer such a threat, which is a process currently unfolding, whatever supplants IS could go through a similar transformation and ultimately metastasize into a more potent challenge than its predecessors.

The blueprint for start-up success as a terrorist organization – evidenced in Iraq and North Africa – is now widely known. After gaining a foothold in a failed state or ungoverned region, the group seeks to latch on to a marginalized ethnic or religious group, exploit local grievances, and lend guidance, resources, expertise, and manpower to the fight.[55] It is not difficult to imagine the Islamic State replicating this formula in any number of places, from Libya to Afghanistan and West Africa. These countries and regions are awash in weapons, and plagued by poor security forces and a weak rule of law, making them the ideal candidates for splinter groups seeking to regenerate and exploit new bases of operations, if they choose to relocate abroad.

The challenge for the international community will be preventing these regenerated slivers from emerging stronger than before. An apt analogy is that the remnants of a largely extinguished fire must be stamped out before the embers can accelerate into a massive conflagration that is difficult to contain. Destroying a terrorist organization – and potentially creating splinter groups in the process – is less important than denying the group the ability to control territory, raise money, and recruit legions of new followers. But this requires a sustained campaign, the consistent allocation of resources, and the political will to continue focusing on the issue long after it has dropped from the news cycle and daily media buzz, replaced by other pressing matters. It has been this last part that has proved capricious in the past. Moreover, despite a laudable effort by the international community to come together in the face of the unprecedented wave of foreign fighters who traveled to conflict zones over the past five years, there is still no universally accepted and agreed-upon strategy either for preventing a similar outflow of aspiring jihadists in the future or for how societies should handle the inevitable return of those who fight, survive, and then seek to come back to their countries of origin – some war-weary, disillusioned, and traumatized; others disengaged, but not deradicalized.

When considering the Islamic State, there are several potential outcomes if the ongoing Coalition counterterrorism campaign proves successful in smashing its core and causing it to splinter. One veritable certainty, however, is that the inclusion of the Islamic State into any future political framework in either Iraq or Syria is a non-sequitur.[56] The Islamic State has not shared any political platform anywhere close to being mildly acceptable to even the most dysfunctional or rogue nation-state. Were a political settlement in either Syria or Iraq to gain traction more broadly, it is possible that elements of the Islamic State

could continue to prosper as a violent criminal organization, relying on extortion, smuggling, and robbery to survive. But a Hezbollah-like political entity is not even a remote possibility, nor does IS seem inclined to favor such a route.

As discussed in chapter 4, al-Qaeda in Syria could prove to be the final death knell of IS in that country, either by defeating its forces militarily or by absorbing the bulk of its remaining fighters into al-Qaeda's ranks. Between HTS and Tanzim Hurras al-Din, there is no shortage of militant Islamist groups which could be possible suitors for militants fleeing IS. Still, if the Islamic State feared it was facing extinction in Syria, its leadership might well decide to relocate the caliphate to Libya, or elsewhere where an existing offshoot might be bolstered.[57] It is possible that, following the atomization of the Islamic State, its remnants could be stamped out by security forces in areas where it currently operates. However, the two primary factors that led to the resuscitation of al-Qaeda in Iraq (AQI) into Islamic State – the Syrian civil war and Baghdad's marginalization of Iraqi Sunnis – show no signs of abating anytime soon, though prospects for the latter are more promising in the near term.

If none of the above futures play out, the United States will need to work with partner nations across the region to disrupt the blueprint that deftly enables splinter groups to reconstitute into more effective fighting forces. This can be accomplished in part by reducing the space for militants to operate and gain traction, including helping governments to address local grievances, promote good governance, and strengthen the rule of law. This will require a true "whole of government approach," including security cooperation in areas such as intelligence, surveillance and reconnaissance, and diplomacy; increased intelligence sharing; and continued punitive measures when necessary. The United States can help provide surveillance of

poorly governed areas to help reduce threats within these territories, while also building the partner capacity of host-nation security forces to help stem migration (and other martial resource) flows to active areas of hostilities.

To the extent possible, the United States should continue working to mitigate the primary factors that led an al-Qaeda splinter to grow into the Islamic State in the first place – namely, pushing hard to end the Syrian civil war and exerting whatever leverage possible to cajole Baghdad into abandoning its overly sectarian stance against Iraqi Sunnis. To some degree, there has been progress on this front under the Abadi government. Without ameliorating what are essentially political issues, even successful counterterrorism tactics will allow room for splinter groups to emerge and grow stronger. There are several other important issues related to splinter groups that counterterrorism forces also need to take into account, including these groups' ability to finance their nascent organizations through a diverse range of activities, disseminate effective propaganda, and exploit new technologies.

Technology, especially technology that enables terrorist groups' ability to talk with one another and communicate their message to a broader audience, is a greater force multiplier in 2019 than it has been at any previous point in history. IS's leveraging of social media provided a tremendous boost to its ability to recruit and organize. It has also vastly improved terrorists' ability to plan and execute virtual plots. As Gartenstein-Ross observed, "Over the past few years, Syria-based IS operatives have found recruits online, spurred them to action, and played an intimate role in the conceptualization, target selection, timing, and execution of attacks. They have also used encrypted communication platforms to assist in bomb-making techniques and provide other forms of technical assistance."[58]

The West must develop a range of strategies to handle the threat posed by these different groups. The "hardcore fighters" who remain in Iraq and Syria will need to be killed or captured by Iraqi security forces and the anti-IS Coalition. The first priority should be detection, which goes hand in hand with increased information sharing and training partner nations to screen and investigate potential terrorists. This suggests an even greater role for multilateral cooperation. Another major hurdle will be marshaling the resources required to monitor, track, and surveil battle-hardened jihadists attempting to blend back into Western society. Efforts by the West to build the partner capacity of host-nation forces in weak and fragile states will not obviate the threat, but will be part of a more comprehensive solution geared toward combating the challenge posed by the "free agents," or roving bands of militants.

The trillion-dollar question is: how do you prevent a similar phenomenon of tens of thousands of people leaving their homes to travel to a war zone to support a violent, non-state armed group? Part of the answer is persuasion, and another part is prevention. Regarding the former, the challenge for Western countries is how to escape what Rik Coolsaet has called the "no-future subculture" that exists in many countries in Europe and elsewhere.[59] This viewpoint holds that French, Belgian, Dutch, and British citizens whose parents or grandparents emigrated from Algeria, Morocco, Somalia, or Pakistan feel no connection to the European societies in which they were raised, even while they have no clear links to their ancestral homelands. This creates an identity crisis which leaves them vulnerable to the allure of extremist interpretations of Islam, while others might see joining IS as a way to define their identities, seek adventure, or openly defy a society and culture they feel separated from to the point of actively wanting to oppose it.

To be fair, in many circles the conversation has grown to include not merely responses to terrorism, but efforts at prevention in the first place. One way states have approached this is to prevent individuals from traveling abroad to conflict zones in the first place through the use of administrative measures, including travel bans and control orders. These have proven to be quite effective in preventing the departure of individuals, although it is critical to establish safeguards and limits around their use.[60] This measure can also lead to unintended consequences, as witnessed with so-called "frustrated foreign fighters." After being denied the ability to travel abroad to wage jihad, they instead seek to conduct attacks in their countries of origin. There are numerous examples of attackers who fit into this category, with cases in the United States, Australia, Canada, Denmark, Spain, and France, to name a few.[61]

The physical entity that was the Islamic State's caliphate is over. Mosul and Raqqa have been retaken and, even though its leader Abu Bakr al-Baghdadi has not yet been killed or captured – at least, at the time of this writing in late 2018 – the core of the Islamic State is decimated. But its message still finds resonance among sub-populations of extremists throughout the world and will continue to do so well into the foreseeable future.

But to defeat IS in the long term, it will take more than measures in the physical world. To counter the threat IS will continue to pose in the future, it is crucial to understand what IS is and what IS is not, where it is truly dangerous and where its power and reach have limits. And, above all else, the Islamic State is an ideology. It represents the embodiment of Salafi-jihadism and all of its undercurrents – anti-American, anti-Jewish, and, of course, anti-Shia. This ideology motivates individuals and groups around the world to conduct attacks in its name, inspiring an amorphous and disconnected cadre of lone

wolves and small groups of jihadists driven to act by its propaganda and overarching messages.

But for all of our acknowledgment of the threat posed by the Islamic State, there are many things it is not. For example, IS is not a monolithic actor, even though many in the West have lumped disparate and diverse threats under the Islamic State banner. This tendency is a legacy of the Cold War, when Washington became comfortable with defining grand strategy in terms of *us versus them.* "Them" now includes a range of state and non-state threats and not all terrorists are the same. Moreover, all Salafi-jihadi terrorist groups are not the same. Defining the Islamic State threat as unitary helps provide a much-needed structure and logic to Western counterterrorism strategy, but it also causes conceptual confusion. In some ways, attempting to make sense of IS is a fool's errand. This is not a centrally managed organization, but rather an opportunistic, disaggregated movement.

The Islamic State is also not an existential threat on the order of the challenge the United States faced throughout the course of the Cold War. IS is not a nuclear-armed nation-state, nor is it a near-peer adversary trained and equipped for conventional military operations. Countering IS demands a sober assessment of the group's organizational and operational capabilities, but, more poignantly, it requires an honest recognition of the international community's ability to affect the future trajectory of this movement. No counterterrorism strategy, no matter how comprehensive or robust, can address the grievances that led to the resuscitation of IS or pacify the virulent ideology that sustains the group.

Eliminating the physical embodiment of IS – the caliphate – is a necessary, but not sufficient, component of winning the long war against the group and in addressing the region's more fundamental challenges. And whatever iteration of violent extremism replaces IS,

the West should be careful to realize that IS is more a symptom of the disease than the underlying cause. The most pragmatic approach to keeping this ideology confined to the margins is working to address the conditions that fueled IS's rise – sectarianism in Iraq and the Syrian civil war – while remaining honest about the threat posed by this ideology and the West's ability to counter this threat wherever it manifests itself over the course of the next generation.[62]

The establishment of the caliphate will be trumpeted by IS as an achievement of meteoric proportions. Indeed, even those opposed to the group and its ideology have to admit that for a violent non-state terrorist organization to establish a proto-state in this day and age is a rare event and a rather brazen, if not ambitious, feat. But it was also an aberration.

The fight against radicalization, extremism, and global jihad is not existential. Now that the caliphate has been crushed, the global jihadist movement will return to its peripatetic past, one characterized largely by infighting amongst militant groups and travel to new battlefields. The pendulum is now swinging away from a globally coordinated effort by centralized terrorist organizations and back to a focus on local and regional conflicts. But even in fragmented and atomized form, these groups present a threat, especially if the Islamic State's ideology persists and successfully convinces a new generation of Muslims that a caliphate is an attainable and desirable objective, and that the means to this end will include the relentless pursuit of never-ending global jihad.

Notes

Introduction

1 Rukmini Callimachi, "To Maintain Supply of Sex Slaves, ISIS Pushes Birth Control," *New York Times*, March 12, 2016.
2 Email exchange with Martha Crenshaw, June 2018.
3 Email exchange with journalist and author of *The Way of the Strangers: Encounters with The Islamic State*, Graeme Wood, June 2018.
4 Although most analysis focuses on the macro-, or group level, it is important not to discard the micro-level view of focusing on lone actors. For more, see Boaz Ganor, Bruce Hoffman, Marlene Mazel, and Matthew Levitt, "Lone Wolf: Passing Fad or Terror Threat of the Future?" in Matthew Levitt, ed., *Neither Remaining Nor Expanding: The Decline of the Islamic State,* Counterterrorism Lectures 2016–2017 (Washington Institute for Near East Policy, 2018), pp. 69–73.
5 https://www.newyorker.com/news/news-desk/isis-jihadis-have-returned-home-by-the-thousands.
6 https://www.usip.org/sites/default/files/The-Jihadi-Threat-ISIS-Al-Qaeda-and-Beyond.pdf, p. 7.

1 The Long Road to the Caliphate

1 See Mustaf Hamid and Leah Farrall, *The Arabs at War in Afghanistan*, London: Hurst & Company, 2015; see also Rodric Braithwaite, *Afgansty: The Russians in Afghanistan 1979–89,* New York: Oxford University Press, 2011.

2 Al Qaeda, Al-Qaeda, Al-Qa'ida, and several other variants are often used interchangeably in the literature. "Al-Qaeda" has been translated variously as the "base of operation," "foundation," "precept," or "method": Bruce Hoffman, "The Changing Face of Al Qaeda and the Global War on Terrorism," *Studies in Conflict & Terrorism*, 27:6, 2004, p. 551.

3 R. Kim Cragin, "Early History of Al-Qa'ida," *Historic Journal*, 51:4, December 2008, pp. 1051–2.

4 Ibid., p. 1056.

5 Brian Michael Jenkins, "Al Qaeda after Bin Laden: Implications for American Strategy," testimony before the Committee on Armed Services Subcommittee on Emerging Threats and Capabilities, United States House of Representatives, June 22, 2011.

6 Assaf Moghadam, "The Salafi-Jihad as Religious Ideology," *CTC Sentinel*, February 15, 2008.

7 Daniel Byman, "Explaining Al Qaeda's Decline," *Journal of Politics*, 79:3, 2017, p. 1107.

8 Brian A. Jackson, "Groups, Networks, or Movements: A Command-and-Control-Driven Approach to Classifying Terrorist Organizations and Its Application to Al Qaeda," *Studies in Conflict & Terrorism*, 29:3, 2006, p. 241.

9 Bruce Hoffman, *Inside Terrorism*, New York: Columbia University Press, 2006, pp. 285–8.

10 Byman, "Al Qaeda's Decline," p. 1107.

11 Seth G. Jones, *A Persistent Threat: The Evolution of al Qa'ida and Other Salafi Jihadists*, Santa Monica, CA: RAND Corp., 2014, p. 10.

12 Ibid., p. 11.

13 Daniel Byman, "Buddies of Burdens? Understanding the Al Qaeda Relationship with Its Affiliate Organizations," *Security Studies*, 23:3, 2014, p. 436.

14 Jones, *A Persistent Threat*, p. 2; see also Katherine Zimmerman, "America's Real Enemy: The Salafi-Jihadi Movement," American Enterprise Institute (AEI), July 2017, p. 4.

15 Douglas E. Streusand, "What Does Jihad Mean?" *Middle East Quarterly*, 4:3, June 1997.

16 Peter Bergen, *The Longest War: The Enduring Conflict Between America and Al Qaeda*, New York: Free Press, 2011, p. 23.

17 David Malet, "Why Foreign Fighters? Historical Perspectives and Solutions," *Orbis*, Winter 2010, p. 105.

18 Cragin, "Early History of Al-Qa'ida," p. 1051.

19 Anonymous, *Imperial Hubris: Why the West is Losing the War on Terror*, Washington, DC: Brassey's, Inc., 2004, p. 129.

20 Bruce Hoffman, "Al Qaeda Trends in Terrorism and Future Potentialities: An Assessment," paper presented at a meeting of the Council on Foreign Relations, Washington, DC Office, May 8, 2003, p. 5.

21 David Aaron, *In Their Own Words: Voices of Jihad*, Santa Monica, CA: RAND Corp., 2008, p. 73.

22 Cragin, "Early History of Al-Qa'ida," p. 1066.

23 Anne Stenersen, *Al Qaeda in Afghanistan*, Cambridge University Press, 2017, pp. 165–75.

24 Jarret Brachman, "The Worst of the Worst," *Foreign Policy*, January 22, 2010.

25 Assaf Moghadam, "How Al Qaeda Innovates," *Security Studies*, 22:3, 2013, p. 477.

26 Bruce Hoffman, "Al Qaeda's Uncertain Future," *Studies in Conflict & Terrorism*, 36:8, 2013, pp. 640–1.

27 Nicholas J. Rasmussen, "Fifteen Years after 9/11: Threats to the Homeland," Statement for the Record: Hearing Before the Senate Homeland Security Governmental Affairs Committee, September 27, 2016.

28 Brian Michael Jenkins, *The Origins of America's Jihadists*, Santa Monica, CA: RAND Corp., 2017, p. 22. A complement to Jenkins's study is Alexander Meleagrou-Hitchens, Seamus Hughes, and Bennett Clifford, *The Travelers: American Jihadists in Syria and Iraq*, Program on Extremism, George Washington University, February 2018. This report focuses on American citizens who either traveled abroad or attempted to travel abroad to join jihadist groups in the Middle East. One of the primary findings is that travelers tend to be male, with an average age of 27, and

are "generally affiliated with IS upon arrival in Syria or Iraq." Minnesota, Virginia, and Ohio are the states with the highest proportional rates of recruitment.

29 Martin Rudner, "Al Qaeda's Twenty-Year Strategic Plan: The Current Phase of Global Terror," *Studies in Conflict & Terrorism*, 36:12, 2013, p. 959. See also Bruce Hoffman, "A First Draft of the History of America's Ongoing Wars on Terrorism," *Studies in Conflict & Terrorism*, 38:1, 2015, p. 81.

30 Daniel Byman, "War Drives Terrorism," *Washington Post*, June 21, 2016.

31 Byman, "Al Qaeda's Decline," pp. 1107, 1113.

32 Daniel Byman, "Judging Al Qaeda's Record, Part I: Is the Organization in Decline?" *Lawfare*, June 27, 2017.

33 Daniel Byman, *Al Qaeda, The Islamic State, and the Global Jihadist Movement: What Everyone Needs to Know*, New York: Oxford University Press, 2015, p. 13.

34 "Al Qaeda: Constitutional Charter, Rules and Regulations," Defense Intelligence Agency, AFGT-2002-600175.

35 Rajan Basra, Peter R. Neumann, and Claudia Brunner, "Criminal Pasts, Terrorist Futures: European Jihadists and the New Crime–Terror Nexus," International Centre for the Study of Radicalisation and Political Violence, November 10, 2016; see also Rajan Basra and Peter R. Neumann, "Crime as Jihad: Developments in the Crime–Terror Nexus in Europe," *CTC Sentinel*, 10:9, October 2017; and, Colin P. Clarke, "Crime and Terror in Europe: Where the Nexus is Alive and Well," International Centre for Counter-Terrorism (ICCT) – The Hague, December 13, 2016.

36 Brian Michael Jenkins, "The al Qaeda-Inspired Terrorist Threat: An Appreciation of the Current Situation," testimony before the Canadian Senate Special Committee on Anti-terrorism, December 6, 2010, p. 6.

37 Brian Michael Jenkins, "Stray Dogs and Virtual Armies: Radicalization and Recruitment to Jihadist Terrorism in the United States Since 9/11," Santa Monica, CA: Rand Corp., p. 14; see also Steven Simon and Jonathan Stevenson, "Al Qaeda's New

Strategy: Less Apocalypse, More Street Fighting," *Washington Post*, October 10, 2010.

38 Leah Farrall, "How Al Qaeda Works," *Foreign Affairs*, March/April 2011.

39 Byman, *Al Qaeda, The Islamic State, and the Global Jihadist Movement*, pp. 47–54.

40 Moghadam, "How Al Qaeda Innovates," p. 467.

41 Farrall, "How Al Qaeda Works."

42 Colin P. Clarke, "The Moderate Face of Al Qaeda," *Foreign Affairs*, October 24, 2017.

43 Martha Crenshaw, "Transnational Jihadism & Civil Wars," *Daedalus*, 146:4, Fall 2017, p. 68.

44 Tricia Bacon, "Hurdles to International Terrorist Alliances: Lessons from Al Qaeda's Experience," *Terrorism and Political Violence*, 29:1, 2017, pp. 79–101.

45 Barak Mendelsohn, *The Al Qaeda Franchise: The Expansion of al Qaeda and Its Consequences*, New York: Oxford University Press, 2016, p. 92.

46 Brian Michael Jenkins, "Al Qaeda in Its Third Decade: Irreversible Decline or Imminent Victory?" Santa Monica, CA: RAND Corp., 2012; see also Rick Nelson and Thomas M. Sanderson, "A Threat Transformed: Al Qaeda and Associated Movements in 2011," Center for Strategic and International Studies (CSIS), February 2011: https://csis-prod.s3.amazonaws.com/s3fs-public/legacy_files/files/publication/110203_Nelson_AThreatTransformed_web.pdf.

47 Bruce Riedel, *The Search for Al Qaeda*, Washington, DC: Brookings Institution Press, 2008, pp. 121–2.

48 Rohan Gunaratna and Aviv Oreg, "Al Qaeda's Organizational Structure and its Evolution," *Studies in Conflict & Terrorism*, 33:12, 2010, p. 1054.

49 Bruce Hoffman, "The Myth of Grass-Roots Terrorism: Why Osama bin Laden Still Matters," *Foreign Affairs*, 87:3, May–June 2008, pp. 133–8. See also Jenkins, "Al Qaeda after Bin Laden."

50 Steve Coll, *Ghost Wars: The Secret History of the CIA, Afghanistan,*

and Bin Laden from the Soviet Invasion to September 10, 2001, New York: Penguin, 2004, pp. 269, 380.

51 Lawrence Wright, *The Looming Tower: Al Qaeda and the Road to 9/11*, New York: Vintage, 2006, pp. 60, 264.

52 Hoffman, "The Changing Face," p. 551.

53 Coll, *Ghost Wars*, p. 474.

54 Rohan Gunaratna, *Inside Al Qaeda: Global Network of Terror*, New York: Berkley Books, 2002, p. 105.

55 Hoffman, "Al Qaeda's Uncertain Future," p. 636.

56 Moghadam, "How Al Qaeda Innovates," p. 469.

57 Gunaratna, *Inside Al Qaeda*, p. 73.

58 Coll, *Ghost Wars*, p. 474.

59 Ali Soufan, *The Black Banners: The Inside Story of 9/11 and the War Against al-Qaeda*, New York: W. W. Norton, 2011, pp. 33-7.

60 Bacon, "Hurdles to Alliances," p. 86.

61 Juan Miguel del Cid Gomez, "A Financial Profile of Al Qaeda and Its Affiliates," *Perspectives on Terrorism*, 4:4, 2010, pp. 4-5.

62 Hoffman, "Changing Face," pp. 551-2.

63 Cragin, "Early History of Al-Qa'ida," pp. 1063-4.

64 Gunaratna and Oreg, "Al Qaeda's Organizational Structure," pp. 1054-64.

65 Fawaz Gerges, *ISIS: A History*, Princeton University Press, 2016, p. 71.

66 Chris Hedges, "Foreign Islamic Fighters in Bosnia Pose a Potential Threat for G.I.'s," *New York Times*, December 3, 1995.

67 David Malet, *Foreign Fighters: Transnational Identity in Civil Conflicts*, New York: Oxford University Press, 2013, pp. 185-6.

68 Evan F. Kohlmann, "The Afghan–Bosnian Mujahideen Network in Europe," Swedish National Defence College, November 28, 1995: www.aina.org/reports/tabmnie.pdf.

69 Mark Urban, "Bosnia: The Cradle of Modern Jihadism?" *BBC News*, July 2, 2015.

70 Cerwyn Moore and Paul Tumelty, "Foreign Fighters and the Case of Chechnya," *Studies in Conflict & Terrorism*, 31:5, 2008, pp. 412-33.

71 Murad Batal Al-Shishani, "The Rise and Fall of Arab Fighters in

Chechnya," *Jamestown Foundation*, January 31, 2006: https://jamestown.org/program/the-rise-and-fall-of-foreign-fighters-in-chechnya.

72 Farrall, "How Al Qaeda Works"; see also Derek Henry Flood, "The Islamic State Raises its Black Flag over the Caucasus," *CTC Sentinel*, June 29, 2015.

73 Lorenzo Vidino, *Al Qaeda in Europe: The New Battleground of International Jihad*, Amherst: Prometheus Books, 2006, p. 203. See also Lorenzo Vidino, "The Arab Foreign Fighters and the Sacralization of the Chechen Conflict," *Al Naklah*, Spring 2006, pp. 1–11.

74 Carlotta Gall and Thomas de Waal, *Chechnya: Calamity in the Caucasus*, New York University Press, 1998, p. 208.

75 Ben Rich and Dara Conduit, "The Impact of Jihadist Foreign Fighters on Indigenous Secular-Nationalist Causes: Contrasting Chechnya and Syria," *Studies in Conflict & Terrorism*, 38:2, 2015, pp. 113–31.

76 Ali Soufan, *Anatomy of Terror*, New York: W. W. Norton, 2017, pp. 175–6.

77 Lorenzo Vidino, "How Chechnya Became a Breeding Ground for Terror," *Middle East Quarterly*, Summer 2005, pp. 1–10: http://foreignfighters.csis.org/history_foreign_fighter_project.pdf.

78 Maria Galperin Donnelly, Thomas M. Sanderson, and Zack Fellman, *Foreign Fighters in History*, Center for Strategic and International Studies (CSIS), April 1, 2017.

79 Mendelsohn, *The Al Qaeda Franchise*.

80 Byman, "Buddies of Burdens?" pp. 431–70.

81 Steven Brooke, "Strategic Fissures: The Near and Far Enemy Debate," in Assaf Moghadam and Brian Fishman, eds., *Self-Inflicted Wounds: Debates and Divisions within al-Qa'ida and its Periphery*, December 16, 2010, p. 45: https://ctc.usma.edu/self-inflicted-wounds.

82 Mendelsohn, *The Al Qaeda Franchise*, p. 110.

83 Bruce Riedel and Bilal Y. Saab, "Al Qaeda's Third Front: Saudi Arabia," *Washington Quarterly*, 31:2, Spring 2008, p. 37.

84 Thomas Hegghammer, "Islamist Violence and Regime Stability in Saudi Arabia," *International Affairs*, 84:4, 2008, p. 713.

85 Mendelsohn, *The Al Qaeda Franchise*, p. 115.

86 Brian Fishman, ed., *Bombers, Bank Accounts, & Bleedout: Al-Qai'da's Road In and Out of Iraq*, Combating Terrorism Center (CTC) at West Point, 2008: https://ctc.usma.edu/bombers-bank-accounts-and-bleedout-al-qaidas-road-in-and-out-of-iraq.

87 Brian Fishman and Joseph Felter, *Al-Qa'ida's Foreign Fighters in Iraq: A First Look at the Sinjar Records*, Combating Terrorism Center (CTC) at West Point, January 2, 2007: https://ctc.usma.edu/al-qaidas-foreign-fighters-in-iraq-a-first-look-at-the-sinjar-records.

88 Patrick B. Johnston, Jacob N. Shapiro, Howard J. Shatz, et al., *Foundations of the Islamic State: Management, Money, and Terror in Iraq, 2005–2010*, Santa Monica, CA: RAND Corp., 2016.

89 Brian Fishman, "Dysfunction and Decline: Lessons Learned from Inside Al-Qa'ida in Iraq," *Washington Quarterly*, March 2009. In 2006, AQI joined the Mujahedin Shura Council (MSC), which was a political–military front for several jihadist organizations, but, as Craig Whiteside notes, the council was "so dominated by AQI to the point that it is possible MSC was a sham organization used to convince Iraqis of its indigenous nature": Craig Whiteside, "The Islamic State and the Return of Revolutionary Warfare," *Small Wars & Insurgencies*, 27:5, 2016, pp. 768–9.

90 James J. F. Forest, Jarret Brachman, and Joseph Felter, *Harmony and Disharmony: Exploiting al-Qa'ida's Organizational Vulnerabilities*, Combating Terrorism Center (CTC) at West Point, February 14, 2006: https://ctc.usma.edu/harmony-and-disharmony-exploiting-al-qaidas-organizational-vulnerabilities; see also Byman, "Buddies of Burdens?" pp. 461–5.

91 Mendelsohn, *The Al Qaeda Franchise*, p. 123. After Zarqawi's death, AQI rebranded itself as the Islamic State of Iraq (ISI), without ever discussing the move with Al Qaeda core leadership.

92 Brian Fishman, "After Zarqawi: The Dilemmas and Future of Al Qaeda in Iraq," *Washington Quarterly*, 29:4, 2006, p. 21.

93 J. Peter Pham, "Foreign Influences and Shifting Horizons: The Ongoing Evolution of Al Qaeda in the Islamic Maghreb," *Orbis*, Spring 2011, pp. 240–54.

94 Geoff D. Porter, "Terrorist Outbidding: The In Amenas Attack," *CTC Sentinel*, 8:5, May 2015.

95 Christopher S. Chivvis and Andrew Liepman, *North Africa's Menace: AQIM's Evolution and the U.S. Policy Response*, Santa Monica, CA: RAND Corp., 2013.

96 Mendelsohn, *The Al Qaeda Franchise*, p. 133.

97 Jean-Luc Marret, "Al Qaeda in the Islamic Maghreb: A 'Glocal' Organization," *Studies in Conflict & Terrorism*, 31:6, 2008, p. 549.

98 Christopher S. Chivvis, *The French War on Al Qa'ida in Africa*, Cambridge University Press, 2015, p. 25.

99 Camille Tawil, *Brothers in Arms: The Story of Al-Qa'ida and the Arab Jihadists*, London: SAQI, p. 195.

100 Nicholas Schmidle, "The Saharan Conundrum," *New York Times Magazine*, February 13, 2009.

101 Chivvis and Liepman, *North Africa's Menace*, p. 4.

102 Manuel R. Torres Soriano, "The Road to Media Jihad: The Propaganda Actions of Al Qaeda in the Islamic Maghreb," *Terrorism and Political Violence*, 23:1, 2010, pp. 72–88.

103 Pham, "Foreign Influences," p. 245.

104 Rukmini Callimachi, "Paying Ransoms, Europe Bankrolls Qaeda Terror," *New York Times*, July 29, 2014.

105 Mendelsohn, *The Al Qaeda Franchise*, p. 134.

106 Eric Schmitt and Saeed al-Batati, "The U.S. Has Pummeled Al Qaeda in Yemen. But the Threat is Barely Dented," *New York Times*, December 30, 2017.

107 Michael Page, Lara Challita, and Alistair Harris, "Al Qaeda in the Arabian Peninsula: Framing Narratives and Prescriptions," *Terrorism and Political Violence*, 23:2, 2011, pp. 150–72.

108 Gregory D. Johnsen, *The Last Refuge: Yemen, Al-Qaeda, and America's War in Arabia*, New York: W. W. Norton, 2013, p. 261.

109 Alexander Meleagrou-Hitchens, "As American as Apple Pie: How Anwar al-Awlaki Became the Face of Western Jihad," The

International Centre for the Study of Radicalisation and Political Violence (ICSR), 2011; see also Scott Shane, "The Lessons of Anwar al-Awlaki," *New York Times Magazine*, August 27, 2015; and Haroro J. Ingram and Craig Whiteside, "The Yemen Raid and the Ghost of Anwar al-Awlaki," *The Atlantic*, February 9, 2017.

110 Bryce Loidolt, "Managing the Global and the Local: The Dual Agendas of Al Qaeda in the Arabian Peninsula," *Studies in Conflict & Terrorism*, 34:2, 2011, pp. 102–23.

111 Byman, "Buddies of Burdens?" p. 452.

112 "Al Qaeda is Losing Ground in Yemen. Yet It is Far from Defeated," *The Economist*, June 10, 2017.

113 Mendelsohn, *The Al Qaeda Franchise*, p. 140. See also Ty McCormick, "U.S. Attacks Reveal Al-Shabaab's Strength, Not Weakness," *Foreign Policy*, March 9, 2016.

114 Daveed Gartenstein-Ross, "The Strategic Challenge of Somalia's Al-Shabaab," *Middle East Quarterly*, 16:4, Fall 2009, pp. 25–36. For a more robust discussion of AIAI, see Kenneth J. Menkhaus, "Somalia and Somaliland: Terrorism, Political Islam, and State Collapse," in Robert I. Rotberg, ed., *Battling Terrorism in the Horn of Africa*, Cambridge, MA: World Peace Foundation, 2005, pp. 35–6.

115 Seth G. Jones, Andrew Liepman, and Nathan Chandler, *Counterterrorism and Counterinsurgency in Somalia*, Santa Monica, CA: RAND Corp., 2016, p. 9.

116 Daniel Benjamin and Steven Simon, *The Age of Sacred Terror: Radical Islam's War Against America*, New York: Random House, 2003, pp. 118–23.

117 Stig Jarle Hansen, *Al-Shabaab in Somalia: The History of a Militant Islamist Group, 2005–2012*, New York: Oxford University Press, 2013, pp. 28–32.

118 Ken Menkhaus and Christopher Boucek, "Terrorism Out of Somalia," Carnegie Endowment for International Peace, September 23, 2010: https://carnegieendowment.org/2010/09/23/terrorism-out-of-somalia-pub-41612.

119 Ken Menkhaus, "Non-State Actors and the Role of Violence in

Stateless Somalia," in Klejda Mulaj, ed., *Violent Non-State Actors in World Politics*, New York: Columbia University Press, 2010, p. 373.

120 David Shinn, "Al Shabaab's Foreign Threat to Somalia," *Orbis*, 55:2, 2011, pp. 203–15. See also Committee on Homeland Security, *Al Shabaab: Recruitment and Radicalization Within the Muslim American Community and the Threat to the Homeland*, Washington DC: Government Printing Office, July 27, 2011, p. 2.

121 Lorenzo Vidino, Raffaello Pantucci, and Evan Kohlmann, "Bringing Global Jihad to the Horn of Africa: al Shabaab, Western Fighters, the Sacralization of the Somali Conflict," *African Security*, 3:4, 2010, p. 224.

122 For more on this, see Richard Shultz and Andrea Dew, *Terrorists, Insurgents, and Militias: The Warriors of Contemporary Combat*, New York: Columbia University Press, 2007; and Clint Watts, Jacob Shapiro, and Vahid Brown, *Al-Qa'ida's (Mis)Adventures in the Horn of Africa*, Combating Terrorism Center, July 2, 2007.

123 Ken Menkhaus, "Al-Shabaab's Post-Westgate Capabilities," *CTC Sentinel*, 7:2, February 2014.

124 Christopher Anzalone, "The Resilience of al-Shabaab," *CTC Sentinel*, 9:4, April 2016.

125 Jason Burke, "Mogadishu Truck Bomb: 500 Casualties in Somalia's Worst Terrorist Attack," *Guardian*, October 16, 2017.

2 The Inner Workings of the Islamic State

1 Byman, "Al Qaeda's Decline," p. 1112.

2 Michael Weiss and Hassan Hassan, *ISIS: Inside the Army of Terror*, New York: Regan Arts, 2015, p. 186.

3 "Islamic State Has Been Stashing Millions of Dollars in Iraq and Abroad," *The Economist*, February 22, 2018.

4 Renad Mansour and Hisham al-Hashimi, "ISIS Inc.," *Foreign Policy*, January 16, 2018.

5 Phil Williams and Colin P. Clarke, "Iraqi and Syrian Networks," in

Kim Thachuk and Rollie Lal, eds., *Terrorist Criminal Enterprises*, Santa Barbara, CA: ABC-CLIO, 2018.

6 Ibid., pp. 27–46.

7 Daniel L. Glaser, "The Evolution of Terrorism Financing: Disrupting the Islamic State," in Levitt, ed., *Neither Remaining Nor Expanding*, pp. 43-7; Daniel L. Glaser, testimony before the House Committee on Foreign Affairs Subcommittee on Terrorism, Nonproliferation, and Trade, and House Committee on Armed Services Subcommittee on Emerging Threats and Capabilities, June 9, 2016; and Center for the Analysis of Terrorism, *ISIS Financing 2015*, Paris, May 2016.

8 Colin P. Clarke, "Drugs & Thugs: Funding Terrorism Through Narcotics Trafficking," *Journal of Strategic Security*, 9:3, Fall 2016; for more on how involvement in narcotics trafficking impacts terrorist groups, see Svante Cornell, "Narcotics and Armed Conflict: Interaction and Implications," *Studies in Conflict & Terrorism*, 30:3, 2007, pp. 207-27.

9 Scott Bronstein and Drew Griffin, "Self-Funded and Deep-Rooted: How ISIS Makes its Millions," *CNN*, October 7, 2014.

10 Stefan Heibner, Peter R. Neumann, John Holland-McCowan, and Rajan Basra, *Caliphate in Decline: An Estimate of Islamic State's Financial Fortunes*, London: The International Centre for the Study of Radicalisation and Political Violence, 2017. See also Rukmini Callimachi, "The Case of the Purloined Poultry: How ISIS Prosecuted Petty Crime," *New York Times*, July 1, 2018.

11 Johnston et al., *Foundations of the Islamic State*.

12 US Central Command, "Coalition Kills Daesh Criminal Leader, Followers," Combined Joint Task Force – Operation Inherent Resolve Public Affairs Office, June 19, 2018.

13 United Nations Security Council, "Twenty-Second Report of the Analytical Support and Sanctions Monitoring Team Submitted Pursuant to Resolution 2368 (2017) Concerning ISIL (Da'esh), Al-Qaida and Associated Individuals and Entities," New York, July 27, 2018, p. 8.

14 Mansour and al-Hashimi, "ISIS Inc."

15 Clarke, "Drugs & Thugs."

16 Heibner et al., "Caliphate in Decline."

17 Colin P. Clarke, Kimberly Jackson, Patrick B. Johnston, et al., *Financial Futures of the Islamic State of Iraq and the Levant*, Santa Monica, CA: RAND Corp., 2017.

18 "Islamic State Ammunition in Iraq and Syria: Analysis of Small-Calibre Ammunition Recovered from Islamic State Forces in Iraq and Syria," London: Conflict Armament Research, October 2014, p. 5.

19 Thomas Maurer, "ISIS's Warfare Functions: A Systemized Review of a Proto-State's Conventional Conduct of Operations," *Small Wars & Insurgencies*, 29:2, 2018, pp. 229–44.

20 "How ISIS Works," *New York Times*, September 16, 2014.

21 C. J. Chivers, "ISIS' Ammunition is Shown to Have Origins in U.S. and China," *New York Times*, October 5, 2014. See also Julia Harte and R. Jeffrey Smith, "Where Does the Islamic State Get Its Weapons?" *Foreign Policy*, October 6, 2014.

22 Kirk Semple and Eric Schmitt, "Missiles of ISIS May Pose Peril for Aircrews," *New York Times*, October 26, 2014.

23 Jamie Crawford, "Report Details Where ISIS Gets Its Weapons," CNN.com, December 14, 2017.

24 "Weapons of the Islamic State: A Three-Year Investigation into Iraq and Syria," *Conflict Armament Research*, December 2017, p. 146

25 Many of the Iraqi soldiers who refused to fight blamed their failure to stand their ground on officers, saying they were deliberately denied the resupply of basic necessities such as food and water: C. J. Chivers, "After Retreat, Iraqi Soldiers Fault Officers," *New York Times*, July 1, 2014.

26 Daniel Trombly and Yasir Abbas, "Who the U.S. Should Really Hit in ISIS," *Daily Beast*, September 23, 2014.

27 Gina Harkins, "5 Things to Know About Islamic State's Military Capabilities," *Army Times*, September 16, 2014.

28 "Arms Windfall for Insurgents as Iraq City Falls," *New York Times*, June 10, 2014.

29 Josh Rogin, "ISIS Video: America's Air Dropped Weapons Now in Our Hands," *Daily Beast*, October 21, 2014.

30 Charlie Winter, "War by Suicide: A Statistical Analysis of the Islamic State's Martyrdom Industry," International Centre for Counter-Terrorism (ICCT) – The Hague, ICCT Research Paper, February 2017.

31 Peter Bergen and Emily Schneider, "Now ISIS Has Drones?" CNN. com, August 25, 2014.

32 Michael S. Schmidt and Eric Schmitt, "Pentagon Confronts a New Threat from ISIS: Exploding Drones," *New York Times*, October 11, 2016.

33 Truls Hallberg Tønnessen, "Islamic State and Technology – A Literature Review," *Perspectives on Terrorism*, 11:6, 2017.

34 Trombly and Abbas, "Who the U.S. Should Really Hit in ISIS."

35 Nigel Inkster, "The Resurgence of ISIS," International Institute for Strategic Studies (IISS), June 13, 2014.

36 Charles Lister, "Profiling the Islamic State," Brookings Institution Doha Center Analysis Paper, No. 13, November 2014, p. 17: www. brookings.edu/research/profiling-the-islamic-state.

37 Carter Malkasian, "If ISIS Has a 3-24 (II): Trying to Write the Field Manual of the Islamic State," *Foreign Policy*, October 7, 2014.

38 Daniel Byman and Jeremy Shapiro, "Homeward Bound? Don't Hype the Threat of Returning Jihadists," *Foreign Affairs*, September 30, 2014.

39 Colin P. Clarke, "Round-Trip Tickets: How Will Authorities Know When Foreign Fighters Have Returned?" *Lawfare*, September 24, 2017, https://www.lawfareblog.com/round-trip-tickets-how-will-authorities-know-when-foreign-fighters-have-returned.

40 Anne Speckhard and Ahmet S. Yayla, "The ISIS Emni: The Origins and Inner Workings of IS's Intelligence Apparatus," *Perspectives on Terrorism*, 11:1, 2017.

41 Lorenzo Vidino, Francesco Marone, and Eva Entenmann, *Fear Thy Neighbor: Radicalization and Jihadist Attacks in the West*, Ledizioni: Italian Institute for International Political Studies (ISPI), 2017, p. 66.

42 Christoph Reuter, "Secret Files Reveal the Structure of the Islamic State," *Der Spiegel*, April 18, 2015.

43 Vera Mironova, Ekaterina Sergatskova, and Karam Alhamad, "ISIS' Intelligence Service Refuses to Die," *Foreign Affairs*, November 22, 2017.

44 Rukmini Callimachi, "How a Secretive Branch of ISIS Built a Global Network of Killers," *New York Times*, August 3, 2016.

45 Michael Rubin, "How Does ISIS Do Intelligence?" American Enterprise Institute, AEIdeas, December 5, 2016.

46 Bruce Hoffman, "The Evolving Terrorist Threat and CT Options for the Trump Administration," in Aaron Zelin, ed., *How Al Qaeda Survived the Islamic State*, Washington Institute for Near East Policy, 2017, p. 11.

47 James R. Clapper, "Worldwide Threat Assessment of the US Intelligence Community," Senate Armed Services Committee, Statement for the Record, February 9, 2016, p. 4.

48 Seth G. Jones, James Dobbins, Daniel Byman, et al., *Rolling Back the Islamic State*, Santa Monica, CA: RAND Corp., 2017.

49 Caleb Weiss and Bill Roggio, "Islamic State Assaults City in Syrian Kurdistan," *FDS's Long War Journal*, September 18, 2014.

50 Email exchange with Aaron Zelin, June 2018.

51 Clarke et al., *Financial Futures*.

52 Yochi Dreazen, "From Electricity to Sewage, U.S. Intelligence Says the Islamic State is Fast Learning How to Run a Country," *Foreign Policy*, August 18, 2014.

53 Jones et al., *Rolling Back the Islamic State*, p. 50.

54 Nicholas J. Rasmussen, "World Wide Threats: Keeping America Secure in the New Age of Terror," Hearing Before the House Committee on Homeland Security, November 30, 2017.

55 Paul Cruickshank, "A View from the CT Foxhole: Nicholas Rasmussen, Former Director, National Counterterrorism Center," *CTC Sentinel*, 11:1, January 2018.

56 Byman and Shapiro, "Homeward Bound?"

57 Lister, "Profiling the Islamic State," p. 17.

58 Callimachi, "How a Secretive Branch of ISIS Built a Global Network of Killers."

59 Bill Roggio and Caleb Weiss, "Over 100 Jihadist Training Camps Identified in Iraq and Syria," *FDD's Long War Journal*, June 21, 2015.

60 Hassan Hassan, "The Secret World of ISIS Training Camps – Ruled by Sacred Texts and the Sword," *Guardian*, January 24, 2015.

61 Graeme Wood, "What ISIS Really Wants," *The Atlantic*, March 2015.

62 Ishaan Tharoor, "It Turns Out Many ISIS Recruits Don't Know Much About Islam," *Washington Post*, August 17, 2016; see also Simon Cottee, "'What ISIS Really Wants' Revisited: Religion Matters in *Jihadist* Violence, but How?" *Studies in Terrorism & Conflict*, 40:6, 2017, pp. 439–54; and Aya Batrawy, Paisley Dodds, and Lori Hinnant, "Leaked ISIS Documents Reveal Recruits Have Poor Grasp of Islamic Faith," *The Independent*, August 16, 2016.

63 Lorne L. Dawson and Amarnath Amarasingam, "Talking to Foreign Fighters: Insights into the Motivations for *Hijrah* to Syria and Iraq," *Studies in Conflict & Terrorism*, 40:3, 2017, pp. 190–210.

64 Lizzie Dearden, "ISIS Releases Video of Child Soldiers Training for Jihad in Syria Camp for 'Cubs of the Caliphate,'" *Independent*, February 23, 2015.

65 John G. Horgan, Max Taylor, Mia Bloom, and Charlie Winter, "From Cubs to Lions: A Six Stage Model of Child Socialization into the Islamic State," *Studies in Conflict & Terrorism*, 40:7, 2017, pp. 645–64.

66 Kinana Qaddour, "ISIS's War on Families Never Ended," *Foreign Policy*, February 1, 2018.

67 Jamie Dettmer, "Germany Alarmed by 'Kindergarten Jihadists,'" *Voice of America*, February 2, 2018.

68 Romina McGuinness, "ISIS Trained Child Soldiers to Launch Attacks on EU, Claims French Jihadist," *Express*, June 29, 2018.

69 Callimachi, "The Case of the Purloined Poultry."

70 Simon Cottee, "ISIS in the Caribbean," *The Atlantic*, December 8, 2016.

71 Robert F. Worth, "The Professor and the Jihadi," *New York Times Magazine*, April 5, 2017.

72 Joby Warrick and Greg Miller, "New ISIS Recruits Have Deep Criminal Roots," *Washington Post*, March 23, 2016.

73 Tamara Makarenko, "Increasingly Vulnerable," *The Cipher Brief*, April 27, 2016.

74 Simon Cottee, "The Challenge of Jihadi Cool," *The Atlantic*, December 24, 2015. See also Thomas Hegghammer, "The Soft Power of Militant Jihad," *New York Times*, December 18, 2015.

75 Hegghammer, "The Soft Power of Militant Jihad."

76 Mary Anne Weaver, "The Short, Violent Life of Abu Musab al-Zarqawi," *The Atlantic Monthly*, July/August 2006.

77 Andrew Higgins, Kimiko de Freytas-Tamura, and Katrin Bennhold, "In Suspects' Brussels Neighborhood, a History of Petty Crimes and Missed Chances," *New York Times*, November 16, 2015.

78 Jean-Charles Brisard and Kevin Jackson, "The Islamic State's External Operations and the French–Belgian Nexus," *CTC Sentinel*, 9:11, 2016.

79 Alissa J. Rubin and Milan Schreuer, "Sole Surviving Suspect in Paris Attacks Stands Trial in Belgium," *New York Times*, February 5, 2018. See also Rory Mulholland and Danny Boyle, "Heroic French Officer Arnaud Beltrame Dies after Switching Himself for Hostage in France Supermarket," *Telegraph*, March 24, 2018.

80 Simon Cottee, "Europe's Joint Smoking, Gay-Club Hopping Terrorists," *Foreign Policy*, April 13, 2016.

81 Matthew Levitt, "My Journey to Brussels' Terrorist Safe Haven," *Politico*, March 27, 2016.

82 Anthony Faiola and Souad Mekhennet, "The Islamic State Creates a New Type of Jihadists: Part Terrorist, Part Gangster," *Washington Post*, December 20, 2015.

83 Terence McCoy, "How ISIS Leader Abu Bakr al-Baghdadi Became the World's Most Powerful Jihadist Leader," *Washington Post*, June 11, 2014.

84 Tim Arango and Eric Schmitt, "U.S. Actions in Iraq Fueled the Rise of a Rebel," *New York Times*, August 10, 2014.

85 Andrew Thompson and Jeremy Suri, "How America Helped ISIS," *New York Times*, October 1, 2014. See also Terrence McCoy, "How the Islamic State Evolved in an American Prison," *Washington Post*, November 4, 2014.

86 William McCants, "The Believer," Brookings Institution, September 1, 2015: http://csweb.brookings.edu/content/resear ch/essays/2015/thebeliever.html.

87 Hannah Strange, "Islamic State Leader Abu Bakr al-Baghdadi Addresses Muslims in Mosul," *Telegraph*, July 5, 2014.

88 Will Cathcart, "The Secret Life of an ISIS Warlord," *Daily Beast*, October 27, 2014.

89 "The Anatomy of ISIS: How the 'Islamic State' is Run, from Oil to Beheadings," *CNN*, September 18, 2014.

90 Ben Hubbard and Eric Schmitt, "Military Skill and Terrorist Technique Fuel Success of ISIS," *New York Times*, August 27, 2014.

91 "How ISIS Works," *New York Times*.

92 Hubbard and Schmitt, "Military Skill and Terrorist Technique Fuel Success of ISIS." See also Ruth Sherlock, "Inside the Leadership of Islamic State: How the New 'Caliphate' is Run," *Daily Telegraph*, July 9, 2014.

93 Eric Schmitt, Rukmini Callimachi, and Anne Barnard, "Spokesman's Death Will Have Islamic State Turning to Its 'Deep Bench,'" *New York Times*, August 31, 2016.

94 Joby Warrick, "ISIS's Second-in-Command Hid in Syria for Months. The Day He Stepped Out, the U.S. Was Waiting," *Washington Post*, November 28, 2016.

95 David D. Kirkpatrick, "ISIS' Harsh Brand of Islam is Rooted in Austere Saudi Creed," *New York Times*, September 24, 2014.

96 David Motadel, "The Ancestors of ISIS," *New York Times*, September 23, 2014.

97 Daveed Gartenstein-Ross and Amichal Magen, "The Jihadist Governance Dilemma," *Washington Post* Monkey Cage Blog, July 18, 2014: https://www.washingtonpost.com/news/monkey-cage/ wp/2014/07/18/the-jihadist-governance-dilemma/?utm_term=. 8a6eb2d717ee.

98 For more on the falling-out between IS and al-Qaeda, see J. M. Berger, "The Islamic State vs. al Qaeda," *Foreign Policy*, September 2, 2014.

99 William McCants, "State of Confusion," *Foreign Affairs*, September 10, 2014.

100 David Ignatius, "The Manual that Chillingly Foreshadows the Islamic State," *Washington Post*, September 25, 2014.

101 Robin Simcox, "ISIS' Western Ambitions," *Foreign Affairs*, June 30, 2014.

102 Daniel Byman, "The State of Terror," *Slate*, June 13, 2014.

103 Aaron Y. Zelin, "ISIS is Dead, Long Live the Islamic State," *Foreign Policy*, June 30, 2014.

104 Joby Warrick, *Black Flags: The Rise of ISIS*, New York: Anchor, 2016, p. 260.

105 Cole Bunzel, "From Paper State to Caliphate: The Ideology of the Islamic State," Brookings Institution, March 9, 2015: https://www.brookings.edu/research/from-paper-state-to-caliphate-the-ideology-of-the-islamic-state.

106 Hassan Hassan, "The Sectarianism of the Islamic State: Ideological Roots and Political Context," Carnegie Endowment for International Peace, June 13, 2016: http://carnegieendowment.org/2016/06/13/sectarianism-of-islamic-state-ideological-roots-and-political-context-pub-63746.

107 Lizzie Dearden, "ISIS: Islam is 'Not Strongest Factor' Behind Foreign Fighters Joining Extremist Groups in Syria and Iraq – Report," *Independent*, November 16, 2016.

108 Email exchange with J. M. Berger, June 2018.

109 Eric Schmitt, "U.S. Secures Vast New Trove of Intelligence on ISIS," *New York Times*, July 27, 2016.

110 Seth G. Jones, "Jihadist Sanctuaries in Syria and Iraq: Implications for the United States," testimony before the Committee on Homeland Security Subcommittee on Counterterrorism and Intelligence, US House of Representatives, July 24, 2014, p. 1.

111 Griff Witte, Sudarsan Raghavan, and James McAuley, "Flow

of Foreign Fighters Plummets as Islamic State Loses Its Edge," *Washington Post*, September 9, 2016.

112 "Foreign Fighters Flow into Syria," *Washington Post*, October 11, 201. See also David D. Kirkpatrick, "New Freedoms in Tunisia Drive Support for ISIS," *New York Times*, October 21, 2014.

113 Peter Neumann, "Suspects into Collaborators," *London Review of Books*, 36:7, April 3, 2014.

114 Tim Arango and Eric Schmitt, "Escaped Inmates from Iraq Fuel Syrian Insurgency," *New York Times*, February 12, 2014.

115 Jytte Klausen, "They're Coming: Measuring the Threat from Returning Jihadists," *Foreign Affairs*, October 1, 2014.

116 Kate Brannen, "Children of the Caliphate," *Foreign Policy*, October 27, 2014.

117 Megan A. Stewart, "What's So New About the Islamic State's Governance?" *Washington Post* Monkey Cage Blog, October 7, 2014.

118 "The Anatomy of ISIS," *CNN*.

119 Aaron Y. Zelin, "When Jihadists Learn How to Help," *Washington Post* Monkey Cage Blog, May 7, 2014.

120 Benjamin Bahney, Howard J. Shatz, Carroll Ganier, et al., *An Economic Analysis of the Financial Records of al-Qa'ida in Iraq*, Santa Monica, CA: RAND Corp., 2010; for more micro-level data on the group's financial bureaucracy, see Benjamin W. Bahney, Radha K. Iyengar, Patrick B. Johnston, Danielle F. Jung, Jacob N. Shapiro, and Howard J. Shatz, "Insurgent Compensation: Evidence from Iraq," *American Economic Review*, 103:3, 2013, pp. 518–22.

121 Howard J. Shatz, "To Defeat the Islamic State, Follow the Money," *Politico*, September 10, 2014.

122 Janine Davidson and Emerson Brooking, "ISIS Hasn't Gone Anywhere – And It's Getting Stronger," Council on Foreign Relations, Defense in Depth, July 24, 2014.

123 Mariam Karouny, "In Northeast Syria, Islamic State Builds a Government," Reuters, September 4, 2014.

124 Jessica Stern and J. M. Berger, *ISIS: The State of Terror*, New York: HarperCollins, 2016, p. 114.

125 William McCants, *The ISIS Apocalypse*, New York: St. Martin's Press, 2015, p. 152.

126 Aaron Zelin, "The Islamic State of Iraq and Syria Has a Consumer Protection Office," *The Atlantic*, June 13, 2014.

127 Graeme Wood, *The Way of the Strangers*, New York: Random House, 2017, p. xxii.

128 Andrew Shaver, "Turning the Lights Off on the Islamic State," *Washington Post* Monkey Cage Blog, October 16, 2014.

129 Sudarsan Raghavan, "Inside the Brutal but Bizarrely Bureaucratic World of the Islamic State in Libya," *Washington Post*, August 23, 2016.

130 Ghaith Abdul-Ahad, "The Bureaucracy of Evil: How Islamic State Ran a City," *Guardian*, January 29, 2018.

131 Aymenn al-Tamimi, "The Evolution in Islamic State Administration: The Documentary Evidence," *Perspectives on Terrorism*, 9:4, 2015; see also Rukmini Callimachi, "The ISIS Files," *New York Times*, April 4, 2018.

132 Brian Dodwell, Daniel Milton, and Don Rassler, *The Caliphate's Global Workforce: An Inside Look at the Islamic State's Foreign Fighter Paper Trail*, Combating Terrorism Center at West Point, April 2016, p. 18: https://ctc.usma.edu/the-caliphates-global-work force-an-inside-look-at-the-islamic-states-foreign-fighter-paper-trail.

133 Shiv Malik, "The ISIS Papers: Behind 'Death Cult' Image Lies a Methodical Bureaucracy," *Guardian*, December 7, 2015.

134 Laura Ryan, "IS is Better Than Al Qaeda at Using the Internet," *Defense One*, October 10, 2014.

135 Ali Fisher and Nico Prucha, "ISIS is Winning the Online Jihad Against the West," *Daily Beast*, October 1, 2014.

136 Rod Nordland, "Iraq's Sunni Militants Take to Social Media to Advance Their Cause and Intimidate," *New York Times*, June 28, 2014. For more on the group's use of social media, see Rita Katz, "Follow ISIS on Twitter: A Special Report on the Use of Social

Media by Jihadists," Insite Blog on Terrorism & Extremism, June 26, 2014.

137 Jacob Siegel, "Has ISIS Peaked as a Military Power?" *Daily Beast*, October 22, 2014.

138 Colin Clarke and Charlie Winter, "The Islamic State May Be Failing, But Its Strategic Communications Legacy is Here to Stay," *War on the Rocks*, August 17, 2017. See also Nafees Hamid, "The British Hacker Who Became the Islamic State's Chief Terror Cybercoach: A Profile of Junaid Hussain," *CTC Sentinel*, 11:4, April 2018.

139 Bennett Seftel, "What Drives ISIS," *The Cipher Brief*, May 5, 2016.

140 Aaron Y. Zelin, "Picture or It Didn't Happen: A Snapshot of the Islamic State's Official Media Output," *Perspectives on Terrorism*, 9:4, 2015.

141 Charlie Winter, "The Virtual 'Caliphate': Understanding Islamic State's Propaganda Strategy," *Quilliam Foundation*, July 2015, p. 28.

142 Charlie Winter and Jordan Bach-Lombardo, "Why ISIS Propaganda Works," *The Atlantic*, February 13, 2016.

143 Daveed Gartenstein-Ross, Nathaniel Barr, and Bridget Moreng, "How the Islamic State's Propaganda Feeds into Its Global Expansion Efforts," *War on the Rocks*, April 28, 2016.

144 Colin P. Clarke and Haroro J. Ingram, "Defeating the ISIS Nostalgia Narrative," Foreign Policy Research Institute (FPRI), After the Caliphate Project, E-Notes, April 18, 2018.

145 Lorraine Ali, "Islamic State's Soft Weapon of Choice: Social Media," *Los Angeles Times*, September 22, 2014.

146 Ezzeldeen Khalil, "Gone Viral: Islamic State's Evolving Media Strategy," *Jane's Intelligence Review*, October 2014, p. 15.

147 Josh Kovensky, "IS's New Mag Looks Like a New York Glossy – With Pictures of Mutilated Bodies," *New Republic*, August 25, 2014. The name "Dabiq" was chosen for the magazine because Dabiq is a small village in Syria that is believed by some IS fighters to be the place where one of the final battles of the Islamic apocalypse will take place. See William McCants, "ISIS Fantasies of an Apocalyptic

Showdown in Northern Syria," Brookings Institution, October 3, 2014: https://www.brookings.edu/blog/markaz/2014/10/03/isis-fantasies-of-an-apocalyptic-showdown-in-northern-syria.

148 Harleen K. Gambhir, "Dabiq: The Strategic Messaging of the Islamic State," *Institute for the Study of War*, August 15, 2014, p. 2.

149 James P. Farwell, "The Media Strategy of IS," *Survival*, 56:6, December 2014 / January 2015, pp. 49–55.

150 Marc Lynch, Deen Freelon, and Sean Aday, "Syria's Socially Mediated Civil War," United States Institute of Peace (USIP), Peaceworks No. 91, 2014, p. 15.

151 Scott Shane and Ben Hubbard, "ISIS Displaying a Deft Command of Varied Media," *New York Times*, August 30, 2014.

152 Jytte Klausen, "Tweeting the *Jihad*: Social Media Networks of Western Foreign Fighters in Syria and Iraq," *Studies in Conflict & Terrorism*, 38:1, 2015, pp. 1–22.

153 Clarke and Winter, "The Islamic State May Be Failing, But Its Strategic Communications Legacy is Here to Stay."

154 Gerges, *ISIS: A History*, p. 270.

155 Greg Miller and Souad Mekhennet, "Inside the Surreal World of the Islamic State's Propaganda Machine," *Washington Post*, November 20, 2015.

156 Mia Bloom, "Constructing Expertise: Terrorist Recruitment and 'Talent Spotting' in the PIRA, Al Qaeda, and ISIS," *Studies in Conflict & Terrorism*, 40:7, 2017, pp. 603–23.

157 Cottee, "The Challenge of Jihadi Cool."

158 J. M. Berger, "How IS Games Twitter," *The Atlantic*, June 16, 2014; see also Simon Cottee, "Why It's So Hard to Stop IS Propaganda," *The Atlantic*, March 2, 2015.

159 Jonathon Morgan and J. M. Berger, "The IS Twitter Census: Defining and Describing the Population of IS Supporters on Twitter," Brookings Institution, March 5, 2015.

160 Jack Moore, "ISIS's Twitter Campaign Faltering Amid Crackdown," *Newsweek*, February 18, 2016. See also Dustin Volz, "Islamic State Finds Diminishing Returns on Twitter: Report," Reuters, February 18, 2016.

161 Elizabeth Bodine-Baron, Todd C. Helmus, Madeline Magnuson, and Zev Winkelman, *Examining ISIS Support and Opposition Networks on Twitter*, Santa Monica, CA: RAND Corp., 2016. Still, others are skeptical at how effective this tactic is over the long term. For a more pessimistic view on the effectiveness of shutting down IS Twitter accounts, see Amarnath Amarasingam, "What Twitter Really Means for Islamic State Supporters," *War on the Rocks*, December 30, 2015.

162 Mia Bloom, Hicham Tiflati, and John Horgan, "Navigating ISIS's Preferred Platform: Telegram," *Terrorism and Political Violence*, 2017, pp. 1-13.

3 The Coming Terrorist Diaspora

1 Margaret Coker, Eric Schmitt, and Rukmini Callimachi, "With Loss of Its Caliphate, ISIS May Return to Guerilla Roots," *New York Times*, October 18, 2017. See also Yaroslav Trofimov, "Faraway ISIS Branches Grow as Group Fades in Syria, Iraq," *Wall Street Journal*, May 18, 2018.

2 Julian E. Barnes, Valentina Pop, and Jenny Gross, "Europe Doesn't Expect Fresh Influx of Returning ISIS Fighters," *Wall Street Journal*, October 17, 2017.

3 Julie Hirschfeld Davis, "Trump Drops Push for Immediate Withdrawal of Troops from Syria," *New York Times*, April 4, 2018.

4 For some of the best works to discuss these differences, see Assaf Moghadam, Ronit Berger, and Polina Beliakova, "Say Terrorist, Think Insurgent: Labeling and Analyzing Contemporary Terrorist Actors," *Perspectives on Terrorism*, 8:5, October 2014; Seth G. Jones, *Waging Insurgent Warfare: Lessons from the Vietcong to the Islamic State*, New York: Oxford University Press, 2017, pp. 8-9; David Kilcullen, "Countering Global Insurgency," *Journal of Strategic Studies*, 28:4, 2005, pp. 597-617; and Hoffman, *Inside Terrorism*, p. 35.

5 The category strategy is consonant with that presented by Jones in *Waging Insurgent Warfare*, ch. 3.

6 Mohamed Fadel Fahmy, "Egypt's Wild West," *Foreign Policy*, August 24, 2011: https://foreignpolicy.com/2011/08/24/egy pts-wild-west-2.

7 Sahar F. Aziz, "Rethinking Counterterrorism in the Age of IS: Lessons from Sinai," *Nebraska Law Review*, 95:2, pp. 307–65.

8 For more on ABM, see Mokhtar Awad and Samuel Tadros, "Bay'a Remorse? Wilayat Sinai and the Nile Valley," *CTC Sentinel*, 8:8, August 2015.

9 Mokhtar Awad, "IS in the Sinai," in Katherine Bauer, ed., *Beyond Syria and Iraq: Examining Islamic State Provinces*, Washington Institute for Near East Policy, 2016, p. 21.

10 Sudarsan Raghavan, "Militant Threat Emerges in Egyptian Desert, Opening New Front in Terrorism Fight," *Washington Post*, March 14, 2018.

11 Erin Cunningham, "Bomb Blast in Egypt's Sinai Peninsula is Deadliest Attack on Army in Decades," *Washington Post*, October 24, 2014; Kareem Fahim and David D. Kirkpatrick, "Jihadist Attacks on Egypt Grow Even Fiercer," *New York Times*, July 1, 2015.

12 Zack Gold, "Sisi Doesn't Know How to Beat ISIS," *Foreign Policy*, November 30, 2017: https://foreignpolicy.com/2017/11/30/ sisi-doesnt-know-how-to-beat-isis.

13 David D. Kirkpatrick, "Secret Alliance: Israel Carries Out Airstrikes in Egypt, With Cairo's O.K.," *New York Times*, February 3, 2018.

14 Mokhtar Awad, "The Islamic State's Pyramid Scheme: Egyptian Expansion and the Giza Governorate Cell," *CTC Sentinel*, 9:4, April 2016.

15 Sudarsan Raghavan and Heba Farouk Mahfouz, "Egypt Launches Major Offensive Against Islamic State Militants," *Washington Post*, February 9, 2018.

16 Loveday Morris, "Islamic State Declares War on Rival Hamas With Video Execution," *Washington Post*, January 4, 2018.

17 Phone interview with Zack Gold, July 2017.

18 Colin P. Clarke, "How Salafism's Rise Threatens Gaza," *Foreign*

Affairs, October 11, 2017: https://www.foreignaffairs.com/articles/israel/2017-10-11/how-salafisms-rise-threatens-gaza.

19 Zack Gold, "Security in the Sinai: Present and Future," ICCT Research Paper, March 2014: https://www.icct.nl/download/file/ICCT-Gold-Security-In-The-Sinai-March-2014.pdf.

20 Mokhtar Awad, "Why ISIS Declared War on Egypt's Christians," *The Atlantic*, April 9, 2017.

21 Declan Walsh, "Attacks Show ISIS' New Plan: Divide Egypt By Killing Christians," *New York Times*, April 10, 2017.

22 Declan Walsh, "Gunmen Kill Police Officer Near St. Catherine's Monastery in Egypt," *New York Times*, April 18, 2017.

23 "Gunman Kills 11 in Attacks on Coptic Church, Christian-Owned Shop in Egypt," Reuters, December 29, 2017.

24 Declan Walsh and Nour Youssef, "Militants Kill 305 at Sufi Mosque in Egypt's Deadliest Terror Attack," *New York Times*, November 24, 2017.

25 Hassan Hassan, "Its Dreams of a Caliphate Are Gone. Now ISIS Has a Deadly New Strategy," *Guardian*, December 30, 2017.

26 Sudha Ratan, "The Trump Administration's New Afghan Problem: The Islamic State," *The Diplomat*, April 3, 2018.

27 Antonio Giustozzi, "Taliban and Islamic State: Enemies or Brothers in Jihad?" Center for Research & Policy Analysis, December 14, 2017: https://www.crpaweb.org/single-post/2017/12/15/Enemies-or-Jihad-Brothers-Relations-Between-Taliban-and-Islamic-State.

28 Zabihullah Ghazi and Mujib Mashal, "Deadly ISIS Attack Hits an Aid Group, Save the Children, in Afghanistan," *New York Times*, January 24, 2018. See also Bart Jansen, "11 Afghan Troops Die in Islamic State Attack on Kabul Military Academy, Latest in Violent Surge," *USA Today*, January 29, 2018.

29 Jawad Sukhanyar and Mujib Mashal, "Twin Mosque Attacks Kill Scores in One of Afghanistan's Deadliest Weeks," *New York Times*, October 20, 2017.

30 "ISIS On Rise in Pakistan," *The Hindu*, January 8, 2018: https://

www.thehindu.com/news/international/isis-on-rise-in-pakistan -report/article22397277.ece.

31 Salman Masood, "Pakistan Reels After Attack on Police Training College Leaves 61 Dead," *New York Times*, October 25, 2016.

32 Borhan Osman, "The Islamic State in 'Khorasan': How it Began and Where It Stands Now in Nangarhar," Afghanistan Analysts' Network, July 27, 2016: https://www.afghanistan-analysts.org/ the-islamic-state-in-khorasan-how-it-began-and-where-it-stand s-now-in-nangarhar.

33 United Nations Security Council, "Twenty-First Report of the Analytical Support and Sanctions Monitoring Team Submitted Pursuant to Resolution 2368 (2017) Concerning ISIL (Da'esh), Al Qaeda and Associated Individuals and Entities," January 26, 2018.

34 Mirwais Harooni and Kay Johnson "Taliban Urge Islamic State to Stop 'Interference' in Afghanistan," Reuters, June 16, 2015.

35 Animesh Roul, "Islamic State Gains Ground in Afghanistan as Its Caliphate Crumbles Elsewhere," *Jamestown Terrorism Monitor*, 16:2, January 26, 2018: https://jamestown.org/program/islamic-state-gains-ground-afghanistan-caliphate-crumbles-elsewhere.

36 Matthew Dupee, "Red on Red: Analyzing Afghanistan's Intra-Insurgency Violence," *CTC Sentinel*, 11:1, January 2018. See also Najim Rahim and Rod Nordland, "Are ISIS Fighters Prisoners or Honored Guests of the Afghan Government?" *New York Times*, August 4, 2018.

37 "Afghan Official: Islamic State Present in at Least 3 Provinces," Associated Press, June 29, 2015.

38 Bennett Seftel, "'Persistent, Expanding and Worrisome': ISIS Rebounds in Afghanistan," *The Cipher Brief*, January 5, 2018.

39 Mujib Mashal, "In Tangled Afghan War, a Thin Line of Defense Against ISIS," *New York Times*, December 25, 2017.

40 Ayaz Gul, "Russia Says About 10,000 IS Militants Now in Afghanistan," *VOA News*, December 23, 2017.

41 Amanda Erickson, "How the Islamic State Got a Foothold in Afghanistan," *Washington Post*, March 21, 2018.

42 Merhat Sharipzhan, "IMU Declares it is Now Part of the Islamic State," *RFERL*, August 6, 2015.

43 Larisa Brown, "UK Jihadis 'Have Joined Slaughter in Afghanistan': Minister Fears 'Porous Borders' Have Allowed Extremists to Leave Syria for the Country," *Daily Mail*, January 29, 2018.

44 Tom O'Connor, "Where Will IS Be in 2018? Iran Says Afghanistan and Pakistan Are Next as Islamic State Loses Iraq and Syria," *Newsweek*, December 12, 2017.

45 Idrees Ali, "Air Strikes Hit Islamic State in Afghanistan Under New Rules: U.S.," Reuters, April 14, 2016.

46 W. J. Hennigan, "Air Force Drops Non-Nuclear 'Mother of All Bombs' in Afghanistan," *Los Angeles Times*, April 13, 2017.

47 Jo Becker and Eric Schmitt, "As Trump Wavers on Libya, an ISIS Haven, Russia Presses On," *New York Times*, February 7, 2017.

48 Noha Aboueldahab, Tarek M. Yousef, Luiz Pinto, et al., "The Middle East and North Africa in 2018: Challenges, Threats, and Opportunities," Brookings Institution, December 21, 2017.

49 Aaron Y. Zelin, "The Islamic State's Model," *Washington Post* Monkey Cage Blog, January 28, 2015.

50 Aaron Y. Zelin, "The Others: Foreign Fighters in Libya," Washington Institute for Near East Policy, Policy Note No.45, 2018.

51 Malek Bachir and Akram Kharief, "The Slow Death of al Qaeda in Algeria," *Middle East Eye*, February 1, 2018.

52 Khalid Mahmoud, "AFRICOM Expects ISIS Attack on Libya's Oil Crescent," *Asharq Al-Aswat*, January 3, 2018; see also Jeff Seldin, "Defense, Intelligence Officials Warn Against Underestimating Islamic State," *VOA News*, December 31, 2017.

53 Aaron Y. Zelin, "The Islamic State's First Colony in Libya," Washington Institute for Near East Policy, PolicyWatch 2325, October 10, 2014.

54 Benoit Faucon and Matt Bradley, "Islamic State Gained Strength in Libya by Co-Opting Local Jihadists," *Wall Street Journal*, February 17, 2015.

55 Johannes Saal, "The Islamic State's Libyan External Operations Hub: The Picture So Far," *CTC Sentinel*, 10:11, December 2017.

56 Frederic Wehrey and Ala' Alrababa'h, "Rising Out of Chaos: The Islamic State in Libya," *Diwan*, March 5, 2015.

57 Paul Cruickshank, Nic Robertson, Tim Lister, and Jomana Karadsheh, "ISIS Comes to Libya," *CNN*, November 18, 2014.

58 Andrew Engel, "The Islamic State's Expansion in Libya," PolicyWatch 2371, February 11, 2015.

59 David D. Kirkpatrick, Ben Hubbard, and Eric Schmitt, "ISIS's Grip on Libyan City Gives It a Fallback Option," *New York Times*, November 28, 2015. See also Jon Lee Anderson, "ISIS Rises in Libya," *New Yorker*, August 4, 2015.

60 Sudarsan Raghavan, "A Year After ISIS Left, A Battered Libyan City Struggles to Resurrect Itself," *Washington Post*, January 8, 2018.

61 Issandr El Amrani, "How Much of Libya Does the Islamic State Control?" *Foreign Policy*, February 18, 2016.

62 For more, see Christopher S. Chivvis, *Toppling Qaddafi: Libya and the Limits of Liberal Intervention*, Cambridge University Press, 2013.

63 "How Real is the Threat of Returning IS Fighters?" *BBC News*, October 23, 2017.

64 Aaron Y. Zelin, "The Islamic State's Burgeoning Capital in Sirte, Libya," Washington Institute for Near East Policy, Policywatch 2462, August 6, 2015. See also Aaron Y. Zelin, "The Islamic State's Territorial Methodology," Washington Institute for Near East Policy, Research Note No. 29, January 2016.

65 Bennett Seftel, "ISIS Grows and Festers in Lawless Libya," *The Cipher Brief*, January 26, 2018.

66 Ryan Browne, "US Strikes ISIS Targets in Libya for a Second Time in Less Than a Week," CNN.com, September 28, 2017.

67 Johannes Saal, "The Islamic State's Libyan External Operations Hub: The Picture So Far," *CTC Sentinel*, 10:11, December 2017.

68 Frederic Wehrey, "When the Islamic State Came to Libya," *The Atlantic*, February 10, 2018.

69 Marielle Ness, "The Islamic State's Two-Pronged Assault on Turkey," CTC Beyond the Caliphate: Islamic State Activity Outside the Group's Defined Wilayat, January 2018.

70 Eric Schmitt, "Thousands of ISIS Fighters Flee in Syria, Many to Fight Another Day," *New York Times*, February 4, 2018. See also Mike Giglio and Munzer Awad, "The Escape: How ISIS Members Fled the Caliphate, Perhaps to Fight Another Day," Buzzfeed, December 19, 2017.

71 Callimachi, "How a Secretive Branch of ISIS Built a Global Network of Killers"; Jack Moore, "Hundreds of ISIS Fighters are Hiding in Turkey, Increasing Fears of Europe Attacks," *Newsweek*, December 27, 2017.

72 Erin Cunningham and Karim Fahim, "Islamic State Claims Responsibility for Istanbul Nightclub Attack," *Washington Post*, January 2, 2017. See also Ahmet S. Yayla, "The Reina Nightclub Attack and the Threat to Turkey," *CTC Sentinel*, 10:3, March 2017.

73 Ahmet S. Yayla, "ISIS Airmail: The Bomb Shipped from Turkey to Australia," *Wall Street Journal*, August 9, 2017.

74 Colin P. Clarke and Ahmet S. Yayla, "Erdogan's Fatal Blind Spot," *Foreign Policy*, February 15, 2018.

75 Hans Nicholas and Mosheh Gains, "Pentagon Confirms U.S. Ground Operations in Yemen," NBCnews.com, December 20, 2017.

76 Alex Horton, "In a First, U.S. Launches Deadly Strikes on ISIS Training Camps in Yemen," *Washington Post*, October 17, 2017.

77 Hassan Hassan, "ISIS Has Stepped Up Campaigns in Yemen, Egypt, and Afghanistan. The Coalition Fighting It Should Be Worried," *The National*, May 23, 2018.

78 Nadwa al-Dawsari, "Foe Not Friend: Yemeni Tribes and Al Qaeda in the Arabian Peninsula," Project on Middle East Democracy (POMED), February 2018.

79 Elisabeth Kendall, "Impact of the Yemen War on Militant Jihad," POMEPS Studies 29: Politics, Governance, and Reconstruction in Yemen, January 12, 2018: https://pomeps.org/2018/01/12/impact-of-the-yemen-war-on-militant-jihad.

80 Sudarsan Raghavan, "Still Fighting Al Qaeda," *Washington Post*, July 6, 2018.

81 Ben Watson, "The War in Yemen and the Making of a Chaos State," *Defense One*, January 28, 2018.

82 Peter Salisbury, "Yemen: National Chaos, Local Order," Chatham House Research Paper, Middle East and North Africa Programme, December 2017, p. 23.

83 Email exchange with Bruce Hoffman, July 2018.

84 Email exchange with Elisabeth Kendall, July 2018.

85 Colin P. Clarke, "Expanding the ISIS Brand," *National Interest*, February 17, 2018.

86 "Malaysia Arrests Two ISIS Militants Over Planned Attacks on Police Stations and Buddhist Monks," *The Straits Times*, January 22, 2018.

87 Jeffrey Gettleman, "A Mysterious Act of Mercy by the Subway Bombing Suspect," *New York Times*, December 18, 2017. See also Sadanand Dhume, "Bangladesh Exports a New Generation of Terrorists," *Wall Street Journal*, December 28, 2017.

88 Jason Burke, "Al Qaeda Moves In to Recruit from Islamic State and Its Affiliates," *Guardian*, January 19, 2018.

89 Daniel L. Byman, "What Happens When ISIS Goes Underground?" Brookings Institution, January 18, 2018: https://www.brookings. edu/blog/markaz/2018/01/18/what-happens-when-isis-goes-un derground.

90 Vera Mironova and Ekaterina Sergatskova, "Will Former ISIS Fighters Help the Rohingya?" *Foreign Affairs*, September 22, 2017.

91 C. Christine Fair, "Political Islam and Islamist Terrorism in Bangladesh: What You Need to Know," *Lawfare*, January 28, 2018.

92 Rukmini Callimachi, "ISIS Seems to Tailor Attacks for Different Audiences," *New York Times*, July 2, 2016.

93 For more on AQIS, see Alastair Reed, "Al Qaeda in the Indian Subcontinent: A New Frontline in the Global Jihadist Movement?" International Centre for Counter-Terrorism (ICCT) – The Hague, ICCT Policy Brief, May 2015: https://icct.nl/publication/al-qaeda-in-the-indian-subcontintent-a-new-frontline-in-the-glob al-jihadist-movement.

94 Fair, "Political Islam and Islamist Terrorism in Bangladesh."

95 Amira Jadoon, "An Idea or a Threat? Islamic State Jammu & Kashmir," Combating Terrorism Center, February 9, 2018: https:// ctc.usma.edu/idea-threat-islamic-state-jammu-kashmir.

96 For more on this subject, see Steve Coll, *Directorate S: The C.I.A. and America's Secret Wars in Afghanistan and Pakistan*, New York: Penguin Press, 2018.

97 Richard C. Paddock, "In Indonesia and Philippines, Militants Find a Common Bond: ISIS," *New York Times*, May 26, 2017.

98 Jeffrey Hutton, "Suicide Bombers Strike Jakarta, Killing 3 Police Officers," *New York Times*, May 25, 2017; Alex Horton, "Family of Suicide Bombers Kills At Least 7 in Indonesia Church Attacks," *New York Times*, May 13, 2017.

99 Michael Peel, "Militant Islamists Shift Focus to Southeast Asia," *Financial Times*, June 18, 2017.

100 Sidney Jones, "How ISIS Transformed Terrorism in Indonesia," *New York Times*, May 22, 2018.

101 Ryan Browne and Barbara Starr, "U.S. Military Official: 50 ISIS Foreign Fighters Captured Since November," CNN.com, December 12, 2017.

102 Edward Delman, "ISIS in the World's Largest Muslim Country," *The Atlantic*, January 3, 2016.

103 Richard C. Paddock, "He Aimed to Fight in Syria. ISIS Had a Broader Plan: Southeast Asia," *New York Times*, September 3, 2017.

104 Joseph Chinyong Liow, "IS in the Pacific: Assessing Terrorism in Southeast Asia and the Threat to the Homeland," testimony before the Subcommittee on Counterterrorism and Intelligence Committee on Homeland Security, House of Representatives, April 27, 2016.

105 Kirsten E. Schultze and Joseph Chinyong Liow, "Making Jihadis, Waging Jihad: Transnational and Local Dimensions of the ISIS Phenomenon in Indonesia and Malaysia," *Asian Security*, 2018: https://www.tandfonline.com/doi/abs/10.1080/14799855.2018.1 424710?journalCode=fasi20.

106 Nava Nuraniyah, "Migrant Maids and Nannies for Jihad," *New York Times*, July 18, 2017.

107 Patrick B. Johnston and Colin P. Clarke, "Is the Philippines the Next Caliphate?" *Foreign Policy*, November 28, 2017.

108 Felipe Villamor, "ISIS Threat in Philippines Spreads in Remote Battles," *New York Times*, October 23, 2017. See also James Griffiths, "ISIS in Southeast Asia. Philippines Battles Growing Threat," CNN.com, May 29, 2017.

109 Lindsay Murdoch, "Marawi Uprising Funded by $1.9 Million from Islamic State," *Sydney Morning Herald*, October 25, 2017.

110 Chandni Vatvani, "9 Suspected Terrorists Arrested in Indonesia," *Channel News Asia*, October 24, 2017.

111 Marielle Ness, "Beyond the Caliphate: Islamic State Activity Outside the Group's Defined Caliphate: Southeast Asia," *CTC Sentinel*, January 2018.

112 Will Edwards, "ISIS' Reach Extends to Southeast Asia," *The Cipher Brief*, August 20, 2017.

113 Email exchange with Zachary Abuza, July 2017.

114 Thomas M. Sanderson, "From the Ferghana Valley to Syria and Beyond: A Brief History of Central Asia Foreign Fighters," Center for Strategic and International Studies, January 5, 2018: https://www.csis.org/analysis/ferghana-valley-syria-and-beyond-brief-history-central-asian-foreign-fighters.

115 Svante Cornell, "Central Asia: Where Did Islamic Radicalization Go?" in Katya Migacheva and Bryan Frederick, eds., *Religion, Conflict, and Stability in the Former Soviet Union*, Santa Monica, CA: RAND Corp., 2018.

116 Mohammed S. Elshimi, "Understanding the Factors Contributing to Radicalisation among Central Asian Labour Migrants in Russia," RUSI Occasional Paper, April 2018: https://www.sfcg.org/wp-content/uploads/2018/04/RUSI-report_Central-Asia-Radicalisation_ENG_24042018.pdf.

117 Thomas F. Lynch III, Michael Bouffard, Kelsey King, and Graham Vickowski, "The Return of Foreign Fighters to Central Asia: Implications for U.S. Counterterrorism Policy," Center

for Strategic Research, Institute for National Strategic Studies, National Defense University, Strategic Perspectives No. 21, October 2016: http://inss.ndu.edu/Portals/68/Documents/strat perspective/inss/Strategic-Perspectives-21.pdf. See also Anna Dyner, Arkadiusz Legiec, and Kacper Rekawak, "Ready to Go? ISIS and Its Presumed Expansion into Central Asia," Polish Institute of International Affairs (PISM), Policy Paper No.19 (121), June 2015.

118 Goktung Sonmez, "Violent Extremism among Central Asians: The Istanbul, St. Petersburg, Stockholm, and New York City Attacks," *CTC Sentinel*, 10:11, December 2017. See also Andrew E. Kramer, "New York Turns Focus to Central Asian Militancy," *New York Times*, November 1, 2017; Sajjan Gohel, "How Uzbekistan Became Ripe Recruiting Territory for ISIS," CNN.com, November 1, 2017.

119 Kim Cragin, "Foreign Fighter 'Hot Potato,'" *Lawfare*, November 26, 2017.

120 Reid Standish, "'Our Future Will Be Violent Extremism,'" *Foreign Policy*, August 1, 2017.

121 Reid Standish, "Scenes from Central Asia's Forever War," *Foreign Policy*, August 7, 2017. See also "Kyrgyzstan: State Fragility and Radicalisation," International Crisis Group, October 3, 2016; and Bruce Pannier, "Are Central Asia's Militants Already Coming Home from the Middle East?" Radio Free Europe / Radio Liberty, May 25, 2018.

122 Eleanor Ross, "Why Extremist Groups are Gaining Strength in Central Asia," *Newsweek*, April 12, 2017. See also Thomas Joscelyn, "The Turkistan Islamic Party's Jihad in Syria," *FDD's Long War Journal*, July 10, 2018; and also Colin P. Clarke and Paul R. Kan, "Uighur Foreign Fighters: An Underexamined Jihadist Challenge," International Centre for Counter-Terrorism – The Hague (ICCT), Policy Brief 8, no. 5, 2017.

123 Jack Moore, "Russia Overtakes Saudi Arabia and Tunisia as Largest Exporter of ISIS Fighters," *Newsweek*, October 24, 2017.

124 Andrew S. Bowen, "ISIS Comes to Russia," *Daily Beast*, July 10, 2015.

125 Ekaterina Sokirianskaia, "Russia's North Caucasus Insurgency

Widens as ISIS' Foothold Grows," *World Politics Review*, April 12, 2016.

126 Colin P. Clarke, "How Russia Became the Jihadists' No. 1 Target," *Politico Magazine*, April 3, 2017.

127 John Campbell, "The Islamic State 'Presence' in the Sahel is More Complicated Than Affiliates Suggest," Council on Foreign Relations (CFR), June 1, 2018.

128 Jacob Wirtschafter and Karim John Gadiaga, "Africa Becomes the New Battleground for ISIS and al Qaeda as They Lose Ground in the Mideast," *USA Today*, October 25, 2017.

129 Wesley Morgan, "Behind the Secret U.S. War in Africa," *Politico*, July 2, 2018.

130 Jacob Zenn, "Boko Haram's Al Qaeda Affiliation: A Response to Five Myths about Boko Haram," *Lawfare*, February 1, 2018.

131 Ryan Browne, "US Wars of Growing African Terror Threat," CNN.com, April 19, 2018. The author is also thankful to Jason Warner for help with estimates of IS fighters in various African affiliates. Email exchanges with Jason Warner, July 2018.

132 Jason Warner and Caleb Weiss, "A Legitimate Challenger? Assessing the Rivalry between al-Shabaab and the Islamic State in Somalia," *CTC Sentinel*, 10:10, November 2017.

133 Jason Warner, "Sub-Saharan Africa's Three 'New' Islamic State Affiliates," *CTC Sentinel*, 10:1, January 2017.

134 Bennett Seftel, "Al Qaeda Thrives Across Weak West African States," *Cipher Brief*, September 14, 2017.

135 Cristina Maza, "ISIS and Al Qaeda Terrorists Increase Attacks on Western Targets in Africa, Report Reveals," *Newsweek*, February 26, 2018.

136 Caleb Weiss, "Al Qaeda Has Launched More Than 100 Attacks in West Africa in 2016," *FDD's Long War Journal*, June 8, 2016. See also Drew Hinshaw and Zoumana Wonogo, "Al Qaeda Attacks in Burkina Faso Kill At Least 30," *Wall Street Journal*, January 17, 2016.

137 Daveed Gartenstein-Ross, Jacob Zenn, Sarah Sheafer, and Sandro Bejdic, "Evolving Terror: The Development of Jihadist Operations

Targeting Western Interests in Africa," Foundation of Defense for Democracies, February 2018: https://www.thefdd.org/analy sis/2018/02/25/evolving-terror-the-development-of-jihadist-ope rations-targeting-western-interests-in-africa.

138 Yaroslav Trofimov, "In Somalia – or Afghanistan – Can Insurgent Defections Change a War's Course?" *Wall Street Journal*, February 8, 2018.

139 Sunguta West, "The Resurgence of al-Shabaab," Jamestown Foundation, Terrorism Monitor, February 8, 2018: https://james-town.org/program/resurgence-al-shabaab.

140 Rukmini Callimachi, "Al-Qaeda Backed Group Has a New Target: Plastic Bags," *New York Times*, July 4, 2018.

141 Warner and Weiss, "A Legitimate Challenger?"

142 Jason Warner and Ellen Chapin, "Targeted Terror: The Suicide Bombers of al-Shabaab," Combating Terrorism Center, February 13, 2018: https://ctc.usma.edu/targeted-terror-suicide-bombers-al-shabaab. Despite this massive death toll, Warner and Chapin's detailed analysis concluded that the attacks actually attempt to avoid targeting non-combatant civilians.

143 Tricia Bacon, "This is Why al-Shabaab Won't Be Going Away Any Time Soon," *Washington Post* Monkey Cage Blog, July 6, 2017.

144 Daisy Muibu and Benjamin P. Nickels, "Foreign Technology or Local Expertise? Al-Shabaab's IED Capability," *CTC Sentinel*, 10:10, November 2017.

145 "The Fight Against the Islamic State is Moving to Africa," *The Economist*, July 14, 2018.

146 Clayton Thomas, "Al Qaeda and U.S. Policy: Middle East and Africa," Congressional Research Service (CRS) Report R43756, February 5, 2018.

147 Olivier Monnier, "Islamic State, al Qaeda Support Fuels Attacks in West Africa," *Bloomberg*, February 5, 2018.

148 "The Social Roots of Jihadist Violence in Burkina Faso's North," International Crisis Group, Report No. 254, October 12, 2017: https://www.crisisgroup.org/africa/west-africa/burkina-faso/254 -social-roots-jihadist-violence-burkina-fasos-north.

149 Caleb Weiss, "Al Qaeda Branch in Mali Claims Burkina Faso Attacks," *FDD's Long War Journal*, March 3, 2018.

150 Jacob Zenn, "Demystifying al Qaeda in Nigeria: Cases from Boko Haram's Founding, Launch of Jihad and Suicide Bombings," *Perspectives on Terrorism*, 11:6, 2017.

151 "IS Affiliate Establishes Stronghold in West Africa," Reuters, April 29, 2018.

152 John Vandiver, "ISIS, Routed in Iraq and Syria, is Quietly Gaining Strength in Africa," *Stars and Stripes*, February 17, 2018.

153 Helene Cooper, "Boko Haram and ISIS Are Collaborating More, U.S. Military Says," *New York Times*, April 20, 2016.

154 Carla Babb, "Congressman Says Africa Next 'Hot Spot' for Islamic State," *VOA News*, December 7, 2017.

155 International Centre for Counter-Terrorism (ICCT) – The Hague, "Foreign Fighters Phenomenon in the EU: Profiles, Threats and Policies," 2016: https://icct.nl/publication/report-the-foreign-fighters-phenomenon-in-the-eu-profiles-threats-policies.

156 Vidino et al., *Fear Thy Neighbor*, pp. 15–16.

157 Marc Hecker and Elie Tenenbaum, "France vs. Jihadism: The Republic in a New Age of Terror," IFRI, January 2017: https://www.ifri.org/en/publications/notes-de-lifri/notes-de-lifri/france-vs-jihadism-republic-new-age-terror.

158 William McCants and Christopher Meserole, "The French Connection," *Foreign Affairs*, March 24, 2016: https://www.foreignaffairs.com/articles/2016-03-24/french-connection.

159 Conrad Hackett, "5 Facts About the Muslim Population in Europe," Pew Research Center, November 29, 2017.

160 Gilles Kepel, Tamara Cofman Wittes, and Matthew Levitt, "The Rise of Jihad in Europe: Views from France," Washington Institute for Near East Policy, PolicyWatch 2806, May 19, 2017: https://www.washingtoninstitute.org/policy-analysis/view/the-rise-of-jihad-in-europe-views-from-france.

161 Laurence Peter, "How France is Wrestling with Jihadist Terror," *BBC News*, July 28, 2016.

162 Mitch Prothero, "Their Parents Fought with ISIS. Now France is

Trying to Figure Out What to Do with Them," Buzzfeed, February 19, 2018.

163 Fidelma Cook and Jake Wallis Simons, "Jihadi Capital of France," *Daily Mail*, November 18, 2015.

164 George Heil, "The Berlin Attack and the 'Abu Walaa' Islamic State Recruitment Network," *CTC Sentinel*, 10:2, February 2017.

165 Daniel H. Heinke, "German Foreign Fighters in Syria and Iraq: The Updated Data and Its Implications," *CTC Sentinel*, 10:3, March 2017.

166 Caroline Copley and Madeline Chambers, "Germany Bans Islamist 'True Religion' Group, Raiding Mosques and Flats," Reuters, November 15, 2016.

167 "Germany Terrorism Prosecution Cases Soar," *Deutsche Welle*, October 22, 2017.

168 Jamie Dettmer, "Germany Alarmed by 'Kindergarten Jihadists,'" *VOA News*, February 2, 2018.

169 Liam Stack, "Terrorist Attacks in Britain: A Short History," *New York Times*, June 4, 2017.

170 Alexander Meleagrou-Hitchens and Seamus Hughes, "The Threat to the United States from the Islamic State's Virtual Entrepreneurs," *CTC Sentinel*, 10:3, March 2017; see also "Who Are Britain's Jihadists?" *BBC News*, October 12, 2017.

171 Michael Kenney, Stephen Coulthart, and Dominick Wright, "Structure and Performance in a Violent Extremist Network," *Journal of Conflict Resolution*, 61:10, 2017, pp. 2208–34.

172 Email exchange with Michael Kenney, June 2018.

173 Lizzie Dearden, "UK Home to Up to 25,000 Islamist Extremists Who Could Pose a Threat, EU Official Warns," *Independent*, September 1, 2017.

174 Michael Holden, "Teacher Tried to Create 'Army of Children' to Launch Terror Attacks in London," Reuters UK, March 2, 2018.

175 Aaron Williams, Kaeit Hinck, Laris Karklis, Kevin Schaul, and Stephanie Stamm, "How Two Brussels Neighborhoods Became a 'Breeding Ground' for Terror," *Washington Post*, April 1, 2016.

176 Paul Cruickshank, "The Inside Story of the Paris and Brussels Attacks," CNN.com, October 30, 2017.

177 Pieter Van Ostaeyen, "Belgian Radical Networks and the Road to the Brussels Attacks," *CTC Sentinel*, 9:6, June 2016.

178 By some accounts, Zerkani was responsible for convincing more than 60 young men to go to fight in Iraq and Syria; see Guy Van Vlierden, "Molenbeek and Beyond. The Brussels Antwerp Axis as Hotbed of Belgian Jihad," in Arturo Varvelli, ed., *Jihadist Hotbeds: Understanding Local Radicalization Processes*, Milan: Italian Institute for International Political Studies (ISPI), 2016.

179 Rik Coolsaet, "Facing the Fourth Foreign Fighters Wave: What Drives Europeans to Syria, and to Islamic State? Insights from the Belgian Case," Egmont Institute, Egmont Paper 81, March 2016, p. 8: www.egmontinstitute.be/facing-the-fourth-foreign-fighters-wave.

180 Teun Voeten, "Molenbeek Broke My Heart," *Politico*, March 23, 2016.

181 Matthew Levitt, "My Journey to Brussels' Terrorist Safe Haven," *Politico*, March 27, 2016.

182 Cynthia Kroet, "Belgium's Molenbeek Home to 51 Groups with Terror Link: Report," *Politico*, March 20, 2017.

183 Thomas Renard and Rik Coolsaet, "Reassessing Belgium's 'Failed' Counterterrorism Policy," *Lawfare*, March 22, 2018. See also Rik Coolsaet and Thomas Renard, "Returnees: Who Are They, Why Are They (Not) Coming Back and How Should We Deal with Them? Assessing Policies on Returning Foreign Terrorist Fighters in Belgium, Germany, and The Netherlands," Egmont Institute, February 6, 2018.

4 From "Remain and Expand" to Survive and Persist

1 Jonathan Spyer, "Welcome to Syria 2.0," *Foreign Policy*, January 25, 2018.

2 Colin P. Clarke, "How ISIS is Transforming," *Foreign Affairs*, September 25, 2017.

3 "Experts: ISIS Still Capable of Recapturing Iraqi Areas," *Ahsarq Al-Awsat*, January 19, 2018.

4 Jones et al., *Rolling Back the Islamic State*.

5 Sune Engel Rasmussen, Nour Alakraa, and Nancy A. Youssef, "ISIS Remnants Fight On, Despite U.S. Campaign," *Wall Street Journal*, July 9, 2018.

6 Rhys Dubin, "ISIS 2.0 is Really Just the Original ISIS," *Foreign Policy*, April 3, 2018.

7 Johnston et al., *Foundations of the Islamic State*.

8 Raja Abdulrahim, "Islamic State Returns to Guerrilla Warfare in Iraq and Syria," *Wall Street Journal*, January 2, 2018. See also Eric Schmitt, "The Hunt for ISIS Pivots to Remaining Pockets of Syria," *New York Times*, December 24, 2017.

9 Hassan Hassan, "Insurgents Again: The Islamic State's Calculated Reversion to Attrition in the Syria–Iraq Border Region and Beyond," *CTC Sentinel*, 10:11, December 2017.

10 Hassan Hassan, "Down but Not Out: ISIL Will Regroup and Rise Again," *The National*, December 25, 2017.

11 Benjamin Bahney and Patrick B. Johnston, "ISIS Could Rise Again," *Foreign Affairs*, December 15, 2017.

12 Borzou Daraghi, "After the Black Flags of ISIS, Iraq Now Faces the White Flags," Buzzfeed, April 1, 2018.

13 Qassim Abdul-Zahra and Susannah George, "Islamic State Haunts Northern Iraq Months After Its Defeat," Associated Press, March 28, 2018. See also "Islamic State Regrouping in Iraqi, Disputed Kurdish Territories," *VOA News*, March 26, 2018.

14 Hassan Hassan, "ISIL Sleeper Cells in Iraq Are a Warning Sign the Extremist Group is Already Reforming," *The National*, March 28, 2018.

15 Vera Bergengruen, "Trump Keeps Saying ISIS Has Been Defeated. But the U.S. Military Says It's Gaining Ground," Buzzfeed, April 17, 2018. See also Hassan Hassan, "ISIS is Ready for a Resurgence," *The Atlantic*, August 26, 2018.

16 Shiraz Maher, "Islamic State is Not Beaten and Will Return," *New Statesmen*, October 17, 2017. See also Sune Engel Rasmussen,

"Online Propaganda Builds Islamic State Brand in the Face of Military Losses," *Wall Street Journal*, August 26, 2018.

17 Sune Engel Rasmussen, "Islamic State Leader Emerges in Audio Message," *Wall Street Journal*, August 22, 2018. See also Hassan, "ISIS is Ready for a Resurgence."

18 Hassan Hassan, "Zawahiri's Statements Reveal Plenty About Syria's Fractured Jihadi Scene," *The National*, November 29, 2017,

19 Charles Lister, "New Opportunities for ISIS and Al Qaeda," in Paul Salem, Bilal Y. Saab, Alex Vatanka, et al., "2018 Middle East Preview: What to Expect," Middle East Institute, January 8, 2018.

20 Gareth Browne, "Al Qaeda's 'Re-Radicalisation' Schools Lure ISIL Fighters in Syria," *The National*, January 20, 2018.

21 Daniel L. Byman, "The Middle East After the Defeat of the Islamic State," Brookings Institution, March 28, 2018: https://www.brookings.edu/blog/order-from-chaos/2018/03/28/the-middle-east-after-the-defeat-of-the-islamic-state.

22 Jones, *Waging Insurgent Warfare*, pp. 18–19.

23 Assaf Moghadam, *Nexus of Global Jihad: Understanding Cooperation Among Terrorist Actors*, New York: Columbia University Press, 2017, p. 168.

24 Christoph Reuter, "'Liberated Areas' of Iraq Still Terrorized By Violence," *Der Spiegel*, March 21, 2018.

25 Sirwan Kajjo, "ISIS: Surging in Syria Again," Gatestone Institute International Policy Council, March 27, 2018: https://www.gatestoneinstitute.org/12097/isis-surging-syria.

26 Rhys Dubin, "Coalition Analysis Warns of Potential Islamic State Resurgence," *Foreign Policy*, January 10, 2018.

27 Michael R. Gordon, "Areas Newly Seized from ISIS Seen at Risk of Backsliding," *Wall Street Journal*, December 12, 2017.

28 Erika Solomon and Asser Khattab, "ISIS 'Far from Finished' as Jihadi Fighters Regroup in Syria," *Financial Times*, February 3, 2018.

29 Jeff Seldin, "IS Fighters Fleeing to Assad-controlled Parts of Syria," *VOA News*, December 27, 2017.

30 Shelly Culbertson and Linda Robinson, *Making Victory Count*

After Defeating ISIS: Stabilization Challenges in Mosul and Beyond, Santa Monica, CA: RAND Corp., 2017.

31 Tamer El-Ghobashy, Mustafa Salim, and Louisa Loveluck, "Islamic State's 'Caliphate' Has Been Toppled in Iraq and Syria. Why Isn't Anyone Celebrating?" *Washington Post,* December 5, 2017.

32 Hassan Hassan and William McCants, "Is ISIS Good at Governing?" Brookings Institution, April 18, 2016: https://www.brookings.edu/blog/markaz/2016/04/18/experts-weigh-in-part-7-is-isis-good-at-governing.

33 Joby Warrick, Will McCants, and Aaron Y. Zelin, "The Rise of ISIS: 'Remaining and Expanding,'" The Washington Institute for Near East Policy, PolicyWatch 2522, November 12, 2015.

34 Email exchange with Haroro Ingram, August 2018.

35 Daniel L. Byman, "Comparing Al Qaeda and ISIS: Different Goals, Different Targets," prepared testimony before the Subcommittee on Counterterrorism and Intelligence of the House Committee on Homeland Security, House of Representatives, April 29, 2015.

36 Clarke and Ingram, "Defeating the ISIS Nostalgia Narrative."

37 Email exchange with Craig Whiteside, August 2018.

38 Colin Clarke and Daveed Gartenstein-Ross, "How Will Jihadist Strategy Evolve as the Islamic State Declines?" *War on the Rocks,* November 10, 2016.

39 Daniel Byman, "Divisions Within the Global Jihad," *Lawfare,* September 29, 2017.

40 Robin Wright, "After the Islamic State," *New Yorker,* December 12, 2016.

41 Tore Refslund Hamming, "Jihadi Competition and Political Preferences," *Perspectives on Terrorism,* 11:6, 2017.

42 Moghadam, "How Al Qaeda Innovates," pp. 466–97.

43 Daveed Gartenstein-Ross, "The Manchester Attack Shows How Terrorists Learn," *The Atlantic,* May 23, 2017.

44 Bridget Moreng, "ISIS' Virtual Puppeteers," *Foreign Affairs,* September 21, 2016; see also Clint Watts, "Inspired, Networked &

Directed – The Muddled Jihad of IS & Al Qaeda Post Hebdo," *War on the Rocks*, January 12, 2015.

45 Daveed Gartenstein-Ross and Madeline Blackman, "ISIL's Virtual Planners: A Critical Terrorist Innovation," *War on the Rocks*, January 4, 2017.

46 Rukmini Callimachi, "Not 'Lone Wolves' After All: How ISIS Guides World's Terror Plots from Afar," *New York Times*, February 4, 2017.

47 R. Kim Cragin and Ari Weil, "'Virtual Planners' in the Arsenal of Islamic State External Operations," *Orbis*, 62:2, 2018, pp. 294–312.

48 R. Kim Cragin, "The November 2015 Paris Attacks: The Impact of Foreign Fighter Returnees," *Orbis*, 61:2, 2017, pp. 212–26. See also R. Kim Cragin, "The Challenge of Foreign Fighter Returnees," *Journal of Contemporary Criminal Justice*, 33:3, 2017, pp. 292–312.

49 Seth G. Jones, "Will Al Qaeda Make a Comeback?" *Foreign Affairs*, August 7, 2017.

50 Clarke, "The Moderate Face of Al Qaeda."

51 Tore Refslund Hamming, "The Al Qaeda – Islamic State Rivalry: Competition Yes, but No Competitive Escalation," *Terrorism and Political Violence*, 2017, p. 3. Salafi characterizes an adherent of an ideological strain in Sunni Islam that seeks to emulate, as purer, the thinking and practices of Muhammad and the earliest generations of Muslims. Jihadists believe that violent struggle against non-Muslims and Muslims they judge as apostate is an important religious duty (Bahney et al., *An Economic Analysis of the Financial Records of al-Qa'ida in Iraq*).

52 Cole Bunzel, "Jihadism on Its Own Terms," Hoover Institution, May 17, 2017: https://www.hoover.org/research/jihadism-its -own-terms.

53 Rik Coolsaet, "Anticipating the Post-Daesh Landscape," Egmont Paper 97, October 2017, p. 9: http://www.egmontinstitute.be/ anticipating-post-daesh-landscape.

54 Hassan, "The Sectarianism of the Islamic State."

55 Thomas Joscelyn, "Islamic State Rescinds One of Its Most

Problematic Religious Rulings," *FDD's Long War Journal*, September 20, 2017.

56 Cole Bunzel, "A House Divided: Origins and Persistence of the Islamic State's Ideological Divide," *Jihadica*, June 5, 2018.

57 R. Green, "Dispute Over Takfir Rocks Islamic State," *MEMRI*, August 4, 2017.

58 Tore Hamming, "The Extremist Wing of the Islamic State," *Jihadica*, June 9, 2016.

59 Byman, "Divisions Within the Global Jihad."

60 Daveed Gartenstein-Ross, Jason Fritz, Bridget Moreng, and Nathaniel Barr, "Islamic State vs. Al Qaeda," New America Foundation, December 4, 2015: https://static.newamerica.org/attachments/12103-islamic-state-vs-al-qaeda/ISISvAQ_Final.e68 fdd22a90e49c4af1d4cd0dc9e3651.pdf.

61 Hamming, "The Al Qaeda – Islamic State Rivalry: Competition Yes, but No Competitive Escalation," fn. 65.

62 Daveed Gartenstein-Ross and Nathaniel Barr, "How Al Qaeda Survived the Islamic State Challenge," Hudson Institute, March 1, 2017: https://www.hudson.org/research/12788-how-al-qaeda-survived-the-islamic-state-challenge.

63 Matthew Phillips and Matthew Valasik, "The Islamic State is More Like a Street Gang Than Like Other Terrorist Groups," *Washington Post* Monkey Cage Blog, November 15, 2017.

64 Colin P. Clarke, "Al Qaeda in Syria Can Change Its Name, But Not Its Stripes," *The Cipher Brief*, March 23, 2017.

65 Charles Lister, "US Officials Just Mislabeled a Syrian Terror Group as al Qaeda. Worse, They're Missing a Far Bigger Threat," *Defense One*, June 1, 2018.

66 Email exchange with Hassan Hassan, August 2018.

67 Clarke, "The Moderate Face of Al Qaeda."

68 Colin P. Clarke, "Expanding the ISIS Brand," *The National Interest*, February 17, 2018.

69 Rukmini Callimachi, "Protest of U.S. Terror Listing Offers a Glimpse of Qaeda Strategy," *New York Times*, November 17, 2016; see also Daveed Gartenstein-Ross and Thomas Joscelyn,

"Rebranding Terror," *Foreign Affairs*, August 28, 2016; and Daveed Gartenstein-Ross and Nathaniel Barr, "Extreme Makeover, Jihadist Edition: Al Qaeda's Rebranding Campaign," *War on the Rocks*, September 3, 2015.

70 Colin P. Clarke and Barak Mendelsohn, "Al Qaeda's Ruthless Pragmatism Makes It More Dangerous Than the Islamic State," Reuters, October 27, 2016.

71 The author is thankful to Bruce Hoffman for this observation.

72 Colin P. Clarke and Chad C. Serena, "Why Syria's War May Be About to Get Even Worse," Reuters, August 25, 2016.

73 Bruce Hoffman, "Al Qaeda's Master Plan," *The Cipher Brief*, November 18, 2015.

74 Eric Schmitt and David E. Sanger, "As U.S. Focuses on ISIS and the Taliban, Al Qaeda Re-emerges," *New York Times*, December 29, 2015.

75 Bruce Hoffman, "Al Qaeda: Quietly and Patiently Rebuilding," *The Cipher Brief*, December 30, 2016.

76 Gartenstein-Ross and Barr, "How Al Qaeda Survived the Islamic State Challenge."

77 The Soufan Center, "The Forgotten War: The Ongoing Disaster in Yemen," June 2018: http://thesoufancenter.org/research/the-forgotten-war-the-ongoing-disaster-in-yemen.

78 Bruce Hoffman, "The Global Terror Threat and Counterterrorism Challenges Facing the Next Administration," *CTC Sentinel*, 9:11, December 2016.

79 Andrew H. Kydd and Barbara F. Walter, "The Strategies of Terrorism," *International Security*, 31:1, Summer 2006, pp. 49–80.

80 Bruce Hoffman, "The Coming ISIS–Al Qaeda Merger: It's Time to Take the Threat Seriously," *Foreign Affairs*, March 29, 2016.

81 Bruce Hoffman, "A Growing Terrorist Threat on Another 9/11," *Wall Street Journal*, September 8, 2017.

82 Assaf Moghadam, "Marriage of Convenience: The Evolution of Iran and al Qaeda's Tactical Cooperation," *CTC Sentinel*, 10:4, April 2017. See also Adrian Levy and Cathy Scott-Clark, "Al Qaeda

Has Rebuilt Itself – With Iran's Help," *The Atlantic*, November 11, 2017.

83 Email exchange with Hassan Hassan, August 2018.

84 Email exchange with Seth G. Jones, July 2018.

85 Email exchange with Bruce Hoffman, July 2018.

86 Tore Refslund Hamming, "With Islamic State in Decline, What's Al Qaeda's Next Move?" *War on the Rocks*, April 27, 2018.

87 Bruce Hoffman, "Al Qaeda's Resurrection," Council on Foreign Relations, March 6, 2018: https://www.cfr.org/expert-brief/al-qaedas-resurrection.

5 After the Caliphate: Preventing the Islamic State's Return

1 Seth G. Jones, Charles Vallee, Nicholas Harrington, and Hannah Byrne, "The Evolving Terrorist Threat: The Changing Nature of the Islamic State, Al-Qaeda, and Other Salafi-Jihadist Groups," Center for Strategic and International Studies: https://www.isis.org/analysis/evolution-salafi-jihadist-threat.

2 Rukmini Callimachi, "ISIS Leader Baghdadi Resurfaces in Recording," *New York Times*, August 22, 2018.

3 Lorne L. Dawson, "The Demise of the Islamic State and the Fate of Its Western Foreign Fighters: Six Things to Consider," International Centre for Counter-Terrorism – The Hague (ICCT), ICCT Policy Brief, June 2018, p. 4.

4 R. Kim Cragin has argued that, contrary to popular belief, most foreign fighters do not die on battlefields or travel from conflict to conflict, but return home. See Cragin, "The Challenge of Foreign Fighter Returnees."

5 Alastair Reed and Johanna Pohl, "Disentangling the EU Foreign Fighter Threat: The Case for a Comprehensive Approach," *RUSI*, February 10, 2017.

6 Simon Cottee, "Pilgrims to the Islamic State," *The Atlantic*, July 24, 2015.

7 Jessica Stern and J. M. Berger, "ISIS and the Foreign Fighter Phenomenon," *The Atlantic*, March 8, 2015.

8 See Callimachi, "Not 'Lone Wolves' After All"; see also Gartenstein-Ross and Blackman, "ISIL's Virtual Planners"; and Alexander Meleagrou-Hitchens and Seamus Hughes, "The Threat to the United States from the Islamic State's Virtual Entrepreneurs," *CTC Sentinel*, 10: 3, March 2017, pp. 1–8.

9 Thomas Hegghammer, "Should I Stay or Should I Go? Explaining Variation in Western Jihadists' Choice between Domestic and Foreign Fighting," *American Political Science Review*, 107:1, February 2013, pp. 1–15.

10 Cragin, "The November 2015 Paris Attacks," pp. 212–26.

11 Callimachi, "How a Secretive Branch of ISIS Built a Global Network of Killers"; see also Hoffman, "The Global Terror Threat and Counterterrorism Challenges Facing the Next Administration."

12 Daniel Byman, "Where Will the Islamic State Go Next?" *Lawfare*, June 22, 2018.

13 United Nations Security Council Counter-Terrorism Committee Executive Directorate (CTED), "The Challenge of Returning and Relocating Foreign Terrorist Fighters: Research Perspectives," April 2018.

14 Radicalisation Awareness Network (RAN) Manual, "Responses to Returnees: Foreign Terrorist Fighters and Their Families," July 2017.

15 "Belgian Investigators Shed Light on Liège Gunman as IS Group Claims Attack," *France 24*, May 30, 2018.

16 Robin Wright, "ISIS Jihadis Have Returned Home by the Thousands," *New Yorker*, October 23, 2017.

17 Yolande Knell, "Inside the Iraqi Courts Sentencing IS Suspects to Death," *BBC News*, September 2, 2017.

18 Will Worley, "At Least 100 European ISIS Fighters 'To Be Prosecuted in Iraq, With Most Facing Death Penalty,'" *Independent*, October 7, 2017.

19 Tanya Mehra, "Bringing (Foreign) Terrorist Fighters to Justice in a Post-ISIS Landscape Part I: Prosecution by Iraqi and Syrian Courts," International Centre for Counter-Terrorism – The Hague (ICCT), December 22, 2017.

20 Hollie McKay, "Syrian Opposition, Out of Jail Space, Fears Threat of Released ISIS Prisoners," *Fox News*, May 29, 2018.

21 Eric Schmitt, "Battle to Stamp Out ISIS in Syria Gains New Momentum, but Threats Remain," *New York Times*, May 30, 2018.

22 Tanya Mehra, "Bringing (Foreign) Terrorist Fighters to Justice in a Post-ISIS Landscape Part II: Prosecution by National Courts," International Centre for Counter-Terrorism – The Hague, January 12, 2018.

23 Jenna Consigli, "Prosecuting the Islamic State Fighters Left Behind," *Lawfare*, August 1, 2018.

24 Margaret Coker and Falih Hassan, "A 10-Minute Trial, a Death Sentence: Iraqi Justice for Iraqi Suspects," *New York Times*, April 17, 2018.

25 Alissa J. Rubin, "She Left France to Fight in Syria. Now She Wants to Return. But Can She?" *New York Times*, January 11, 2018.

26 Ben Hubbard, "Wives and Children of ISIS: Warehoused in Syria, Unwanted Back Home," *New York Times*, July 4, 2018.

27 Jamie Grierson and Caelainn Barr, "Police Facing Surge in Extremists Released from Jail, Analysis Finds," *Guardian*, June 3, 2018.

28 Anthony Loyd, "A Close Encounter with British ISIS Jihadis," *New Statesman*, June 20, 2018.

29 Paul Sonne, Devlin Barrett, and Ellen Nakashima, "U.S. and Britain Are Divided Over What to Do with Captured IS Fighters," *Washington Post*, February 14, 2018.

30 Kevin Baron, "US-Backed Syrian Force Holding 'Hundreds' of Foreign Fighters," *Defense One*, February 1, 2018.

31 Tanya Mehra, "Bringing (Foreign) Terrorist Fighters to Justice in a Post-ISIS Landscape Part III: Collecting Evidence from Conflict Situations," International Centre for Counter-Terrorism – The Hague, June 12, 2018.

32 Christophe Paulussen and Kate Pitcher, "Prosecuting (Potential) Foreign Fighters: Legislative and Practical Challenges," International Centre for Counter-Terrorism – The Hague (ICCT), ICCT Research Paper, January 2018.

33 Department of Justice, Office of Public Affairs, "Former Iraqi Terrorists Living in Kentucky Sentenced for Terrorist Activities," Press Release, January 29, 2013.

34 Georgia Holmer and Adrian Shtuni, "Returning Foreign Fighters and the Reintegration Imperative," United States Institute for Peace (USIP), Special Report 402, March 2017.

35 Georgia Holmer, "What to Do When Foreign Fighters Come Home," *Foreign Policy*, June 1, 2015.

36 Arsla Jawaid, "From Foreign Fighters to Returnees: The Challenges of Rehabilitation and Reintegration Policies," *Journal of Peacebuilding and Development*, 12:2, 2017, pp. 102–7; see also Andrew Higgins, "For Jihadists, Denmark Tries Rehabilitation," *New York Times*, December 13, 2014.

37 Lucy Williamson, "How France Hopes to Help Radicals Escape Jihadist Net," *BBC News*, February 28, 2018.

38 Fabian Merz, "Dealing with Jihadist Returnees: A Tough Challenge," Center for Security Studies (CSS), Report no. 210, June 2018.

39 "How Belgium Copes with Returning Islamic State Fighters," *The Economist*, December 19, 2017.

40 Charles Lister, "Returning Foreign Fighters: Criminalization or Reintegration?" Brookings Institution Policy Briefing, August 2015.

41 Jessica Trisko Darden, "Compounding Violent Extremism? When Efforts to Prevent Violence Fail," *War on the Rocks*, June 6, 2018.

42 Humera Khan, "Why Countering Extremism Fails," *Foreign Affairs*, February 18, 2015.

43 Walle Bos et al., "Capacity-Building Challenges: Identifying Progress and Remaining Gaps in Dealing with Foreign (Terrorist) Fighters," International Centre for Counter-Terrorism – The Hague (ICCT), ICCT Policy Brief, May 2018.

44 Dipesh Gadher, "Generation Jihad: The British Children Brutalised by Terror," *The Times*, March 25, 2018.

45 Kinana Qaddour, "ISIS's War on Families Never Ended," *Foreign Policy*, February 1, 2018.

46 Jacob Olidort, "Inside the Caliphate's Classroom: Textbooks, Guidance Literature, and Indoctrination Methods of the Islamic State," The Washington Institute for Near East Policy, Policy Focus 147, August 2016.

47 Clarke and Ingram, "Defeating the ISIS Nostalgia Narrative."

48 Robin Simcox, "Children of the Caliphate: Victims or Threat?" *Lawfare*, December 10, 2017.

49 Joana Cook and Gina Vale, "From Daesh to 'Diaspora': Tracing the Women and Minors of Islamic State," International Centre for the Study of Radicalisation (ISCR), 2018.

50 Liesbeth van der Heide and Jip Geenen, "Children of the Caliphate: Young IS Returnees and the Reintegration Challenge," International Centre for Counter-Terrorism – The Hague (ICCT), ICCT Research Paper, August 2017.

51 Patrick B. Johnston, "Does Decapitation Work? Assessing the Effectiveness of Leadership Targeting in Counterinsurgency Campaigns," *International Security*, 36:4, Spring 2012, pp. 47–79.

52 Ben Connable and Martin C. Libicki, *How Insurgencies End*, Santa Monica, CA: RAND Corp., 2010.

53 Eric Schmitt, "ISIS May Be Waning, But Global Threats of Terrorism Continue to Spread," *New York Times*, July 6, 2018.

54 Anne Gearan and Dan Lamothe, "From Iraq to Syria, Splinter Groups Now Larger Worry Than Al Qaeda," *Washington Post*, June 10, 2014.

55 Audrey Kurth Cronin, "How al Qaeda Ends: The Decline and Demise of Terrorist Groups," *International Security*, 31:1, Summer 2006, pp. 7–48.

56 Jonathan Powell, "Negotiate with ISIS," *The Atlantic*, December 7, 2015.

57 Brian Michael Jenkins and Colin P. Clarke, "In the Event of the Islamic State's Untimely Demise . . .," *Foreign Policy*, May 11, 2016.

58 Email exchange with Daveed Gartenstein-Ross, August 2018.

59 Coolsaet, "Anticipating the Post-Daesh Landscape," p. 22.

60 Berenice Boutin, "Administrative Measures against Foreign

Fighters: In Search of Limits and Safeguards," International Centre for Counter-Terrorism – The Hague (ICCT), December 16, 2016.

61 Daniel Byman, "Frustrated Foreign Fighters," Brookings Institution, July 13, 2017.

62 Andrew Liepman and Colin P. Clarke, "Demystifying the Islamic State," *U.S. News & World Report*, August 19, 2016.

Index

Abaaoud, Abdelhamid 57, 103
al-Abadi, Haider 155
Abdeslam, Salah 56
ABM (Ansar Bait al-Maqdis) 73
Abu Sayyaf Group (ASG) 4, 24, 88,
    90, 91
al-Adnani, Abu Muhammad
    59
affiliate groups 125, 126
  Algeria 33
  al-Shabaab 95, 97
  AQAP 35, 73
  AQI 14
  Boko Haram 95
  counterterrorism 72
  existing jihadi groups 29–30
  Iraq 31–2
  ISKP 77
  Kashmir 87
  Libya 80, 81–2
  networks 13–14, 54
  North Africa 34
  relocation 2, 5, 6, 151
  Sinai Peninsula 73, 74
  al-Suri 108
  Syria 39–40, 119
  Yemen 36, 73
  al-Zarqawi 118
  see also franchise operations;
    splinter groups
Afghan Arabs 3, 137
Afghanistan
  al-Qaeda 3–4, 25, 27
  bin Laden 10, 137

deradicalization 147
foreign fighters 10
global jihadism 24
Islamic State 29, 52, 70, 71
jihadism 6, 78
Shiite Muslims 76–7
Taliban 24, 76
USA 4, 29, 78–9
wars of attrition 22
  see also Soviet-Afghan War
AFPAK (Afghanistan and Pakistan)
    76–9
Africa 94–6
  see also East Africa; North Africa;
    Sub-Saharan Africa; West Africa;
    specific countries
African Union Mission in Somalia
    (AMISOM) 38, 96
AFRICOM (US African Command)
    95, 98
Afwaj al-Muqawama al-Lubnaniya
    (AMAL) 151–2
AIAI (al-Itihaad al-Islamiya) 36
airline attacks 35
Alawites 60
Aleppo 50, 111
Algeria 25
  affiliate groups 33
  al-Qaeda 29, 30, 33–4
  AQIM 33, 34
  foreigners targeted 97
  GIA 32
  GSPC 30
  Islamic State 70, 80

Algeria (*cont.*)
  jihadism 6
  splinter groups 152
al-Qaeda 11–12, 13–14, 160–1n2
  Afghanistan 3–4, 25, 27
  Algeria 29, 30, 33–4
  alliances 21–2
  and al-Shabaab 4, 14, 30
  Arab Spring 124, 131–2
  bin Laden ix, x, xi, 22
  Constitutional Charter 19
  core 39–40
  expansion 29–30, 129–30
  financial infrastructure 25–6
  franchise operations 4–5, 21–2
  future developments 129–33
  ideology 128, 132
  insurgency 21–2
  Iraq 29, 31–2, 63
  and Islamic State x, xii, 7–8, 109,
    115–16, 117–29, 132
  networks 19, 38, 61–2
  organizational structure 23–6,
    61–4
  propaganda 46
  rebranding 120–1
  rebuilding 132–3
  Salafi-jihadism 3, 11, 13, 127–9
  Shiite Muslims 122–3
  Somalia 3–4, 29
  strategic decision-making
    20–2
  Syria xi, 119–21, 123, 125, 154
  tactics 114–15, 117, 124
  Yemen xi, 4–5, 29, 34–6, 84, 85,
    121, 124
  see also affiliate groups; franchise
    operations; splinter groups; al-
    Zawahiri
al-Qaeda in Iraq: *see* AQI
al-Qaeda in the Arabian Peninsula:
  see AQAP
al-Qaeda in the Indian Subcontinent
  (AQIS) 87, 190n93
al-Qaeda in the Islamic Maghreb: *see*
  AQIM

al-Shabaab
  affiliate groups 95, 97
  and al-Qaeda 4, 14, 30
  Somalia 14, 30, 36–8, 95
  splinter groups 95, 151
  suicide bombings 96–7
  violence 96–7, 195n142
AMAL (Afwaj al-Muqawama al-
  Lubnaniya) 151–2
ambushes 5, 28, 40, 72, 107
AMISOM (African Union Mission in
  Somalia) 38, 96
Amri, Anis 57, 101
Anas, Abdullah 10
al-Anbari, Adnan 58
Ansar Bait al-Maqdis (ABM) 73
Ansar Dine 14, 95
Ansar Sharia 124
Ansar al-Sharia Libya 14, 80
Ansaru 95
antiquities smuggling 42, 43
apostasy 60, 116
apostate regimes 16, 24, 67, 113, 122
apps 5, 67
AQAP (al-Qaeda in the Arabian
  Peninsula)
  affiliated 35, 73
  as franchise 4, 14, 30
  and Islamic State 97
  Yemen 35–6, 60, 73–4, 83–4
  al-Zawahiri 35–6
AQI (al-Qaeda in Iraq)
  as affiliate 14
  as franchise 4, 30
  and Islamic State 39, 154
  and MSC 167n89
  sectarianism 32, 119
  Shiite Muslims 30
  split 60
  and TWJ 32
  al-Zarqawi 56, 62–3, 106
  al-Zawahiri 119
AQIM (al-Qaeda in the Islamic
  Maghreb) 32
  as affiliate 14
  Algeria 33, 34

Boko Haram 95
criminal activities 34
as franchise 4, 30, 36
Libya 80
AQIS (al-Qaeda in the Indian
Subcontinent) 87, 190n93
Arab Spring xi, 39, 72, 117, 124,
131–2
Armed Islamic Group (GIA) 32
Arnaout, Enaam 27–8
ASG: see Abu Sayyaf Group
Asia 4
see also Central Asia; South Asia;
Southeast Asia; specific countries
al-Asiri, Ibrahim Hassan 35
al-Assad, Bashar 110–11, 121, 138
assassinations 47, 75, 96–7, 110
Australia 55, 83, 122, 138, 157
al-Awlaki, Anwar 16, 35, 113
Azzam, Abdullah 10, 15

Baathists 48, 58
al-Baghdadi, Abu Bakr
bin Laden 58
as Caliph 58, 61, 157
and extremists 116
influence of ix, 57, 108, 128–9, 136
purges 47–8
and al-Zawahiri 58, 108
Bahney, Benjamin 107
Bangladesh 70, 87
"Baqiya wa Tatamaddad" slogan
67–8, 111
Barbaros, Abu Abdel Aziz 27
Bedouins 72, 74
beheadings 1, 60, 66, 123
Belgium 99, 103–4, 140, 146
see also Brussels attacks
Belkacem, Fouad 103
Benevolence International
Foundation (BIF) 27–8
Bengazhi 81
Berlin Christmas market attack 57,
82, 101
BIF (Benevolence International
Foundation) 27–8

Bilaad al-Shaam 125
bin Laden, Osama
Afghan Arabs 137
Afghanistan 10, 137
al-Qaeda ix, x, xi, 22
Arab Spring 117
and al-Baghdadi 58
death of 10, 11–12, 130
EIJ 24
Somalia 36
Sudan 24–5
on USA 10, 15–16
Yemen 25
and al-Zarqawi 32
and al-Zawahiri 11, 108
Boko Haram 95, 98–9
Borough Market attack 102
Bosnia 3–4, 6, 25, 27–8, 134
Bouhlel, Mohamed Lahouaiej 57
brainwashing 53, 59–60, 101,
148–50
Brussels attacks 5, 48, 56, 59, 103
Bunzel, Cole 115
Burkina Faso 95–6, 97, 98
burning alive 1, 123
Byman, Daniel 14, 30, 36, 113

caliphate ix, x, 2, 17, 66
al-Qaeda 18–19
children 148–50
collapse of 2, 3, 61, 63, 69, 82,
88–9, 130, 135, 136–7, 157
establishing 1, 11, 50, 116–17, 118,
134–5
foreign fighters returning 99
global jihadism 50–1, 136–7
Islamic State ix, 18, 61, 159
Libya 154
nostalgia of 112–13
virtual 54, 108
Callimachi, Rukmini 1, 48–9, 83
Caucasus 6, 14, 70, 93–4
Central Asia 6, 91–4
Charlie Hebdo attacks 36, 57
Chechnya 3–4, 6, 24–5, 27, 28–9,
134

children
  brainwashing 53, 59–60, 101, 148–50
  Cubs of the Caliphate camps 53
  recruitment of 102–3
  suicide bombers 63
Choudry, Anjem 102
Christians 73, 75, 89
civilians attacked 38, 73, 195n142
Cold War 45, 158
Combating Terrorism Center 90
Consumer Protection Authority 64
Coolsaet, Rik 55, 104, 116, 156
Coulibaly, Ahmed 57
countering violent extremism (CVE)
    programs 147
counterinsurgency 7, 72, 74
Counter-IS Coalition 44
  see also Western Coalition
counterterrorism x
  affiliate groups 72
  al-Qaeda rebranding 120–1
  Belgium 103–4
  and counterinsurgency 7, 72
  effects of 152, 155
  Europe 17, 102
  foreign fighter returnees 8
  Indonesia 88–9
  sanctions 43–4
  Saudi Arabia 31
  Southeast Asia 90
  splinter groups 3, 8–9, 135, 151, 155
  technological innovations 131
  USA 23
  Western Coalition x, xi, 123, 133, 153–4
  see also intelligence services
Cragin, Kim 92
Crenshaw, Martha 1
crimes against humanity 141, 144
criminal activities
  AQIM 34
  foreign fighters 62
  funding from 41, 42, 55, 56

jihadist networks 55, 114–15
  recruits 20
crucifixion 1, 123
Crusader-Zionist alliance 16, 136
Cubs of the Caliphate camps 53
Culbertson, Shelly 111
CVE (countering violent extremism)
    programs 147

Dabiq 67, 181–2n147
Damascus 110
Dayton Accords 25, 28
Democratic Republic of Congo
    (DRC) 6, 151
Denmark 99, 146, 157
deradicalization 135, 145, 146–7
dis videos 118
disengagement 135, 138, 145, 153
disillusionment 20, 137–8, 153
do-it-yourself terrorism 20–1, 108
Domodedovo Airport suicide attacks 94
DRC (Democratic Republic of
    Congo) 6, 151
drones 4, 46–7
Droukdal, Abdelmalek 34
drownings 1

East Africa 94, 96–7
East Turkestan Islamic Movement 14
Egypt
  geopolitics 75
  insurgency 73–4
  Islamic State 6, 70
  and Libya 73
  Morsi 72
  sectarianism 75
  support for 25
  al-Zawahiri 24
  see also Sinai Peninsula
EIJ (Egyptian Islamic Jihad) 11, 24, 75
Emni 7, 48–9, 59, 107
Emwazi, Mohammed 102
"the enemy of my enemy is my
    friend" 126

environmental measures 96
Eritrea 25
Ethiopia 36–7, 96
ethnic cleansing 27
Euphrates River 42, 69, 106–7
Europe 17–18, 33, 99–104, 143, 145–6
  see also specific countries
European Parliament report 55
executions 49, 58, 66, 102, 155
extortion 42, 44, 123, 154

Facebook 66, 68
failed states xi, 25, 79–80, 130, 152
far enemy concept 16, 24, 122
Finland 99
Fishman, Brian 32
foreign fighter returnees
  caliphate 99
  counterterrorism 8
  Denmark 146
  families 135, 143
  ideology 137–8, 146
  operational 138–9
  prosecution of 139–44
  rehabilitation 144–8
  Syrian trials 141
  Turkey 139
  USA 143
  Western Coalition 67, 134, 136,
    137–9, 156
foreign fighters
  Afghanistan 10
  capacity-building efforts 147–8
  criminal activities 62
  from Europe 17–18, 99, 143
  and families 135
  global jihad 21, 62
  in Iraq 32, 134, 137
  killed 136
  in Libya 81–2
  Pakistan 24
  post-caliphate 106–7
  prevention 135, 156–7
  recruitment of 4–5
  Russia 93–4
  in Syria 62, 134, 137–8, 141

from the US 143, 162n28
West Africa 95
Former Soviet Union (FSU) 92
Fort Hood shootings 35
Foundation of Defense for
  Democracies 96
France 33, 55, 56–7, 99, 100–1, 146
  see also Paris attacks
franchise operations 2, 4–5, 14,
    29–38
  against West 20–1
  bin Ladenism x
  expanding 22, 70–2
  Libya 80
  networks 54
  preference divergence 8
  Salafi-jihadism 11, 14, 151
  Sinai Peninsula 73
  South Asia 85–7
  see also affiliate groups; splinter
    groups
FSU (Former Soviet Union) 92

Garissa attack, Kenya 38
Gartenstein-Ross, Daveed 114, 123,
    155
Gaza 74–5
"General Guidelines for Jihad" (al-
  Zawahiri) 117
genocide 144
geographical factors 17–18, 24, 72,
    75, 82, 88, 89, 125
geopolitics xi, 25, 75, 79–80, 126–9,
    152
Gerges, Fawaz 27, 67
Germany 33, 53, 57, 99, 101
  see also Berlin Christmas market
    attack
GIA (Armed Islamic Group) 32
Glaser, Daniel 41–2
Global Coalition to Defeat ISIS 9
global jihadism ix, x–xi, 2, 11–17,
    26–9
  Afghanistan 24
  Africa 94–5
  al-Qaeda 19, 38

global jihadism (*cont.*)
  caliphate 50–1, 136–7
  fight against 159
  in flux 111–12
  foreign fighters 21, 62
  franchise groups and affiliates
    29–38
  goals and objectives 17–20
  ideology x–xi, 14–17, 122
  intensification 129–31
  organizational structure 23–6
  potential defeat of 134
  strategy 113–14
  technological innovations 114–15
Global War on Terror xi–xii, 10, 130,
  134
Godane, Ahmed 37
gradualism 113
Group for Support of Islam and
  Muslims (JNIM) 95, 98
GSPC (Salafist Group for Preaching
  and Combat) 30, 32, 33
guerrilla-style tactics 47, 70, 72, 84–5,
  106
Gunaratna, Rohan 24

Hamas 74–5
Hamming, Tore 116
Hapilon, Isnilon 91
Haque, Umar 102–3
Hasan, Nidal 35
Hassan, Hassan 106–7, 108
  ISIS: Inside the Army of Terror 128
al-Hayali, Fadel 58
Hay'at Tahrir al-Sham (HTS) 119, 154
Hegghammer, Thomas 31, 55
Hezbollah 46, 52, 121, 151
hisbah 62
hit-and-run attacks 5, 40
Hizb ut-Tahrir al-Islam (HuT) 93
Hizb-ul-Mujahideen (HM) 87
Hoffman, Bruce xi, 14, 49, 125, 129
Horgan, John G. 53
Horn of Africa 36, 95, 96–7
hospitals targeted 77
Houthi rebels 85

HTS (Hay'at Tahrir al-Sham) 119, 154
Huckabee-Sanders, Sarah 69–70
human resources 61–4
human rights groups 143
humanitarian efforts 66–7
Hussain, Junaid 102
Hussein, Saddam 48, 58
HuT (Hizb ut-Tahrir al-Islam) 93

Ibn Taymiyyah 15
ICU (Islamic Courts Union) 36
identity crisis 156–7
ideology
  al-Qaeda 128, 132
  foreign fighter returnees 138,
    146
  global jihadism x–xi, 14–17, 122
  Islamic State 5, 38, 59–61, 66, 110,
    128, 132, 135, 148, 157–9
  jihadism 109, 115–17
  operational capabilities 128
  Salafism 12, 14–17
  Saudi Arabia 145
  social media 66
  splinter groups 152
  USIP 145
Idlib 50, 124
IEDs (improvised explosive devices)
  75
Imarat Kavkaz 14
improvised explosive devices (IEDs)
  75
IMU (Islamic Movement of
  Uzbekistan) 13, 24, 76, 78, 91–2,
  93
In Defence of Muslim Lands (Azzam)
  15
India 6, 29, 86, 87
indoctrination 28, 53, 59, 61, 109,
  148, 150
  see also brainwashing
Indonesia 6, 13, 70, 88–9, 90
Instagram 66, 67
insurgency 7, 21–2, 70, 72, 73–4, 89,
  109–10, 130
insurgency theorists 16–17

intelligence services
  Counter-IS Coalition 44
  Emni 7, 48-9, 59, 107, 129
  foreign fighter returnees 137
  Germany 53
  information sharing 17, 130-1, 154
  and law inforcement 25-6, 67, 104, 115
  and military 90
  Pakistan 88
  United Kingdom 102
  USA 51-2
International Centre for Counter-Terrorism 150
International Commissions of Inquiry 144
Interpol 140
Inter-Services Intelligence (ISI) 88
Investigative Team, UNSC 144
Iran 93, 121-2, 128, 131-2
Iraq
  al-Qaeda 29, 31-2, 63
  civil war 21
  foreign fighters in 32, 134, 137
  guerilla-style tactics 106
  insurgency potential 109-10
  Islamic State 6-7, 11, 69, 108, 132-3, 140-1, 144
  sectarianism 4, 104
  Shiite Muslims 107-8
  soldiers 172n25
  Sunni Muslims 57-8, 63, 106, 154, 155
  Tawhid wal Jihad 30
  training camps 53
  US troops 62-3, 69-70, 85, 106, 108
  war crimes 141
  weapons hoarded 106
  White Flags 107
  Yazidis 1
  al-Zarqawi 30, 31-2
  see also AQI; ISI
IS: see Islamic State
ISI (Inter-Services Intelligence) 88
ISI (Islamic State in Iraq) 4, 39-40

ISIS: Inside the Army of Terror (Hassan) 128
ISKP (Islamic State in Khorasan Province) 76, 77, 78
Islamic charities 27
Islamic Courts Union (ICU) 36
Islamic Movement of Uzbekistan: see IMU
Islamic State (IS) 4-5, 7-8
  Afghanistan 29, 52, 70, 71
  Algeria 70, 80
  and al-Qaeda x, xii, 7-8, 109, 115-16, 117-19, 126-9, 132
  and AQI 39, 154
  Bangladesh 87
  caliphate ix, 18, 61, 159
  Egypt 6, 70
  financing 41-4, 55, 56, 152
  future developments 105, 129-33
  hisbah 62
  human resources 63-4
  humanitarian efforts 66-7
  ideology 5, 38, 59-61, 66, 110, 128, 132, 135, 148, 157-9
  intelligence service 48-9
  Iraq 6-7, 11, 69, 108, 132-3, 140-1, 144
  leadership 57-9
  municipal services 63
  networks of command 58-9
  operational capabilities 5, 40-53
  opportunism 109-11
  organizational capabilities 5, 54-68, 107
  outsourcing attacks 77
  propaganda 46, 65-8, 89, 123, 135-6
  purges 47-8
  recruitment xi, 20, 89
  Salafi-jihadist movement 59-60, 93-4, 127-9, 157-8
  sectarianism 44, 118, 122-3,159
  Shiite Muslims 60, 61, 122-3
  social media 1-2, 5, 40, 54, 65, 66-8, 136, 155, 180-1n136
  Somalia 70, 95

Islamic State (*cont.*)
  splintering 57, 69, 150–1
  state building 49, 61, 63–4, 104,
    130, 134–6
  strategy 111–15
  Syria 1, 6–7, 11, 69, 132–3
  takfirism 59, 116–17
  Twitter 65, 183n161
  US Army and Marine Corps
    Counterinsurgency Field
    Manual 48
  violence 60, 118, 120, 131–2
  weapons 44–7
  Yazidi girl 1
  Yemen 6, 71, 83
  al-Zarqawi 118–19
  al-Zawahiri 118
  see also affiliate groups; bin Laden;
    franchise operations; splinter
    groups
Islamic State in Iraq (ISI) 4, 39–40
Islamic State in Khorasan Province:
  see ISKP
Islamic State in Somalia, Kenya,
  Tanzania, and Uganda 95
Islamic State in West Africa (ISWA)
  98
Islamic State of Iraq and Syria 39–40
Islamic Youth Shura Council 80
Israel 16, 73, 74
ISWA (Islamic State in West Africa)
  98
al-Itihaad al-Islamiya (AIAI) 36
Ivory Coast 95–6, 97

Jabhat al-Nusra (JN) 14, 36, 39–40,
  48, 53, 67, 119
Jabhat Fateh al-Sham 119
Jaish-e-Mohammed (JeM) 87
Jama'at al-Tawhid wal-Jihad (TWJ)
  31–2
Jamaat of Central Asian Mujahidin
  93
Jarabulus crossing 50
JeM (Jaish-e-Mohammed) 87
Jemmah Islamiyah 4, 13, 75, 88

Jenkins, Brian Michael 11–12, 18
jihadi cool 55, 68
jihadism xi–xii
  Afghanistan 6, 78
  attacks in Europe 99
  criminal networks 55, 114–15
  free-agents 5–6
  ideology 109, 115–17
  infrastructure for 78
  networks 19
  opportunism 24
  Russia 91–2
  sectarianism 109
  Sunni Muslims 15, 50, 115–17,
    202n51
  in USA 18
  see also global jihadism
JN: *see* Jabhat al-Nusra
JNIM (Group for Support of Islam
  and Muslims) 95, 98
Johnston, Patrick 107
al-Jolani, Mohammed 125
Jones, Seth: *Waging Insurgent
  Warfare* 109
Jordan 24, 25, 27, 32, 62
al-Joulani, Abu Muhammad 39–40
JustPaste.it 67

Kampala bombings 37–8
Karimov, Islam 91
Kashmir 87–8, 131–2
Kassem, Abu 57–8
Katibah Nusantara 89
Katibat al-Battar al-Libiyah (KBL) 80
al-Kattab, Ibn 28
Kazakhstan 92–3
KBL (Katibat al-Battar al-Libiyah)
  80
Kenya 36, 38, 95
Kepel, Gilles 55
Kerchove, Gilles de 102
Khalid bin al-Walid Army 110
Khorasan Group 125
kidnapping 34, 42, 43
Al-Kifah 27
killing of unbelievers 60

Knights of Martyrdom 66–7
Knights Under the Prophet's Banner (Zawahiri) 28–9
Konig, Emilie 142–3
Kurds 7, 46, 48, 60, 142–3
Kyrgyzstan 93

Lashkar-e-Jhangvi (LEJ) 77
Lashkar-e-Taliba (LeT) 76, 87
Lebanon 21, 25, 121, 151–2
LEJ (Lashkar-e-Jhangvi) 77
LeT (Lashkar-e-Taliba) 76, 87
Levitt, Matthew 56
Liberation Tigers of Tamil Eelam (LTTE) 151
al-Libi, Abu Yahya 16
Libya
   AQIM 80
   caliphate 154
   and Egypt 73
   Islamic State 6, 52, 70, 71, 79–82
   jihadists 99
   Salafism 81
   state-building 64
   support for 25
   taxation 64
Libyan Islamic Fighting Group (LIFG) 13
Liège killings 140
LIFG (Libyan Islamic Fighting Group) 13
London attacks 102
lone wolf terrorists 20, 59, 157–8
looting 42, 45
Louay, Abu 57–8
LTTE (Liberation Tigers of Tamil Eelam) 151

Maalbeek metro station 103
Madrid train bombings 33
Maghreb 32, 73, 80, 97
   see also AQIM
MAK (Maktab al-Khidamat) 10, 11
Mali 14, 21, 95, 97–8, 115, 121
The Management of Savagery (Naji) 60, 107

Manchester concert bombing 82, 102
Marawi 89, 90, 91
martyrdom 66, 92, 149
Masasen, Hans-Georg 101
Mattis, James 79
media 35, 41, 65–8
   see also social media
medical expenses 63–4
Mehra, Tanya 141
Mendelsohn, Barak 22
Metrojet Flight 9268 73
MILF (Moro Islamic Liberation Front) 88
Mogadishu car-bombing 38
Moghadam, Assaf 21
Mohammed, Khalid Sheikh 24
Molenbeek 56, 103
Moro Islamic Liberation Front (MILF) 88
Morocco 56, 80, 156
Morsi, Mohammed 72
Moscow Metro suicide bombing 94
Mosul
   census 64
   city charter 60
   foreign fighters 99
   Iraqi security forces 106
   kids' fun day 63
   looting 42
   as operational base 50
   post-caliphate 2, 130, 136, 157
al-Mourabitoun 95
Mozambique 95, 151
MSC (Mujahedin Shura Council) 167n89
Mubarak, Hosni 24
El Mudžahid Battalion 27
al-Muhajiroun 102
mujahedin 10, 27
Mujahedin Shura Council (MSC) 167n89
Muslim Brotherhood 15
Muslims persecuted 27, 85–7
Myanmar 6, 85–7

Naji, Abu Bakr 113
   The Management of Savagery 60,
      107
narcotics 42, 43
National Counterterrorism Center
   (NCTC) 18
New York City pipe bomb 86
New York Times 1
New Yorker 6
Nice truck attack 57, 100
Niger 95, 98
Nigeria 96, 98
non-governmental organizations
   144, 145
North Africa 4, 6, 34
Northern Ireland 152
nostalgia narrative 149
Nusra: *see* Jabhat al-Nusra (JN)

Office of Borders and Immigration
   82
oil fields 43, 44, 51
oil sales 42-3

Pakistan 4, 24, 25, 76-9, 88
Papa Noel: *see* Zerkani, Khalid
Paris attacks
   Belgian ringleader 103
   casualties 100, 115, 138-9
   Charlie Hebdo 36, 57
   Islamic State 5, 48, 49-50, 56, 59
Parsons Green Underground
   bombing 102
Patriotic Europeans Against the
   Islamization of the West
   (PEGIDA) 101
People's Protection Units (YPG) 110
Petraeus, David 35
Philippines xi, 6, 24 5, 70, 71, 00-9
police training college attack 77
Politico 103
PREVENT 143
prison 62, 100, 135, 139-40, 146
propaganda 46, 65-8, 89, 123, 135-6,
   139-40, 149
prosecutions 139-44

public relations 65-8
public services 63, 64
Putin, Vladimir 93, 94

Qaddafi, Muammar 80, 81
al-Qaqaa, Abu 62-3
Qutb, Sayyid 15

Radicalisation Awareness Network
   (RAN) 139-44
radicalization
   Belgium 104
   Central Asian workers 92
   France 55, 100, 146
   Indonesia 89
   mujahedin 27
   prison 100, 135, 139-40
   recruitment 20, 136
   United Kingdom 53, 102-3
railroad explosion 94
ramming attacks 40, 57, 65
RAN (Radicalisation Awareness
   Network) 139-44
RAND Corporation 68, 111
rapprochement 127-9
Raqqa 2, 49-50, 54, 112, 130, 136,
   157
Rasmussen, Nicholas 18
recidivism 135, 145
recruitment 4-5
   children 102-3
   criminal activities 20
   Europeans 54-7
   Islamic State xi, 20, 89
   online 155
   radicalization 20, 136
   records 48, 54
   training 52-3
   weapons 45
rehabilitation 144-8
Reina nightclub shootings 83
religious extremism 55
Renard, Thomas 104
Risen Alive 66-7
Riyadh compound bombings 30
robbery 42

Robinson, Linda 111
Rohingya Muslims 85–7
Roy, Olivier x, 55
Royal United Services Institute
    (RUSI) 92, 130, 152, 154
rule of law 92, 130, 152, 154
RUSI: see Royal United Services
    Institute
Russia 28–9, 91–2, 93–4

safe havens xi, 3, 17, 37, 41, 49–52,
    79, 80
Salafi-jihadist movement
    al-Qaeda 3, 11, 13, 127–9
    East Africa 94
    franchise operations 11, 14, 151
    ideology 12, 14–17
    Islamic State 59–60, 93–4, 127–9,
        157–8
    Somalia 37
    statistics 134
    Sub-Saharan Africa 151
    Sunni Muslims 202n51
    Turkey 83
    weak regimes 115
    Yemen 85
Salafism 12, 14–17, 53, 81, 115
Salafist Group for Preaching and
    Combat: see GSPC
sanctions 43–4
Saudi Arabia 24–5, 28, 29–31, 85,
    131–2, 145
Save the Children 76
Scandinavia 55
SDF (Syrian Democratic Forces) 110,
    141
sectarianism x, 6
    AQI 32, 119
    Egypt 75
    Iraq 4, 104
    Islamic State 44, 118, 122–3, 159
    jihadism 109
    Philippines 89
September 11 terrorist attacks ix, 3,
    10, 23
sexual slavery 1

sharia law 36, 60, 98, 116–17, 123
Sharia4Belgium 102, 103
Shiite Muslims
    Afghanistan 76–7
    al-Qaeda 122–3
    AQI 30
    in Iran 93
    in Iraq 107–8
    Islamic State 60, 61, 122–3
    al-Zarqawi 32
    see also Sunni-Shiite conflict
al-Shisani, Ali Fathi 28
al-Shishani, Omar 58
Sinai Peninsula 6, 7, 8–9, 29, 52, 70,
    71, 72–5
Sirte 81–2, 134
el-Sisi, Abdel Fattah 73–4
slavery 1
sleeper cells 88–9, 108
social media
    feuding 116, 118
    ideology 66
    Islamic State 1–2, 5, 40, 54, 65,
        66–8, 136, 155
Somalia
    al-Qaeda 3–4, 29
    al-Shabaab 14, 30, 36–8, 95
    civil wars 21
    Ethiopia 36–7
    Islamic State 70, 95
    Salafi-jihadist movement 37
    suicide bombing 37
    support for 25
    USA 21, 36
Soufan Group 91
SoundCloud 67
South Asia 85–8
Southeast Asia 6, 29, 52, 88–91
Soviet-Afghan War 3, 10, 12, 26–7, 28,
    134, 137
Spain 33, 99
Special Forces program 22, 49, 52–3
splinter groups
    Algeria 152
    al-Shabaab 95, 151
    Boko Haram 95

splinter groups (*cont.*)
counterterrorism 3, 8–9, 135, 151, 155
failed states 152
HTS 119
ideology 152
reconstituting 135, 152–3, 154–5
state-building 49, 61, 63–4, 104, 130, 134–6
Sub-Saharan Africa 94–6, 151
Sudan 3–4, 24–5
Sufism 28, 75
suicide attacks 45, 46
al-Shabaab 96–7
Boko Haram 98
children 63
Domodedovo Airport 94
Indonesia 88–9
ISKP 76–7
Manchester concert 102
Moscow Metro 94
reliance on 47, 75, 76–7, 127
Sinai Peninsula 75
Somalia 37
Sunni Muslims
co-opted 109–10
disenfranchisement 51
eliminated 60
factions 93
in Iraq 57–8, 63, 106, 154, 155
jihadists 15, 50, 115–17, 202n51
Yemen 84
see also Sunni-Shiite conflict
Sunni Triangle 110
Sunni-Shiite conflict 119, 128, 131–2
al-Suri, Abu Musab x, 16, 108, 113
surveillance 46, 48, 154–5
Sweden 99
al-Sweidawi, Adnan 58
Syria
affiliated groups 39–40, 119
al-Qaeda xi, 29, 119–21, 123, 154
Arab Spring 39
children sent to Europe 53
civil war 4, 93, 115, 119, 138, 155, 159

detainee camps 143
foreign fighters in 62, 134, 137–8, 141
insurgency potential 109–10
Islamic State 1, 6–7, 11, 69, 132–3
Jabhat al-Nusra 14
Kurds 142–3
oil fields 43
as safe haven 51–2
Turkey 50, 110
US troops 69–70
see also al-Assad, Bashar
Syrian Army 47
Syrian Democratic Forces (SDF) 110, 141

Tajikistan 25, 28, 92
takfirism 59, 116–17
Tal Abayd crossing 50
Taliban 24, 76
Tanzania 94
Tanzim Hurras al-Din 119–20, 125, 154
tatarrus 116–17
Tawhid wal Jihad 30
Tawil, Camille 33
taxation 42, 43, 51, 64, 123
technicals 46
technological innovations 114, 131
Tehrik-i-Taliban Pakistan (TIP) 77
Telegram 68
terrorism 20–1, 23–4, 40–1, 49–50, 73, 108
see also specific locations
TFG (Transitional Federal Government) 38
Thailand 152
Tigantourine gas facility 33
Tigris River 110
TIP (Tehrik-i-Taliban Pakistan) 77
TIP (Turkestan Islamic Party) 93
Tønnessen, Truls Hallberg 46
Transitional Federal Government (TFG) 38
travel bans 157
Trinidad and Tobago 55

Trump, Donald 69–70, 79, 84
Tunisia 70, 80, 82
Turkestan Islamic Party (TIP) 93
Turkey 41, 50, 82–3, 110, 139
al-Turkmani, Abu Muslim 57–8
Twitter 65, 68, 183n161
TWJ (Jama'at al-Tawhid wal-Jihad)
    31–2

Uganda 37–8, 95
Ullah, Akayed 86
ummah 15, 17, 66, 113
United Arab Emirates 85
United Kingdom 102–5
    GSPC 33
    jihadist attacks 82, 99, 102
    possible extremists 150
    PREVENT 143
    prosecutions 141
    recruitment 55, 102–3
United Nations Security Council 43,
    144
United States of America ix
    in Afghanistan 4, 29, 78–9
    attacks on ix, 3, 10, 18, 23, 86
    bin Laden 10, 15–16
    counterterrorism 23
    Crusader–Zionist alliance 136
    Defense Department 84
    embassies bombed 36, 94
    foreign fighters from 143,
        162n28
    Global War on Terror xi-xii, 10,
        130, 134
    intelligence service 51–2
    in Iraq 62–3, 69–70, 85, 106, 108
    IS recruits 55
    and Israel 16
    jihadism 18
    Kurds 46
    Lebanon 21
    Somalia 21, 36
    State Department 70
    surveillance 154–5
    Syria 69–70
    Syrian Democratic Forces 110

US African Command (AFRICOM)
    95, 98
US Army and Marine Corps
    Counterinsurgency Field
    Manual 48
USIP (United States Institute for
    Peace) 145
Uyghur Islamic Party of Eastern
    Turkestan 93
Uzbeks 91, 92, 123
    see also IMU

vehicle-borne improvised explosive
    devices (VBIEDs) 5, 40, 46
vehicular terrorism 5, 40, 65
virtual caliphate 54, 108
virtual planner model 114

Waging Insurgent Warfare (Jones)
    109
Wahhabism 28, 60
war crimes 141–2, 144
weapons 44–7, 98–9, 106
West Africa 70, 71, 95, 97–9
Western Coalition 113
    counterterrorism x, xi, 123, 133,
        153–4
    deradicalization 145
    foreign fighter returnees 67, 134,
        136, 137–9, 156
    information sharing 156
    technological innovations 114,
        131
Westgate Mall attack 38
Westminster Bridge attack 102
WhatsApp 67
White Flags 107
Whiteside, Craig 112–13
Wilayat Qawqaz 93
wilayats 7, 80
winning hearts and minds 115, 117,
    124
women's role 1, 55, 101
Wood, Graeme 2, 53, 64
Wright, Robin 6
al-Wuhayshi, Nasir 35

Yaryshmardy ambush 28
Yazidi girl 1
Yemen
    affiliate groups 36, 73
    al-Qaeda xi, 4–5, 29, 34–6, 84, 85,
        121, 124
    AQAP 35–6, 60, 73–4, 83–4
    bin Laden 25
    civil war 21, 115
    Houthi rebels 85
    Islamic State 6, 71, 83
    local tribes 36
    Salafi-jihadism 85
    Sunni Muslims 84
YPG (People's Protection Units) 110
Yugoslavia, Federal Republic of 27–8

al-Zarqawi, Abu Musab
    affiliate groups 118
    AQI 56, 62–3, 106
    bin Laden 32
    Iraq 30, 31–2
    Islamic State x, 118–19

leadership ix, x, 4, 106
and Shiites 32
short-/long-term gains 120
and al-Zawahiri 32
al-Zawahiri, Ayman
    AQAP 35–6
    to AQI 119
    and al-Baghdadi 58, 108
    and bin Laden 11, 108
    Egypt 24
    "General Guidelines for Jihad" 117
    GSPC 33
    as ideologue 16–17
    on Islamic State 118
    al-Joulani 39–40
    Knights Under the Prophet's
        Banner 28–9
    leadership 13–14, 22, 124–6
    Qutb 15
    violence 60
    and al-Zarqawi 32
Zelin, Aaron 50–1, 80
Zerkani, Khalid 56, 103, 198n178

Introduction

On a grey and drizzly day in January 2017, on the steps of the Capitol Building in Washington, DC, the newly elected president of the United States gave a speech unlike any of his predecessors. It had the anger and frustration of the political fringes, but it came from the political mainstream. In his inaugural speech, the new "Leader of the Free World" said:

> For too long, a small group in our nation's Capital has reaped the rewards of government while the people have borne the cost. Washington flourished – but the people did not share in its wealth. Politicians prospered – but the jobs left, and the factories closed. The establishment protected itself, but not the citizens of our country. Their victories have not been your victories; their triumphs have not been your triumphs; and while they celebrated in our nation's Capital, there was little to celebrate for struggling families all across our land. That all changes – starting right here, and right now, because this moment is your moment: it belongs to you.

The election of Donald Trump is in many ways illustrative of what this book is about: the mainstreaming and normalization of the far right in general, and the populist radical right in particular, in the twenty-first

century. As I finish this manuscript, in May 2019, three
of the five most populous countries in the world have a
far-right leader (Brazil, India, and the US) and the biggest
political party in the world is the populist radical right
Indian People's Party (BJP). Within the European Union
(EU), two governments are fully controlled by populist
radical right parties (Hungary and Poland), another four
include such parties (Bulgaria, Estonia, Italy, Slovakia),
and two are held up with support of a populist right
party (Denmark and the United Kingdom).[1] And in the
latest European elections, far-right parties increased
their presence in the European Parliament yet again,
albeit modestly, as they had done in the previous
elections in 2014 and 2009.

A lot has changed since I started working on the far
right in the late 1980s, as a student at the University
of Leiden in the Netherlands, when the far right was
still primarily a phenomenon of the political margins.
Neo-Nazi groups could barely protest in the streets
without being arrested and anti-immigration parties
barely registered in the polls. Today, the far right is
closely connected to the political mainstream; and in
more and more countries it is becoming the political
mainstream. Let me illustrate this disturbing transfor-
mation with three (European) examples.

In 1982, thousands of protesters filled the square in
front of the Dutch parliament in The Hague. Carrying
signs that read "They Are Back" and "Racism is Hate
Against Humans," they protested against one man,
Hans Janmaat, leader of the misnamed Center Party,
who, with fewer than 70,000 votes (0.8 percent), had
entered the Second Chamber. Fast-forward more than
three decades, and the Dutch parliament counts twenty-
two (out of 150) far-right Members of Parliament
(MPs), installed without any protests, while the main
right-wing government parties advance and implement
policies that are fully anchored in the Center Party's

main point of controversy: "The Netherlands is not an immigration country. Stop immigration!"

In 1999, the Austrian Freedom Party (FPÖ) gained its biggest electoral success to date, coming second with 26.9 percent of the vote in the parliamentary elections. When the party entered the government the next year, it was met by mass demonstrations and an international boycott. When the FPÖ returned to government in 2018, few Austrians came out to demonstrate, while the international community embraced the coalition with virtually no protest.

And, finally, in France, most French people responded with horror when the leader of the National Front (FN), Jean-Marie Le Pen, made the 2002 presidential run-offs with 16.9 percent of the national vote. In response, turnout for the second round increased substantially, keeping Le Pen at 17.8 percent, less than one percent higher than in the first round. Fifteen years later, his daughter Marine made the second round with 21.3 percent. This time (even) fewer French people voted in the second round and Le Pen increased her support to 33.9 percent. With Marine Le Pen almost doubling her father's 2002 score, most French people were relieved rather than upset. At least she didn't win.

These examples illustrate the fundamental differences between the so-called "third wave" and "fourth wave" of the postwar far right. The third wave, roughly from 1980 till 2000, saw the rise of electorally successful populist radical right parties, although they were largely reduced to the political margins, as mainstream parties excluded them from political coalitions and often minimized "their" issues, notably immigration and European integration. In the fourth wave, which roughly started in the twenty-first century, radical right parties have become mainstreamed and increasingly normalized, not just in Europe, but across the world. And even extreme right parties have emerged, as extreme right sentiments (like antisemitism, historical revisionism, and racism) are openly flirted with in the media and politics.

The so-called "refugee crisis" of 2015 played a special role in this development. I put the term in quotes because whether or not it was indeed a crisis is more a matter of personal judgment than objective condition. The EU had the financial resources to deal with even these record numbers of asylum seekers, although for years it had neglected to build an infrastructure to properly take care of them. Mainstream media and politicians *chose* to frame the influx of asylum seekers as a "crisis," thereby providing ammunition to the already mobilized far right.

The "refugee crisis" was not the initial cause of the mainstreaming of the far right, in Europe or beyond, but it has definitely functioned as a catalyst for the process. Anti-immigration demonstrations have become a common occurrence on the streets of major European cities, while far-right violence against anti-fascists, immigrants, the LGBTQ community, and refugees has increased sharply. From Germany to the US, law enforcement and intelligence agencies warn of a growing far-right terrorist danger, often after decades of downplaying this threat.

This book aims to give an accessible and concise overview of the fourth wave of the postwar far right. While it includes several original observations which will also be of interest to more expert readers, this book is first and foremost written for a non-academic audience; for people who follow the news, are concerned about the rise of the far right, but feel that media accounts provide too little detail and insight, while academic and non-academic books are too complex or simply too long. It draws on more than a quarter-century of scholarship, including my own, and simplifies and summarizes this in ten clearly structured chapters.

My hope is that after reading this book, the reader will feel better equipped to assess the key challenges that the far right poses to liberal democracies in the twenty-first century and to feel empowered to defend liberal democracy against these challenges. But before she can do this, we have to address one of the most confusing and frustrating aspects of the academic and public debate on the topic: terminology.

Terminology

The ideas and groups at the heart of this book are described with an ever-growing myriad of terms, often used interchangeably, yet without a clear definition or explanation of the differences and similarities. While issues of terminology might sound like a purely academic matter, they are crucial to politics and the public debate. For instance, in countries like Germany, "extreme right" groups can be banned, while "radical right" groups cannot.

It is true that most of the defining and terming is done by outsiders, that is, academics, anti-fascists, and journalists, rather than by the far right itself, but this is not to say that it does not care about terminology. Leaders from prominent far-right parties, like the FN (now National Rally, RN) and FPÖ, have taken academics and journalists to court for describing them as "fascist," for example. Others have proudly proclaimed themselves to be populists, and sometimes even racist, albeit often after redefining the term more favorably. For example, Matteo Salvini, leader of the Northern League (LN; now just League) and Italy's interior minister, said that while "populist" was used as an insult, for him, it was a compliment. And former Breitbart News CEO and Trump advisor Steve Bannon told FN activists at a party gathering, "Let them call you racists. Let them call you xenophobes. Let them call you nativists. Wear it as a badge of honor."

There is no academic consensus on the correct terms for the broader movement and the various subgroups within it. Moreover, the dominant term has been changing throughout the postwar era. In the first decades, these movements were primarily described in terms of "neo-fascism," which changed to "extreme right" in the 1980s, "radical right" in the 1990s, some form of "right-wing populism" in the early twenty-first century, as well as "far right" in more recent years. This development reflects changes both within the movement itself and in the scholarly community that studies it.

Most academics agree that the movement is part of the broader *right*, but disagree over what that exactly means. The terms "left" and "right" date back to the French Revolution (1789–99), when supporters of the king sat to the right of the president of the French parliament and opponents to the left. This means that those on the right were in favor of the *ancien régime*, marked by its hierarchical order, while those on the left supported democratization and popular sovereignty. After the Industrial Revolution, the left–right division became mainly defined in terms of socio-economic policies, with the right supporting a free market and the left a more active role of the state, although alternative meanings remained popular – such as religious (right) versus secular (left). In more recent decades, left–right has become more defined in socio-cultural terms, with the right standing for either authoritarianism (versus the left's libertarianism) or nationalism (versus the left's internationalism) – or, in the terms of RN leader Marine Le Pen, "patriot–globalist."

While these various interpretations differ on many points, they do share an essential core, which has been captured most accurately by the Italian philosopher Norberto Bobbio,[2] who defines the key distinction between left and right on the basis of their view on (in) equality: the *left* considers the key inequalities between people to be artificial and negative, which should be overcome by an active state, whereas the *right* believes that inequalities between people are natural and positive, and should be either defended or left alone by the state. These inequalities can be (believed to be) cultural, economic, racial, religious, or however defined.

This book is not concerned with the so-called "mainstream right," such as conservatives and liberals/ libertarians, but only with those on the right who are "anti-system," defined here as hostile to liberal democracy. This is what I call the *far right*, which is itself divided into two broader subgroups. The *extreme right* rejects the essence of democracy, that is, popular sovereignty and majority rule. The most infamous example of the extreme right is fascism, which brought to power German *Führer* Adolf Hitler and Italian *Duce* Benito Mussolini, and was responsible for the most destructive war in world history. The *radical right* accepts the essence of democracy, but opposes fundamental elements of *liberal* democracy, most notably minority rights, rule of law, and separation of powers. Both subgroups oppose the postwar liberal democratic consensus, but in fundamentally different ways. While the extreme right is revolutionary, the radical right is more reformist. In essence, the radical right trusts the power of the people, the extreme right does not.

Given the prevalence of the term *populism* in contemporary political discussions, let me quickly clarify both my understanding of that term and its relationship to the far right. I define populism as a (thin) ideology that considers society to be ultimately separated into two homogeneous and antagonistic groups, the pure people and the corrupt elite, and which argues that politics should be an expression of the *volonté générale* (general will) of the people (see also chapter 2). At least in theory, populism is pro-democracy, but anti-liberal democracy. Consequently, the extreme right is, by definition, not populist, while the radical right can be – and, in the twenty-first century, predominantly is.

Outline of the Book

This book focuses predominantly on the fourth wave, that is, on the far right in the twenty-first century. While I aim to present the far right in its diversity, including both the extreme right and the radical right, the emphasis will be on the most important ideas, organizations, and personalities of the contemporary period, that is, populist radical right leaders and parties. The first set of chapters focuses primarily on the far right itself (chapters 1–5), while the second deals with the far right within the (mostly western democratic) political context (chapters 6–8).

Chapter 1 provides a concise chronological overview of the four waves of postwar far-right politics. Chapter 2 introduces the key ideologies and issues of the contemporary far right. Chapter 3 focuses on the organizational structure of the far right, distinguishing between far-right parties, social movement organizations, and subcultures. Chapter 4 shifts the focus to the people within the far right, more specifically leaders, members and activists, and voters. Chapter 5 examines the main forms of mobilization, that is, elections, demonstrations, and violence.

The next three chapters situate the far right within its (western democratic) political context. Chapters 6 and 7 discuss the causes and consequences of the recent rise of the far right, summarizing some of the key academic and public debates – such as economic anxiety versus cultural backlash – and highlighting the broad variety of far-right challenges that western democracies are facing today. Chapter 8 reviews the different ways in which democracies have responded to the rise of the far right. Chapter 9 looks at the role of gender within the far right, relating it to most of the aspects discussed in the previous chapters. Finally, chapter 10 ends the book with twelve theses that highlight key characteristics and novelties of the fourth wave of the postwar far right.

1

History

In 1945, the world started to recover from the second world war in thirty years. An estimated 75 to 85 million people were killed, and many more were seriously injured. Europe was in ruins. Nazi Germany and the Soviet Union bore the brunt of the destruction, but almost all European countries were severely affected by collaboration, destruction, and occupation. Millions of minorities had perished in the Nazi annihilation and concentration camps, most notably Jews, Roma and Sinti (commonly referred to by the derogatory term "Gypsies"), homosexuals, and communists.

As the European continent was recovering from one division, between fascists and anti-fascists, it was entering another one, between communists and anti-communists. The Cold War separated Europe into a capitalist and (largely) democratic West and a socialist and authoritarian East. This division preceded the Second World War, and the two sides were only brought together by the shared threat of fascism, because anti-fascism was one of the few values communists and liberal democrats shared (despite the cynical pact that

Hitler and Stalin struck between 1939 and 1941). Yet, as soon as fascism was destroyed, the two became mortal enemies again.

The anti-fascist consensus would survive the Cold War, even though there were fundamental national and regional differences in the ways in which countries dealt with the far right in the postwar era. In communist states, all "fascist" ideas and movements were banned, as were all other non-communist ideas and movements. Most East European collaborators and fascists were killed in the war and the postwar repression or were able to escape to, primarily, the Americas, where they integrated into broader anti-communist émigré communities, which often already held very right-wing ideas.

While most western democracies also went through a short period of, partly extrajudicial and violent, repression of local fascists and collaborators, particularly in countries that were occupied by Nazi Germany, many had more ambivalent legal restrictions on far-right ideas and movements. Countries that had not been occupied, like the UK and US, introduced virtually no restrictions, while others, notably Germany and Italy, officially banned "neo-fascist" ideas and movements (see chapter 8). Despite different legal systems, and social pressures, the general lesson of the Second World War was "never again." It was a sentiment that was also at the heart of the process of European integration, which aimed to integrate economies and pool sovereignty to create a bulwark against nationalism.

Three Waves of the Postwar Far Right, 1945–2000

In 1988, the German political scientist Klaus von Beyme[1] identified three waves of far-right politics in postwar Western Europe. While there is some debate about the exact characteristics and time periods of the different waves, his model does provide at least a rough sketch of the ways in which the far right fared in the second half of the twentieth century.

Neo-Fascism, 1945–55

In the direct aftermath of the defeat of fascism, far-right politics was backward- rather than forward-looking. Given that almost all far-right activists and groups had collaborated with the fascists during the war, far-right politics was almost universally rejected – and in some countries, like Germany and the Netherlands, all nationalisms were perceived negatively. Most Europeans who had either ideologically supported, or opportunistically collaborated with, the fascist regimes adapted to the new democratic reality either by becoming apolitical or by working within the democratic parties and system.

The small group of fascists who remained loyal to the cause, and who were not or no longer imprisoned, worked mainly at the margins of society. They were mostly described as "neo-fascists," but there was really not much new to them. They were old fascists who remained loyal to the old ideology, who organized primarily within social organizations, providing camaraderie and social support for the "heroes" and martyrs" of the fascist cause. Among the more important groups were those providing support for former Eastern Front fighters (mostly Waffen-SS) and their families, such as the Belgian Saint-Martin Fund and the German Mutual Aid Association of Former Waffen-SS Soldiers – millions of children and wives had lost their fathers and husbands and were left without a state pension because their countries considered them traitors.

As far as (neo-)fascists wanted to remain politically active, they had to operate in a hostile legal and political climate. Even when cautious not to be openly neo-fascist, far-right organizations led by former (high-ranking) fascists rarely achieved popular support and often forced significant state repression. Most of the political parties did not contest elections, and even if they did, they would remain well under the electoral threshold of parliamentary representation. Several (neo-)fascist parties were banned in the 1950s, including the German Socialist Reich Party (SRP) in 1952 and the Dutch National European Social Movement in 1956.

The main exception was the Italian Social Movement (MSI), which was led by a former Fascist government official, Giorgio Almirante, and made little secret of its credentials – the initials allegedly signified "*Mussolini Sei Immortale*" (Mussolini, You Are Immortal). Although the new Italian Constitution explicitly stated, "It shall be forbidden to reorganize, under any form whatsoever, the dissolved Fascist party," the MSI entered parliament in 1948 and remained represented until its transformation into the "post-fascist" National Alliance in 1995. It even provided parliamentary support for the short-lived Tambroni government in 1960.

Outside of Europe, neo-fascist ideas were often represented in East European émigré organizations in the Americas and Australia. This was strengthened by the influx of former fascist activists and politicians, particularly from collaborationist regimes in Croatia, Hungary, and Slovakia, after the end of the Second World War. In Latin America, some more or less relevant groups were strongly influenced by the far-right regimes of Antonio Salazar's Estado Novo in Portugal and, in particular, Francisco Franco's Falange in Spain.

In an attempt to break away from their national marginalization, some fascist leaders tried to organize at the international level. The most famous attempt was the European Social Movement (ESM), inspired by the success of the MSI, which was founded at a congress in Malmö (Sweden) in 1951. While it brought together the most well-known far-right activists of that period, as well as representatives of the most relevant far-right parties (including the MSI and SRP), the ESM remained marginal in its short life, becoming moribund in 1957. The same applied to all other attempts at far-right collaboration, including the various attempts to develop a European nationalism by people like the British fascist Oswald Mosley (also involved in the ESM) and the US attorney and polemicist Francis Parker Yockey, founder of the ambitiously named European Liberation Front, which existed from 1949 till 1954.

Right-Wing Populism, 1955–80

Small neo-fascist groups continued to exist on the margins of western societies, but the ensuing decades saw the rise of a variety of right-wing populist parties and politicians, which were defined by opposition to the postwar elites rather than allegiance to a defeated ideology and regime. Former fascists played a role in many of these parties, but they were not neo-fascist in terms of either ideology or personnel. First and foremost, these parties revolted against postwar conditions, most notably the marginalization of the rural peripheries and the development of the welfare state.

While there had been some earlier right-wing populist parties, like the National Agricultural Party in Ireland and the Common Man's Front in Italy in the 1940s, the defining movement was the Defense Union of Shopkeepers and Craftsmen, better known as the Poujadists, after its leader Pierre Poujade. Poujadism did include several features of fascism, including a strong focus on the leader and a strident anti-parliamentarism – Poujade called the *Assemblée Nationale* "the biggest brothel in Paris" – but was not openly anti-democratic.

It became a mass movement almost overnight, counting some 400,000 members in 1955, and gaining fifty-two seats in the 1956 elections under the name of Union and French Fraternity, When General Charles de Gaulle founded the Fifth Republic in 1958, the Poujadists quickly disappeared from French politics, although they would leave an important legacy: Jean-Marie Le Pen was the leader of its youth movement and was elected as the youngest parliamentarian in French postwar history in 1956 (a feat his granddaughter, Marion Maréchal-Le Pen, would repeat in 2012).

There were similar rural populist parties after the Poujadists, most notably the Farmers' Party in the Netherlands, but the most important right-wing populist parties that emerged later in the second wave had a different profile. In 1973, the Progress Party took the Danish political establishment by surprise, scoring 15.9 percent of the vote in its first-ever election – the party was founded just the previous year by the idiosyncratic lawyer and TV personality Mogens Glistrup. Also in 1973, a similar party, initially named Anders Lange's Party for a Strong Reduction in Taxes, Duties, and Public Intervention but renamed Progress Party in 1977, gained a more modest 5 percent in Norway. Both Progress Parties are best described as "neoliberal populist," however, railing against high taxes and big government – the Danish party wanted to scrap defense altogether, presenting as its policy an answering machine message stating "we surrender" in Russian.

In addition, some new far-right parties were founded that were hybrids, that is, combinations of old extreme right (often neo-fascist) and new radical right ideas and personnel. Possibly the first such party was the Swiss National Action for People and Nation, founded in 1961, but the most important, and enduring, was the National Democratic Party of Germany (NPD), founded in 1964. While founded by former Nazi officials, the

NPD focused primarily on postwar issues, including the most important theme of the future: non-European immigration. Similarly, the British National Front (NF), a crudely racist party, founded from a merger of smaller groups in 1967, had some localized impact in the late 1970s organizing behind slogans like "Stop Immigration" and "Make Britain Great Again."

In the United States, right-wing populism mainly operated within the broader anti-communist movement, whose most (in)famous representatives were the John Birch Society and Senator Joseph McCarthy. It got a second wind in the presidential campaign of Republican Senator Barry Goldwater, which ended disastrously, but provided the germ for the birth of a new, more radical, conservative subculture. The most significant radical right moment, however, was the 1968 presidential run of Alabama governor George Wallace, under the heading of the American Independent Party. Running on an explicitly racist agenda, vehemently defending racial segregation, Wallace was the only third-party candidate to win states in the postwar era – indeed he won no less than five, all in the former confederate South. This was part of a broader racist opposition to desegregation in the former Confederate states, which included the infamous Ku Klux Klan (KKK), which had flourished twice before, in the late 1860s and 1920s, and now, in its third iteration, grew back to roughly 50,000 people in the 1960s, as well as the more respectable Citizens' Council, with an estimated membership of ca. 250,000.

Radical Right, 1980–2000

The first significant wave of far-right politics in Western Europe started in the early 1980s, picking up real steam only in the 1990s. Fueled by unemployment and mass immigration, although with a lag effect of almost a decade, radical right parties started to slowly but steadily enter national parliaments. The earliest was the Flemish Bloc (VB), which entered the Belgian parliament as an electoral alliance in 1978, followed by the Dutch Center Party in 1982. Both parties had modest support, around 1 percent, translating into one representative in the highly proportional electoral systems of their respective countries. In 1986, the French FN, which had been founded fourteen years earlier and had so far contested national elections unsuccessfully, profited from a change in the electoral system to translate its 9.6 percent of the vote into thirty-five parliamentary seats. Two years later, France changed back to its previous majoritarian system, which accomplished what it meant to do: the FN scored an identical percentage, but gained zero seats.

In addition to various new radical right parties, such as The Republicans in Germany and the Sweden Democrats (SD), the third wave included former mainstream parties, such as the FPÖ in Austria and the Swiss People's Party (SVP), which were transformed into populist radical right parties by new (official or unofficial) party leaders – Jörg Haider and Christoph Blocher, respectively. These parties proved much more durable than previous far-right parties – the MSI excluded – and, with some exceptions, remain relevant today.

After the fall of communism in 1989, the far right also emerged in various post-communist countries, although initially in more specifically regional forms. It included parties like the Croatian Party of Rights and the Slovak National Party (SNS), which harked back in ideology and even some personnel to fascist parties of the 1930s and 1940s, as well as parties that merged far-right features with communist nostalgia, like the Greater Romania Party. At the same time, far-right politicians got elected on lists of non-far-right parties, such as the Bulgarian Socialist Party, the Communist Party of the Russian Federation, and Solidarity Electoral Action in Poland.

By the turn of the century, the populist radical right had become the dominant ideology within the European far right. Although there were national and regional differences – for example, opposition to non-European immigration was less important in the East, while opposition to Roma was mostly absent in the West – almost all relevant far-right parties combined nativism, authoritarianism, and populism (see chapter 2). They railed against immigrants and/or indigenous minorities as well as European and national elites, while presenting themselves as the voice of the people who said what the people think.

Only a few populist radical right parties contested elections in the 1980s, scoring on average just 2.3 percent in the countries in which they participated – 1.1 percent in Europe overall. By contrast, most European countries had at least one far-right party contesting elections in the 1990s, gaining on average 4.4 percent (see the table below). The differences between Eastern and Western Europe were significantly smaller than was generally assumed, although the highest score in Eastern Europe was much higher than in Western Europe: 45.2 percent in Croatia versus 26.9 percent in Switzerland.

While electoral and organizational volatility was high, with parties emerging and disappearing rapidly, particularly in the extremely unstable party systems of Eastern Europe, several populist radical right parties started to establish themselves within national political systems in the 1990s. For instance, the FN, LN, and VB all became part of the established parties in their respective countries, even if they mostly remained outside of the political establishment. Owing to still limited electoral success, however, as well as ideological, personal, and

Average vote for far-right parties in national parliamentary elections in EU member states, 1980–2018 (by decade)

Years	Average vote (%)	No. countries	No. parties
1980–9	1.1	17	8
1990–9	4.4	28	24
2000–9	4.7	28	24
2010–18	7.5	28	34

Note: The averages of the table are based on the twenty-eight countries that were members of the European Union in 2018. The score for the 1980s only reflects West European states, as Eastern Europe was still under communist rule at that time. *Source*: Parlgov.

tactical differences, the European far right was largely unable to come together transnationally. Political groups in the European Parliament tended to include only some parties, and were short-lived because of disagreements within and between them (see chapter 3).

Outside of Europe, far-right parties started to become important players within the fragmented Israeli party system – with parties like Moledet and Tkuma, which entered parliament as part of the electoral alliance National Union in 1999. And while the neo-fascist Kach party of Rabbi Meir Kahane, as well as its successor Kahane Lives, were banned by the state in 1994, Kahanism would become the dominant strand in the Israeli far right in the fourth wave. In South Africa, openly racist organizations like the Afrikaner Resistance Movement lost support after the end of the apartheid regime in 1994, spiraling increasingly into an orgy of political violence.

Far-right groups existed only on the margins in the US, although some politicians tried to build a basis within the Republican Party – such as former KKK Grand

Wizard David Duke and "paleoconservative" journalist and politician Patrick "Pat" Buchanan. In Australia, Pauline Hanson was elected as an Independent in 1996 after the Liberal Party of Australia had disendorsed her because of derogatory remarks about Indigenous Australians. The following year, she founded her One Nation Party (ONP), which had some initial successes, but also suffered much internal division and strife. Most prominently, in 1980, the BJP was founded in India on the basis of the Bharatiya Jana Sangh and Janata Party, which would soon challenge the dominance of the hegemonic Congress Party.

The Fourth Wave, 2000–

The far right entered a fourth wave in the twenty-first century, electorally and politically profiting from three "crises": the terrorist attacks of September 11, 2001 (and beyond), the Great Recession of 2008, and the "refugee crisis" of 2015. All the western democracies were affected, albeit in different ways, shaking the national and international political status quo, and giving rise to an unprecedented wave of Islamophobic and populist protest.

What characterizes the fourth wave, and differentiates it from the third wave, is the mainstreaming of the far right. While far-right politics was largely considered out of bounds for mainstream parties and politicians after 1945, with some notable exceptions (such as Eastern Europe in the 1990s and the US South in the 1960s), this is no longer the case today. In more and more countries, populist radical right parties and politicians are considered *koalitionsfähig* (acceptable for coalitions) by mainstream right, and sometimes even left, parties. Moreover, populist radical right (and even some extreme right) ideas are openly debated in mainstream circles, while populist radical right policies are adopted, albeit it generally in (slightly) more moderate form, by mainstream parties.

Another characteristic of the fourth wave is the heterogeneity of the far right, even within the subgroup of successful political parties. While the usual suspects still constitute the core – that is, the populist radical right parties that emerge from outside the political mainstream – they are complemented by a dizzying array of new far-right parties. The most important are transformed conservative parties, such as the Alliance of Young Democrats–Hungarian Civic Alliance (Fidesz) and Law and Justice (PiS) in Poland. Western European mainstream parties had transformed into radical right parties before, but the FPÖ and the SVP did this in opposition, while Fidesz and PiS transformed while in government. Even more shocking is the emergence of extreme right parties in national parliaments, such as the neo-Nazi Golden Dawn (XA) in Greece and the People's Party – Our Slovakia (ĽSNS), which was renamed Kotleba – People's Party Our Slovakia in 2015, after its leader Marian Kotleba.

Even when limiting our analysis to populist radical right parties, that is, the usual suspects, we see a fundamental change in the twenty-first century. First of all, most of the parties significantly increased their support. Far-right parties gained on average 4.7 percent of the vote in the first decade of the twenty-first century, and 7.5 percent in the second, that is, 2010–18 (see the table above). Second, populist radical right parties broke through in countries that had previously resisted them, like Germany and Sweden, or where they had remained relatively marginal, like Hungary and the Netherlands. Third, many populist radical right parties have numbered among the biggest parties in their country. In fact, several parties are, or have been at one time, the biggest party in their country in nationwide elections and polls, including the Danish People's Party (DF), Fidesz, the FN, PiS, and the SVP.

Radical right parties also became more relevant for government formation. First and foremost, more and more parties entered government, and in a variety of ways. Some, like Fidesz and PiS, were able to constitute governments by themselves – something only the Croatian Democratic Union[2] had been able to achieve in the third wave. Several others became official partners in coalition governments with non-far-right parties, such as the FPÖ in Austria, National Union Attack in Bulgaria, Popular Orthodox Rally in Greece, and LN in Italy. Finally, a few parties supported minority governments of non-far-right parties, generally getting a stricter immigration policy in return – as was the case with the DF in Denmark (2001–11 as well as 2016–19) and the Party for Freedom (PVV) in the Netherlands (2010–12).

And while the far right already had agenda-setting power during the third wave, leading often to a tougher discourse on immigration and immigrants, though more rarely to a toughening of policies, this has increased significantly during the fourth wave (see chapter 7). In the wake of the three "crises" of the early twenty-first century, radical right politics has become largely detached from populist radical right parties. Many (right-wing) parties now advance a nativist, authoritarian, and populist discourse, including Euroscepticism, Islamophobia, and opposition to "do-goodism" and "political correctness." From Austrian chancellor Sebastian Kurz to his British counterpart Theresa May, mainstream politicians are no longer just paying lip service to populist radical right policies, they are actually introducing stricter policies on immigration, integration, and terrorism themselves.

And the relevance of the far right is no longer limited to Europe either, if it ever was. A democratically elected far-right leader currently governs three of the five biggest countries in the world. In the case of Jair Bolsonaro in Brazil and Donald Trump in the US, they came to power on the list of non-far-right parties. In India, Prime Minister Narendra Modi is the leader of the BJP, the party representative of the well-established and -organized Hindutva movement, which includes violent, extremist groups like the National Volunteer Organization (RSS), of which Modi has been a member since he was eight years old. And in Israel, long-term prime minister Benjamin Netanyahu has brought his right-wing Likud party more and more in line with his various far-right coalition partners.

Was the Tea Party movement a populist radical right movement or a mainstream right-wing movement with populist radical right groups and individuals? Is the Republican Party in the US (still) a mainstream right-wing party with a far-right leader or has Trump successfully transformed the party in his image? Where does Britain's Conservative Party stop and the United Kingdom Independence Party (UKIP) or Brexit Party begin? Is there still a fundamental difference between Fidesz and the Movement for a Better Hungary (Jobbik), the original far-right party in Hungary, which in the past years has campaigned on a more moderate platform than the officially "conservative" Fidesz? The mainstreaming of the far right – in terms of ideology, politics, and organization – that characterizes the fourth wave has made the borders between the radical right and the mainstream right – and in some case left, as in the Czech Republic and Denmark – more and more difficult to establish.

2

Ideology

When we think about the far right, we tend to think
about ideological features like antisemitism and racism,
as well as political issues like immigration and security.
Although the far-right movement is highly diverse,
even within the two major subgroups, extreme right
and radical right, there are many ideological features
and political issues that are shared across groups and
parties. This chapter first discusses the key ideologies
within the extreme right, that is, fascism and Nazism,
and the key ideological features of the (populist) radical
right, that is, nativism, authoritarianism, and populism.[1]
It then discusses how these ideological features play out
in the major issues of the far right of the fourth wave:
immigration, security, corruption, and foreign policy.
Its views on gender will be discussed in chapter 9.

Ideology

Extreme right ideologies believe that inequalities are
natural and outside of the purview of the state. They

celebrate difference and hierarchy, and their core feature is elitism, which holds that some groups and individuals are superior to others and should therefore have more power. There are many different extreme right groups and ideas, which often disagree more than they agree. For example, absolutist monarchists and racists agree that the basis of power is blood, but the former refer exclusively to royal lineage, the latter to alleged racial differences. Some theocrats believe that the highest power comes from a "Holy Book," like the Bible or the Talmud, while fascists position it in the person of the leader. In this book, I focus exclusively on far-right groups that base their identity primarily on ethnic or racial categories, which means that those groups that are primarily monarchist or religious, and for which ethnic and racial distinctions are secondary or irrelevant, are not discussed.

The most important extreme right ideology is fascism, a syncretic ideology which draws on various left- and right-wing anti-democratic traditions. Historical Italian fascism, often referred to as Fascism with a capital "F," held that ultimate power rested in the leader, who was the embodiment of the nation and state. For fascists, the state is not just a legal institution, it is an ethical, organic, and spiritual entity which requires full loyalty and submission. In essence, fascism is totalitarian, in that it wants full control of society. Every aspect of life is to be controlled by the party/state and there is absolutely no space for independence. Unsurprisingly, fascism rejects democracy. Hitler stated that "democracy is the foul and filthy avenue to communism," while Mussolini rejected it as "electoralism."

Instead, fascism offers a "Third Way," which goes beyond liberalism and socialism. This is reflected in its economic doctrine of corporatism, in which society is organized in corporate groups, such as those of agriculture and the military, which are meant to work together, in an organic manner, to the benefit of the state. Fascism wants to realize a national "rebirth" and create a "new man," physically fit and ideologically pure, unbound by old hierarchies of class and heritage. As an ideology, fascism also believes in actions over words as well as war over peace. It believes that violence is power, and war not only is the natural state of life, but also purifies and regenerates the nation and state.

German fascism, better known as National Socialism or Nazism, shares many core features with (Italian) Fascism, but is more explicitly and fundamentally antisemitic and racist. Whereas fascists see the main entity as the state, a legal category, Nazis see it as the race, a supposedly biological category. Nazis believe that there are several different races and that the Aryan race is superior to all others. It is the right of the superior *Übermenschen* (superhumans) to dominate, and even exterminate, the inferior *Untermenschen* (subhumans). In the Nazis' worldview, Jews are seen as both morally and physically inferior, yet economically and politically powerful. Nazis claim that the actions and ideas – and especially "conspiracies" – of "the Jews" infect the Aryan race with moral and racial disease – hence their portrayal as rats (i.e. vermin) in propaganda such as the infamous 1940 movie *Der Ewige Jude* (*The Eternal Jew*).

It is important to situate the racism of the Nazis in its historical context. In the early twentieth century, antisemitism and racism were broadly accepted within German, and European, societies and even within parts of the scientific community. After the horrors of the Second World War, racism became largely unacceptable, and in some countries even illegal, while the whole concept of "race," and the existence of different "races," was mostly rejected. Instead, ingroups were increasingly defined in non-biological terms, most notably "ethnic groups" or "nations," which are both primarily cultural categories. A group of mainly French radical right activists, commonly known as the *nouvelle droite* (see chapter 3), developed a new ideology, which they termed *ethnopluralism*. Dismissed by opponents as merely "new racism," ethnopluralism argues that people are divided into ethnic groups, which are equal but should remain segregated. Whether implicitly or explicitly, ethnopluralism has become a core ideological feature of most relevant European radical right groups today.

That said, racism is not dead. It is still prominent within the extreme right (e.g. neo-Nazis and white supremacists) and even radical right politicians will at times slip into a racial or racist discourse. For instance, Martin Helme, the son of the leader of the Estonian Conservative People's Party (EKRE), and currently Estonian minister of finance, said on a Tallinn TV talk show, on recent riots and ethnic conflicts in Sweden, "Our immigration policy should have one simple rule: if you're black, go back." He also said, "I want Estonia to be a white country." Similarly, Thierry Baudet, leader of the new Dutch party Forum for Democracy (FvD), said in a discussion on the "refugee crisis" in 2015, "I don't want Europe to Africanize" and "I would really like Europe to stay dominantly white and culturally as it is now."

Whether informed primarily by racism or ethnopluralism, one of the key ideological features of the far right, and the dominant feature of the contemporary populist radical right, is *nativism*, a combination of nationalism and xenophobia. It is an ideology that holds that states should be inhabited exclusively by members of the native group (the nation) and that non-native (or "alien") elements, whether persons or ideas, are fundamentally threatening to the homogeneous nation-state. The core idea of nativism is best summarized in the slogan "Germany for the Germans, Foreigners Out," which became infamous as a rallying cry at the often-violent anti-refugee rallies of the early 1990s.

The ultimate goal of the populist radical right is an *ethnocracy*, that is, a democracy in which citizenship is based on ethnicity. It wants to (re)create this monocultural state by closing the borders to immigrants and giving "aliens" a choice between assimilation or repatriation. Those who are unwilling to assimilate, that is, become "native," must be expelled to the country they (or their ancestors) came from. However, populist radical right groups disagree about the scope of assimilation. Some believe that only "related" ethnic groups can assimilate – for example, only other (white) Europeans can become German or Hungarian – while others mainly hold that Islam is incompatible with their nation, meaning that Muslims cannot assimilate into "western" societies.

Within nativism, antisemitism and Islamophobia play particularly important roles. *Antisemitism*, hostility to or prejudice against Jews, was the key prejudice of the far right in the early twentieth century, and remains central to many extreme right groups today. However, many populist radical right groups and parties, particularly in Western Europe, are not antisemitic and some have even become philosemitic (pro-Jewish), seeing Israel as the ideal ethnocracy and Jews as natural allies in the struggle against Islam. *Islamophobia*, an irrational fear of Islam or Muslims, has become the defining prejudice of the far right of the fourth wave. In this view, Islam is equated with Islamism, that is, an extremist political interpretation of Islam, and Muslims are seen as hostile to democracy and to all non-Muslims – Islamophobes often proudly declare themselves to be "kuffars" or "infidels."

The term *authoritarianism* is often used to describe non-democratic leaders or political systems, but I use it

Islamophobic anti-Obama protester at Tea Party rally in Mishawaka, Indiana, in 2009. (Photo by author.)

in different manner, in line with a long tradition in social psychology. Here, authoritarianism refers to the belief in a strictly ordered society, in which infringements on authority are to be punished severely. Authoritarians see almost all "problems," including drug addiction or perceived sexual deviancy, as essentially law-and-order issues which can only be countered by a tough punitive approach and prevented by reintroducing "moral" or "traditional" education in schools.

Populism, finally, is the buzzword of the twenty-first century, but that prominence is in part a consequence of its conceptual confusion. I define populism as a (thin) ideology that considers society to be ultimately separated into two homogeneous and antagonistic groups, the pure people and the corrupt elite, and which argues that politics should be an expression of the *volonté générale* (general will) of the people. In essence, populists claim that the mainstream parties are working together to keep the people, of which the populists are the voice (i.e. the *vox populi*), from power. Indian prime minister and BJP leader Narendra Modi gave a good example in a speech in April 2018 when he declared that the Congress Party is for the elite (*namdaar*), whereas the BJP is for the people (*kaamdaars*).

In short, the far right consists, broadly, of two groups, the extreme right and the radical right, which hold fundamentally different positions on democracy. Whereas the extreme right rejects the essence of democracy – the idea of political equality and government by popular majority – the (populist) radical right supports democracy, at least in theory, but fundamentally challenges key institutions and values of liberal democracy, including minority rights, rule of law, and separation of powers. Hence, the difference between the two is not merely quantitative – in the sense that the extreme right is a more radical/extreme form of the radical right – it is also qualitative.

The different far-right groups and parties are acutely aware of this and often amplify their internal differences to sell themselves to potential followers. In general, extreme right groups attack radical right parties as corrupt and weak, "bourgeois" sellouts to the political establishment, who value acceptance by the political establishment, as well as individual material spoils, over their ideals. For their part, radical right parties denounce extreme right groups as full of crazies who are politically ineffective and/or dangerously violent. Many far-right groups spend more time denouncing their far-right "competitors" than their "real" enemies within the political establishment.

Rarely do they present each other as two sides of the same struggle. In fact, both accuse the other of undermining its righteous struggle. The radical right argues that the extreme right, through its ideological extremity and violent actions, discredits the broader struggle, while the extreme right holds that the radical right, because it works within the system, compromises the essence of the struggle, settling on compromises that uphold the fundaments of the despised political system.

Themes

During the third wave, the far right was often portrayed as a single-issue movement, exclusively concerned with immigration. This is incorrect. Immigration remains the key political issue for most far-right groups, particularly in Western Europe and North America, but it is only one of several issues that they campaign on. While there are many ideological and national variations, four political issue clusters are central to all far-right groups and parties around the globe: immigration, security, corruption, and foreign policy.

Immigration

The immigration issue includes two separate but related issues: immigration and integration. Immigration proper has long been one of the core issues of almost every far-right group in Europe and North America, but occasionally also features prominently in some countries in other regions (such as Brazil and Japan). Populist radical right parties typically claim that "mass immigration" constitutes an existential threat to their nation and state, while extreme right groups are more concerned about race, claiming that western countries are facing a "white genocide" because of mass immigration and state-sponsored multiculturalism.

In the twenty-first century, the conspiracy theory of "The Great Replacement" is at the heart of much of the anti-immigration rhetoric of the populist radical right – and, increasingly, the mainstream right. Popularized by French writers Jean Raspail and Renaud Camus, but building upon an antisemitic and racist tradition dating back to the late nineteenth century, the thesis holds that "the West" is being overrun by a "tidal wave" of non-Western immigration. Populist radical right politicians believe that mass immigration is not driven by poverty in developing countries, but organized by progressive politicians in the developed countries, who either hate their own nation or try to compensate for their lost electorate – which partly went to the populist radical right – by "importing" new voters. In recent years, strongly pushed by Hungarian premier Viktor Orbán, the Jewish US-Hungarian billionaire philanthropist George Soros has been seen as the evil genius in this conspiracy, reflecting a modern-day version of the infamous antisemitic classic *The Protocols of the Elders of Zion*.

Obviously, both "native" and "alien" are subjective terms. In the view of the far right, one is not simply native because one has citizenship of a country. In fact, many of the so-called "aliens" are born and bred in the "native" country, despite being falsely referred to as "immigrants" (not just by the far right). The key far-right "Other" of the twenty-first century is "the

Muslim," not just in Europe, but also in India and Israel as well as among many new groups in North America. Far from being exclusive to the far right, Islamophobia, and specifically a fear of "Islamization," dominates far-right propaganda, in which domestic and foreign developments are combined with conspiracy theories based on dubious statistics or simplistic narratives.

While many populist radical right politicians try to express their nativism in the largely neutral terms of ethnopluralism, they almost always argue or imply that the "native" culture is superior to the "alien" one(s). The far right describes "aliens" almost exclusively in derogatory terms. For example, BJP president Amit Shah claimed that Bangladeshi immigrants in India are "infiltrators" and "termites," Jewish Home leader, and then Israeli minister of education, Naftali Bennett referred to asylum seekers as "illegal infiltrators," and Brazilian president Jair Bolsonaro has called (Venezuelan) immigrants "scum of the earth."

Security

Far-right groups are obsessed with "security," but they interpret the concept much more broadly than just the physical security of individuals. Security refers both to individuals and to collectives, most notably the nation or race, and has a cultural, economic, and physical component. Almost every political issue is perceived through the lens of a "threat to the natural order," creating insecurity, which has to be dealt with by an iron hand. Whether it is drugs, immigration, or unemployment, the solution is found in authoritarian policies, celebrating the stick and criticizing the carrot. However, security almost always has a nativist component to it, given that "aliens" are seen as the key source of natives' insecurity.

Take the issue of crime, one of the most prominent themes in their propaganda. For the far right, crime is first and foremost an "alien" issue, in the sense that it almost exclusively focuses on (alleged) crimes committed by "non-natives." A striking example of this nativist fixation on crime is the Victims of Immigration Crime Engagement Office, an agency President Trump created within the Department of Homeland Security – itself an illustration of the securitization of immigration that followed the terrorist attacks of 9/11 in most western countries. Much far-right propaganda mentions "aliens" almost only as criminals and the few "native" crimes that are acknowledged are predominantly corruption cases by "progressive" political elites (see below).

According to the far right, crime is rampant, and increasing because of immigration and the "naïve" and "weak" policies of established politicians. Its propaganda is filled with selective and suggestive stories about "immigrant crime," or, in racial terms, "black-on-white crime," mostly from tabloids and right-wing media, which it presents as just the tip of the iceberg. When confronted with data that show that crime levels are actually decreasing, and are relatively low, as is the case in many western democracies, it tends to dismiss them as lies (e.g. Donald Trump's "fake news") produced by "the corrupt elite" and their "politically correct" minions to cover up the failures of multicultural society.

Key to the far right's programs around the globe are tough law and order issues, which it often shares with other right-wing groups, most notably conservatives. For the far right, crime is not related to socio-economic conditions – except if committed by poor "natives" – and has to be confronted with ruthless law enforcement. It therefore calls for more police on the streets and tougher sentences – but is divided on the death penalty – as well as less "political meddling" in law enforcement. Many groups also emphasize the need for schools to return to teaching youths discipline, respect, and "traditional values," notably the importance of the heterosexual family.

They link the issue of security to both elites (populism) and minorities (nativism). The youth are supposedly "indoctrinated" by left-wing teachers and academics who corrupt their innocent minds with "cultural Marxism" and other "perverse" ideas (see below). And it is because of the corruption or weakness of mainstream politicians that crime is rampant, and people feel insecure. For example, in India in 2018, Modi attacked the local Congress party in the state of Karnataka for interfering with the Lokayukta, an anti-corruption ombudsman organization, linking this directly to security: "In Karnataka there is no law, there is no order. The Lokayukta is not safe, how can the common people be safe." Similarly, in Brazil, during his 2018 presidential campaign, Bolsonaro proclaimed in one interview: "If a police officer kills ten, fifteen, or twenty alleged criminals with ten or thirty bullets each, he needs to get a medal and not be prosecuted."

However, the only way to truly stop the rise of crime, according to the far right, is to stop immigration. After all, in its world, crime is an almost exclusively "alien" phenomenon. Hence, Trump and other US nativists emphasize the crucial importance of building a wall on the southern border with Mexico – implying, against empirical evidence, that most crime in the US is committed by Latin American immigrants – while in the Netherlands Geert Wilders of the PVV campaigned from 2010 with the slogan "more security, less immigration." The most powerful, and racist, visualization of this mix of authoritarianism and nativism is the infamous campaign poster of the SVP in which a group of white sheep kick a black sheep off the Swiss flag under the slogan "creating security."

While the interrelation between crime and immigration has been a staple of the far right since at least the 1980s, the connection to the issue of terrorism is a more recent phenomenon. In the post-9/11 world, terrorism and Islam have been closely linked, in both mainstream and far-right discourse. Far-right groups rarely use the term "terrorism" for anything else than Islamist political violence, often minimizing, if not outright defending, "anti-immigrant" violence – or far-right-inspired violence against other groups, including representatives of left-wing groups and the state. For the far right, terrorism is closely related to immigration and multiculturalism. France's Marine Le Pen even went so far in 2017 as to call multiculturalism a weapon for Islamic extremists and claim that (multicultural) France has become "a university for Jihadists."

Corruption

While far-right propaganda primarily targets ethnic and racial "Others," internal and external to the country, the issue of corruption is almost exclusively linked to people from the in-group. Corruption is often mixed with authoritarianism, nativism, and, particularly, populism. It is a particular "elite" who are connected to corruption. On the one hand, it is the powerful, notably mainstream politicians, but also often economic elites, who are accused of stealing from the people. On the other hand, it is a political elite, broadly described as "the left," who are accused of corrupting the nation with "postmodernist" and "cultural Marxist" ideas – both terms, but particularly the latter, having strong antisemitic overtones. As Britain's UKIP tweeted in December 2018, "Make no mistakes, the EU wants to control your thoughts through your speech to spread its Postmodernist Neo-Marxist ideology."

Of course, in many countries, financial corruption by economic and political elites is a real and serious issue. For example, Bulgarian or Italian populist radical right parties don't have to invent scandals as their countries have long been plagued by widespread corruption. At the same time, even in these countries, many politicians are not corrupt – while several populist radical right parties (e.g. LN and RN) and politicians (e.g. Bolsonaro and Trump) have been linked to corruption too. But even in countries that are broadly acknowledged as not corrupt, like Estonia or Sweden, populist radical right parties use almost identical accusations. Far-right groups also argue that "the elite" corrupt the political system by electoral fraud. For example, both BJP president Shah and US president Trump have pushed the unsubstantiated claim that millions of "illegal immigrants" have been voting in elections in their respective countries.

Elites are also charged with corrupting the minds of the people, particularly of women (see chapter 9) and the youth. Far-right politicians from across the globe have accused academics, artists, and journalists not just of being elitist or left-wing, but also of being "anti-national": that is, traitors of the nation, the worst insult for a nationalist. For instance, Jewish Home politicians regularly attack progressive civil society organizations like the New Israel Fund, while the BJP has harassed domestic and foreign NGOs, including the Ford Foundation and Greenpeace, and has accused left-wing professors of having "occupied" academia and turned the youth against the nation. Extreme right politicians tend to substitute nation for race, but make similar claims, although they have a particular obsession with "race-mixing," which they consider a form of genocide. A special role in "white genocide" conspiracy theories is almost always reserved for "the Jews," who are alleged to mastermind all such plots in order to submit the white race to their power.

Foreign Policy

The far right lives in a dog-eat-dog world in which international relations are a zero-sum game: everyone is out for their own success, and so when one wins, the others lose. This is not to say it opposes any international cooperation, or does not care about other countries (or nations), but rather that this is always at best secondary to national (or racial) concerns – hence, Trump's "America First" policy has many national variants. Moreover, far-right groups have always been very suspicious of, and mostly outright hostile to, supranational organizations, from the strong EU to the much weaker United Nations (UN). But as much as they criticize the existing world order, they don't really have clear alternative visions, let alone one unified vision.

Irredentism, or the claim on some "lost" territory, plays a major role in the political program of many far-right groups, particularly in Central and Eastern Europe, where borders have shifted repeatedly in the past century. For instance, with the 1920 Treaty of Trianon, Hungary lost almost two-thirds of its territory – something that all the country's far-right organizations are obsessed with reversing. From Fidesz to the 64 Counties Youth Movement, they claim to represent all "ethnic Hungarians" – including the millions of Hungarian speakers in Romania, Serbia, Slovakia, and Ukraine – and strive to reunite all Hungarian territories.

Similarly, the struggle for Greater Israel (*Eretz Yisrael*) is at the heart of almost all Israeli far-right groups, while far-right organizations in India and Japan are focused on border disputes with Pakistan and China, respectively. The far right in Russia has a particularly dazzling myriad of irredentist fantasies, from a Eurasian Empire to a renewed Soviet Union under (explicit) Russian leadership. The most extreme is that of Vladimir Zhirinovsky, the longest-serving leader of a major far-right party in the world, the terribly misnamed Liberal Democratic Party of Russia. He once stated that he dreams of a time "when Russian soldiers can wash their boots in the warm waters of the Indian Ocean."

A second obsession of most far-right groups is supranational organizations, which are seen as a first step towards (cosmopolitan) one-world government. While most far-right groups are not fond of the UN, almost only US groups make a big issue out of this largely toothless organization. Conspiracy theories about secret plans to invade and occupy the US – ranging from Agenda 21 to black helicopters – reach deep inside the conservative movement, while far-right groups see the dawn of a "New World Order," after former President George H.W. Bush's famous "slip of the tongue" in a 1992 speech. Israeli far-right groups consider the UN to be an antisemitic organization, dominated by Arab states, and intent on destroying the State of Israel. And in his maiden speech to the Australian parliament in 2016, Australian ONP senator Malcolm Roberts called upon his country to leave the "socialistic, monolithic" UN.

Unsurprisingly, the actually powerful EU is a major concern for the European far right, which considers it a threat to national sovereignty. As Euroscepticism started to spread among European publics in the wake of the 1992 Maastricht Treaty, most far-right groups and parties became more outspoken and radical in their opposition to the EU. This has only increased after the so-called "refugee crisis" of 2015, as German chancellor Angela Merkel's pro-refugee policy and the EU's (ultimately unsuccessful) refugee redistribution plan infuriated the far right. This sentiment is clearly expressed in a 2018 tweet by Santiago Abascal, the leader of the newest stars in the European populist radical right firmament, the Spanish party Vox, who ranted against "the globalist oligarchy, freeloading on [public] budgets, which hopes to impose failed models on the people, [and] now dedicates itself to demonizing democracy and the sovereignty of nations."

During the third wave, most populist radical right parties were on the defensive with respect to European integration. Only a few openly called for their country to exit the EU, but almost all parties believed that the integration process had gone too far, particularly after the signing of the Maastricht Treaty, and wanted to roll back newer initiatives and stop further integration. The EU was seen as a hostile and remote bureaucracy in which "nationalist" forces had no voice. As a consequence of their growing electoral successes and political relevance in the fourth wave, populist radical right parties have become more ambitious and bold with regard to the EU. This is particularly true for populist radical right leaders in Central and Eastern Europe, who see their own countries as the "bulwark of Christianity" (PiS leader Jarosław Kaczynskí in Poland) and "the future of Europe" (Fidesz leader Viktor Orbán in Hungary).

Today, few relevant populist radical right parties still want to leave the EU. Both Marine Le Pen and Geert Wilders had shifted to an exit position in 2013, only to muddle it later on – partly due to the European backlash to the incompetent handling of Brexit by the British government. Most populist radical right parties remain Eurosceptic, however, wanting to "reform" the EU into a looser and more democratic organization which returns national sovereignty to its member states. Still, they differ on the fundamental nature of the future Europe. Ethnic nationalist parties like the Belgian VB want a "Europe of Nations," but state nationalist parties like France's RN and Spain's Vox prefer a "Europe of Fatherlands" (i.e. current states), fearing separatism at home. And while Fidesz and PiS call for a "Christian Europe," most West European populist radical right parties are much less comfortable with a continent defined in explicitly religious terms.

Finally, far-right parties are deeply divided on how the world should be ordered. During the Cold War, many radical right parties, somewhat grudgingly, supported the western NATO alliance, while most extreme right groups proposed a post-fascist Third Way. Today, many are worried about a unipolar world dominated by the US, even under President Trump, and embrace a stronger Russia to counter US hegemony. True to visions of French grandeur, Marine Le Pen has proposed a nationalist Washington–Paris–Moscow axis between her, Trump, and Putin. But many East European far-right groups, like EKRE and PiS, are deeply Russophobic and prefer a US-dominated world. Similarly, in India Modi seems fairly supportive of a dominant US, for now, while in Brazil Bolsonaro has vowed to work with Trump, in particular to oppose China's growing power.

The Role of Religion

Far-right ideologies can be combined with all religions as well as with a non-religious and even anti-religious position. Italian Fascism was initially anti-religious, but shifted to a more non-religious position after coming to a pragmatic agreement with the Vatican. Most contemporary European populist radical right groups are at best culturally Christian, in the sense that they consider Christianity, or a specific denomination (e.g. Roman Catholicism), as part of the national culture. Some go even a step further, arguing that one specific religion is part of the nation. For example, the DF's program states that "the Danish Evangelical Lutheran Church is the Church of the Danish people," while SD leader Jimmie Åkesson has said that the Church of Sweden should be reinstated as a state church. In light of the rising importance of Islamophobia, many populist radical right parties have become more outwardly Christian, embracing Christianity or more vaguely "Judeo-Christian values," without becoming truly religious parties. For instance, the Austrian FPÖ, which was founded as an anti-clerical party, has recently become a staunch defender of orthodox Catholics like former St. Pölten bishop Kurt Krenn, a vocal opponent of Islam and Muslim immigration.

The link between the far right and Christianity is strong in the US, at least on the populist radical right. Politicians from Pat Buchanan to Sarah Palin have defined the US as a "Christian nation" and have emphasized the importance of Christianity to politics. On the extreme right, the KKK has always been deeply religious, changing from exclusively Protestant to inclusively Christian over time (see vignette 1). However, many extreme right groups are only nominally Christian, or even explicitly anti-Christian, arguing that Christianity is "Jewish." For instance, groups like the now almost defunct Aryan Nations adhere to Christian Identity, an antisemitic and racist form of "Christianity," in which whites are the true "Chosen People" and all non-whites are seen as soulless "mud people."

Outside of the US, some far-right groups and politicians are openly Christian in a religious way. Bolsonaro ran with the initial slogan "Brazil above everything, and God above us all." The Polish PiS is deeply Catholic and closely associated with the most nationalist and orthodox elements of the Polish Catholic Church. It has argued that the "European Constitution" should include a reference to "God," and has made its orthodox interpretation of Catholicism a leading principle in many of its education, family, and health policies. The small neo-fascist New Force in Italy is fundamentalist Catholic and strives for the "recovery of Christian religiosity" and "faith in the Catholic Church."

In general, ties between the far right and religion are closer in Orthodox Christian countries, from Greece to Russia, given that most Orthodox Churches are national churches and have strong nationalist traditions. In Romania, small neo-Guardist groups remain loyal to an esoteric combination of mysticism and Orthodoxy – a faith which in the early twentieth century defined the original Legion of the Archangel Michael, more popularly known as the Iron Guard. In Ukraine, several far-right groups, like Svoboda and C14, support the schismatic Orthodox Church of Ukraine, which split from the official Ukrainian Orthodox Church, an autonomous branch of the Russian Orthodox Church, in 2018.

In contrast, there are quite strong pagan, and explicitly anti-Christian, strands within the European far right too. The French *nouvelle droite* is officially pagan, arguing that "Judeo-Christian monotheism" has become secularized. Following the German philosopher Friedrich Nietzsche, its main thinker, Alain De Benoist, argued in his book *On Being a Pagan* (1981) that Christianity must be destroyed, and a new "Indo-European" paganism should be created. Various extreme right groups also hark back to (alleged) pre-Christian beliefs, including various forms of *Ásatrú* (heathenry). In the late twentieth century, Odinism, and particularly its racial form, Wotanism, which worships Nordic gods like Odin and Thor, became popular among some neo-Nazi groups. Elements of Wotanism can also be found in some Christian Identity groups, as well as the now practically defunct "Creativity" movement, while some extreme right groups even practice Satanism.

Hindutva ideology is perhaps the most perfect mix of nativism and religion. Going back to the classic text *Essentials of Hindutva* (1923) by Vinayak Damodar Savarkar, it replaces purely religious Hinduism with more nationalist *Hindu Rashtra*, that is, the Hindu nation. Initially, it also had a strong racist component, referring to the *Arya* (Hindu race), as Savarkar was strongly influenced by European fascism, particularly Nazism. While contemporary Hindutva groups like the BJP and RSS no longer (openly) support fascism or biological racism, they remain committed to a staunchly xenophobic Hindu nationalism. With the exception of some specific groups that are seen as part of the Hindu fraternity (e.g. Buddhists and Sikhs), Hindutva groups consider non-Hindus like Christians and Muslims as threats to the Hindu nation and an obstacle to the desired Hindu state (Hindustan).

Buddhism has long been seen as an exceptional religion, untainted by religious fanatics or violent nationalists. This image was shattered by recent events in Myanmar. While the government and military mostly justify the brutal repression of the Muslim Rohingya in terms of national security, far-right groups like the decentralized 969 Movement and the Organization for the Protection of Race and Religion, as well as extremist leaders like monk Ashin Wirathu, want to punish everyone who "insults" Buddhism. This includes, by definition, people of other religions. Far-right Buddhists have not only been involved in violent pogroms against the Rohingya minority, but have also branded Myanmar human rights groups as "traitors on national affairs" and accused them of being backed by foreign groups.

Unsurprisingly, the connection with religion is very strong among the Jewish far right, given their ethno-religious definition of the nation. With few exceptions

– notably Israel Our Home, which caters primarily to secular Russian immigrants – Israeli far-right groups combine ethnic nationalism with religious Judaism. The National Religious camp, mainly represented by Jewish Home and its most recent split, New Right, has long based its struggle for the annexation of "Judea and Samaria" (the West Bank) on the biblical argument that God gave the Land of Israel to its Chosen People (the Jews). The most extreme fusion of Israeli nationalism and Jewish religion is Kahanism, which combines fascism with religious fundamentalism. According to the late Rabbi Meir Kahane, not only should Israel occupy the whole "Land of Israel," but also only (real) Jews should inhabit it, and all non-Jews should be (forcefully) expelled.

One of the few clear examples of a far-right Muslim movement, at least in the essentially nativist sense defined here, is the Turkish Nationalist Action Party (MHP). Initially a secularist party, it embraced Islam in the 1970s, arguing "We are as Turk as the Tengri mountain and as Muslim as the Hira mountain. Both philosophies are our principles." In the 1980s, the Idealist faction broke off and founded the Grand Unity Party, which combines Turkish nationalism with Islamism. Islam plays a central role in Malay nationalism too. While the former ruling United Malays National Organization combines Malay nationalism with a multinational society, albeit with decades of racial politics, it is increasingly struggling with more radical Malay nationalists, who believe only Muslims can be real Malays, and who attack non-Muslims (notably Chinese, Christians, and Hindus).

Vignette 1: Shifting "Us" and "Them"

All far-right ideologies are built around a strict us-versus-them opposition, but both the *us* and the *them* can change over time. As groups have come to consider different "Others" as threatening, they have changed not only the "them," but also the "us." This is the case not just across different groups, but even within similar groups.

A good example of these shifting identities is the KKK, which wreaked havoc in the US South in the late 1860s. Founded by former Confederate soldiers, the Klan claimed to defend the White Anglo-Saxon Protestant (WASP) Southerner and targeted both African Americans and Yankees in the South (derogatively referred to as "carpet-baggers"), although they primarily killed the former. The second KKK, which emerged in the early twentieth century, was not merely a Southern phenomenon. No longer opposing Yankees, it was particularly successful above the Mason–Dixon line, including in Indiana and Illinois. Still hating African Americans (and Jews), the new Klan now mainly railed against Catholic immigration from Europe. The third and current iteration of the KKK, a mostly Southern reaction to the civil rights movement of the 1960s, is still deeply antisemitic and racist, but primarily defends "Christian whites" instead of only WASPs. They increasingly overlap with neo-Nazi groups, which have replaced the Nazis' "Aryan" race with the broader "white" race, thereby no longer excluding Slavs and other non-Germanic whites.

A more recent transformation of us and them identities can be seen in the fourth wave, in which the main enemies of the populist radical right have become Islam and Muslims. While it defined "immigrants" primarily in ethno-national terms in the 1980s and 1990s, the largely similar "aliens" are mainly described in ethno-religious terms today – an important, legal, difference is that most of the former were indeed immigrants, whereas most "aliens" today are actually citizens, born and raised in Western Europe or the US. In the post-9/11 world, and the ongoing "War on Terror," Turks and Moroccans in Germany and the Netherlands, or Bengalis and Pakistanis in the UK, have become (just) Muslims. Unsurprisingly, this has led many far-right groups to emphasize or even rediscover their own religious roots, redefining the "us" more in terms of Christian or "Judeo-Christian civilization."

But the "us" can even change in national terms. The FPÖ was founded in the 1950s as a Great German party, defining Austrians as part of the German nation, and rejecting the construct of an Austrian nation as an "ideological monstrosity." But in the 1980s, in its attempt to increase electoral support, the FPÖ shed its Great German ideology and redefined itself as the party of "Austrian patriots." Similarly, Umberto Bossi founded the LN in staunch opposition to the Italian state. The party later even invented its own nation, Padania, with a new currency, flag, and passport. But when Matteo Salvini took over in 2013, he rebuilt the moribund LN as an Italian party, downplaying regionalism (and Padania) as well as attacks on Southern Italians, and prioritizing attacks on Muslims and, more recently, refugees. Salvini

even dropped "Nord" from the party name, successfully campaigning as Lega (League) with the slogan "Italians first" in the 2018 parliamentary elections.

3

Organization

Far-right politics comes in a broad variety of forms, not just in terms of ideology and issues, but also in types of organizations. Some groups have millions of supporters, others just a handful. Some are purely intellectual, others primarily violent. Some are, organizationally speaking, more similar to mainstream political parties like Britain's Conservative Party or Labour Party, others to US criminal gangs like the Bloods and the Crips.

There are many different ways to slice up the far right organizationally, and none of them is perfect. I roughly follow the distinction introduced by the German political scientist Michael Minkenberg,[1] although with slightly different terminology, distinguishing between political parties, social movement organizations, and subcultures. Simply stated, political parties run for elections, social movement organizations do not, and while parties and social movement organizations are reasonably well-organized groups, subcultures are not.

In the following sections, I describe the main characteristics and representatives of the different organizational structures within the contemporary far right. It is not an attempt to be exhaustive, and by the time you read this, some might already be dated. Many far-right organizations are still very fluid and temporal; they come and go and sometimes even change roles (e.g. from party to social movement organization). The chapter ends with a discussion of the international collaboration of the far right, a topic of grandiose speculation, but whose reality is much more modest.

Political Parties

In their most essential form, political parties are political groups that contest elections to public office. Given that most democracies are party democracies, in which almost all crucial political positions are occupied by people elected on a party ticket, far-right political parties are at the core of the fourth wave. They contest elections in the vast majority of western democracies, and are getting elected to a majority of their national parliaments. At the same time, far-right parties differ in many ways. Leaving aside ideological differences, which have been addressed previously, far-right parties differ in terms of organizational structure, often but not always a consequence of their respective age. The two extremes are the Indian BJP, which resembles the mass party of the mid-twentieth century, and the Dutch PVV, which literally is a one-man party.

Founded in 1980, the BJP is the main party-political representative of the *Sangh Parivar* (Family of Organizations), the broader Hindu nationalist (*Hindutva*) movement that organizes and represents tens of millions of people across the globe. The BJP has dominated two right-wing coalition governments in India and currently controls many of the country's most populous and important states. It claims to have almost

BJP supporters riding motorbikes carrying BJP flags in New Delhi, India, after winning the 2014 parliamentary election. (Source: Arindam Banerjee/Dreamstime.com/2014.)

one hundred million members, which would make it the biggest political party in the world – even bigger than the Chinese Communist Party. It is a cadre-based party that draws its leadership from the party and the broader *Sangh Parivar*, while its members are organized in hundreds of local, regional, and state branches, including a host of auxiliary organizations, including for farmers, students, and workers, as well as for women, youth, and, interestingly, minorities. "Non-Resident Indians" and other BJP supporters residing outside of India are organized in the Overseas Friends of Bharatiya Janata Party, which claims branches in forty countries across all inhabited continents.

In sharp contrast, the PVV is the most extreme example of a leader-party, given that Geert Wilders is not just the leader of the party, he literally *is* the party. Wilders was a rising backbencher for the conservative People's Party for Freedom and Democracy in the Netherlands who faced pushback for his increasingly strident opposition to Islam and Turkish EU membership. In 2005, he split from the party, continuing for the rest of the legislative period as Group Wilders, before founding the PVV the next year. The party has only two statutory members, Wilders and a foundation of which he is the only member.

All other far-right parties fall somewhere in between these two extremes, with modest levels of membership and organization, and a relatively small cadre of party activists who are almost independent from the party membership. Many parties are dependent upon state funding, which is linked to electoral results and/or parliamentary seats, explaining why few far-right parties survive outside of parliament. In most cases, when they cannot get a foothold in parliament, they remain parties in name only, functioning mainly as political organizations, which rarely contest elections, and never with significant success.

Compared to most mainstream political parties – be they left, right, or center – far-right parties have an organizational structure that is more centralized and leader-centric. Such a structure is not uncommon for new parties, but far-right parties rarely truly democratize. Some hold elections for the party leader among their members, but they are "guided" at best, with the leadership strictly controlling the election procedures and vetting "suitable" candidates from an in-crowd of party cadres. This often leads to frustration and rebellion, but also ensures a relatively smooth transfer of power with relatively marginal changes in ideology, organization, and personnel. Hence, contrary to the popular image of the "flash party," surviving for just one or two elections, several far-right parties have survived initial electoral defeats and internal struggles and are now successfully established within their respective political systems.

Social Movement Organizations

There are a myriad of far-right groups beyond political parties, which range from well-structured, well-funded organizations with hundreds of thousands of members to marginal groupuscules so tiny that they could fit in one bedroom. Many of these organizations are part of a larger social movement, to which they bring some level of structure and permanence. While all organizations share a far-right ideology, they have very different activities, agendas, and constituencies. I focus here primarily on intellectual, media, and political organizations.

Intellectual Organizations

The far right is not a particularly intellectual movement – in fact many far-right groups are openly anti-intellectual, considering all "intellectuals" to be "cultural Marxists" (see chapter 2). But there are some organizations that focus on developing and innovating far-right ideas and educating primarily far-right activists. This includes both specific organizations within the more successful political parties, which organize thematic conferences and summer schools to educate their cadres, and groups that focus exclusively on education, for example by publishing books and magazines.

The most important intellectual far-right movement is the *nouvelle droite* (New Right), a very loosely structured movement of individuals and magazines that spans the globe. These "Gramscians of the Right" believe a political victory can only follow cultural hegemony, which is to be achieved by actively changing the political discourse. They position themselves as anti-1968ers, being both inspired and triggered by the success of the New Left of that period. In many ways, the *nouvelle droite* has copied New Left strategies and tactics, albeit somewhat less successfully (for now).

Its origins lie in the Research and Study Group for European Civilization (GRECE), founded in 1968, whose major figure is Alain De Benoist. The *nouvelle droite* has been instrumental in modernizing classic far-right thinking by replacing classic racism, based on biology and superiority, with ethnopluralism, based on ethnicity and (alleged) equality. It argues that cultures are equal but different, and people can only fully flourish within their own culture, which it associates with a set of traditions. Consequently, it opposes multi-culturalism, which it, paradoxically, considers racist. More recently, the Identitarian movement has taken the *nouvelle droite*'s ideas out of the boring constraints of magazines and think tanks and combined it with media-genic street politics (see vignette 3 in chapter 5).

The US has a broad range of right-wing think tanks, some of which spread core beliefs of the far right. These include anti-immigration organizations like the Federation for Immigration Reform, and allied groups like the Center for Immigration Studies and Numbers USA, which have become fully mainstreamed under the Trump presidency. Similarly, Islamophobic organizations like Frank Gaffney's Center for Security Policy and National Security Advisor John Bolton's Gatestone Institute have become key players in the Trump administration, showing the partial overlap between radical right and (neo-)conservative ideologies and policies – notably in a shared Islamophobia and distrust, or even rejection, of multinational organizations like the UN. At the same time, so-called "alt right" organizations, like Jared Taylor's American Renaissance and Richard Spencer's National Policy Institute, have remained solidly excluded, even during the Trump presidency.

In recent years, far-right activists have also tried to establish their own educational initiatives. Many

European parties were already organizing "summer universities," particularly to educate and socialize their most promising members (their current and future cadres). For example, the FN has been organizing summer universities throughout France for decades, while the VB, and its youth wing, Flemish Interest Youth, has done the same, moving around Europe (including Austria, Croatia, France, and Spain). Most of these gatherings are more summer camp than university, particularly when organized for youth, with a host of physical activities combined with lectures by far-right speakers from inside and outside of the respective party.

More recently, Marion Maréchal-Le Pen, Marine Le Pen's niece, stepped back from active party politics within the FN to establish the Institute of Social Sciences, Economics, and Politics in Lyon. The goal of the new institute is to "detect and train the leaders of tomorrow who will have the courage, intelligence, discernment and competence to act effectively ... in the service of society." Earlier, in Poland, the far right, ultra-orthodox Catholic priest Tadeusz Rydzyk, who previously had supported the League of Polish Families (LPR) and is now close to PiS, founded the College of Social and Media Culture in Torún in 2001. Its graduates have taken prominent places in the private and public Polish media, particularly when PiS is in power.

Media Organizations

The far right has always had its own media organizations, but most were part of larger, or simply better-financed, parties and movements. This applies both to newspapers like the *Deutsche National-Zeitung*, which was published by Dr. Gerhard Frey, the leader of the small German People's Union party, or *Éléments* and *Nouvelle École*, published by GRECE. Most of these publications had a relatively limited audience, reaching not much beyond the (dedicated) membership of their parent organizations.

During the fourth wave, many new far-right media organizations have emerged as a consequence of two developments: (1) the emergence of social media; and (2) the success and mainstreaming of the populist radical right. As soon as the Internet took shape in the 1990s, far-right entrepreneurs saw the advantages for the movement and established a significant presence. Among the first, and for a long time most important, was the *Stormfront* website, operated by ex-KKK leader Don Black, which functioned for many years as the hub for global neo-Nazis and white supremacists. The US far right is highly active online, including through websites like the radical right *Breitbart News*, the neo-Nazi *Daily Stormer*, the conspiratorial *Info Wars*, and the white supremacist *V-DARE*. In Canada, *Rebel Media* functions as an equivalent of *Breitbart News*, while *GeenStijl* (No Style) could be seen as a less professional Dutch equivalent (albeit, technically, a predecessor).

There are a host of European far-right online and offline media too, claiming to provide "real" or "uncensored" news, particularly on the far right's favorite issues like crime, corruption, European integration, and immigration. Some of the more prominent include the Czech *Parlementní Listy* (Parliamentary List), the German *Junge Freiheit* (Young Freedom), the Polish *Gazeta Polska* (Polish Newspaper), and the Spanish *Caso Aislado* (Isolated Case). Outside of Europe and North America, some key far-right media include *Arutz Sheva* (Israel National News) in Israel, *OPEN Magazine* in India, and the online web portal *R7* in Brazil.

Many of the primarily Islamophobic media websites, like *The Brussels Journal*, *Gates of Vienna*, and *Voice of Europe*, claim to be "conservative," which in part reflects the growing ideological and personal convergence between conservative and populist radical right subcultures on issues like immigration and Islam. This convergence, or transformation, has also made some established conservative media into voices of the populist radical right. In Hungary, almost all public and private media have come under the control of the radical right government, and now function as Viktor Orbán's propaganda instruments (see vignette 4 in chapter 7).

Political Organizations

Most far-right groups are political groups, or at least aspire to influence the politics of their country. In fact, some are fairly similar to political parties, in that they have a formal membership, an ideological program, and a fairly sophisticated organizational structure. What distinguishes them from political parties is that they don't contest elections – or have stopped doing so. But the borders are porous, as some political (and social) organizations will occasionally contest elections, at least in some localities, even if they mainly organize non-electoral activities (see chapter 5).

The bulk of far-right political organizations are marginal, with at best a few dozen activists and only a local or online presence. They perform mostly a social function, providing a (safe) meeting space for politically likeminded people, and rarely engage in public activities. This applies as much to the various *Kameradschaften* (Comraderies) in Germany as to the KKK in the US. Even slightly bigger organizations, like the now banned National Action in the UK and the National Socialist Movement in the US, organize only a few, badly attended, rallies, even if they can be responsible for serious violence.

But there are also much bigger and more powerful far-right political organizations, which influence party politics, sometimes even in countries without a strong far-right party. A good example is Japan Conference (Nippon Kaigi), founded in 1997, and with a membership of around 38,000 people, organized in some 230 local branches. Japan Conference is devoted to constitutional revision and historical revisionism, wanting to re-establish Japan as a military power and restore the country's (and emperor's) honor by "changing the postwar national consciousness," which is based on the "illegitimate" Tokyo War Crimes tribunals of 1946–8. While not a political party itself, it is a major player within the Liberal Democratic Party, Japan's dominant political party. A staggering fifteen of the eighteen members of the third Abe Cabinet (2014–18) were members of Japan Conference, including Prime Minister Shinzō Abe, while the organization also claimed 289 of the 480 members of the Japanese parliament.

In recent years, we have seen a few national, and even transnational, organizations that have been reasonably successful in street politics. The English Defence League (EDL) organized various Islamophobic rallies in England, which attracted at times thousands of protesters. Mixing far-right and hooligan cultures, the EDL quickly became a media sensation, leading to offshoots in Europe, North America, and Australasia. However, in recent years it has suffered from declining numbers of demonstrators and internal power struggles. Similarly, Patriotic Europeans Against the Islamization of the Occident (PEGIDA) took the media by storm, despite attracting a sizeable crowd only in Dresden, in the east of Germany, its city of origin. A somewhat similar group in Japan is the Association of Citizens Against the Special Privileges of *Zainichi*, the Korean minority in Japan. Better known as Zaitokukai, it was founded in 2007, and has a volatile, loosely defined and structured, membership that peaked at around 15,000.[2] While Zaitokukai is mostly active on the Internet, it has organized many, mainly smaller, demonstrations against the alleged privileges of the *Zainichi* as well as immigration and immigrants more generally.

Subcultures

Subcultures are groups within the larger national culture that share an identity, values, practices, and cultural objects. Within a subculture, people's common identity is based upon a perceived similar culture (including ideas and symbols) rather than an institutional affiliation. This is not to say that subcultures never include (strong) institutions. Examples of national far-right subcultures are the *Nemzeti Rock* (national rock) subculture in Hungary – which includes a large number of festivals, groups, and even radio stations – and the *Uyoku dantai* in Japan, a loose network of far-right groups that are particularly known for their *gaisensha*, that is, buses and vans covered in propaganda slogans and fitted with loudspeakers, which drive through the streets in small convoys.

There are very few truly far-right international subcultures. In most cases, the far right is part of a broader subculture, either as individuals or as a sub-subculture. Owing to the media obsession with the far right, it can come to define broader subcultures in the public imagination, even if it actually constitutes a (loud and violent) minority, as used to be the case with football hooligans and remains the case with skinheads. In the following section, I will discuss some of the more relevant and well-known far-right subcultures as well as some subcultures with a significant far-right presence.

"Alt-Right"

The so-called "alt-right," short for alternative right, is a somewhat unfortunate term which has gained popularity in the US and beyond in recent years. It was popularized by Richard Spencer, a well-educated white nationalist, with the aim of bringing together as broad a group of "race realists" as possible. Aware that ideologies and terms like white nationalism and white supremacy scared away many, particularly better-educated, people because of their negative connotations, Spencer used the term "alt-right," which broke out of its shadow as a consequence of the rise of Donald Trump and, in particular, Hillary Clinton's ill-advised "alt-right" speech of August 2016.

The essence of the "alt-right" is best captured by the Southern Poverty Law Center, a US anti-racist group, which described it as "a set of far-right ideologies, groups and individuals whose core belief is that 'white identity' is under attack by multicultural forces using 'political correctness' and 'social justice' to undermine white people and 'their' civilization."[3] As with all subcultures, there are only a handful of significant groups or organizations. One of the few organizations with some durability is Spencer's marginal National Policy Institute, a self-described "independent organization dedicated to the heritage, identity, and future of people of European descent in the United States and around the world."

What sets the "alt-right" apart from other far-right subcultures is that it is almost exclusively an online phenomenon. And even online it has a minimal organizational infrastructure. There are some online magazines, like *American Renaissance* (Jared Taylor), *Counter Currents* (Greg Johnson), and *Taki's Magazine* (named after founder Taki Theodoracopulos), but most alt-right activity is unorganized and anonymous and takes place on broader platforms like *4chan* and *Reddit*. It consists mostly of trolling people on social media, like Facebook and Twitter, by posting misogynist and racist memes or posts. There is a significant overlap with other amorphous online subcultures, most notably the gamer world and the so-called "manosphere" (see chapter 9), all dominated by younger, more educated, white males.

Emboldened by Donald Trump's election to the presidency in 2016, even though it has a complicated relationship to him, the "alt-right" tried to create an offline presence. The most successful event was the "Unite the Right" rally in Charlottesville, Virginia, in August 2017. It attracted roughly 1,000 people, although mostly from more traditional neo-Nazi and white supremacist groups like various Klans and the National Socialist Movement, and ended in violence and the murder of counter-protester Heather Heyer. Since then, "alt-right" rallies have rarely attracted more than a few dozen protesters, in addition to many more anti-fascists, and in March 2018 Spencer abandoned his intended university speaking tour after a few months, fed up with anti-fascist violence and legal battles with reluctant university administrators.

Today the "alt-right" remains a mostly anonymous online phenomenon. While international in scope, the subculture is very focused on the Anglo-Saxon world, most notably the US. Even bloggers and vloggers from other countries, like the Swedish–US couple Hendrik Palmgren and Lara Lokteff, of the website *Red Ice*, and Canadian Lauren Southern, formerly of *Rebel Media*, primarily address a US audience. This is even the case for the Swedish businessman Daniel Friberg, who has financed far-right projects in the US – including the website *AltRight.com*.

Football Hooligans

In terms of core demographics, far-right groups, football supporters, and street violence all disproportionately attract young, white, working-class males. The existence of far-right football hooligans is therefore not overly surprising, but its relevance has been significantly overplayed in alarmist media accounts and sensationalist hooligan literature. While much violence was more or less spontaneous, involving fluid groups of ever-changing football supporters, there were also more organized groups of hooligans, so-called "firms," which created a shadowy subculture and structure with their own codes and clothes. Among the most notorious British firms with a strong far-right presence were the Headhunters (Chelsea FC), the Inter City Firm (West Ham United), the Service Crew (Leeds United), and the Soul Crew (Cardiff City).

Far-right hooliganism migrated to the European continent in the 1980s, where local hooligans largely mimicked British firms. Some big European clubs with infamous far-right hooligans are/were Borussia Dortmund and Hansa Rostock (Germany), Hellas Verona and SS Lazio (Italy), FC Feyenoord and FC Groningen (the Netherlands), and Espanyol and Real Madrid (Spain). The problem is much bigger in Eastern Europe, however, where clubs like Dynamo Zagreb (Croatia), Ferencvaros (Hungary), Legia Warsaw (Poland), Spartak Moscow (Russia), and Karpaty Lviv (Ukraine) are notorious for their far-right support. Only a few non-European clubs are known for their far-right ultras. The best known is Beitar Jerusalem in Israel, whose far-right hooligans, known as *La Familia*, are infamous for their "Death to Arabs" chants.

Most West European states have clamped down on hooliganism in general, and far-right hooliganism in particular, through bans on far-right and hooligan symbols as well as stadium bans for violent fans in the late twentieth century. But in recent years, football hooligans have again become involved in far-right actions, mostly outside of football stadiums. For example, Chemnitz FC hooligans played a major role in anti-refugee demonstrations and violence in the East German city in 2018, while hooligans of Dutch club PSV were involved in attacks on anti-racist protesters at a *Sinterklaas* event in Eindhoven that same year. Football hooligans have also founded their own Islamphobic "anti-extremist" organizations, notably the British Democratic Football Lads Alliance and the German Hooligans Against Salafists, which have organized demonstrations with several thousands of participants.

Skinheads

The skinhead subculture emerged in London in the 1960s, as a working-class alternative to the middle-class hippie subculture. Building upon other subcultures, including the mostly black rude boys and the mostly white mods, the initial skinhead subculture was multiracial and relatively apolitical. Musically diverse, from ska to punk, skinheads stood out because of their shaved heads and a specific, and relatively strict, dress code, including Dr. Martens boots, Fred Perry polo shirts, bleached jeans, and narrow braces.

In the 1970s, part of the skinhead movement became increasingly associated with the far right, in particular Britain's National Front, which was one of the first anti-immigrant parties to contest elections in postwar Europe. NF activist Ian Stuart Donaldson (a.k.a. Ian Stuart) was instrumental in the creation of the far-right skinhead subculture, as was his band, Skrewdriver, whose record and song "White Power" is the unofficial anthem of the movement. Far-right skinheads developed a somewhat different dress code, shedding much of the rude boys' culture, but still look largely identical to other skinheads, including anti-racist skins (Skinheads Against Racial Prejudice), also known as "redskins."

Although most media conflate the skinhead movement with the far right, the vast majority of skinheads are non-political or anti-racist. The "Nazi skin" movement peaked in the 1980s in much of Western Europe, and in the 1990s in North America, and has declined sharply since. In part because of the negative public image of skinheads, far-right subcultures have increasingly diversified, and mainstreamed, in terms of music and style. Today, far-right skinheads mainly remain prominent in Eastern Europe, including in the Czech Republic, Poland, Russia, and Serbia. But there are even small neo-Nazi skin subcultures in non-white countries, including Mongolia and Malaysia.

In essence, the far-right skinhead movement is mainly a subculture, without strong organizations of its own, existing primarily online and mobilizing around specific concerts. It is built around a combination of cultural and political markers, expressions of which mainly exist online and around concerts in fashion and music.

International Collaboration

Despite alarmist accusations by some anti-fascists, and sensationalist stories by journalists, international collaborations between far-right activists and organizations have never been particularly successful. This applies to both the extreme right and the radical right, and for similar reasons. First, the far right has limited resources. Second, it is a very volatile political phenomenon, with only a few relatively stable organizations. Third, many groups have dominant leaders, who are not used to collaborating or sharing power. Fourth, while many far-right activists express serious interest in, and solidarity with, far-right brethren in other countries, their nationalism (and nativism) can lead to insurmountable differences of opinion. For instance, the Croatian and Serbian far right each dream of a largely similar territory – Greater Croatia for the former, Greater Serbia for the latter – while many West European far-right activists and groups look down on East Europeans, and several East European far-right groups are strongly anti-German.

International collaboration is intrinsic to neo-Nazis and white nationalists, whose "nation" is defined racially and therefore more internationally. But most of these groups already struggle to organize nationally, let alone internationally. Consequently, within the extreme right, international collaboration rarely goes beyond personal connections between a few specific individuals from Western Europe and North America, and sporadic events (like conferences and concerts), despite grandiose names like the World Union of National Socialists. In some cases, international collaboration is based more on a franchise model, where various "branches" use a similar name, but coordination and collaboration between the branches are minimal. This is particularly the case within the neo-Nazi skinhead world and applies to both the UK-centric Blood and Honour (B&H), founded by Ian Stuart Donaldson, and the US-centric Hammerskin Nation.

Only a few extreme right international collaborations have some relevance in the twenty-first century. The Nordic Resistance Movement (NMR) is a pan-Nordic neo-Nazi movement with branches in five Nordic countries: Denmark, Finland, Iceland, Norway, and Sweden – in the latter it is even a political party. While individual branches have at best modest support, they regularly mobilize dozens, and in Sweden hundreds, of mostly young people and have been linked to street violence. In 2017, the NMR mobilized some five hundred members in Sweden's second-largest city of Gothenburg, but in the same year its Finnish branch was banned by a district court.

The latest iteration of an extreme right Euro-party is the seriously misnamed Alliance for Peace and Freedom (APF), founded in 2015 and currently counting nine member parties from eight countries. Only two have national representations: L'SNS and XA are represented in both their respective national parliaments and the European Parliament. The APF's 2018 conference in Milan, Italy, was held in a fairly small room and featured speakers from eight marginal extreme right groups from Eastern and Western Europe.

The situation is only slightly better for the populist radical right. Most of the newer Islamophobic initiatives share (part of) a name rather than an organization. This applies to the various EDL-inspired "Defence Leagues," PEGIDAs, and Soldiers of Odin, a likely short-lived pan-European initiative of anti-Islam vigilantes. For decades, the FN/RN has been at the heart of collaboration between Europe's far-right parties, but with only modest success. Despite significant financial rewards for cross-national collaboration from the EU, populist radical right parties have always been divided and poorly organized within the European Parliament.

The Group of the European Right (1984–9) was the first official far-right group in the European Parliament, including just the MSI, FN, and the Greek National Political Union – for a short time the Ulster Unionist Party was also affiliated. It was succeeded by the Technical Group of the European Right (1989–94), in which the FN replaced the MSI with Germany's new The Republicans (REP), while the Belgian VB took the place of the Greeks, who did not get reelected. When REP lost its European representation in 1994, after years of infighting and splits, most remaining far-right MEPs sat as independents ("Non-Inscrits") for the subsequent terms – although some were accepted in broader right-wing Eurosceptic groups, like Independence/Democracy (LPR) and the Union for Europe of the Nations (e.g. DF and LN).

To ensure an official political group, and its material benefits in the future, Jean-Marie Le Pen had founded Euronat in 1997, a loose and largely ineffective organization of which almost twenty far-right parties were a member at some point. Its first new attempt, the loose group Identity, Tradition, Sovereignty, was short-lived, from January till November 2007. Euronat was, for all purposes, succeeded by the European Alliance for Freedom (EAF) in 2010, which had at its core the FN, FPÖ, LN, PVV, and VB. But even though far-right parties won in the 2014 European elections, as they had done in 2009, it would take Marine Le Pen until 2015 to constitute a new official political group, Europe of Nations and Freedom (ENF). ENF replaced the EAF, which was officially dissolved in 2016, mainly by adding some dissident MEPs from assorted far-right parties. After the modestly successful 2019 European elections, the ENF is to be replaced by a new group, more aligned with Matteo Salvini than Marine Le Pen, which has attracted some new member parties (e.g. the AfD and the DF), but other parties prefer to stay in more established right-wing Eurosceptic groups – like the European People's Party (Fidesz), European Conservatives and Reformists (e.g. FvD, PiS), and Europe of Freedom and Direct Democracy (e.g. Brexit Party) – while extreme right MEPs remain in the Non-Inscrits group (L'SNS and XA).

Outside of Europe, international connections are mainly limited to fairly undeveloped and fluid networks of neo-Nazis. There are many personal connections between far-right activists, but they rarely develop

into institutional collaboration. And even though both
Russian president Putin and US president Trump are
sympathetic to radical right parties and politics, they
have largely kept their distance. Trump is only relatively
close to ex-UKIP and now Brexit Party leader Nigel
Farage, while Putin's (former) party United Russia has
so far only signed official cooperation agreements with
the FPÖ and the League. Israeli right-wing parties,
including Likud, have recently strengthened ties to
several European populist radical right parties (including
Fidesz, LN, and PVV), but remain cautious towards the
RN and continue to reject the FPÖ.

Vignette 2: CasaPound

Most far-right organizations fall within only one of
these categories – political parties, social movement
organizations, or subcultures – but some are more
fluid, combining subcultural aspects with organi-
zational structures and even contesting elections.
A group that brings all three types of organization
together is CasaPound Italy (CPI), which identifies
itself as a "fascist movement." Named after the
modernist poet and fascist ideologue Ezra Pound,
CPI has its ideological origins in historical fascism,
most notably the Labour Charter (1927) and the
Manifesto of Verona (1943), although it emerged
institutionally out of the neo-fascist subculture of
postwar Italy.

Founded in 2003 as CasaPound, the group
has its institutional origins in the squatting of a
building in Rome. Taking its cue from the radical
left squatting movement of previous decades, the
group used its squat as a base to build a broader
support base, housing activists and organizing

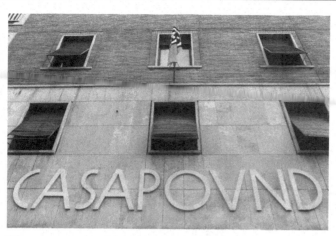

The squat-turned-headquarters of CasaPound Italy in Rome, Italy.
(Source: Jose Antonio/Italian Wikipedia/2014.)

concerts and lectures to the public. In 2008 it changed its name to CasaPound Italy and officially became a "social organization," to emphasize its focus on the housing issue and (nativist) welfare, that is, only for "real" Italians. Today CPI is present in almost all Italian regions, having more than 150 local branches, owning bookshops and pubs as well as online radio and TV channels. It publishes magazines like *Fare Quadrato* and *L'Occidentale*, as well as a new newspaper, *Il Primato Nazionale*, and has set up a network of "non-conventional" squats throughout Italy. It even has its own band, ZetaZeroAlfa (ZZA), founded by Gianluca Iannone, the founding father of CPI.

CPI counts several thousands of activists, including a youth wing, the Student Block. Since 2013, the group has also contested elections, national and local and regional, though so far with little success. In 2018, CPI gained just 1 percent of the vote in the parliamentary elections. In line with its fascist ideology and roots, the organization continues to prioritize extra-parliamentary activities, however, including social activities like providing food to (exclusively) Italian citizens. Given its emphasis on martial beliefs and behavior, it is unsurprising that CPI has been involved in political violence, including clashes with anti-fascists as well as terrorist attacks, like the killing of two Senegalese immigrants in Florence, in 2011, by a CPI sympathizer.

4

People

The far right consists not only of groups, but also of people. The international far right has two stereotypical types of supporters: the grumpy old, white racist – immortalized by the characters of Archie Bunker in the 1970s US sitcom *All in the Family* and Alf Garnett in the UK sitcom *Till Death Us Do Part* – and the heavily tattooed, violent, young Nazi skin, whose pictures accompany virtually every news story about the far right. What both have in common is that they are lower educated, white, male, and upset about "Others." While this particular section of the population is indeed overrepresented within the far right, the movement is, however, much more diverse. This chapter discusses the leaders, members and activists, and voters of the far right.

Leaders

Jean-Marie Le Pen (b. 1928) is in many ways the quintessential far-right leader: white (or majority ethnicity/

race), male, straight, older, authoritarian, charismatic, crude, violent, and with a military background. In his heyday, Le Pen was a mesmerizing speaker, drawing crowds in the thousands who paid to hear him speak. I saw him in Paris in 1986, during the only period the FN had a sizeable representation in parliament. The National Assembly was rather empty, as all other parties boycotted FN speeches, leaving just one MP to report back, so Le Pen was mainly grandstanding for his own faction. Thundering about the corruption of the "Gang of Four" (the other parties) and the dangers of multiculturalism, he captivated not just his own party representatives but many in the public stands too. Almost twenty years later, I saw him again, at an event organized by a student club in Ghent, Belgium. Le Pen was now old, bitter, and boring. He had overstayed his welcome by at least a decade.

Far-right leaders come in many types and only few are as powerful as Jean-Marie Le Pen used to be. To be fair, there is no shortage of the Le Pen-type of leader. Brazil's president Jair Bolsonaro (b. 1955) and XA leader Nikolaos Michaloliakos (b. 1957) are very similar to the French leader, both also having a military background, while US president Donald Trump (b. 1946) hits all the notes except for the military – Trump famously had five draft deferments to keep him out of the Vietnam War. But they are rapidly becoming a minority in an increasingly diverse pool of far-right leaders. Sure, the majority is still white, male, older, and straight, but so are most party leaders. In fact, far-right leaders are increasingly mirroring the leaders of mainstream parties in other aspects too: college-educated, professional politicians who have come through the ranks of the party.

Two good examples are Jimmie Åkesson and Tom Van Grieken, the leaders of Sweden's SD and Belgium's VB, respectively. Åkesson (b. 1979) was briefly active within the youth wing of the mainstream right Moderate Party

Donald Trump and Jair Bolsonaro hold a joint press conference in the Rose Garden of the White House in 2019. (Source: Official White House Photo by Tia Dufour/ Flickr/2019.)

before joining the SD youth wing. He was first elected at the age of nineteen to a local council, and has been a full-time party politician since. Similarly, Van Grieken (b. 1986) joined the VB at a young age, founded a youth branch in his home town, and got elected to his local council at the age of twenty. He then became leader of the national youth branch before moving up to national party leader a few years later. At just twenty-eight years old, he became the youngest party leader in Belgian history. Åkesson and Van Grieken are both products of their political party, and each helped mainstream their party with their idealized son-in-law image.

Most of the current leaders of successful populist radical right parties are a bit older but have fairly similar characteristics and trajectories. Matteo Salvini (b. 1973), who transformed Italy's moribund LN, comes from an upper-middle-class family, attended university

– although, like Åkesson, did not finish because he entered politics – and then worked full-time for the party. Norbert Hofer (b. 1971), who almost won the Austrian presidency for the FPÖ in 2016, grew up in an upper-middle-class, conservative household before working his way up through the ranks of the party, including as a close advisor to then party chairman Heinz-Christian Strache.

Outside of Europe, the profile is not that much different either. India's Narendra Modi (b. 1950) mainly differs from other leaders because of his modest family background, but he also joined the far-right movement at a (very) young age, and started working as a *pracharak* (campaigner) for the extremist RSS at the age of twenty-one. From there, he rose through the ranks of the RSS before being assigned to the BJP. Petrus (Pieter) Groenewald (b. 1955), leader of the white nationalist Freedom Front Plus in South Africa, joined the leading pro-apartheid National Party as a student, and built a long political career in a host of pro-apartheid parties before co-founding his own party in 1994. Similarly, Antonio Kast (b. 1966) was a long-time member and parliamentarian for the conservative Independent Democratic Union in Chile, before running as an independent in the 2017 presidential election (winning 10 percent of the vote) and founding the radical right movement Republican Action in 2018. And Naftali Bennett (b. 1972) was first active within Likud, including as Benjamin Netanyahu's chief of staff, before founding several far-right movements and ultimately joining and leading Jewish Home and then New Right.

But not all far-right leaders fit the stereotype. First and foremost, there is a growing group of female party leaders (see also chapter 9). Most famous among them, of course, is Marine Le Pen (b. 1968), Jean-Marie's youngest daughter, and his hand-picked successor within the RN – a choice he has openly regretted many times since, as she has marginalized both him and his legacy. Against the inherited leadership of Le Pen stand the self-made careers of women like Pia Kjærsgaard (b. 1947) and Pauline Hanson (b. 1954), founders and longtime leaders of Denmark's DF and Australia's ONP, respectively. Even some extreme right organizations have (had) female (deputy) leaders, like Jayda Fransen (b. 1986) of Britain First and Anne Marie Waters (b. 1977) of For Britain.

There are even some leaders who are (more or less) openly gay, albeit it more in right-wing populist parties than in more traditional far-right parties. The most famous openly gay leaders were undoubtedly Pim Fortuyn (b. 1948), who was murdered weeks before his first Dutch national election in 2002, and Michael Kühnen (b. 1955), the notorious leader of Germany's Action Front of National Socialists/National Activists (ANS/NA), who died of AIDS in 1991. Currently, the most high-profile gay far-right leader is Alice Weidel (b. 1979), who leads the Alternative for Germany (AfD) together with Alexander Gauland. Weidel is probably the most atypical far-right leader today: female and lesbian, she worked for Goldman Sachs and speaks Mandarin, and lives partly abroad (in Switzerland) with her non-white partner, who was born in Sri Lanka, and their two adopted children.

Finally, there are even leaders who are not part of the majority ethnic or racial group. This is virtually impossible in the more openly racist extreme right groups, but less problematic within primarily Islamophobic radical right groups. Here, the almost exclusively "Other" is the Muslim, and the "us" is defined in terms of both national and international characteristics, that is, "Judeo-Christian values." Hence, one of the key EDL organizers was a British Sikh, Guramit Singh Kalirai, while an "Afro-Cuban" man, Enrique Tarrio, is president of the Miami chapter of the extreme right "Western chauvinist" Proud Boys group.

Some even make it to national leader, such as Tomio Okamura (b. 1972), who was born in Tokyo to a half-Japanese, half-Korean father and a Czech mother. After growing up in Japan, he moved to the Czech Republic, where he started various more or less successful businesses before embarking on a political career. Okamura was elected as an independent to the Czech Senate in 2012 and created his own party, Tomio Okamura's Dawn of Direct Democracy, a year later. After successful national elections in 2013, the party split, and Okamura founded a new party, Freedom and Democracy, which became the most successful populist radical right party in Czech history in 2017. Okamura has used his own ethnic background as a cover against racism accusations over his bigoted statements, such as calling upon Czechs to walk their pigs in front of mosques.

Members and Activists

Political organizations are notoriously secretive about their membership, in terms of both identity and numbers. This is even more the case for far-right organizations, which assume, rightly, that their members want to remain anonymous because of the associated stigma. Consequently, we have little systematic research on the topic. Most studies are based on interviews with an unrepresentative sample of more dedicated members, namely activists, or participant observations of far-right meetings.

Over the years, I have observed several far-right meetings myself, ranging from demonstrations and party meetings to more casual social meetings, like barbeques and concerts. My personal impressions largely overlap with those of others, albeit with some national and organizational particularities. Overall, activists in Europe seem to be almost exclusively white, predominantly male, and lower middle class rather than working class. In terms of age, there was a big difference between extreme right groups (mostly youngish) and radical right parties (mostly older, i.e. fifty-five-plus).

An early study of the small and short-lived populist radical right Center Democrats in the Netherlands, for example, found that its members were predominantly male, older, working class, non-religious, and from the more urbanized west of the country.[1] A survey among participants of LN and SVP rallies found fairly similar profiles, although they were not as old, and LN participants were better educated than at least the average far-right voter.[2]

Membership in non-party organizations is even harder to track. Not only are these groups much smaller, less organized, and often local or at best regional, but their "members" tend to be transient, with people moving in and out of specific groups and sometimes even the broader subculture. Most studies find that groups that are more extreme in terms of actions and ideology, most notably violent neo-Nazi groups, are even more predominantly male and working class, and tend to be much younger, that is, on average between fifteen and twenty-five years old, with the exception of the leadership, who are often in their thirties and early forties. While women are present, they often have more supportive roles, both to the male members and, if relevant, to their children (see chapter 9).

The picture is a bit different for online-oriented organizations, although anonymity makes this group even harder to study. A Japanese study of a small number of *Netto Uyoku* (Internet right-wing) activists found that the vast majority were white collar, had a regular form of employment, and were enrolled in university or had been at one time. An online study of US "alt-right" supporters showed that they were predominantly male (two-thirds) and white (almost all), while three-quarters had voted for Donald Trump in 2016.[3]

Scholars have distinguished different trajectories of far-right activists, depending on why they joined and remained active. They distinguish, for example, between *revolutionaries*, who have a lifelong commitment to far-right politics; *converts*, who used to believe, and sometimes were active, in mainstream politics before converting to far-right politics; *wanderers*, who have been active within a broad variety of far-right and non-far-right groups; and *compliants*, who claim that their far-right activism is not of their own choosing but because of circumstances beyond their control – most often family connections. The largest group among members (and voters) is the converts, whereas leaders are more often revolutionaries. Compliants are more common among women than men (see also chapter 9).

Voters

Since the beginning of the third wave in the early 1980s, scholars have been studying the electoral support of far-right parties in detail. This section discusses the attitudinal and socio-demographic characteristics of far-right supporters – their motivations will be addressed in more detail in chapter 6. The "typical" voter of far-right parties in Western Europe is white, male, young(ish), moderately educated, and concerned about immigrants and immigration. However, the typical far-right voter constitutes only a minority of the electorate of far-right parties, particularly for the more successful parties. Moreover, in most countries, a majority of people with these characteristics vote for parties other than those of the far right.

West European far-right parties initially attracted small groups of dissatisfied, mainstream right-wing voters, disproportionately petty bourgeois and self-employed men. Their electoral breakthrough in the 1990s was a consequence of the "proletarianization" of their electorates. Parties like the FN and FPÖ became workers' parties, as growing numbers of white workers increasingly felt abandoned, if not outright betrayed, by social democratic parties, whose "Third Way" transformation included not just an embrace of the market economy but also a defense of cosmopolitan values. In fact, in the late 1990s, both parties were more popular among (white) workers than the social democratic parties in their respective countries. Today, even smaller parties, like the AfD and PVV, are among the stronger "workers' parties" in their respective countries.

As far-right parties are becoming more and more successful, their electorates keep transforming, becoming increasingly heterogenous. Already in the early 1990s, French scholars would divide the FN electorate into different groups, based on their previous voting behavior and political attitudes, including the more working-class "leftist Lepenists," the largely amorphous "neither/nor-ists (*ninistes*)," and the predominantly (petty-)bourgeois "rightists."[4] Others differentiate between "protest" and "support" voters, based on whether they mainly vote *for* the far right or *against* the other parties (see also chapter 6). The situation is even more complex in conservative-turned-radical right parties, like Fidesz or the SVP, let alone for mainstream parties run by far-right leaders, like Bolsonaro and Trump, which combine characteristics of both electorates. For instance, one recent study[5] distinguished between five types of Trump voters: American Preservationists (20 percent), Staunch Conservatives (31 percent), Free Marketeers (25 percent), Anti-Elites (19 percent), and the Disengaged (5 percent). While the last two fit with general far-right electorates, the first three more resemble conservative electorates.

In short, the more popular the far-right group, the more diverse its support base. While the public image of *the* far-right supporter is still a stereotypical white, working-class man, the far right draws leaders, activists, and voters from all walks of life. And the most successful populist radical right parties have transformed from working-class parties in the third wave to so-called "*Volksparteien*" (people's parties), reflecting almost all subgroups of the population, in the fourth wave.

5

Activities

The far right engages in three main types of activities: elections, demonstrations, and violence. Populist radical right parties usually attract rather modest crowds in demonstrations, but increasingly large numbers of voters in elections. In contrast, extreme right groups rarely contest elections successfully, if at all, and attract usually even smaller numbers onto the streets. And where populist radical right parties and groups tend to be primarily non-violent, extreme right activists and groups are more often involved in political violence.

For much of the postwar period, organized far-right terrorist groups were rare, as far-right political violence remained mostly limited to more or less random and spontaneous attacks by far-right mobs – with the exception of more organized anti-immigrant and anti-Roma "pogroms" in East Germany and Eastern Europe in the 1990s. In the wake of the so-called "refugee crisis" (2015) in Europe, and the election of Donald Trump (2016) in the US, far-right demonstrations and rallies have increased in frequency and size, while political violence has become more common and deadly. After decades of being blind in the right eye, worsened by the obsessive focus on jihadi terrorism after 9/11, law enforcement and intelligence agencies in a growing number of countries are now warning against the growing threat of far-right terrorism.

Elections

Elections are the most important form of mobilization within democracies. They determine who will represent us and, therefore, are the ultimate forum for achieving political influence. But they are also a great way to achieve visibility in the media, given that elections always receive close coverage. Finally, elections provide an opportunity to attain significant financial resources.

While election campaigns cost political parties money, in many countries they are compensated by the state, often based on either the number of votes or the number of seats they receive in (national) elections. Moreover, once parties gain representation in legislative bodies, at the national, subnational, or supranational level, they have access to even more media coverage and financial resources. Particularly for many far-right activists, being a legislator, or even legislative assistant, is a fairly easy and well-paid job compared to their non-political careers.

Almost all far-right parties contest elections, although some smaller, often extreme right parties do so only intermittently. For example, the Icelandic National Front contested the 2016 national election, but withdrew from the 2017 national elections. On average, far-right parties currently gain around 7.5 percent of the national vote in Europe (see the table below). Their results range from just a handful of votes to an outright majority of the electorate. For instance, Identity Ireland got less than 0.05 percent in the 2016 Irish elections (a grand

*Average vote (%) for far-right parties in National and
European parliamentary elections in EU member states,
1980–2018 (by decade)*

Decade	National elections	European elections
1980–9	1.1	2.4
1990–9	4.4	4.3
2000–9	4.7	5.6
2010–18	7.5	7.6

Source: Parlgov.

total of 181 votes overall), yet Fidesz won 49.3 percent
in the 2018 Hungarian elections.

It is broadly believed that far-right parties do better
in second-order elections than in first-order elections:
that is, elections that determine the constitution of the
national executive. The idea is that people vote with
their heart when it matters, but with their boot when it
does not. However, on average, far-right parties achieve
relatively similar scores in elections for the national
(first-order) and European (second-order) parliament.
They tend to do worse in local and regional elections,
mainly because many far-right parties do not have the
institutional capacity to contest elections across the
country. At the same time, they often peak in tradi-
tional local strongholds in subnational elections, such
as in Antwerp in Belgium (VB), Gujarat in India (BJP),
Nord-Pas-de-Calais-Picardie in France (RN), or Skåne
in Sweden (SD).

The most successful far-right parties today are often
former mainstream right-wing parties that have trans-
formed into populist radical right ones. East Central
European parties like Fidesz and PiS are among the
most recent examples, but they were preceded by
the FPÖ and SVP in Western Europe. Outside of the

European context, Likud in Israel is an important, but often overlooked, case. These parties profit from a so-called "reputational shield," that is, their origins protect them from a far-right stigma, as at least part of the national, and international, media and politics continue to perceive them as conservative long after their transformation into the populist radical right. In most cases, their radicalization has helped rather than hurt them in elections.

Far-right candidates often do better in presidential elections than their party does in parliamentary elections, but they rarely win. The most successful far-right politicians ran as candidates for a non-radical right party, like Jair Bolsonaro of the Social Liberal Party in Brazil and Donald Trump of the Republican Party in the US. Because they polarize the population, meaning that most people either really like or dislike them, far-right politicians tend to be unsuccessful in systems that use a two-round majoritarian system. The best example is France, where both Jean-Marie (2002) and Marine Le Pen (2017) made it into the second round but were then soundly defeated. However, even here things are changing, as FPÖ candidate Norbert Hofer was only narrowly defeated in the second round of the 2016 Austrian presidential elections.

Far-right groups and parties have mixed successes in referendums. Many countries set high thresholds for referendums, which means the far right is unable to organize a referendum, or people's initiative, by itself. In 1993, the FPÖ tried to organize an anti-immigration "Austria First" referendum, which remained not more than a modestly successful petition. In 2016, several populist radical right activists and groups in the Netherlands successfully forced the reluctant Dutch government to organize an advisory referendum on the Ukraine–EU Association Agreement. Although they won the valid referendum, with 61 percent voting against the Agreement and a 32 percent turnout, the Dutch government by and large ignored the outcome. However, the campaign became the launch pad of several successful and unsuccessful political careers, most notably that of Thierry Baudet and his FvD.

The most organic relationship between the far right and referendums exists in Switzerland, famous for its direct democracy. Although the SVP is officially part of the Swiss government, a peculiarity of the Swiss Constitution, it regularly uses popular initiatives (*Volksinitiative*) to try to block national and local legislation, particularly with regard to EU membership and immigration. SVP strongman Christoph Blocher even co-founded a special organization for this purpose in 1986, the Campaign for an Independent and Neutral Switzerland, which, although officially non-partisan, has long acted hand in glove with the SVP in its campaigns.

Demonstrations

For many far-right organizations, particularly those not contesting elections, demonstrations are their most important activity. The German scholar Fabian Virchow has described demonstrations and marches as "politico-emotional events" which perform a multitude of important functions for the groups participating. They "not only bring together otherwise loosely organized small groups in an emotional collective but also serve to organize, educate, and indoctrinate the followers of the far right."[1]

Different demonstrations perform different functions and require different levels of mobilization and organization. Larger groups and movements (hope to) organize large demonstrations to influence public opinion through the media and put political pressure

XA protest in Athens, Greece, 2017.
(Photo by author.)

on mainstream parties. Smaller groups often organize relatively small events, involving only a few activists, with the exclusive aim of attracting the attention of the mainstream media, which will then spread their message to a much broader audience. The Identitarian movement is particularly adept at staging mediagenic events (see vignette 3). More extreme groups, like the NMR in Scandinavia or the Proud Boys in the US, organize demonstrations largely to provoke confrontations with anti-fascists and the police, in an attempt to strengthen an almost military camaraderie through action (see also chapter 9).

A typical extreme right demonstration in Western Europe is held in a provincial town, gathering a few dozen activists, almost all (white) males between fifteen and forty years old, surrounded by at least as many (riot) police, even more (freelance) journalists, and at least twice as many "anti-fascist" counter-protesters. Radical right demonstrations can attract larger crowds, and fewer counter-protesters, but still tend to be remarkably rare and small, particularly given the media hype surrounding them. While far-right groups have organized demonstrations on many different issues, such as against austerity measures in Italy or against the Obama administration in the US, they are mostly related to immigration and integration.

Anti-Islam demonstrations have become a common occurrence throughout Europe, but not only there (see, e.g., India or Israel). There are two groups that have become synonymous with these demonstrations, the EDL in the UK and PEGIDA in Germany, which have inspired dozens of offshoots in their own countries and beyond, such as the Canadian Defence League and Norwegian Defence League, or LEGIDA (in Leipzig, Germany) and PEGIDA USA. In reality, few if any of these offshoots have come close to the success of the original. This itself, however, was already quite limited: the EDL never brought more than 3,000 people onto the streets for a single demonstration, while PEGIDA peaked at some 25,000 in Dresden.

In Eastern Europe, far-right demonstrations can be significantly bigger and largely unopposed. This is in part because they act under the cloak of respectability, attracting both far-right and mainstream protesters. For example, in 2017, some 60,000 people attended the annual Independence Day march in Warsaw, which was led by three far-right groups. The next year, for the centenary of Polish independence, the PiS government joined the far-right-organized march, rather than organizing its own, and the crowd peaked at around 200,000. And in Ukraine, tens of thousands of far-right activists regularly march through the streets of Kyiv, sometimes in torchlight processions, to commemorate old and new far-right heroes, including those of the neo-Nazi Azov Battalion, which fights against the Russian-backed occupation of Crimea.

In the wake of the "refugee crisis," we have seen a sharp increase in bottom-up and spontaneous anti-refugee protests. Many of these demonstrations were purely local in scope, with one single issue: preventing the settlement of (new) refugees in the community. While far-right groups often tried to hijack these protests, after they were reported in national or regional media, many local protesters would reject them as "extremists" and/or "outsiders." Particularly in East Central Europe, small, local, spontaneous protests grew into larger, national demonstrations. New or old far-right groups often played an important role in the mobilization and organization of these rallies. For example, the organizer of the main anti-refugee demonstration in Bratislava in 2015, one of the biggest postcommunist demonstrations ever held in the Slovak capital, worked closely together with the neo-fascist L'SNS, while, at a rally in Prague the same year, the leader of the (now dissolved) Bloc Against Islam sang the national anthem together with Czech president Miloš Zeman, a former social democrat who has more recently moved to the radical right.

Outside of Europe, far-right demonstrations have become more popular too. After deteriorating relations between Japan and South Korea, the anti-Korean activist online group Zaitokukai organized more than a thousand rallies throughout Japan between April 2012 and September 2015. Although most rallies were relatively small in terms of attendance, some turned violent, and the movement enjoyed (tacit) support among high-ranking politicians of the dominant Liberal Democratic Party. In India, the large Hindutva movement regularly pulls off massive demonstrations. For example, in 2018, in Kolkata, some 70,000 people assembled to mark the tenth anniversary of the founding of the anti-Muslim Hindu Samhati nationalist movement. In Brazil, the run-up to the 2018 presidential elections saw huge rallies in support of Bolsonaro across the country. In contrast, while Trump has attracted decent crowds at his rallies, both before and after his election, pro-Trump demonstrations rarely achieve impressive numbers, particularly compared to the anti-Trump demonstrations.

Violence

The far right is commonly associated with violence, be it larger populist radical right parties or smaller extreme right groups and individuals. However, those who primarily perpetrate far-right violence have traditionally not been the leaders within politically relevant organizations but (small groups of) individuals who have at best a peripheral association with the far-right movement. Nevertheless, in recent years far-right violence has become more planned, regular, and lethal, as terrorist attacks in, among others, Christchurch (New Zealand), Pittsburgh (US), and Utøya (Norway) show. And in the wake of the "refugee crisis," more and more countries are growing increasingly concerned about the rise of far-right terrorist groups such as the German National Socialist Underground.

There are a few far-right parties for which political violence is an integral part of their action repertoire. The Greek neo-Nazi party XA has been linked to a string of violent attacks on immigrants and political opponents. The party is even accused of having (had) a secret shadow organization to attack people perceived as "enemies of the Greek nation." The youth wing of the Turkish MHP, commonly known as the Grey Wolves, has terrorized party opponents in Turkey as well as Turkish emigrant communities abroad. And Rabbi Kahane's Kach party in Israel started as a violent group in the US, the Jewish Defense League, which was involved in several terrorist attacks. Today, it remains active in several countries, and members have been linked to political violence in Canada and France, among other countries.

In many countries (including Germany, India, Sweden, and the US), the far right has been responsible for more political violence than the far left, or than ethnic and religious minorities. The Norwegian terrorism scholar Jacob Aasland Ravndal[2] of the Center for Research on Extremism (C-REX) at the University of Oslo calculated that there were 578 far-right violent incidents in Western Europe in the period 1990–2015, including 190 deadly incidents causing 303 deaths. During roughly the same period in the US (1990–2013), far-right activists killed 368 individuals in a total of 155 ideologically motivated homicides.[3] Of course, this only scratches the surface of the real violence, or the threat thereof, let alone its perception by targeted communities.

Most far-right violence (i.e. violence inspired by far-right ideas) targets people who are perceived as "aliens" (e.g. ethnic minorities, immigrants, refugees) or "degenerates" (e.g. [alleged] feminists, gays, leftists, homeless people). The stereotypical perpetrator is a young(ish) white male, often intoxicated, who attacks the victim in a quasi-spontaneous manner. Sometimes larger groups of individuals go on quasi-spontaneous violent rampages, triggered by local incidents or rumors. Anti-Roma pogroms have a long history in East Central Europe, as do anti-Muslim and anti-Sikh pogroms in India. And as noted in chapter 3, in 2018, a violent mob led by football hooligans went on a hunt for "foreigners" in the East German city of Chemnitz after a Cuban-German man was stabbed to death following an altercation with two suspected refugees.

Far-right terrorism has become a growing threat in recent years. So-called "lone wolves," presumed solitary actors, who are nevertheless often significantly influenced by broader far-right subcultures, particularly online, have committed the bulk of the high-profile cases of far-right terrorism. The Norwegian terrorist who killed seventy-seven and injured 319 in an Oslo bombing and Utøya shooting spree in 2010 published a long, ranting "manifesto" that drew heavily from populist radical right politicians and far-right online sources.[4] And the Australian terrorist who killed fifty and seriously wounded fifty more at two mosques in Christchurch (New Zealand) in 2019 actually named his manifesto "The Great Replacement," after a conspiracy theory popular with both conservative and far-right circles (see chapter 3). Some "lone wolves" were actually linked to actual far-right organizations, like the failed LN candidate who injured six immigrants during a shooting spree in Macerata (Italy) in 2018.

The most infamous recent example of a true far-right terrorist organization was the National Socialist Underground in Germany, which consisted of three core members, and is held responsible for ten murders, three bombings, and fourteen bank robberies. In the UK, the neo-Nazi group National Action was officially banned as a terrorist organization in 2016 after many of its members had been accused, and some convicted, of threatening or using violence against minorities and political opponents. In France, in 2018, the authorities dismantled a small far-right terrorist group, the Operational Forces Action, which was believed to be on the verge of carrying out terrorist attacks against Muslims in the country. And in India, the Hindu extremist group Abhinav Bharat, deemed too extremist even by the Sangh Parivar, has been linked to several deadly bombings between 2006 and 2008.

Far-right paramilitary groups are particularly prone to political violence, including outright terrorism. Most European paramilitary units are uniformed but (officially) not armed. Several were set up by far-right political parties, such as the Hungarian Guard, the banned but still operating paramilitary wing of Jobbik; the LN's Green Shirts (*camicie verdi*) in Northern Italy; and the National Party's National Guard in the Czech Republic. While these groups rarely engage in overt physical violence, their mere presence – in formation, often wearing black uniforms with black boots, carrying torches and accompanied by dogs – is aimed at terrorizing targeted populations (mostly immigrants and Roma).

Similarly, in the wake of the "refugee crisis" several new militias emerged in Europe. For example, the Soldiers of Odin have been "patrolling" the streets in cities in several West European countries, mostly in Scandinavia, while in Central and Eastern Europe, groups like the Czech National Home Guard and the Slovenian Stajerska Gang claim to protect local populations against immigrants and refugees. The situation is most dangerous in Ukraine, however, where activists who fight within openly far-right units like the Azov Battalion, now integrated into the Ukrainian National Guard, have started to threaten to use their war experience and weapons "to use force to establish order that will bring prosperity to every Ukrainian family!"

US paramilitary units, more broadly known as militias, are always heavily armed because of the country's gun culture and lax firearms laws. Right-wing militias soared in the 1990s, but decreased significantly in the wake of the Oklahoma City Bombing of 1995. Under President Barack Obama, the number of militias again rose sharply, while they have been further emboldened by Trump's presidency. Traditionally, militias have been strongly anti-government, particularly towards the federal government, and many have been involved in threats and violence against the (federal) state and its representatives. However, when Trump entered the White House, many militias changed from anti-government to pro-government, at least staunchly pro-president. Some (new) groups, like the Oath Keepers and Three Percenters, have even threatened violence if President Trump were to be impeached.

There is significant overlap with the so-called "sovereign citizens" movement, a very loose network of individuals and groups who believe that the local sheriff is the highest authority in the land. Sovereign citizens have been responsible for dozens of shootings in the US, mostly in response to arrest attempts or traffic stops by law enforcement agents. Germany has an equivalent in the form of the *Reichsbürgerbewegung* (Reich Citizens' Movement), who reject the legitimacy of the Federal Republic of Germany and believe the Weimar Constitution of 1919 is still valid. While much less armed and deadly than its US brethren, *Reichsbürger* have been involved in several shoot-outs with law enforcement too.

Arguably, the most powerful violent far-right group in the world is the RSS, a paramilitary organization with a claimed membership of 5–6 million, which is very close to India's ruling BJP. The RSS was banned under British rule and was outlawed three times following independence because of its involvement in political violence and terrorism. The last RSS ban was in 1992, lifted a year later, because of its alleged role in the demolition of the Babri Masjid mosque, which led to various ensuing riots with a total death toll of some 2,000. Since the BJP regained power in 2014, Hindutva militants, often organized within the myriad of RSS groups, have been prominently involved in violence against perceived national enemies, including eaters of cow meat – the cow is a holy animal in the Hindu faith – and the largest religious minority in the country, Muslims.

Vignette 3: The Identitarians

The Identitarians are a pan-European far-right movement which started with the Identitarian Bloc in France in 2003. The movement only took off internationally with the founding of its youth wing, Generation Identity, in 2012. It is currently active across Europe, including in Austria, the Czech Republic, Germany, Ireland, Italy, and the UK. Although various US "alt-right" groups don the Identitarian mantle, like Identity Evropa, there are significant ideological differences, and personal connections are relatively limited and strained – with some exceptions, such as US activist Brittany Pettibone and Canadian activist Lauren Southern.

Ideologically, the Identitarian movement is derived from the *nouvelle droite*, inspired by its main thinkers, Alain De Benoist and the late

Austrian Identitarian movement activists block the border crossing near Spielfeld, Austria, in 2015. (Source: Johanna Poetsch/istock/2015.)

Guillaume Faye. They present themselves as an anti-'68 movement, opposing the "cultural Marxism" and "multiculturalism" of the "left-liberal elite." As a product of the twenty-first century, however, their main "Other" is the Muslim, who is officially opposed on cultural grounds. The central agenda of the Identitarian movement is to oppose the alleged "Islamization" of Europe and to renew the birth rate and identity of European nations. Or, in the words of Markus Willinger, one of its key activists, "We don't want Mehmed and Mustafa to become Europeans." While it officially subscribes to ethnopluralism, and its slogan is "0 percent racism, 100 percent identity," the boundaries between biological and cultural arguments in the movement have become increasingly porous.

Although the *nouvelle droite* has always remained a purely "intellectual" movement, to the frustration of many less intellectual, and particularly younger, supporters, the Identitarian movement is much more diverse in its forms of mobilization. On the one hand, a few Identitarian groups and (former) leaders have contested elections, including in Croatia and France, if so far without any success. On the other hand, while rejecting accusations of extremism and violence, the movement's supporters have been accused of threatening left-wing activists and critical journalists, and the German Federal Office for the Protection of the Constitution is officially surveilling the group because it believes its activities "go against the liberal basic democratic order."

The Identitarian trademark action is a short, mediagenic protest, in which small groups of activists (often just a handful) generate significant media attention by briefly occupying a popular public space – often by exposing a large banner with a short and catchy slogan, symbols unrelated to the classic far right, and easily recognizable colors and fonts. Many journalists are completely enamored with the Identitarians, labeling them "hipster fascists" and providing them with disproportionate and fairly uncritical coverage. The movement's biggest action to date was "Defend Europe," where they crowdsourced more than $178,000 to purchase a large ship (renamed *C-Star*) in an attempt to obstruct human rights organizations from helping refugees in the Mediterranean Sea. Although the action was an organizational disaster, it achieved its prime goal: generating massive media attention.

6

Causes

The academic and public discussions over the reasons behind the success of the far right entail various debates, which resurface across different geographical regions and time periods with depressing frequency. The election of Donald Trump saw many of these old debates being rehashed, in particular in the US, often with no knowledge of or reference to the volumes of articles and books already devoted to them in Europe in the 1990s or even in the US in the 1960s.

In most cases, positions in the debates are not as fundamentally opposed as their protagonists make them out to be. Some are actually interrelated, at times to the extent that they can barely be disentangled empirically, while others are complementary, explaining different subsets of far-right support. In the first section, I discuss four of the most prominent debates: protest versus support; economic anxiety versus cultural backlash; global versus local; and leader versus organization. The second section focuses on the demand side of far-right politics, arguing that, while the extreme right is fairly unconnected to mainstream politics, the populist radical right is better seen as a radicalization of mainstream politics. The chapter ends with a discussion of the role of the media, which functions as both a friend and foe of the far right.

The Debates

It is no surprise that a controversial and polarizing phenomenon like the far right would give way to longstanding and heated debates in both academia and the broader public. While most of these debates are universal in nature, they are shockingly national in terms of detail. As a consequence, people are reinventing the wheel after every breakthrough of a far-right party in a new country, drawing few, if any, lessons from debates and experiences in other countries. This was most painfully shown in the wake of the rise of Donald Trump, which brought these debates to the center of political debates around the globe.

Protest versus Support

The first time I came across this debate was more than thirty-five years ago, after the tiny radical right Center Party had gained almost 10 percent of the vote in the Dutch city of Almere, at that time unflatteringly known as a "white flight" town for the Amsterdam working and middle classes. As the Netherlands had long defined itself as a uniquely non-nationalist country, covering its own history of collaboration in the Second World War with an obsessive focus on Nazi Germany, the success of the Center Party took the country by surprise and caused a major shock and discussion among politicians and pundits alike.

The key question of the protest versus support debate is: do voters of far-right parties express mainly protest *against* the established parties or support *for* the far-right parties? The idea is that a protest voter does not really believe in a far-right ideology, but uses the far-right party to protest against the behaviour and policies of the established parties. In contrast, the support voter actually holds far-right ideas and has chosen the far-right party because it is closest to his/her own ideology.

Academic studies show that many voters of far-right parties are very dissatisfied with (established) political parties, but even more are very negative about immigration and immigrants. Obviously, many voters of other parties hold xenophobic sentiments too – particularly, but not exclusively, voters of mainstream right-wing parties – while anti-establishment sentiments are even more widespread among non-voters. But far-right parties tend to have higher percentages of anti-establishment and anti-immigration voters than all other parties. Some studies also show that these sentiments are more important to them than to voters of other parties.

In short, most studies provide circumstantial evidence for both the protest and the support thesis. This is not at all surprising. There is a perfectly logical third position, namely that voters of far-right parties *both* protest against the established parties *and* support the far-right parties. After all, when someone holds far-right ideas, they will not just support the party that holds those ideas, but also oppose the parties that hold opposite ideas. Moreover, protest voters can become support voters when they see the far-right party achieving policies they support.

It is important to note that the protest versus support debate is not politically neutral. Many people argue that protest is a morally acceptable position, whereas

A banner in California as remnant of Donald Trump's successful presidential campaign of 2016.
(Source: Quinn Dombrowski/Flickr/2016.)

support is not. From the Center Party in the Netherlands in 1983 to Donald Trump in the US in 2016, debates about "far-right voters" have been battlegrounds for mainstream politicians and pundits to push through their own political agenda. Many on the protest side reduce *the* far-right voter to a white, working-class male who has "legitimate concerns" over his cultural identity and economic position. In contrast, many on the support side of the debate paint a similarly stereotypical far-right voter as an ideological racist who scapegoats "the Other" for his/her own (perceived) woes. This leads us to the second key debate.

Economic Anxiety versus Cultural Backlash

Simply stated, this debate is about whether people vote for far-right parties because of economic or cultural reasons. The economic anxiety argument holds that far-right voters are first and foremost responding to economic stress caused by "neoliberal globalization." Whether they are objectively poor or simply feel poor, these stereotypical far-right voters are seen as the "losers of globalization" who protest against their absolute or relative deprivation. The cultural backlash argument holds that these far-right voters mainly protest against another aspect of neoliberal globalization, namely mass immigration and the rise of a multicultural society, which they believe threatens their cultural identity.

It is clear that both theories have much in common, most notably the root cause of the phenomenon (i.e. neoliberal globalization), and see the far-right vote mainly as a protest, although cultural backlash proponents in particular don't exclude the possibility of support either. Decades of academic research have shown that cultural backlash is much more important than economic anxiety, and more recent research on the Trump electorate has once again confirmed this. In short, there are few far-right voters who are informed only by economic anxiety, while there are many who are only expressing a cultural backlash.

But the two are much more complementary than opposite. It is the socio-cultural translation of socio-economic concerns that explains most support for far-right politics. Egged on by nativist narratives in the political and public debates (e.g. "immigrants are taking your jobs *and* your benefits"), many far-right voters link immigration to economic problems, either for them personally or for the region or state they live in. Consequently, they think that limiting immigration, or assimilating immigrants, will improve their economic plight. This is most clearly expressed in welfare chauvinism, that is, the support for a welfare state for one's "own people," which is a major issue for most far-right parties and voters alike.

Global versus Local

The third debate is, again, connected to the previous ones, but focuses primarily on the locus of explanation: that is, whether the phenomenon is primarily global or local. In the most extreme terms, some people explain support for the far right in exclusively, or primarily, general terms, while others believe that each far-right group has to be explained individually and uniquely. Broadly stated, global arguments prioritize the demand side of far-right politics, such as economic anxiety and cultural backlash, while local arguments emphasize supply-side factors, like a charismatic leader and party organization (see below).

The most popular global argument is (neoliberal) globalization. As the most recent iteration of modernization theory, it entails that globalization has caused winners and losers and the latter vote for far-right parties either to punish the established parties (protest), which they hold responsible for globalization, or to put a halt to globalization (including immigration) and "get our country back" (support). Unsurprisingly, global arguments are mostly used by those who try to explain *the* success of the far right – recently more popularly referred to as "the rise of populism" – ignoring other globalized countries that do not have successful far-right parties (e.g. Ireland or Japan).

Local arguments primarily focus on the so-called "Political Opportunity Structure" (POS) within which far-right organizations operate, such as the electoral system and the legal framework. They also emphasize the supply side of far-right politics, including the behavior of both mainstream and far-right groups. For example, scholars have long agreed that openly extreme right parties could not succeed in the postwar era, but recent electoral successes by neo-Nazi parties like XA and L'SNS have proven this to be untrue. Similarly, the idea that majoritarian "first-past-the-post" electoral systems provide an effective barrier to far-right politics has been weakened by the recent elections of Bolsonaro and Trump.

There is no doubt that global factors help to explain why far-right politics can find more or less receptive audiences during certain time periods and in particular geographical regions, but far-right success is first and foremost a consequence of political supply, most notably from far-right leaders and organizations themselves. Even when unemployment and immigration levels are high, they must be defined as a threat to the national identity or state, and caused by "Others," to profit far-right actors. Quite often it is not far-right actors who do this, but rather tabloid media and opportunistic mainstream politicians, without necessarily arguing that far-right organizations provide solutions. In fact, they often combine support for a radical right narrative with opposition to radical right organizations – see, for example, *Bild Zeitung* in Germany or *The Sun* in the UK.

But the mainstream media and mainstream politics have created a fertile breeding ground for far-right groups to exploit by putting their issues at the top of the agenda and framing them in their way (see chapter 7). So we are not just talking about immigration, rather than about education or health care, but we are talking about it as a "problem" or even a "threat." This legitimizes far-right groups, but also makes them look competent, as they have been saying this for years and most of their programs deal with this exact issue. When mainstream parties fail to deliver on issues like crime and immigration, either by choice or through incompetence, far-right parties become attractive alternatives. If far-right parties can offer relatively serious leaders, organizations, and propaganda, rather than small bands of infighting hooligans, they can become an attractive alternative for those voters most concerned about these issues.

Leader versus Organization

The fourth debate shifts the focus to the internal supply side of far-right politics, that is, what the far right offers potential supporters. Discussions about the far right traditionally put much emphasis on "the leader," a consequence of the fact that the contemporary far right is still often perceived as a twenty-first-century version of twentieth-century fascism. Fascism is based on the *Führerprinzip* (leadership principle) – where the leader is the personification of the party, the people, and the state – and much literature on fascism explains its support almost exclusively through the charismatic leader, an exceptional human being who commands the quasi-religious support of a devoted following.

This is very much at odds with the mainstream understanding of postwar democratic politics, in which political organizations, notably political parties, are seen as the key political actors. It is organizations, rather than individuals, that dominate democratic politics. That is not to say that individual leaders like Angela Merkel or Justin Trudeau do not play a role, but they function within the relatively tight constraints of an institutional political context, most notably their own political parties.

It is true that the far right has known many remarkable political leaders: both of radical right parties, like Jean-Marie Le Pen (FN) and Jörg Haider (FPÖ), and of extreme right organizations, like Michael Kühnen (ANS/NA) or Ian Stuart Donaldson (B&H). These leaders personify the organization, at least in the media, adding a personal story to the more abstract political ideology and organization. But for all the media attention that these mediagenic leaders generate, and the speculation about *"l'effect Le Pen"* (the Le Pen effect) and *"Führerparteien"* (leader parties), in most cases parties trump leaders.

Research shows that while leaders can pull in new supporters, they mostly either leave or become supporters of the organization, so that when the two go different ways, the vast majority stay loyal to the organization. This was most perfectly illustrated in Austria in 2005 when Jörg Haider, the allegedly charismatic leader of the FPÖ, decided to split from "his" party, but the vast majority of voters chose party over leader. In the parliamentary elections the following year, the FPÖ received 11 percent of the vote, while Haider's new Alliance for the Future of Austria gained only 4 percent.

Individual leaders play a more dominant role in many far-right groupuscules, like skinhead groups or neo-Nazi *Kameradschaften* (Comradeships). After all, here the formal organization is minimal and the group is not much more than the sum of the individuals. Local groups especially are often based primarily on the activism and charisma of one or a few men or women. Sometimes this becomes painfully clear: for example, when the leader moves to another area and the old group disappears but a new group emerges in the leader's new town. Still, even in smaller groups that are not locally based, leaders are much less dominant than received wisdom holds. Supporters come and go when leaders stay, and supporters stay when leaders go. In the end, most far-right activists in smaller groups are looking for a community and camaraderie, based around a provocative ideology, not a charismatic leader or surrogate father.

The Breeding Ground

During most of the first three waves of the postwar far right, the general assumption was that there was little demand for far-right politics. After all, it was, implicitly or explicitly, linked to historical fascism and the destruction of the Second World War. Much of the academic research on the postwar far right was based on this assumption, which two German social scientists termed the "normal pathology thesis" in an influential, if somewhat obscure, 1967 publication.[1] The thesis holds that only small parts of the population in western democracies support far-right ideas under normal conditions and that this only increases dramatically during times of crisis. This 5 to 10 percent of the population constitute a so-called "normal pathology," a relatively stable and constant presence of people who are ideologically unconnected to the political mainstream.

At least until the early 1990s, the normal pathology thesis seemed to be confirmed by the lack of mass support for far-right parties and politicians across Western Europe and North America. This led to an almost exclusive focus on the so-called demand side of far-right politics. The main question that drove the academic and public debate was: why would anyone support the far right? But as populist radical right parties started to gain significant electoral support in some European countries in the late 1990s, the thesis started to show its limitations. The focus shifted more to the supply side of far-right politics, and a new research question emerged: what kind of far right party is successful?

Simply stated, while the extreme right is indeed a normal pathology, largely unconnected to the political mainstream, the populist radical right is better seen as a pathological normalcy: that is, a radicalization of the political mainstream.[2] Extreme right groups tend to have a niche audience, as anti-democratic, antisemitic, and racist ideas are not just outside of the mainstream, they are rejected by vast majorities of the population in most countries. Moreover, in many countries, fascism is seen as the definition of evil, which means that any group or ideology that is related to it, let alone relates itself to it, is considered unacceptable. Consequently, few extreme right parties are electorally successful – although recent successes in some European countries, like Greece and Slovakia, seem to indicate that this is changing, as memories of the Second World War fade. At the same time, most openly (neo-)fascist groups recruit from a narrow part of the population, mostly lower educated, young men, who are attracted by the outsider and violent image of the far right.

In sharp contrast, most, if not all, countries have a fertile breeding ground for populist radical right ideas and organizations. Nativist, authoritarian, and populist attitudes are widespread, with often pluralities, and sometimes even majorities, expressing support for key populist radical right policies like less immigration, tougher sentences, and fewer perks for politicians. This is not to say that populist radical right values are identical to mainstream values or are shared by the majority of the populations. Rather, the radical right is a *radicalization* of the political mainstream, whose program is, in slightly more moderate form, supported by large sections of the population – and, in the fourth wave, growing sections of the political mainstream (see the next chapter).

Populist radical right values are disproportionately supported by specific subsets of the populations, particularly lower educated, working-class males from the majority "ethnic" or "racial" group. However, because of the postindustrial revolution and mass immigration, these groups are becoming a smaller part of the population in most western democracies. At the same time, younger generations, as well as minorities, are much more accepting of diversity, which could become a problem for future mobilization of the far right. Still, most populist radical right parties mobilize only a (small) part of their potential electorates. The reasons for this have to do with the supply side of politics: that is, the political context in which populist radical right parties mobilize and the product that they offer. However, all of this plays out within the context of a seemingly almighty media.

The Role of the Media

The media are both friend *and* foe of the far right. This can be explained, in part, by the ambiguity and heterogeneity of the media. The media *are* rather than *is*, in the sense that they entail a broad plethora of individuals and institutions, which share very different goals and ideologies. Clearly, Fox News and the *New York Times* do not share many objectives, except, perhaps, making a profit. It is this overarching goal of the media which explains much of the ambiguous position of most media outlets towards the far right.

On the one hand, most media are not far right, and many even consider the far right a danger to democracy. On the other hand, they know that the far right sells. A picture or video of a group of skinheads with Nazi tattoos is therefore considered too good to waste. Editors know it will attract "eyeballs," which means revenue, and will therefore make it into a story. But because stories need to be "newsworthy," they often inflate the importance of the far right. A small group of fairly isolated and marginalized neo-Nazis become "a symptom" of a deeper societal phenomenon.

At the same time, mediagenic far-right politicians like Jair Bolsonaro, Nigel Farage, or Donald Trump have been endlessly interviewed, even at points in their careers when they were (still) marginal in the polls, because media know they provide spectacle. To justify the exposure, journalists will often be overly critical, and even combative, arguing that they "hold them to account." What happens, however, is not just that readers and viewers are exposed to their ideas, but that some will sympathize with the "underdog" far-right politician who is "unfairly attacked" by the "arrogant elite."

The fourth wave is characterized by the mainstreaming and normalization of the far right, which is particularly visible in the media. More and more mainstream media not only push the agenda of the radical right, but also are increasingly open and supportive of radical right politicians and parties. For all purposes, the British *Daily Express* was the unofficial newspaper of UKIP between 2013 and 2018, while Fox News has largely functioned as Trump's media cheerleader since he came to power in January 2017. But even "high-quality" media have changed tune significantly, normalizing populist radical right and Islamophobic politicians by employing them as columnists and occasional op-ed writers or through the presentation of them in sympathetic articles and soft-ball interviews. This is most notable in conservative media, like *Elsevier* in the Netherlands or *The Spectator* in the UK, but also in liberal media, like *de Volkskrant* in the Netherlands or the *New York Times* in the US. The most extreme example, however, is the opinion page of the *Wall Street Journal*, which regularly publishes far-right politicians (like Geert Wilders) and even officially endorsed Bolsonaro in the 2018 presidential elections.

There is a lot of debate on how influential *the* media are in politics. Decades of research shows that most people barely follow the news, and those who do are not easily swayed. In short, media coverage does not so much change issue positions, but it does determine which issues voters deem important. In this agenda-setting role, the media are increasingly supporting the populist radical right, by adopting its frames and issues as well as its voices. When the media almost exclusively focus on issues like crime, corruption, immigration, and terrorism – at the expense of, for instance, education, housing, and welfare – populist radical right policies and parties are indirectly made more relevant. This happened, for example, in the 2017 German parliamentary elections, when the AfD bounced back in the polls after the mainstream media focused on the one televised debate between the Christian Democrat leader Angela Merkel and the Social Democrat leader Manfred Schulz on Turkey, terrorism and internal security, and Islam.

However, media mainstreaming can also hurt the electoral support of populist radical right parties. As "populist radical right issues" dominate the public agenda, and media present their frames as "common sense," mainstream parties will start to adopt populist radical right positions, albeit in (slightly) more moderate form, which could keep voters from jumping ship or even have some radical right voters move (or return) to the mainstream right. What is essential here is whether the populist radical right *owns* the issue. Issue ownership means that voters associate a certain issue position with a particular party. If a populist radical right party owns the issue of opposition to European integration or immigration in a country, increased salience for these issues will benefit them. If they do not, other parties could profit (too).

The fourth wave of the postwar far right coincides with the ascendance of social media, which is often said to have changed the world forever. Not a major political event goes by without people claiming that social media caused it: from the Arab Spring to Trump's election victory. In fact, Trump's election is a good example of how social media really works. While his phenomenal Twitter following helped him get his message out, Trump had acquired his following because of his prominence in the traditional media – most notably his show *The Apprentice* on one of the three major national TV channels – and his social messages were brought into the living room of the average American by traditional media, including CNN and the *New York Times*.

Social media does play an important role for the far right, because it provides an opportunity to circumvent traditional media gatekeepers and push your way into the public debate. Many far-right parties and politicians have recognized the disruptive opportunities of social media, and mastered, or even pioneered, certain outlets and techniques. For example, Heinz-Cristian Strache (FPÖ) has used Facebook much more effectively than any other Austrian politician, while Geert Wilders (PVV), at least initially, and Matteo Salvini (League), have been highly effective on Twitter. Smaller far-right groups like CasaPound Italy and the Identitarians have been disproportionately effective on social media, undoubtedly helped by the fact that several of their leaders work(ed) in advertisement and communication.

However, the reach of social media remains mostly limited to the converted, or curious, without amplification by mainstream media. Given that many journalists live on Twitter, and some mistake their timeline for a representative sample of the real world, savvy far-right social media operators, from Matteo Salvini to Richard Spencer, have been able to reach a much bigger audience than their own followers.

Social media plays the biggest role for subcultures, some of which exist almost exclusively on the Internet. This is the case, first and foremost, for the "alt-right" (extreme right) and "alt-lite" (radical right), which are predominantly US-based, but have a broad international following and impact. The Internet allows isolated individuals to engage with each other and feel part of a bigger movement, often without having to face pushback for their far-right ideas, because they can operate anonymously and within homogenous social media bubbles. Moreover, these bubbles also function as echo chambers, which amplify the reach and intensity of the message, attracting some new followers and radicalizing old ones.

In the end, the relationship between the media and the far right is complex but changing. The media have always been both friend and foe to the far right. But whereas almost no significant media organizations were sympathetic to the far right during the third wave, several major right-wing media outlets are now closely associated with it: most notably Fox News and President Trump. Moreover, the far right has been normalized in many other media, including liberal newspapers. While social media has played a role, by further eroding the traditional media gatekeeper function, it has been more important for smaller and more marginal extreme (or "alt") right groups and subcultures than for bigger and successful populist radical right parties.

7

Consequences

In a 2012 lecture entitled "Three Decades of Populist Radical Right Parties in Western Europe: So What?," I concluded that the populist radical right was a "relatively minor nuisance" to liberal democracy in Western Europe and that the main challenge (still) came from the political mainstream. Moreover, I argued that "even in the unlikely event that PRRPs [populist radical right parties] become major players in West European politics, it is unlikely that this will lead to a fundamental transformation of the political system."[1] While I believe this conclusion still largely holds, I foresaw neither the extent of the political mainstreaming of the populist radical right nor the transformation of some of this "political mainstream" into full-fledged populist radical right parties.

A Question of Power

The consequences of far-right politics depend not only on the power of the far right (i.e. whether it is in government by itself, in coalition with non-far-right actors, or in opposition) but also on the political context within which it operates. Consolidated liberal democracies (like the UK and US) can potentially be impacted most, as they constitute the antithesis of the far right, but they might also prove more resilient to the far-right challenge. In contrast, less consolidated liberal democracies (like Brazil, India, and Israel) might change less, but more easily and quickly. While *direct* impact is somewhat easier to determine, most far-right groups primarily have *indirect* impact: that is, working through mainstream media and politics to achieve their goals.

Far-Right Governments

Until the beginning of the twenty-first century, the far right had only been in power in non-democracies like Franco's Spain or Pinochet's Chile, or replaced very young and fragile democracies like Weimar Germany or postcommunist Croatia. In this century, we see a growing number of populist radical right leaders and parties coming to power in more or less consolidated liberal democracies, such as Brazil, Hungary, and Poland. In most of these cases, however, the populist radical right status of these parties is debated, in academia and society, as they used to be (considered) mainstream right-wing parties.

When the populist radical right comes to power in a liberal democracy, it tries to move the country in an illiberal direction, undermining the independence of courts and the media, snubbing minority rights, and weakening the separation of powers. The level of success and control depends primarily on the strength of the populist radical right party and the complexity of the political system. Helped by a constitutional majority and a simple political system, for instance, Fidesz has encountered little opposition in establishing its "illiberal state" (see vignette 4 below), whereas PiS faces a bigger challenge, lacking a constitutional majority and operating in a more complex political system.

But the illiberal democracy populist radical right parties try to establish is of a special kind, namely an ethnocracy, a nominally democratic regime in which the dominance of one ethnic group is structurally determined. In the most extreme form, an ethnocracy would mean the expulsion of all "aliens," but only some extreme right groups openly support this. The FN laid out the blueprint of its preferred ethnocracy in its infamous Fifty-Point Program of 1991 – elaborated upon by VB leader Filip Dewinter in his Seventy-Point Program a year later – which included, among other things, a "national preference" for "native" French, segregated welfare states for "natives" and "aliens," and the rejection of religious rights for Islam and Muslims. In short, it would create a multi-ethnic France in which "non-natives," including immigrants and French citizens, would be reduced to second-class residents.

The most infamous case of an ethnocracy was undoubtedly Apartheid South Africa; incidentally, a regime that found great support within the global far right and whose demise is often bemoaned. More recently, in July 2018, Israel officially declared its state an ethnocracy, as its parliament – dominated by a coalition of radical right parties – passed the Nation-State Law, which enshrines Israel as "the national home of the Jewish people." Despite pressure from Hindutva extremists, the BJP-led National Democratic Alliance government has so far not officially defined India as "Hindustan," that is, a nation of Hindus, even though many prominent members see the country that way.

The illiberal pressures of far-right governments change not only the polity, but also everything and everyone within it. Other parties are forced to choose whether to collaborate with or oppose the government, which determines whether they get the carrot or the stick. Parties that collaborate run the risk of becoming coopted – like various regional parties within the BJP-dominated National Democratic Alliance – while those that oppose face increasing state pressure and repression. One of the most remarkable effects has been seen in Hungary, where the original far-right party, Jobbik, has rebranded itself as a mainstream party in light of Fidesz's radical right turn.

Far-Right Coalitions

It is rare that the far right is in power by itself, but populist radical right parties are more and more often part of broader coalition governments. In some cases, the populist radical right dominates the coalition, as in India, and possibly in Israel, where an increasingly radical right Likud has long governed coalitions with (other) radical right parties. To a certain extent, one could consider the Trump administration a radical right-dominated coalition, given that it includes both radical and mainstream right members and depends on Congressional support from the equally divided Republican Party. Similarly, in Brazil, President Bolsonaro has to govern without a majority in parliament as his own Social Liberal Party commands only a minority of seats in both houses.

In most cases, the radical right party is the junior partner in the coalition, while the senior partner delivers the premier and dominates the government. The senior partner is often an established liberal democratic party – such as the right-wing Austrian People's Party or the left-wing Bulgarian Socialist Party – but can also be a new, populist (but not far-right) upstart – like Forza

Italia or the Five Star Movement in Italy. In general, coalition governments primarily reflect the policies and priorities of the senior party, and coalitions with populist radical right parties are no exception to this rule.

That said, the senior partner has often moved more towards the junior party in the run-up to the government formation, which means that "its" policies and priorities are, at least in part, those of the populist radical right. Moreover, these governments are coalitions, which means that compromises have to be made and that even the senior party has to accept some power-sharing and scrutiny from other power holders. Ultimately, while these governments do show illiberal, and particularly nativist, impulses, most of the more radical policies are either watered down in the national government or parliament, and sometimes at the federal or local level, or shot down by the courts. One can see this clearly in the US, where President Trump has experienced serious opposition from Congressional Republicans, as well as independent judges, with regard to his controversial "Muslim ban" or "Voter Fraud Commission."

In some cases, populist radical right parties have been the support party of a minority government, which means that they enter into an agreement with the government party/ies to provide them with majority support in parliament. In exchange, they tend to get prominent positions within parliament, for example chairmanships of important committees, as well as policy concessions. Sometimes, far-right parties can have at least as much influence as a support party than as an official coalition party. The best example of this is the DF, which supported a series of right-wing minority governments in Denmark (2001–11, 2016–19), significantly tightening immigration law and strengthening integration requirements.

Far-Right Oppositions

Most opposition parties have only limited policy power, given that government parties make the vast majority of laws. However, they can, and do, set the political agenda, determining what issues are discussed and how they are framed. This is particularly the case for far-right parties that have a significant parliamentary representation. As party systems have fragmented, and far-right parties have increased their success, many countries have much larger coalitions these days, which sometimes include all major mainstream parties, leaving the far right as the largest opposition party in the country (e.g. the AfD in Germany).

There is no doubt that the far right is increasingly successful in agenda-setting, often (unintentionally) helped by opportunistic mainstream politicians and sensationalist mainstream media. In many European countries, it has been able to keep the "immigration" issue at the top of the agenda, while framing it as a threat and integration as a problem. Similarly, European integration is now almost universally discussed as having gone too far, requiring the return of national compe-tencies, and terms like "establishment" and "elite" have largely become disqualifiers.

Until recently, far-right opposition parties mainly affected the discourse of mainstream parties, and to some extent governments. Given that the content of the policies did not change that much, a growing gap between discourse and policies emerged, which only furthered political dissatisfaction and support for populist radical right parties and policies. This is in part what led to the victory of Donald Trump in the Republican primaries – a man who said he would really do what the other Republicans had only talked about doing.

Domestic Consequences

I will assess the political impact of the far right on both national and international politics. With regard to the domestic consequences of far-right politics, I will discuss the impact first on the people (notably public opinion), then on policies, and finally on polities (i.e. the political systems). In the next chapter, on "responses," the specific consequences for other political parties will be addressed. In vignette 4, the specific case of Viktor Orbán's Hungary will be analyzed, the first example of a populist radical right state in the twenty-first century, and increasingly the model of far-right actors across Europe (and beyond).

The People

Virtually all far-right groups aim to influence public opinion, although for a broad variety of goals and through a broad variety of means. Where some neo-Nazi skins use music to attract supporters and violence to intimidate opponents, populist radical right parties focus more on elections and policies to achieve similar aims. Extreme right groups tend to have relatively little success in winning people over to their openly racist and undemocratic ideas, but their violence can have a chilling effect on the population, especially on groups targeted by them. Particularly in some East European towns and cities, extreme right groups have terrorized "alien" populations to create what East German neo-Nazis call *national befreite Zone* (nationally liberated zones), that is, areas "cleansed" of (perceived) immigrants and other ethnic minorities (such as Roma).

As targeted groups feel less safe in the public space, they will also become more critical towards key political and state institutions, from parliament to police. The targeted populations often already have significant distrust of state agencies, particularly law enforcement (because of discrimination and violence), which means they won't report incidents or ask for protection. Often, they believe police officers sympathize with far-right groups too. This is not without reason. In many countries (e.g. France and Greece), police officers disproportionately support populist radical right parties and, particularly at the local level, personal connections with far-right groups and individuals are tight.

But growing support for populist radical right parties will have a similar effect on targeted populations, who will start to perceive significant parts of both society and the state as hostile to their interests, if not their outright presence. This will be even stronger when populist radical right parties are mainstreamed and normalized in broader society, let alone when they participate in (national and local) governments. In the end, this could lead these targeted populations to lose trust in the whole political system.

The relationship between public opinion of the general population and populist radical right parties is more complex than is often assumed. Public opinion is both a cause and consequence of their electoral success, although there is much stronger evidence for the former than the latter. Most populist radical right parties achieve their electoral breakthrough from the political margins, being almost absent from the mainstream media. Given that their ideology is closely related to mainstream values, rather than fundamentally opposed to them (see chapter 6), they do not have to change people's minds. What they need is for the public debate to shift to their topics, and use their frames, which often happens without the populist radical right playing a major role in the process.

Still, there is little empirical evidence that this all significantly influences public opinion. While surveys show an increase in anti-establishment sentiments and Euroscepticism in much of Europe, anti-immigrant sentiments were already high – even in countries that had little immigration before 2015 – and seem to be slightly decreasing in Western Europe, as younger people become more comfortable with diversity. Similarly, in the US, opposition to immigration has been declining since (at least) 1995, while support for immigration has been rising, and Trump's presidency has done nothing to stop this. Within the EU, we even see some signs of a liberal democratic backlash to far-right success. For example, support for the EU has gone (back) up after Brexit, and is particularly high in Hungary and Poland, despite, or maybe because of, deeply Eurosceptic populist radical right governments.

The biggest effect is not on issue positions but on issue salience: that is, how important people think an issue is – and perhaps also on the intensity of their position. This is a direct consequence of the emphasis put on issues in the media, which is again related to choices by both mainstream and radical right politicians. Overall, however, the far right's effect on public opinion is mostly indirect, through agenda-setting, and largely dependent upon the political mainstream (media and politics) adopting its issues and frames uncritically. For instance, the EU-wide Eurobarometer surveys have shown for years the high salience of issues like immigration and terrorism, even in countries where both phenomena are minor to non-existent.

The Policies

Despite the fact that the populist radical right has set the political agenda in many European countries during most of the twenty-first century so far, words have spoken louder than actions for much of the time. Mainstream parties of the right *and* left have moved significantly to the right in terms of their discourse on corruption, crime, European integration, and immigration, but made mainly cosmetic policy changes. For instance, while British prime minister David Cameron and French president Nicolas Sarkozy declared multiculturalism a failure, they toughened some integration criteria and demands, but did not fundamentally change immigration or integration policies. Similarly, while many North European prime ministers criticized the EU for being too powerful and out of touch, and promised to oppose a next bailout, they did not provide clear alternative European futures and, inevitably, supported future bailouts. The political scientist Antonis Ellinas has called this strategy "to play and then retract the nationalist card."[2]

The so-called "refugee crisis," in combination with a spike in jihadist terrorism in Western Europe, has quickly closed the gap between discourse and policy. In response to German chancellor Angela Merkel's *Willkommenspolitik* ("Welcome Politics") in 2015, opening Germany and thereby much of the EU to asylum seekers, Hungarian prime minister Viktor Orbán led a nativist backlash of a growing coalition of member states. Central and East European countries were the most overt and vocal in their opposition to non-European immigration, and most radical in their new anti-immigration policies – including the building of fences and the criminalization of undocumented immigrants – but many West European governments were happy to follow their lead. Several of the most strident anti-immigrant governments are dominated by the populist radical right (e.g. Hungary, Poland), but others are not (e.g. Austria, Denmark, Slovakia), and some even officially exclude populist radical right parties from the government (e.g. the Czech Republic, the Netherlands).

Outside of Europe, radical right parties and politicians have also mainly affected counter-terrorism and immigration policies. President Trump has finally passed his "Muslim ban," albeit in moderated form and after significant judicial and political opposition; continues his pressure to build a (larger) wall at the southern border with Mexico; and even plans a significant overhaul of legal immigration, which would prioritize European immigrants. Israel has become even less open to asylum seekers, and has adopted the Nation-State Law, which further marginalizes Arab Israelis. And while the BJP-led Indian government has mainly focused on (neoliberal) economic policies, it did try to pass a nationwide "beef ban," playing to Hindu nationalist and Islamophobic sentiments, which was struck down by the Supreme Court in 2017. In addition, with regard to the millions of "illegal immigrants" in India's northeast, the government has said that Hindu migrants from Bangladesh should be protected, but Muslims who are found to be illegal should be expelled.

The Polities

Until recently, far-right parties did not affect their respective polities either, at least not in more fundamental terms. Studies showed that while governments with populist radical right participation tried to undermine independent courts or media, and abolish minority rights (notably for Muslims), they were generally opposed by coalition partners, civil society organizations, and independent courts. Given that they lacked a parliamentary majority, let alone a constitutional one, they would be dependent upon coalition partners, which either did not share their objectives, or feared the populist radical right would abuse their new powers. So, while independent courts and media would be criticized, and immigrant and minority rights would be weakened, this would not be much different from other right-wing governments in surrounding countries.

The situation has changed in recent years, particularly in certain Central and East European countries (such as Hungary and Poland), but also in India, Israel, and the US. The main challenges come primarily from conservative-turned-populist radical right parties and politicians. Ever since he entered the White House, President Trump has relentlessly criticized journalists and judges who oppose him, suggesting new measures to curtail their independence. But, to date, he has tried to change his political environment primarily by replacing the personnel rather than the institutional structure. In Poland, the new populist radical right government has mounted a frontal attack on the courts and media, but has been resisted by civil society, judges, opposition parties, and the international community. PiS is trying to follow the "Budapest model," but lacks Orbán's constitutional majority and, so far, staying power. What a populist radical right government looks like we can see in Hungary, which Orbán has transformed from a liberal democracy into a competitive authoritarian regime, devoid of independent courts and media, as well as free and fair elections (see vignette 4).

International Consequences

A think tank report on "the populist challenge to foreign policy," of which I was a co-author, concluded only a few years ago that "Europe's troublemakers" had only modest influence on foreign policy and the international community.[3] Adding insult to injury, it was published just a few months before a majority of Brits decided to leave the EU, undoubtedly one of the most important foreign policy decisions in Europe in the twenty-first century. While the EU referendum was primarily a consequence of internal divisions within the Conservative Party, UKIP's electoral competition played a role in David Cameron's call for an EU referendum, and UKIP's anti-immigrant campaign played a major role in making Brexit a reality.

Although the Brexit vote was a major foreign policy success for the far right, the consequent incompetence and infighting over the type of Brexit and post-Brexit world desired are emblematic of the foreign policy divisions within the far right. In sharp contrast to the sensationalist media narratives about a nationalist international, far-right groups are fundamentally divided over the most basic foreign policy issues. What brings them together, by and large, is a disdain for the current global order, defined by cultural, economic, and political integration (even if more in theory than practice).

Consequently, European populist radical right parties, and (coalition) governments, are increasingly able to frustrate international collaboration, like the UN's Intergovernmental Conference on the Global Compact for Immigration in Marrakesh (2018), and sometimes even block it, like the EU refugee resettlement plan (2017), but they cannot fundamentally change it, let alone create an alternative global order. This will probably not change after the 2019 European elections, even when a new populist radical right Eurosceptic super-group emerges, because the individual parties always put national over European interests. And their national interests, both inside and outside of the EU, differ significantly, and often oppose each other: for instance, some are from countries that are net payers to the EU (e.g. the FPÖ and FvD), while others are from net receivers (e.g. Fidesz and Vox).

Even President Trump has mainly limited the US role in international organizations and treaties, including

NATO and the UN, rather than seeking to abolish or transform them. And in the few cases where he has withdrawn the US, such as from the Paris Agreement on Climate Change (2017) or the UN Human Rights Council (2018), this has been supported by neoconservatives as much as by the radical right in the Republican Party. Trump has also repeatedly disappointed foreign far-right allies by lukewarm support, and sometimes even critique, of their own pet projects – from Brexit to Greater Israel. In fact, in response to Trump's erratic "America First" foreign policy, support for closer cooperation within the EU and NATO has increased rather than decreased, to the dismay of much of the European far right.

Vignette 4: Orbán's Hungary

Helped by corruption scandals in the Socialist government, and division and infighting within the liberal democratic camp, Viktor Orbán returned to power with a massive victory in the 2010 elections. During its eight years of opposition, Fidesz had created a parallel society and state, sustained by a myriad of "civic circles" (*Polgari Körök*) and partisan media. Despite radical, and at times even violent, opposition to the Socialist government, Fidesz had campaigned on a relatively vague, national conservative agenda. But emboldened by an unexpected constitutional majority, Orbán wasted little time in implementing a program that has transformed Hungary from a liberal democracy into an "illiberal state."

Orbán has reduced parliament to a partisan rubber-stamping institution, which does little else than uncritically introduce and pass

Viktor Orbán speaks at the European People's Party
congress in Bucharest, Romania, in 2012.
(Source: European People's Party/Flickr/2012.)

government-initiated legislation. He has weakened
non-majoritarian institutions, from courts to tax
offices, by limiting their power and stacking them
with cronies. He has criticized independent civil
society organizations and media, frustrating their
operations by new legislation and withdrawal of
state funding. A network of businessmen associated
with Fidesz, and more specifically Orbán himself,
started to buy up most of the Hungarian media,
folding some (including the well-regarded newspaper
Népszabadszág) and eventually consolidating the
others and donating them to an "independent"
national foundation, run by a loyalist. Today, with
the exception of one TV station (RTL Klub) and a
few websites, the Hungarian media are completely
under Orbán's control.

While Orbán had largely stayed out of major
international debates in his first term after

returning to power, he has become a major European player in the wake of the "refugee crisis," successfully taking on Angela Merkel and blocking the EU's proposed refugee redistribution plan. Now openly embracing populist radical right positions, Orbán has transformed Hungary into an illiberal democracy, using nativist campaigns against asylum seekers to marginalize his remaining political opponent, Jobbik, while intensifying an antisemitic campaign against the Jewish US-Hungarian philanthropist George Soros to curtail civil society and drive out the Central European University. With his recent move to create a parallel, partisan judiciary, overpowering the nominally independent judiciary, Hungary is no longer liberal or democratic. It has become a competitive authoritarian state, which allows an increasingly embattled and harassed opposition to exist only on the political margins.

The fact that Hungary could transform from a liberal democratic into a far-right authoritarian regime within the EU, which was founded to prevent the emergence of exactly such regimes, is a painful illustration of politics in the fourth wave. First, it shows the transformation of a mainstream right-wing party into a populist radical right one. Second, rather than meeting broad opposition from the European political mainstream, as would have happened during the third wave, Fidesz was protected by the mainstream right European People's Party, the main political group in the European Parliament. Third, while Orbán is a loud and open Eurosceptic, his approach to the EU is offensive rather than defensive. He does not want to leave the EU; he wants to transform it in Hungary's image.

8

Responses

I rarely give a public lecture where I am not asked the question, "What can we do to defeat the far right?" Understandably, many people are not so much interested in the various actions, ideologies, and organizations of the far right, but are mainly concerned about its negative impact on liberal democracy, and the perceived incompetence, and unwillingness, of mainstream parties to deal with it. I share this interest, both as an academic and as a citizen, but have to admit that, even after more than two decades, I still do not have the answer.

Around the world, countries approach the far right, and political extremism more generally, in different ways, depending on a broad range of factors, such as the country's history, the strength of the liberal democratic system, and the perceived threat of the far-right challenge. This chapter will discuss the key responses by the state, political parties, and civil society. It ends with a short discussion of the crucial question: do they work?

The State: Between the German and the US Models

The essence of a liberal democratic system is not just majority rule, but also the protection of minority rights. While today the term "minority" is mainly associated with "ethnic" or "racial" groups, in legal terms it extends to a much broader range of categories, including political minorities. However, not every state tolerates political minorities to the same extent. With regard to the far right, the distinction between the German and the US models is the most relevant.

Although the US has a long history of far-right politics, including a toxic mix of authoritarianism and racism, these are mostly associated with mainstream, and so supposedly democratic, parties. Fascist and quasi-fascist movements and personalities – such as the German American Bund and Father Charles Coughlin – were quite popular in the early twentieth century, but were seen as "imported" and "Un-American." And except for the attack on Pearl Harbor, the country remained free from fascist(-linked) territorial destruction, let alone occupation.

This specific historical context explains in part why the US has remained so tolerant to the far right, which, like all other political groups, is protected by the iron-clad First Amendment of the US Constitution: "Congress shall make no law respecting an establishment of religion, or prohibiting the free exercise thereof; or abridging the freedom of speech, or of the press; or the right of the people peaceably to assemble, and to petition the Government for a redress of grievances." Freedom of speech is sacrosanct in the US, at least it has been since the late 1960s, and protects even the most extreme organizations and speech. The most famous example of this is the so-called "Skokie

Affair" of 1977, when the National Socialist Party of America wanted to march through Skokie, Illinois, a Chicago suburb with a particularly large number of Jewish inhabitants, including Holocaust survivors. The American Civil Liberties Union challenged the village's ban on the march, and the use of Nazi uniforms and swastikas, arguing it infringed on the party's First Amendment rights. In the end, the Supreme Court ruled in agreement with the American Civil Liberties Union and the National Socialist Party of America.

This stands in sharp contrast with the Federal Republic of Germany, which was built as a direct response to the Weimar Republic, which was considered, in hindsight, too tolerant to survive a significant (right-wing) extremist challenge. Consequently, the new postwar German state was constructed to prevent the far right from ever coming to power by democratic means again. The Federal Republic is a so-called *wehrhafte Demokratie* (militant democracy), in which the main political institutions (executive, legislature, and judiciary) are given extensive powers and duties to defend the liberal democratic orders.

Most importantly, social groups that are deemed "hostile" to the liberal democratic order can be banned by the interior minister – although they can appeal the decision in court – while "hostile" political parties can be banned (only) by the fiercely independent Federal Constitutional Court. Consequently, hundreds of extreme right groups have been banned, often small neo-Nazi *Kameradschaften*, but only one extreme right party, the Socialist Reich Party, in 1952. The NPD has been threatened by a party ban for most of its (long) existence. It survived a first court case in 2001–3, when the Federal Constitutional Court dismissed the case because the party was so full of informants and infiltrators that the Court could not accurately distinguish between the party and the state.

In another attempt, a few years later, the Court did declare the party "hostile to the Constitution" and urged parliament to starve it of public funds, but also refused to ban it.

Importantly, the differences between the German and the US models exclude the use of violence. In all countries, including the US, the state monitors potentially violent groups, including on the far right. However, across the globe, anti-racist activists and left-wing politicians have long complained that the state, and particularly intelligence and law enforcement services, are "blind on the right eye": that is, they ignore or minimize the threat from far-right violence. Since the terrorist attacks of 9/11, many states have refocused their priorities, and thereby resources, on jihadi terrorism, often to the detriment of investigating far-right terrorism. For instance, in the Netherlands, only one person within the Dutch General Intelligence and Security Service remained responsible for "extremism" (including the far right) post-9/11.

The situation in the US is particularly disturbing in this respect. In the wake of the 9/11 attacks, the newly created Department of Homeland Security had forty analysts for jihadi terrorism and a mere six for "domestic non-Islamic terrorism," which includes left-wing terrorism and so-called "ecoterrorism" too. When the Department published a report on "right-wing terrorism" in 2009, in which it warned against possible terrorist attacks by military veterans (like the man who was responsible for the Oklahoma City bombing in 1995), the conservative backlash was so fierce that Homeland Security Secretary Janet Napolitano offered an official apology. The next year, the team responsible for the report was dissolved and the major analyst left in frustration, claiming only two members were left analyzing the far right. Despite the increase in far-right violence in the US, which has been more deadly and regular than jihadi terrorism since 9/11, the situation has continued to deteriorate. In recent years, the Trump presidency has withdrawn funding from several anti-far-right violence initiatives and has used the term "terrorism" exclusively for (alleged) jihadist perpetrators.

The Parties: From Demarcation to Incorporation

As politics in most western democracies is first and foremost party politics, the question of how liberal democratic parties should deal with far-right parties is crucial to the broader question of how to respond to the far right. Among the myriad of different approaches, we can distinguish between four prominent and distinct ones: demarcation, confrontation, cooptation, and incorporation.[1]

Demarcation

Demarcation means that liberal democratic parties exclude far-right parties from their political interactions. They try to ignore them and continue with their day-to-day politics as if the far-right party (or parties) does not exist. For much of the postwar era, this was the de facto approach towards the various small radical right parties in all western democracies; although some (openly) extreme right parties and groups were banned, particularly in the first decade of the postwar era. Once populist radical right parties started to increase their electoral support, other parties were forced to take a more explicit, and formal, position. Most mainstream parties officially declared populist radical right parties to be outside of the democratic realm and therefore excluded them from the political game.

After yet another "Black Sunday," that is, an electoral victory of the radical right Flemish Bloc (later Flemish Interest, VB), all other parliamentary parties in Flanders, the Dutch-speaking northern part of Belgium, came together and formally agreed to constitute a so-called *cordon sanitaire* around the VB. Officially, the cordon had a fairly limited mandate: it excluded any political coalition, on whatever level of government, with the VB. Unofficially, it excluded not only the party, but also its main issue (immigration), and thereby the major concern of its voters. Despite ups and downs in the electoral successes of the VB, the *cordon sanitaire* has not been broken since its (second) introduction in 1992.

Political parties in many western democracies still practice demarcation today, though only Belgium has an official *cordon sanitaire*. The AfD is excluded in Germany, the RN in France, the PVV in the Netherlands (except for 2010–12), and the SD in Sweden. But in all these countries, for a variety of reasons, the unofficial cordons are starting to show cracks, with growing dissent particularly among local and regional politicians of mainstream right-wing parties. In the end, demarcation, be it official or not, is always more strategic than ideological. Whenever it becomes expedient for a specific party to break the cordon, it will, arguing it has outlived its purpose, because the populist radical right party is allegedly no longer outside of the liberal democratic order, or that it is undemocratic to marginalize certain voters.

Confrontation

A confrontation strategy entails an active opposition to far-right parties and, most often, their policies. This is mostly limited to very small or very extreme parties, such as the NPD in Germany and XA in Greece. They are mainly confronted on their most extreme positions – such as anti-democracy, antisemitism, historical revisionism, and racism – and are attacked for their (alleged) propensity for violence, whether through incitement or actual violent actions. These confrontations mainly have symbolic value, and are sometimes even shared by radical right parties, in an attempt to show that they are "moderate" and not far right. The most cynical example is Fidesz, which regularly uses the specter of an "extreme right" Jobbik-dominated Hungary to silence domestic and, particularly, foreign critics of its own radical right policies.

While confrontations with small or extreme parties have overall low benefits, but also low costs, this is not so for confrontations with large or populist radical right parties. First of all, if the far-right party is big, it could be a potential coalition partner, or at least could be used as such in coalition negotiations with other parties. This applies especially to mainstream right parties, which are often facing a mainstream left party that does have acceptable left coalition partners: that is, Green and even some radical left parties. If center-right parties exclude far-right parties *a priori*, they weaken their own hand in the coalition negotiations with center-left parties.

Second, and more important, confrontations could push away potential voters, who are choosing between the mainstream and populist radical right, and even some of the mainstream's own voters. While few voters will be lost over opposition to anti-democratic or antisemitic positions, this is no longer the case with illiberal, and especially Islamophobic, positions. Hence, if a mainstream party confronts a populist radical right party over its anti-immigrant or anti-Islam agenda, it could be perceived as (too) pro-immigrant and pro-Islam by mainstream voters, including their own.

Not surprisingly, then, confrontation has become less and less common in the twenty-first century as populist radical right parties have become more successful electorally and more relevant politically. The main parties that continue to openly confront populist radical right parties are the Greens and some social liberal parties, like the Dutch Democrats 66 and the French "The Republic on the Move!" of President Emanuel Macron, which have little overlap in potential voters. If mainstream parties still confront populist radical right parties, they focus almost exclusively on the leaders, while acknowledging the "legitimate concerns" of their "misguided" voters, which brings us to the third strategy.

Cooptation

At least since the late 1990s, cooptation has become the dominant model of interaction in western democracies. This means that liberal democratic parties exclude populist radical right parties, but not their ideas. This is a logical consequence of the opportunistic confrontation strategy that many mainstream parties adopted when populist radical right parties increased their electoral support and political power. Cooptation exists in different forms and gradations. Almost all major European leaders have criticized "multiculturalism," including German chancellor Angela Merkel, who at the same time remains staunchly opposed to the normalization of the AfD (let alone the NPD). Similarly, more conservative politicians, like John Howard in Australia or Bart De Wever in Belgium, have made their career attacking their radical right opponents, while simultaneously adopting much of their program.

Initially, liberal democratic parties primarily adopted populist radical right discourse, problematizing

European integration and multiculturalism, without substantially changing their policies. The only real change in the late twentieth century was in terms of refugee policies as a consequence of populist radical right opposition to the sudden influx of refugees from the Yugoslav civil war in the early 1990s. In the early twenty-first century, the gap between discourse and policy grew wider, until several developments, most notably terrorist attacks and the so-called "refugee crisis" (often linked in both populist radical right and mainstream right discourses), led to a slew of authoritarian and nativist policies from mainstream governments (see chapter 7).

Incorporation

Incorporation means that not just populist radical right positions, but also populist radical right parties, are mainstreamed and normalized.[2] The first time this happened in postwar Europe was in 1994, in Italy, where right-wing populist Silvio Berlusconi created a coalition government with the "post-fascist" National Alliance and the populist radical right LN. The government came after a complete implosion of the existing party system and lasted only eight months, after which the LN pulled the plug.

In 2000, the FPÖ entered a coalition government with the conservative Austrian People's Party, which led to massive pushback in Austria and Europe. Egged on by the Austrian Social Democrats, which had negotiated in secret with FPÖ too, hundreds of thousands of Austrians took to the streets to demonstrate against the "fascist" government. The (then) fourteen other EU member states had tried to prevent the coalition with a strong statement, saying they would "not promote or accept any bilateral official contacts at a political level" with a government including the FPÖ. In the end, the EU-14 only boycotted the FPÖ ministers and appointed a committee of three "wise men," which recommended that the sanctions should be lifted. Despite mutterings from some EU member states, and the Austrian Social Democrats, the sanctions were lifted after less than a year.

When the FPÖ returned to government in 2018, there were much smaller demonstrations in Austria, and no EU government boycotted FPÖ ministers. This time the FPÖ was able to get the coveted foreign minister position, but decided to appoint the independent former diplomat and political analyst Karin Kneissl to prevent international boycotts (only Israel boycotts her). It was an indication of the normalization of incorporation. Populist radical right parties have been in coalition governments in many different countries and supported minority governments in several more.

The increasing incorporation of populist radical right parties is, both directly and indirectly, a result of their growing electoral relevance – and, at least as important, the public perception of their rise, which is inflated by sensationalist media accounts. On the one hand, populist radical right parties are now so big in many countries that excluding them from government creates increasingly high costs for particularly mainstream right-wing parties – that is, either Grand Coalitions with the main center-left party, which means sharing more power, or coalitions with two or three other parties, which tend to be more ideologically diverse and (therefore) less politically stable. On the other hand, many mainstream right-wing parties have been moving to the right for over a decade, particularly on socio-cultural issues, so that the populist radical right is increasingly its most logical coalition partner in terms of ideological fit.

Civil Society: Between Non-Violent and Violent Resistance

Beyond the state and political parties, civil society groups play a major role in responding to the rise of the far right. Where political parties increasingly prefer cooptation and incorporation, particularly in the fourth wave, this is much less the case for civil society organizations. Few religious or trade union organizations have coopted nativist or populist rhetoric, and even those that no longer exclude or confront far-right groups and individuals at best tolerate rather than incorporate them, accepting them but not their ideologies. Particularly in the public image, civil society is still primarily characterized by demarcation and confrontation.

Demarcation

Many civil society organizations bar their members from being active within far-right organizations or, at the very least, from being candidates for far-right parties or leaders of far-right groups. This has traditionally been the case for almost all trade unions, which have long been among the best organized and most vocal opponents of the far right. Union members who stood in elections for populist radical right parties would be expelled, while union leaders who expressed sympathy for populist radical right parties would be forced to choose between the union and the party. This applied to most Christian democratic and social democratic unions – and even more so for communist unions. As a consequence, some populist radical right parties tried to create their own trade unions, particularly within sectors that are known to be sympathetic to the far right. In the late 1990s, the FN created unions for police officers (FN-Police) and prison guards (FN-Pénitentiaire), but both were ruled unlawful by the French Supreme Court of Appeal. In countries where the far right is more mainstreamed, some trade unions are close or sympathetic to major far-right parties, like the Indian Workers' Union, the labor wing of the RSS, which has over 6 million members.

While most trade unions continue to officially oppose the far right in the fourth wave, there are significant national and sectoral differences. For example, in countries where the populist radical right has been mainstreamed, if not outright normalized, like Denmark, trade unions mainly try to ignore the elephant in the room. In countries where the populist radical right is not yet a serious player, however, like (until a few years ago) Germany and the US, trade unions are (or were) still resolute in their demarcation. However, even in the US, there are sectoral differences within the broader trade union movement, depending, to a large extent, on how widespread support for Donald Trump is within the specific union's membership.

Similarly, while far-right groups, both parties and social movement organizations, were excluded from cultural, political, and social events in most European countries during the third wave, particularly in the western part, this *cordon sanitaire* is rapidly breaking down and has even largely disappeared in some countries. For example, far-right publishers are now routinely represented at international and national book fairs after decades of exclusion, even though, like the Antaios stand of "new right" ideologue and publisher Goetz Kubitschek at the 2017 Frankfurt Book Fair, they are largely shunned.

Confrontation

Although tacit toleration, rather than open incorporation, is becoming more and more common during the fourth wave, confrontation remains an important part of civil society responses to the far right. Some of the largest demonstrations in recent years have been, directly or indirectly, against the far right, from the explicitly anti-racist demonstration in Berlin in 2018, attracting almost a quarter million of people, to the more implicitly anti-far-right Women's Marches across the US, mobilizing between 3 and 5 million people in 2017.

In addition to the occasional large anti-racist demonstrations, there are smaller but more regular "anti-fascist" demonstrations. While the former are often reactions to far-right events, but organized in a different space and time, the latter are direct confrontations with the far right. The various counter-demonstrations also have different goals, from showing the far right that they are not welcome in a town, or showing the broader public that the far right does not represent the majority, to preventing the far right from organizing and spreading its "message of hate."

As noted in chapter 5, most far-right demonstrations are confronted with much bigger anti-fascist counter-demonstrations. There are many pictures of "demonstrations" by a few dozen far-right activists surrounded by ten to twenty times as many anti-fascists, separated by an often massive police force. This has been the case for every hyped "alt-right" rally in the US, including the deadly "Unite the Right" rally in Charlottesville in 2017. But it is also the case for most demonstrations of the EDL and PEGIDA, and certainly their many unsuccessful local and international offshoots. For instance, even in Dresden, the only city where PEGIDA has at times mobilized tens of thousands of supporters, counter-demonstrators almost always matched if not exceeded its numbers.

Anti-fascists come in many different guises. The media image is that of a black-clad, young and violent, mostly male anarchist, who hates both "fascism" and "the state." This so-called "black bloc" is often only a small minority of larger counter-demonstrations, despite featuring prominently in media reports, but more significant among smaller counter-demonstrations, particularly against more violent extreme right groups. The "black bloc" resembles the fascists it battles in the streets in many ways, from demographics (young, male) to fashion (black hoodies, combat boots) to strategy (confrontational and violent). In some cases, the relationships between individual anti-fascists and fascists are so close that they have each other's phone numbers and communicate outside of demonstrations.

Anti-fascist demonstrations and demonstrators are generally not violent, although violence is more common on the margins of the demonstrations and the movement. It is this threat of violence that gives the anti-fascists, and particularly the "black bloc," such a high media profile. It consequently also transforms irrelevant far-right events, from invited speeches at universities to small local protests, into high-profile media events, as we have seen in the US in the past years (e.g. in Berkeley, California, and Portland, Oregon). This symbiotic relationship, as well as the spiral of (potential) violence associated with it, is a bone of contention within the broader anti-fascist and particularly anti-racist movement.

Do These Responses to the Far Right Work?

Which approach works best depends on a broad variety of objective and subjective conditions, including the history of a country, the political culture, the strength of both liberal democracy and the far-right group, and the control/role of the media. But, more than anything, it depends on what the key objective of the approach is. This is itself linked to what the understanding of (liberal) democracy is; more specifically, whether one believes that the intolerant should be tolerated.

If the key objective is to minimize the direct impact of far-right groups, nothing is more effective than a ban. An oft-heard argument against banning extreme right groups is that this would drive their members underground and into terrorism. While this argument is popular, the empirical evidence is so far inconclusive. Only a tiny portion of the population is willing to use violence to advance its political goals, and while this group might be somewhat bigger among members of the far right, it is still very small. Moreover, most far-right violence is more or less spontaneous, rather than premeditated, and far-right terrorists are not disgruntled former members of now banned groups or parties.

Banning far-right parties is also the best way to prevent them from winning votes, and consequently influencing other parties and potentially policies, presuming it is done before they achieve their electoral breakthrough. But banned parties can re-emerge in more moderate forms, at least in terms of their public image, without having changed their ideology. This was the case, for example, with the Flemish Bloc, which reinvented itself as Flemish Interest after a 2004 conviction had made its political functioning virtually impossible. Except for the name and party color, which changed from orange to yellow, the two VBs were near identical in terms of ideology and leadership. At least initially, the party even profited from the "ban" in electoral terms, although it might have led to its decline later on, when voters increasingly looked for alternatives that were more acceptable to other parties.

Moreover, where do we draw the line in terms of which ideas and organizations should be banned? While majorities might agree on the banning of openly neo-Nazi parties, contemporary populist radical right parties are much closer to the political mainstream, and therefore considered less, or not, problematic. And even if the French were to agree on banning a party like, say, Marine Le Pen's RN, on the basis of its nativist agenda, what would be the legal argument to not ban mainstream parties like the (French) Republicans, which have copied much of the discourse and policies of the Le Pens over the past decades?

Assuming we accept at least the right of populist radical right parties to exist legally, but we want to limit their electoral success and therefore political impact, which of the four approaches works best? In general, demarcation works best, but only under certain conditions. First and foremost, all major parties must engage in it. Second, the media must be supportive of it. And, third, the timing must be right. The populist radical right party must not be too big or important to coalition formation – because it can then lead to "anti-far-right" coalitions that are too large and ineffective. The key challenge of the *cordon sanitaire* is, however, to exclude far-right parties, but not their issues – which is different from their issue frames and positions.

In Belgium and Sweden, for example, the exclusion of the far-right party went hand in hand with rendering the issue of immigration almost taboo, despite real and perceived grievances within the population. This led to the eventual electoral breakthrough, and then continued growth, of the SD in Sweden, while other parties moved into the VB's territory in Flanders: first the right-wing populist List Dedecker and later the conservative, Flemish nationalist New Flemish Alliance. While it seemed that the cordon had at least continued to marginalize the VB, if no longer its issues and issue positions, its recent return indicates that this might just have been temporary.

Confrontation with radical right parties has rarely been used, at least not by the most important parties (i.e. the mainstream right and left), which compete with them electorally. If mainstream politicians attacked radical right leaders and parties, they mostly did this in combination with acceptance of their issue positions, albeit in somewhat more moderate form, or with their voters' "legitimate grievances." In other words, confrontation was really cooptation. Even the genuine confrontation of Green and social liberal parties did not necessarily harm the populist radical right, as it raised the salience of "their" issues and made them more central to the electoral campaign and political struggle. Collaboration, finally, tends to mainstream and normalize both radical right parties and their policies – although this does not have to be permanent (e.g. the Dutch PVV was excluded and marginalized again after withdrawing its support from the right-wing coalition government in 2012).

Exclusion by civil society organizations can limit the full mainstreaming of far-right organizations, at least temporarily, but, as many trade unions have found out, it does not prevent their members from supporting far-right ideas and parties. Moreover, while massive anti-racist demonstrations might have given solace and support to some of the targeted populations, who see that at least large parts of the population do not stand with the far right, they have not stopped the rise of populist radical right parties. And while anti-fascists can rightly claim some successes in the fight against the far right, not least owing to their (threats of) violence – for example, as noted in chapter 3, Richard Spencer abandoned his university speaking tour in the US in part because of anti-fascist violence – they also help to keep marginal far-right groups in the public eye, providing massive free media attention for their groups and ideas.

In the end, what works best depends on so many cultural and organizational factors that it makes little sense to look for a silver bullet. A political party like the Dutch PVV, with just one member, requires a different approach than not just a violent subculture like the US sovereign citizens, but also a political party like the Austrian FPÖ, which is deeply rooted in a centuries-old nationalist subculture. And a still relatively small opposition party in a consolidated liberal democracy, like the AfD in Germany, constitutes a fundamentally different challenge than a far-right president in a more fragile democracy, like Bolsonaro in Brazil. As such, if we are looking for a more effective response, the key probably lies in using different combinations of the existing approaches.

9

Gender

Like all political phenomena, the far right is deeply gendered. However, it is gendered in a much more complex manner than its often simplistic and stereotypical public image suggests. This should not be that surprising by now, given the heterogeneity of the far right that we have so far encountered. So, while it is true that men dominate the far right overall, there are more than enough exceptions, including female leaders like Marine Le Pen. And while traditional images of masculinity are central to many far-right groups and subcultures, think only of militias and skinheads, this is less the case in populist radical right parties in Northern Europe, for example.

This chapter looks at the importance of sex and gender in the various aspects that have been discussed in the previous chapters. Simply stated, sex is biologically determined, while gender is socially constructed. Sex is about men and women, gender about masculinity and femininity. Genders are socially constructed in a hierarchical and oppositional manner. Masculine traits are valued more than feminine traits and masculinity (strong) is defined in opposition to femininity (weak). As with all social constructions, gender is closely related to (sub)cultures, meaning that interpretations of femininity and masculinity will differ between and within countries. They are influenced by a host of different factors, including education, ideology, and religion.

The first section of this chapter looks at the different views of gender roles within the far right and discusses the importance of sexism. The second section looks at the representation of men and women according to the various *levels* (i.e. leaders, activists, and supporters) and their involvement in the different *types* of activities (i.e. elections, demonstrations, and violence) of far-right organizations. The last two sections look at the role of gender in the consequences as well as the causes of and responses to far-right success.

Ideology and Issues

The far right's views on gender (and sexuality) are, first and foremost, shaped by its nativism – be it ethnically or racially defined. Ideologically, the far right espouses a view that the German sociologist Andreas Kemper[1] has termed *familialism*: "a form of biopolitics which views the traditional family as a foundation of the nation, and subjugates individual reproductive and self-determination rights [of women in particular] to the normative demand of the reproduction of the nation."[2] Or, in the words of a leaflet of a local branch of the League in Italy, to celebrate International Women's Day no less, women have "a great social mission to fulfill in regard to the survival of our nation."

There are some important differences in the interpretation of familialism, however. Most far-right groups hold a traditional view on women, in which they are exclusively seen as mothers (or mothers-to-be). This means that women are discouraged from working, let alone from having a career. Instead, the state is to materially support non-working mothers and large families. Particularly in Western Europe, many far-right groups hold so-called "modern traditional" views on women, in which working women are tolerated, and even supported, but preferably after their child-rearing has ended. Many populist radical right parties in Northern Europe cannot even be described as modern traditional, given that they openly promote women's rights and don't prioritize motherhood. But their claim that gender equality has been achieved in their country betrays a relatively conservative outlook, at least within their national political context.

Traditionally, the far right mainly expressed so-called *benevolent sexism*, in which women are seen as morally pure and physically weak. This means that (good) women should be adored by men, as women are necessary to make men complete – through the heterosexual family, the heart of the nation or race. But it also means that women should be protected by (real) men, which is implicitly captured in the infamous "Fourteen Words" of one of the founding members of the neo-Nazi terrorist group The Order: "We must secure the existence of our people and a future for white children." He would later add fourteen more words: "Because the beauty of the White Aryan woman must not perish from the earth."

This means that views on both femininity *and* masculinity are very traditional. Real men work, preferably physical labor, and are aggressive and muscular, to protect "their" women. The family is heterosexual and male-dominated, in terms of authority and finances, although women are often ascribed a particular moral weight, which keeps the more aggressive, even animalistic, aspects of their men in check. First and foremost, however, the woman is the womb of the nation, the mother of children, responsible for morally and physically raising the next generation.

More recently, *hostile sexism* has become more overt within the far right, particularly online. Hostile sexism objectifies and degrades women, who are often viewed as trying to control men through feminist ideology or sexual seduction. Whereas benevolent sexism sees women as morally pure and physically weak, hostile sexism considers them morally corrupt and politically powerful. The growing prominence of hostile sexism within the far right is partly related to strong ties between the "manosphere" and the "alt-right." It is widespread within online subcommunities – from gamers (e.g. Gamergate) to "incels" (involuntary celibates) and "pickup artists" – where politicized rape fantasies are openly debated. But hostile sexism has also entered party politics, for example in the new Dutch party FvD, whose leader, Thierry Baudet, has supported "pickup artist" Julian Blanc's claim that women want to be "overwhelmed" and "dominated" by men.

Benevolent and hostile sexism have different views not just on femininity but also on masculinity. In benevolent sexism, the man is physically strong, muscular and powerful. He is not threatened by women. In contrast, in hostile sexism, men consider themselves to be threatened by women, even if mainly implicitly and politically, rather than explicitly and physically. But in certain online communities, men self-identify as "beta males," physically weak and unattractive to women, in contrast to the traditionally masculine "alpha male." These views are closely related to a combination of *toxic masculinity* – in which manhood is defined by violence, sex, status, and aggression – and *misogyny* – a hatred of women – which is omnipresent online but also offline.

Most far-right groups present some combination of elements of benevolent and hostile sexism, which is generally referred to as *ambivalent sexism*. While online "alt-right" groups primarily express hostile sexism, most populist radical right parties, particularly in Western Europe, mainly emphasize benevolent sexism in their official propaganda, even if leading members express hostile sexism towards women who do not live up to their sexist ideals – such as female advocates of (Muslim) immigrants, lesbians, and feminists.

Irrespective of their gender views, or form of sexism, virtually all far-right groups see contemporary feminism negatively. While many Northern European radical right parties speak positively of the original feminists, even they claim that feminism has gone "too far" or is no longer necessary, because gender equality has been achieved – although it is now said to be threatened by Muslim immigrants. Outside of Northern Europe, most far-right groups, but also many conservative groups, argue that feminists are an intolerant and oppressive group (so-called "femiNazis") that wants to control society by imposing "a new form of totalitarianism."

Feminism, like homosexuality, is portrayed as a (mortal) threat to the nation by many far-right groups. There are two, closely integrated, strands of this argument. First, feminism is claimed to undermine the traditional family and thereby the survival of "the nation" – a major concern of the far right in Eastern Europe, where countries are facing rapidly declining birth rates. Second, feminism is considered to be "alien" to the national culture, and often even portrayed as a "weapon" by which foreigners try to weaken the nation – quite often these foreigners are (mostly) Jews, like George Soros.

The other main threat to the nation, and especially its women, is seen as "alien" men. Far-right propaganda is filled with images and stories that play off the age-old western racist stereotypes of (Muslim and non-white) men as animalistic and hyper-sexual predators. Moreover, in line with so-called *femonationalism*, women and women's rights are claimed to be under threat of an "invasion" of Muslims and "Global Islam." As Marine Le Pen wrote in a January 2016 op-ed in the French daily *L'Opinion*, "I am scared that the migrant crisis signals the beginning of the end of women's rights." The far right increasingly targets "native" women in its propaganda, arguing that it is their only defense against "Islamization" and subsequent subjugation.

Similarly, many far-right groups are staunchly homophobic, opposing the "homosexual agenda" that is alleged to threaten the nucleus of the nation, the heterosexual family. When the Polish Supreme Court sided with an LGBTQ organization that was denied

Women of the Identitarian movement demonstrating against a planned refugee shelter in Graz, Austria. The banner reads "Protecting women means closing the borders." (Source: Johanna Poetsch/istock/2016.)

service by a print shop in 2018, the PiS minister of justice responded, "The Supreme Court in this case spoke against freedom and acted as a state oppressor by servicing the ideology of homosexual activists." Various far right leaders have made homophobic remarks, including Brazilian president Bolsonaro, who said that he would be unable to love his son if he was gay and that he would "prefer that he would die in an accident," or Jean-Marie Le Pen, who said in a 2016 interview with *Le Figaro*, "Homosexuals are like salt in soup. If there isn't enough it's a bit bland; when there's too much, it's inedible."

But more and more West European radical right groups and parties accept homosexuality and homosexuals. Some organizations, such as the EDL in the UK and the AfD in Germany, have (un)official groups for their LGBTQ members, while a few even have openly homosexual leaders, like AfD co-leader Alice Weidel. These groups consider homosexuals a potential new electorate for their Islamophobic propaganda. Espousing so-called *homonationalism*, groups like the EDL or PVV argue that LGBTQ rights, which are defined as part of "national culture," are threatened by Muslim immigration and that the far right is the only one to defend them. As failed UKIP leader Anne Marie Waters tweeted: "I'm a gay woman who values my freedom, believe me, Islam is out to get me."

People and Actions

Although the typical far-right leader, if *he* even exists, is both male and hyper-masculine (see chapter 3), particularly within European populist radical right parties few still meet that stereotype in the twenty-first century. Leaders increasingly either are female or do not conform to traditional notions of masculinity.

Where older male leaders like Jean-Marie Le Pen or Jair Bolsonaro personified the stereotypical "political soldier," younger leaders like Gabor Vona (Jobbik) and Tom Van Grieken (VB) look more like eternal students or stereotypical ideal sons-in-law, often patient and smiling in interviews rather than angry and belligerent. Perhaps the most illustrative example of the new far-right man is Jimmie Åkesson, who stepped back as SD leader for several months in 2014 in order to battle burnout. Similarly, US "alt-right" leader Richard Spencer, whom mainstream media regularly praise for his fashion sense – the progressive US magazine *Mother Jones* described him as "an articulate and well-dressed former football player with prom-king good looks and a 'fashy' (as in fascism) haircut" – has openly expressed his disdain for physical confrontations.

In addition, there are more and more leading women within far-right groups and parties. Several populist radical right parties have (had) female leaders, including Alice Weidel (AfD), Giorgia Meloni (Brothers of Italy), Pauline Hanson (ONP), Pia Kjærsgaard (DF), Frauke Petry (AfD), and, of course, Marine Le Pen (RN). Other groups and parties have women within their leadership, like Barbara Pas (VB) and Magdalena Martullo-Blocher (SVP). While most parliamentary delegations of populist radical right parties have few women, although the percentage tends to go up when the total numbers of seats for the party increases, they are often fairly similar to other (smaller) right-wing parties.

As populist radical right parties largely reflect the sex bias and gender roles of conservative parties, many extreme right groups and subcultures are fairly similar to their non-far-right and non-political equivalents. For example, there are similarities in socio-demographics of "fascist" and "anti-fascist" groups as well as far-right and non-political skinheads – all predominantly younger and male. What is unique to the far right, however, is

Marine Le Pen speaks at a rally for the 2014 European elections under the slogan "Yes to France, No to Brussels." (Source: TV Patriotes/Flickr/2014.)

the gender gap in the membership and particularly the electorate, which is often roughly two to one or sixty–forty male-to-female. Populist radical right parties therefore have a much larger gender gap than all other parties, with the notable exception of Green parties (which are disproportionately supported by women). In contrast, Christian democratic and conservative organizations and parties tend to have slightly more female than male members and supporters – in part because women live longer and tend to be more religious.

Women are underrepresented on the far right not only in terms of voting, but also in terms of demonstrating and, particularly, using violence. While larger demonstrations, particularly of Islamophobic groups like the EDL and PEGIDA, can have a sizeable minority of female participants, most smaller demonstrations by extreme right groups are almost exclusively male. Women can be involved in far-right political violence, particularly in its usual, more spontaneous racist form, but very few are among the convicted perpetrators. Almost all premeditated far-right violence, including terrorist attacks, is committed by male lone wolves or small cells of men. A notable exception is Germany's National Socialist Underground, in which one of the three core members was a woman, although she was allegedly not personally involved in the murders.

Consequences

Until recently, we had little idea what the gendered effects of far-right rule would be, given that populist radical right parties were at best junior coalition parties in broader right-wing governments. They often shared their (modern) traditional gender views with their dominant, mainstream right coalition partners. Consequently, these governments did not stand out from other conservative ones. This is changing rapidly in the fourth wave, however, as more and more populist radical right parties come to power.

In Hungary, radical right prime minister Viktor Orbán has enshrined familialism in the new constitution, which asserts that Hungary "shall protect the institution of marriage as the union of a man and a woman" because the family is "the basis of the nation's survival." Similarly, the PiS government in Poland has adopted a policy of "family mainstreaming," which puts the heteronormative family at the core of "the political rules of the government."[3] In addition to the promotion of traditional gender roles, including by relatively generous state subsidies, staunch opposition to abortion is a key aspect of (far-right) familialism. So are attacks on groups and individuals promoting feminism (or homosexuality), who are depicted as "traitors" or "agents of a transnational lobby." Populist radical right governments in Hungary and Poland have actively targeted women's rights NGOs with new tax legislation as well as with raids of offices and arrests of activists.

Unsurprisingly, many far-right groups, as well as many conservative groups, have targeted the academic discipline of Gender Studies, which they consider a "pseudoscience" that undermines the traditional family structure. Putting words into deeds, the Orbán government banned the two existing Gender Studies programs in Hungary in 2018, arguing that "people are born either male or female and we do not consider it acceptable for us to talk about socially constructed genders, rather than biological sexes." At the same time, the recently privatized Corvinus University has started an "Economics of Family Policy and Public Policies for Human Development" program, undoubtedly hoping to profit financially from the government's family mainstreaming agenda.

Similarly, far-right governments have undermined the position and rights of the LGBTQ community. Within hours of his inauguration, Brazilian president Bolsonaro, long known for his homophobic remarks, stripped LGBTQ concerns from the Human Rights Ministry and named Damares Alves, an ultraconservative pastor, as minister of women, family and human rights, and indigenous people. Alves argues that diversity policies have threatened the Brazilian family and that there will be "no more ideological indoctrination of children and teenagers in Brazil" under the new administration. "Girls will be princesses and boys will be princes." Many of these policies and views are also promoted by the Trump administration, although they are largely in line with existing Republican Party policies, and seen as more a priority of Vice-President Mike Pence than President Trump.

But the far right can also affect societal norms outside of parliament. Traditionally, far-right violence was strongly gendered. Consistent with benevolent sexism, and traditional views of masculinity, physical violence of the stronger male against the weaker female was frowned upon. Consequently, not only were perpetrators of far-right violence disproportionately male, so were their victims. To be clear, this applies exclusively to "political violence," given that "domestic violence" and sexual assault are serious problems within many far-right groups, including among leading members of populist radical right parties – one only has to think of Trump's infamous *Access Hollywood* tape, in which he brags about grabbing women by the pussy. Moreover, far-right men (and women) often and openly engage in verbal and even physical attacks on "native" women who associate with "alien" men – for many neo-Nazi and white nationalist groups, "race mixing" makes (mainly) women part of the "white genocide."

Given that hostile sexism considers women politically powerful, male violence against women has become more acceptable and frequent. This is particularly the case with verbal violence, but increasingly also with physical violence. For instance, in many "alt-right" online communities particular vitriol is reserved for women who do not live up to their misogynist standards. But more recently women have also become the prime target of physical violence by far-right incels. Most prominently, a twenty-two-year-old man killed six and seriously injured fourteen before committing suicide in Isla Vista, California, in 2014. The killer, who referred to himself as "The Supreme Gentleman," had distributed a 141-page document online hours before his attack, expressing his deep-rooted loathing of women and his intense frustration over his virginity. This not only made him into a hero within online far-right and incel communities, it also inspired several other deadly misogynist attacks, including the ones in Toronto, Canada, and Tallahassee, Florida, both in 2018.

Causes and Responses

Paradoxically, while men are overrepresented within the far right, almost all research on gender within the far right focuses on women. Similarly, while traditional gender roles and (benevolent or hostile) sexism are often mentioned as reasons for why women would feel less attracted to the far right, they are less often mentioned, and rarely elaborated upon, as reasons why men are more attracted. However, it makes sense that these gendered views play a bigger role in attracting men *to* the far right than in repelling women *from* it. After all, they blend in with other far-right ideological features, which believe in the superiority of the white (or major ethnicity) heterosexual male.

Similarly, the masculine image of the far right, portrayed by both its supporters and its opponents, will be disproportionately attractive to men – particularly less educated and older men. While many women, with similar characteristics, also hold traditional gender views, this masculine image will not necessarily entice them to become active within these groups. Moreover, the association of the far right with violence deters many women, but attracts certain men. Extreme right groups are often attractive to young men who desire a sense of martial camaraderie strengthened by (occasional) violent confrontations with anti-fascists.

Most far-right groups also mainly call upon men, rather than women, to become politically active. It is up to men to "secure the existence of our people and a future for white children." Extreme right groups portray *active* strong men as defenders of *passive* weak women. Some propaganda tries to mobilize men by attacking them for not protecting "their" women from murder and rape by "alien" men and even try to shame those not yet active by pointing out that, as a consequence of their (feminine) passivity, some women have to engage in (masculine) struggle. Populist radical right parties provide fairly similar messages in a more subtle and less violent manner.

In the far-right worldview, it is natural for men to be politically active. This is generally not the case for women. Consequently, far-right women often justify their political activism in terms of motherhood. They become members of far-right organizations because they are "afraid for the future of my children." Even several female far-right leaders use this traditional trope. Sarah Palin presented herself in the 2008 US presidential campaign as a "hockey mom," while Pauline Hanson saw herself as the mother of her nation, stating in 1998 that "Australia is my home and the Australian people are my children." But not only are far-right women more often reluctantly political, they also more often claim to be accidentally political. Interviews with activists of far-right groups and parties, in Europe and the US, find that almost all men claim to have made a conscious choice to become active, whereas a significant minority of women say it was because of a relative, or that they, more or less accidentally, ended up within the movement.

Just as benevolent sexism creates space for women as mothers, hostile sexism provides opportunities for women who meet its ideal of femininity. Female online "alt-right" stars like American Lana Lokteff (from website and TV station *Red Ice*) and Canadian Lauren Southern (formerly of *Rebel Media*) are young women who sell a far-right message through their image of a hyper-sexualized, Nordic beauty. Similarly, some of their male counterparts, like Lokteff's Swedish husband Henrik Palmgren and his countryman Marcus Folin (a.k.a. "The Golden One"), portray the traditional masculinity of the (mythical) Nordic Viking.

Unsurprisingly, given the large female support for mainstream right-wing groups and parties, sexism is not the main reason why women support the far right at (much) lower levels than men. Neither is the popular misperception that women are less nativist and authoritarian, or have a "natural" solidarity with other marginalized groups. Many surveys show that, in general, women hold largely similar views to men on crime, immigration, and terrorism, among many other issues. Consequently, when they support far-right parties, women do so for by and large the same reasons as men: opposition to immigration and concerns about crime and insecurity.

What sets female voters apart from male voters is their lower political self-confidence (efficacy) and their much lower tolerance for violence. In almost all national cultures, and subcultures, the far right is associated with violence – be it because of its actions, its self-presentation (clothes and symbols), or sensationalist media coverage. In much of the postwar era, even the non-violent populist radical right was considered outside of the political mainstream, ideologically and socially unacceptable. Consequently, even many women who hold authoritarian and nativist attitudes do not support far-right groups and parties either because of the (association with) violence or because they do not feel confident enough to support a socially unacceptable group.

This is changing, however. Women are increasingly becoming as politically self-confident as men. Moreover, during the fourth wave, the far right, and particularly the populist radical right, is increasingly mainstreamed and normalized. Many populist radical right groups and parties have "softened" their image, by using softer colors and symbols, more mainstream clothes and fashion, and more prominent women. The best example of this is the *dédiabolisation* (de-demonization) strategy of Marine Le Pen, who has barely moderated her party ideologically, but has provided it with a more "feminine" and therefore "softer" image. For instance, during her 2017 presidential campaign, she used only her first name Marine – trying to detach herself from the more extreme and violent reputation of her father – and used the symbol of a rose rather than the party's flame (which has strong fascist overtones).

There are, of course, risks to a more "feminine" image for far-right groups. While it might attract some, loosely committed, women, it could turn off more committed men, who are attracted to the far right exactly because of its "masculine" image. This is particularly the case for smaller extreme right organizations, like skinhead or neo-Nazi groups, which function more like a (criminal) gang than a (political) party for the mostly male members.

Given the partly different motivations for joining far-right groups, or (not) voting for populist radical right parties, of men and women, responses to the far right should include a gender perspective. For example, while highlighting the violent character of the far right could keep women from joining, it might make certain men keener to join. Similarly, some research shows that personalizing nativism and racism, by including detailed and personal experiences by the victims, is very effective with girls and women, but less so with boys and men. And exit programs for far-right activists have to think about alternative activities and groups that are attractive to boys and men who hold traditional interpretations of masculinity, but without strengthening them – let alone toxic masculinity. Finally, such programs need to address the sense of insecurity and nostalgia that underpins the male supremacy enshrined in, but largely obscured by, white supremacy.

10

Twelve Theses on the Fourth Wave

I want to finish this short book with twelve theses that illustrate and summarize the most important aspects and developments of the contemporary far right. Most of these are unique to the fourth wave of the postwar far right, which roughly started at the beginning of the new century, illustrating that we are dealing with a different political context than in the third wave of the late twentieth century. While the far-right phenomenon is roughly the same as in the third wave, at least in ideological terms, the political context in which it operates has changed dramatically – partly because of the actions of the far right, but mainly because of actions and developments outside of its direct impact.

1 The Far Right Is Extremely Heterogeneous

We often speak about *the* far right as if it is a homogeneous entity, identical within time and space. But the far right is plural rather than singular. It differs significantly on a broad range of factors, most notably ideology:

for example, the anti-democratic extreme right versus the anti-liberal democratic radical right. The far right mobilizes in different types of organizations (e.g. parties, social movement organizations, subcultures) and through various types of activities (e.g. elections, demonstrations, violence) – although several individual activists are involved in multiple types of organizations and activities. Some groups and subcultures are global, many are national, and most are only regional or even local. Moreover, there is no one-on-one relationship between type of ideology and type of organization: there are extreme right parties (e.g. XA) and radical right movements (e.g. PEGIDA).

But even within the most relevant subcategory of the far right, that is, populist radical right parties, differences are at least as pronounced as similarities. The parties differ in terms of age, electoral success, history and legacy, leadership, organization, and political relevance. There are poorly organized parties with an extreme right history and little electoral success, like the Portuguese National Renovator Party, but also well-organized, decades-old parties which are among the most successful parties in their country, like France's RN or India's BJP. They include parties that emerged on the extreme right, like Sweden's SD, as well as transformed conservative parties, like Fidesz and Switzerland's SVP.

2 The Populist Radical Right Is Mainstream(ed)

While the extreme right remains largely marginal and marginalized, the populist radical right has become mainstreamed in most western democracies. Mainstreaming takes places because populist radical right parties and mainstream parties address increasingly similar issues and because they offer increasingly similar issue positions. The change can come from movement by the populist radical right (moderation), by the mainstream (radicalization), or by both at the same time (convergence).

At the beginning of the third wave, populist radical right parties were seen as "niche parties" which mainly addressed socio-cultural issues like crime and immigration. In contrast, mainstream parties competed primarily on the basis of socio-economic issues like taxation and unemployment. But in the last two decades, socio-cultural issues have come to dominate the political agenda. In most European countries, as well as in Australia and the US, the political debate is dominated by socio-cultural issues and so-called "identity politics," including a more or less explicit defense of white supremacy in the face of the increasing politicization of ethnic and religious minorities. Consequently, socio-cultural issues are no longer niche as mainstream parties now also prioritize them over socio-economic issues, at least in their electoral campaigns. One could even argue that today socio-economic issues have become niche.

But mainstream and populist radical right parties not only address the same issues, they also increasingly offer similar issue positions. Research shows that this is the consequence more of the radicalization of mainstream parties than of the moderation of populist radical right parties. In fact, over recent decades, the populist radical right has barely moderated, not even when in government. Instead, mainstream parties have radicalized, moving further towards the (populist radical) right in terms of, first and foremost, immigration and integration, but also law and order, European integration (or international collaboration more generally), and populism.

The salience of socio-cultural issues like immigration and terrorism, as well as the radicalization of mainstream parties, is obviously related to specific political events, such as jihadist terrorist attacks and the so-called "refugee crisis," but it is important to remember that these events are politically framed: that is, the influx of more than a million asylum seekers to Europe in 2015 could have been debated as a humanitarian tragedy instead of a threat to national culture and sovereignty. Whereas many mainstream parties primarily adopted populist radical right discourse before, they are now increasingly adopting their frames and, therefore, policies too. This has significant broader consequences for contemporary politics.

As socio-cultural issues have come to dominate the political agenda, and mainstream parties have increasingly adopted the frames of the radical right, it comes as little surprise that populist radical right parties have increased not only their electoral support but also their political impact. In fact, in some countries they do not even have to be (officially) part of the government to dictate a significant part of its agenda, most notably immigration and integration policies, such as in the Czech Republic, France, or the UK. It is important to remember that this is taking place as populist radical right parties are still, in almost all countries, a political minority – on average the third biggest party in the country.

3 Populist Radical Right Politics Is No Longer Limited to Populist Radical Right Parties

As a consequence of mainstreaming, populist radical right politics is no longer (primarily) limited to populist radical right parties. Statements that used to be exclusive to populist radical right parties in the third wave have become "common sense" in the fourth wave. This started out relatively moderate. For instance, mainstream leaders from (then) French president Nicolas Sarkozy to German chancellor Angela

Merkel have stated that multiculturalism has failed, while (then) Czech president Václav Klaus and Dutch prime minister Mark Rutte have argued that European integration has gone too far and the EU has become a "bureaucratic moloch" that threatens democracy in the member states. In the US, (neo)conservatives in the Republican Party, including Texas senator Ted Cruz, were parroting far-right conspiracy theories about the UN (and the alleged "New World Order") well before President Trump brought them into the White House.

But decades of authoritarian and nativist responses to jihadist terrorist attacks, as well as the so-called "refugee crisis" of 2015, have led to a change not just in discourse, but also in policies. Many political leaders in Central and Eastern Europe have likened the "refugee crisis" to a Muslim invasion, some even calling for the monitoring of all Muslims in their country, while a majority of Republican governors in the US supported a "Muslim ban." Even countries that do not have a strong far-right opposition party, like Australia or Slovenia, have mainstream (right-wing) parties that advocate for strong nativist policies. In fact, Australia's brutal refugee policy has become an inspiration for populist radical right parties across Europe.

4 The Boundaries Have Become Blurred

One of the consequences of the mainstreaming of populist radical right parties, and the growing separation between policies and parties, is that the boundaries between mainstream (right-wing) and populist radical right parties have become increasingly porous. For instance, compared to their predecessors (the Union for a Popular Movement and the FN) in the third wave, the differences between France's Republicans and the RN in the fourth wave are marginal. Similarly, what makes parties like the Israeli Likud and US Republican Party mainstream right, but parties like the Danish DF or the Norwegian Progress Party populist radical right? These issues are even more pronounced in much of Eastern Europe, with parties like the Croatian Democratic Union, Latvia's National Alliance, or the Slovenian Democratic Party.

This is an important question, both morally and politically, and needs to be more openly and critically discussed in academic and public debates. For decades, the far right has been externalized, associated with amoral and marginalized groups. By definition, mainstream parties were not populist radical right and did not implement populist radical right policies. This meant that, mostly implicitly, it was assumed that the only challenge to liberal democracy came from outside, not inside, the political mainstream. It is clear that this can no longer be upheld. Many of the immigration policies that have been proposed, and even implemented, by mainstream parties, including of the left wing (e.g. the Hollande and Renzi governments in France and Italy, respectively), are virtually identical to those exclusively proposed by populist radical right parties in the third wave. They are steeped in an authoritarian, nativist, and/or populist worldview, irrespective of whether these mainstream parties have adopted them for opportunistic reasons or have truly transformed ideologically.

5 The Populist Radical Right Is Increasingly Normalized

It should come as little surprise that, as the boundary between mainstream and populist radical right politics becomes more and more blurred, the populist radical right is becoming increasingly normalized. To be clear, the extreme right is still mostly rejected, although even that is changing. For instance, Brazilian president Bolsonaro has openly flirted with military government, while US president Trump has defended "alt-right" protesters in Charlottesville. And the world's largest party, the Indian BJP, is part of a Hindutva subculture that includes openly extremist and violent groups. Nevertheless, in most cases, support for the extreme right within the political mainstream is either muted or, if voiced, still broadly opposed.

In sharp contrast, populist radical right parties, and particularly ideas, are increasingly tolerated, and even embraced, by business, civil society, economic, media, and political circles. This has reached new levels in the wake of Brexit and Trump in 2016, which saw an outpouring of understanding for "working-class voters" that was often framed within an outright populist narrative. The common people ("Somewheres") were the political victims of an out-of-touch elite ("Anywheres"). This frame is not just pushed in right-wing media, notably Murdoch-owned media in Anglo-Saxon countries, but also enthusiastically embraced by liberal media. Leaving aside that it reduces populist radical right support to the working class, which is empirically incorrect, it reduces the working class to just whites and nativists, another problematic simplification.

The argument that populist radical right voters are protest voters, rather than supporters of a radical right agenda, has been present since the beginning of the third wave in the early 1980s. What sets the fourth wave apart is that whereas they used to be portrayed as gullible and misguided, they are now increasingly portrayed as the voice of common sense. In populist terms, it is "the people" (reduced to radical right voters) who are "authentic" and "moral," and "the elite" (i.e. all mainstream parties) who are "cosmopolitan" and "corrupt." To be sure, this is not (yet) the dominant narrative, but it has made serious inroads in both conservative and liberal circles, including within academia.

6 The Extreme Right Are a Normal Pathology, the Populist Radical Right a Pathological Normalcy

During most of the postwar era, the far right was seen as a "normal pathology" of western democracy, that is, a premodern phenomenon, ideologically unconnected to modern democracy, and supported by just a small minority of the population. In reality, the so-called "normal pathology" thesis was always at best partly true. Overall, it did apply to the extreme right, as support for (open) racism and, particularly, non-democratic regimes was indeed limited to a small minority of the population in most countries.

The populist radical right, on the other hand, is much more a pathological normalcy, that is, a radicalization of mainstream values, supported by sizeable minorities, if not outright pluralities and majorities. Surveys from Austria to the US and Brazil to India show that large parts of the population hold authoritarian, nativist, and populist attitudes. Moreover, these attitudes are clearly related to mainstream ideologies and values, like anti-establishment sentiments as well as support for the nation-state and for law-and-order policies. This is not to say that the majority, or even plurality, of the populations in western democracies support a populist radical right ideology, or that there is no significant difference between the ideologies of mainstream and populist radical right parties. Rather, the difference is primarily a matter of *degree* rather than *kind*. The populist radical right does not stand for a fundamentally different world than the political mainstream;

rather it takes mainstream ideas and values to an illiberal extreme.

7 The Rise of the Populist Radical Right Is About Dealignment Rather Than Realignment (For Now)

When Green and New Left parties were making inroads into the political systems of Western Europe and North America, political scientists argued that we were experiencing a process of both dealignment and realignment. In other words, not only were people breaking their old ties to established parties (dealignment), they also were forcing new bonds with the Green and New Left parties (realignment). Similarly, many commentators have argued that the white working class has exchanged social democratic for populist radical right parties.

Despite remarkably high levels of loyalty among populist radical right voters in the 1990s, particularly for the FN and FPÖ, both parties suffered great losses in the early 2000s. And while they have bounced back since, it is clear that realignment is partial at best. More than half of the people who voted for Marine Le Pen in the first round of the 2017 presidential elections did not come out to vote for the FN in the legislative elections two months later. This is even clearer in the case of most other radical right parties, particularly in Central and Eastern Europe, whose support has been shown to be highly volatile – except for the conservative-turned-populist radical right parties in Hungary and Poland, which have been able to use state resources to keep their support base, at least for now. The consequence of this development is that, even if populist radical right parties return to electoral marginality in the near future (which is, however, unlikely), the party systems will not return to their stable origins.

8 The Far Right Is a Gendered Phenomenon

As with all political phenomena, the far right is gendered, but in a complex, multifaceted way. Most far-right groups are ambivalent sexist: that is, combining aspects of both benevolent sexism and hostile sexism. Even when they put "their" women on a pedestal, women who do not conform to benevolent sexist (in terms of reproduction or sexuality) or nativist/racist norms (by dating outside of their culture or "race") are met with virulent hostility. Similarly, while more traditional interpretations of masculinity predominate, in which men are expected to be strong protectors of weak women, toxic masculinity, in which mental and sexual frustration is taken out on independent and "opinionated" women, is increasingly prominent, particularly within far-right and related online communities (such as the "incels" and the "manosphere"). Toxic masculinity has also made women primary targets in some far-right political violence.

Almost all far-right groups subscribe to familialism, which sees women as mothers and, as such, as essential to the survival of the nation/race. Beyond that, far-right gender norms are mostly culturally determined. Almost all far-right groups hold more traditional gender norms within their own national cultural context. But the modern traditional views within the Northern European far-right groups, which support working women and often accept abortion and divorce, would be considered progressive in many Southern countries and are fundamentally at odds with the traditional views of most far-right groups there, which see women exclusively as mothers.

Far-right propaganda is rife with femonationalism: that is, the use of women and feminist arguments (like gender equality) in support of nativism, in particular

Islamophobia. Women (and girls) are portrayed as vulnerable, threatened by "aliens" (domestic or foreign), and dependent upon the protection of "their" (masculine) men. It is only within the context of Islamophobia that far-right groups defend gender equality and women's rights, juxtaposing an egalitarian "West" against a misogynist "Islam." Given that they argue that gender equality has been achieved, even North European populist radical right parties tend to vote against gender equality policies, rejecting women's quotas as "tokenism," because "real women" don't need the state to protect their equality. In power, most far-right parties have tried to weaken feminist groups, and marginalize or oppose gender mainstreaming, instead creating and subsidizing a familialist, right-wing infrastructure.

The far right is still a predominantly male and masculine phenomenon in terms of leaders, members, and voters. This is particularly the case in smaller extreme right groups, in which a kind of martial camaraderie and an image and practice of violence attract a specific subset of men, while at the same time repelling most women. But things are changing. Female leaders are becoming more common and visible, don't always live up to the traditional image of femininity – this applies in particular to Marine Le Pen (RN) – while more and more male leaders are breaking with the traditional masculine image, like Jimmie Åkesson (SD) or Tom Van Grieken (VB). Given that the main reason for the underrepresentation of women within the far right is its association with violence, which is much more rejected by women than by men, this change in leadership, as well as the mainstreaming and "softening" of its propaganda, could make at least populist radical right parties more attractive to women – a still largely underutilized electorate.

9 No Country Is Immune to Far-Right Politics

For a long time, we have believed that certain countries or societies are immune to far-right politics. Americans and Brits claimed that their countries were exceptions, being inherently democratic, already having withstood fascist temptations in the early twentieth century. Dutch and Swedes believed their societies were so liberal that populist radical right parties could never take root there. And many believed that Germany had been so profoundly impacted by the Holocaust trauma and its impressive *Vergangenheitsbewältigung* (dealing with history) that far-right forces could never regain popular support within its repressive militant democracy. Similarly, commentators have long argued that the (fresh) memory of the right-wing authoritarian Franco regime explained the absence of a successful populist radical right party in Spain.

We now know that this was wrong. And even if there are still countries with unsuccessful far-right parties, like Canada or Portugal, this is more a supply than a demand issue. These countries have a fertile breeding ground for populist radical right politics too. They just have not yet been confronted with the right populist radical right party or political entrepreneur for their specific political context. How quickly this can change we are seeing in Spain, for example, where Vox has done what several other far-right parties before it failed to do. Admittedly helped by specific circumstances, including tensions around Catalonian independence and massive corruption scandals within the conservative Popular Party, Vox has rapidly achieved not just electoral success, but also political relevance.

10 The Far Right Is Here to Stay

The far right is here to stay. This even applies to the extreme right, which also survived the repressive aftermath of the 1945 defeat of the fascist movements and regimes that originally inspired it. To be clear, there are few indications that extreme right parties or politicians are returning to political power. Even in Greece, which probably resembles Weimar Germany more than any other democracy, the neo-Nazi XA is remarkably stable at roughly 5–7 percent of the vote. That said, extreme right actors and ideas have recently been praised by two of the most powerful men in the world, Brazilian president Bolsonaro (military dictatorship) and US president Trump ("alt-right" demonstrators in Charlottesville). Moreover, antisemitism and racism have returned to the center of the political debate, be it more implicitly in traditional media or more explicitly on social media.

In addition, there is a clear increase in both verbal and physical extreme right violence. Threats of violence by far-right activists and (anonymous) trolls remain commonplace on social media, although many platforms have recently become more repressive and vigilant, slowly but steadily tightening the virtual space within which the extreme right can operate. Both verbal and physical violence have exploded in the wake of the "refugee crisis," leading to insults and violence against both "aliens" and "natives" who are considered supportive of them. After decades of obsessing over jihadi terrorism, to the detriment of (other) domestic terrorist threats, many countries are increasingly warning against the growing threat of far-right terrorism. So far, most major attacks have been perpetrated by single attackers but even these individuals were tightly connected to the larger far-right virtual community.

Given that it is fundamentally related to mainstream values, albeit in a radicalized manner, and its more recent success is linked to structural changes and speaks to prominent issues, there is little reason to assume the populist radical right has reached its electoral or political peak. But while the support for populist radical right *ideas* within society is relatively stable, many populist radical right *parties* still have very volatile electorates. This is because the saliency of their *issues* is dependent upon the broader political context and varies in time and space. After all, politics is, first and foremost, local rather than global.

In the long term, however, the populist radical right is facing serious challenges. While its key issues – related to cultural, economic, and political integration – will remain relevant for some time to come, many societies are changing rapidly, becoming more diverse and more accepting of diversity. The US is expected to become a majority minority country within the coming decades, and while most European countries are nowhere near this, several of its major cities are. Moreover, while many populist radical right parties are profiting from resentment in the geographical periphery, as a new urban–rural divide has reasserted itself in many countries, most countries are still (sub) urbanizing, as the rural population is ageing and declining. Surveys show that younger generations and urban populations are much more accepting of the multicultural reality, which will make them less likely to support populist radical right ideas and parties. However, as long as younger people vote at much lower rates than older people, mainstream politicians will continue to cater more to the latter than the former.

11 There Is No Single Best Way to Deal with the Far Right

Given that the far right is highly diverse, there is no best way to deal with it. First of all, violent groups require a different strategy than non-violent groups. Dealing with the violent far right, which is predominantly extreme right, is primarily a law enforcement issue. Most countries already have the required laws on the books, and sufficient personnel in the state apparatus. What many lack is the willingness to acknowledge the threat of the far right and use their repressive resources to deal with it. Importantly, even violent far-right groups and individuals should be fought within the limits of liberal democracy, as excessive infringement of human rights and the use of force not only could create a violent backlash, but also would weaken liberal democracy as such, making the cure worse than the disease.

Non-violent far-right ideas and groups should be mainly addressed by educational and political initiatives. Given its limited support, the extreme right poses a much smaller challenge than the much more popular populist radical right. Neither pure exclusion, nor pure inclusion works. The former limits the liberal democratic space, while the latter weakens liberal democracy from within. Some argue that the best approach is to mix the two (cooptation), that is, exclude the groups but include the ideas, but developments in countries like Belgium and France show that this does little to stem the growth of populist radical right parties, while it makes their ideas and policies even more influential, given that they are now pushed by mainstream parties.

As the far right is always primarily a product of local and national conditions, the best way to deal with its challenge will always need to be developed in line with these conditions. For instance, whether you face a one-man party (PVV) or a mass party (BJP) has major consequences for how to construct a counter-response. Similarly, the far right poses a different type of threat in a parliamentary than a presidential system, or whether in opposition or in (coalition) government. This does not mean that each country, or locality, should reinvent the wheel. We can learn from each other, and across national and even continental boundaries. But, ultimately, the strategy should be local or national if it is to succeed.

12 The Emphasis Should Be on Strengthening Liberal Democracy

The ultimate goal of all responses to the far right should be the strengthening of liberal democracy. Put simply, only fighting the far right does not necessarily strengthen liberal democracy, but strengthening liberal democracy will, by definition, weaken the far right. That the two do not always go hand in hand is not always acknowledged. Limiting free speech or the right to demonstrate not only infringes on the democratic rights of far-right activists, it undermines these rights in general, and thereby the liberal democratic regime. This is not even to speak of the tendency for repressive measures aimed at one group to be later applied to other groups, including some that are neither radical nor right.

This is not the place to develop strategies in much detail. But let me suggest at least some guiding principles. First, we should be better at explaining why liberal democracy is the best political system we currently have, and how it protects *all* its discontents. To do this, we should be better informed, and more explicit, about the inherent tensions of the system, most notably between majority rule and minority rights. Second, we should develop and propagate positive political alternatives, based on a host of liberal democratic ideologies (i.e. Christian democrat, conservative, Green, liberal, and social democrat). Third, we should reclaim the political agenda on the basis of our own political programs. Rather than following the far right's issues, let alone their frames, we should address the issues that concern us, as well as the majority of the population, and posit our own, ideologically informed, positions. Obviously, this should not exclude any important issues, including those currently associated with the far right (like crime, corruption, and immigration). Fourth, we should set clear limits to what collaborations and positions are consistent with liberal democratic values – ideally *before* we are confronted with a significant far-right challenge. Only if we believe in liberal democracy can we defend it!

Notes

Introduction

1 The far-right parties in question are the Patriotic Front (Bulgaria), DF (Denmark), EKRE (Estonia), Fidesz (Hungary), the League (Italy), PiS (Poland), the SNS (Slovakia), and the Democratic Unionist Party (UK).

2 N. Bobbio, *Left and Right: The Significance of a Political Distinction*, University of Chicago Press, 1997.

Chapter 1 History

1 K. von Beyme, "Right-Wing Extremism in Western Europe," *West European Politics*, 11(2), 1988, pp. 1–18.

2 The Croatian Democratic Union transformed into a non-far-right party after the death of its powerful party leader, Croatian President Franjo Tudjman, in 1999. In more recent years, it has been one of several right-wing parties in the Western Balkans to be inspired by the illiberal turn of Viktor Orbán in Hungary.

Chapter 2 Ideology

1 For a more elaborate discussion of my terminology, see C. Mudde, *Populist Radical Right Parties in Europe*, Cambridge University Press, 2007.

Chapter 3 Organization

1 M. Minkenberg, *The Radical Right in Europe: An Overview*, Bertelsmann Stiftung, 2011.

2 See N. Higuchi, *Japan's Ultra-Right*, Trans Pacific Press, 2016.
3 From the SPLC website: *https://www.splcenter.org/ fighting-hate/extremist-files/ideology/alt-right*.

Chapter 4 People
1 M. Esser and J. van Holsteyn, "Kleur bekennen: over leden van de Centrumdemocraten," in J. van Holsteyn and C. Mudde (eds.), *Extreem-rechts in Nederland*. Sdu, 1998.
2 D. Albertazzi and D. McDonnell, *Populists in Power*, Routledge, 2015. I thank Duncan McDonnell for sharing some additional LN and SVP data with me.
3 See, respectively, Higuchi, *Japan's Ultra-Right*; and P.S. Forscher and N. Kteily, "A Psychological Profile of the Alt-Right," *PsyArXiv*, August 9, 2017.
4 See, for example, N. Mayer, *Ces Français qui votent Le Pen*, Flammarion, 2002.
5 E. Elkins, "The Five Types of Trump Voters: Who They Are and What They Believe," Democracy Fund, 2017, available at: *https://www.voterstudygroup.org/ publications/2016-elections/the-five-types-trump-voters*.

Chapter 5 Activities
1 F. Virchow, "Performance, Emotion, and Ideology: On the Creation of 'Collectives of Emotion' and Worldview in the Contemporary German Far Right," *Journal of Contemporary Ethnography*, 36(2), 2007, pp. 147–64 (p. 147).
2 J.A. Ravndal, "Right-Wing Terrorism and Violence in Western Europe: Introducing the RTV Dataset," *Perspectives on Terrorism*, 10(3), 2016, available at: *http://www.terrorismanalysts.com/pt/index.php/pot/ article/view/508/1008*.
3 See the paper by J.D. Freilich, S.M. Chermak, J. Gruenewald, and W.S. Parkin, "Far-Right Violence in the United States: 1990–2013," START, 2014, available at: *http://www.start.umd.edu/pubs/START_ECDB_FarRight Violence_FactSheet_June2014.pdf*.
4 I do not mention the names of far-right terrorists as

personal fame is one of the main motivations for their actions and creates a cult of personality that inspires potential other terrorists.

Chapter 6 Causes

1 See E.K. Scheuch and H.D. Klingemann, "Theorie des Rechtsradikalismus in westlichen Industriegesellschaften," *Hamburger Jahrbuch für Wirtschafts- und Gesellschaftspolitik*, 12 (1967), pp. 11–29.
2 I have developed the "pathological normalcy" thesis in more details in C. Mudde, "The Populist Radical Right: A Pathological Normalcy," *West European Politics*, 33(6), 2010, pp. 1167–87.

Chapter 7 Consequences

1 C. Mudde, "Three Decades of Populist Radical Right Parties in Western Europe: So What?," *European Journal of Political Research*, 52(1), 2013, pp. 1–19 (p. 1).
2 A.A. Ellinas, *The Media and the Far Right in Western Europe: Playing the Nationalist Card*, Cambridge University Press, 2010, p. 218.
3 R. Balfour et al., *Europe's Troublemakers: The Populist Challenge to Foreign Policy*, European Policy Center, 2016, available at: *http://www.epc.eu/documents/uploads/pub_6377_europe_s_troublemakers.pdf?doc_id=1714.*

Chapter 8 Responses

1 The categorization of party responses to the far right comes from M. Minkenberg, "The Radical Right in Public Office: Agenda-Setting and Policy Effects," *West European Politics*, 24(4), 2001, pp. 1–21.
2 On coalition formation with radical right parties, see S.L. de Lange, "New Alliances: Why Mainstream Parties Govern with Radical Right-Wing Populist Parties," *Political Studies*, 60(4), 2012, pp. 899–918.

Chapter 9 Gender

1 A. Kemper, *Foundation of the Nation: How Political Parties and Movements Are Radicalising Others in Favour of Conservative Family Values and Against Tolerance,*

Diversity, and Progressive Gender Politics in Europe, Friedrich Ebert Stiftung, 2016.

2 See W. Grzebalska and A. Pető, "The Gendered Modus Operandi of the *Illiberal* Transformation in Hungary and Poland," *Women Studies International Forum*, 68, 2019, pp. 164–72 (p. 167).

3 Ibid., p. 168.

Chronology

1948: MSI enters Italian parliament for the first time.

1951: ESM founded in Malmö, Sweden.

1952: SRP banned in Germany.

1956: National European Social Movement banned in the Netherlands.

Poujadists enter French parliament, including Jean-Marie Le Pen.

FPÖ founded in Austria.

1961: National Action for People and Nation founded in Switzerland.

1964: NPD founded in Germany.

1968: George Wallace wins five states in US presidential elections.

GRECE founded in France.

1972: FN founded in France.

1973: Progress Party enters Danish parliament for the first time.

Progress Party enters Norwegian parliament for the first time.

1977: Christoph Blocher becomes leader of Zurich branch of SVP.

US Supreme Court rules in the Skokie case.

1978: VB enters Belgian parliament as part of electoral list.

1979: VB officially founded as political party.

1980: BJP founded in India.

1982: Center Party enters Dutch parliament for the first time.

1984: Group of the European Right founded in European Parliament.

1985: XA founded in Greece.

1986: FN gains thirty-five seats in French parliament.

Jörg Haider becomes leader of FPÖ.

1987: B&H founded in the UK.

1988: SD founded in Sweden.

1989: Technical Group of the European Right founded in European Parliament.

SNS founded in Czechoslovakia.

1990: Franjo Tudjman elected president of Croatia.

SNS enters Czechoslovak parliament for the first time.

1991: LN founded as political party in Italy.

Greater Romania Party founded.

1992: RSS banned in India.

Liberal Democratic Party of Russia founded.

SNS enters coalition government under Vladimír Mečiar.

Greater Romania Party enters Romanian parliament for the first time.

Belgian parties introduce *cordon sanitaire* against VB.

1993: Ban against RSS in India lifted.

Liberal Democratic Party of Russia enters Russian parliament for the first time.

Greater Romania Party enters coalition government under Nicolae Văcăroiu.

B&H founder Ian Stuart Donaldson dies in car crash.

1994: LN enters coalition government under Silvio Berlusconi.

Kach party banned in Israel.

1995: MSI transforms into National Alliance.

DF founded as split from Progress Party in Denmark.

Far-right terrorist kills 168 people in bombing in Oklahoma City, US.

1996: BJP forms coalition government in India.

1997: ONP founded in Australia.

Japan Conference (Nippon Kaigi) founded.

1998: DF enters Danish parliament for the first time.

1999: National Union alliance enters Israeli parliament.

EDL founded in the UK.

2000: FPÖ enters coalition government under Wolfgang Schüssel.

Popular Orthodox Rally founded in Greece.

2001: LN returns to power in third Berlusconi government.

DF supports Danish right-wing minority government.

2002: Jean-Marie Le Pen qualifies for second round of presidential elections.

2003: CPI founded in Italy.

Identitarian Bloc founded in France.

Jobbik founded in Hungary.

2004: Flemish Bloc dissolved in Belgium, succeeded by Flemish Interest.

2005: Jörg Haider splits from FPÖ and founds Alliance for the Future of Austria.

2006: Geert Wilders founds PVV, enters Dutch parliament.

SNS enters coalition government under Robert Fico in Slovakia.

2007: Identity, Tradition, Sovereignty founded in European Parliament.

2008: Jörg Haider dies in car crash.

LN enters coalition in fourth Berlusconi government.

John McCain picks Sarah Palin as running mate in presidential elections.

2009: Tea Party launched in response to bailouts by US government.

2010: SD enters Swedish parliament for the first time.

Fidesz regains power in Hungary with constitutional majority.

Jobbik enters Hungarian parliament for the first time.

Far-right terrorist kills seventy-seven in Oslo bombing and Utøya shooting in Norway.

L'SNS founded in Slovakia.

EAF founded in European Parliament.

2011: Marine Le Pen becomes leader of FN.

Popular Orthodox Rally participates in government in Greece.

2012: Generation Identity founded in France.

XA enters Greek parliament for the first time.

EKRE founded in Estonia.

2013: Matteo Salvini becomes leader of the LN.

AfD founded in Germany.

Marian Kotleba elected governor of Banská Bystrica region in Slovakia.

Vox founded in Spain.

2014: PEGIDA founded in Germany.

BJP returns to power in India.

DF, FN, and UKIP become biggest national parties in European elections.

2015: Jean-Marie Le Pen expelled from FN.

EKRE enters Estonian parliament for the first time.

ENF founded; replaces EAF.

Frauke Petry becomes leader of AfD.

APF officially founded.

2016: Donald Trump wins presidential elections in the US.

Norbert Hofer (FPÖ) almost wins Austrian presidential elections.

UK votes to leave EU in referendum.

L'SNS enters Slovak parliament for the first time.

2017: "Unite the Right" rally in Charlottesville, Virginia.

Marine Le Pen qualifies for, and loses, the presidential run-off in France.

Alexander Gauland and Alice Weidel become co-leaders of AfD.

FPÖ enters coalition government under Sebastian Kurz.

2018: LN drops "Northern" and becomes League.

Jair Bolsonaro wins presidential elections in Brazil.

National Front (FN) is renamed National Rally (RN).

League enters populist government coalition under Giuseppe Conti.

Likud-dominated government passes Nation-State Law.

2019: Far-right terrorist kills fifty in attack at two mosques in Christchurch, New Zealand.

Vox enters Spanish parliament for the first time.

EKRE enters coalition government under Jüri Ratas.

Austrian government falls over FPÖ scandal.

Brexit Party, Fidesz, League, PiS, and RN become biggest parties in European elections.

Glossary

"Alt-right" "a set of far-right ideologies, groups, and individuals whose core belief is that 'white identity' is under attack by multicultural forces using 'political correctness' and 'social justice' to undermine white people and 'their' civilization" (Southern Poverty Law Center).

Ambivalent sexism a combination of benevolent sexism and hostile sexism.

Antisemitism hostility to or prejudice against Jews.

Authoritarianism the belief in a strictly ordered society, in which infringements on authority are to be punished severely.

Benevolent sexism the belief that women are morally pure and physically weak, deserving adoration and in need of protection by strong men.

Democracy a political system based on popular sovereignty and majority rule.

Ethnocracy   a nominally democratic regime in which the dominance of one ethnic group is structurally determined.

Ethnopluralism   the belief that people are divided into ethnic groups which are equal but should remain segregated.

Euroscepticism   dissatisfaction about the process of European integration and the institution of the European Union.

Extreme right   ideologies that believe that inequalities between people are natural and positive and that reject the essence of democracy.

Familialism   the belief that the traditional family is the foundation of the nation and individual reproductive and self-determination rights are secondary to the reproduction of the nation.

Far right   a combination of both the extreme right and the radical right.

Fascism   a totalitarian ideology that offered a "Third Way" beyond liberalism and socialism based on economic corporatism, an ethical state, a national rebirth, an all-powerful leader, and the cleansing qualities and natural state of violence and war.

Femonationalism   the use of women and women's rights in support of nativism, in particular Islamophobia.

Homonationalism   the use of homosexuals and gay rights in support of nativism, in particular Islamophobia.

Hostile sexism   considers women to be morally corrupt and politically powerful, trying to control men through feminist ideology or sexual seduction.

Islamophobia   an irrational fear of Islam or Muslims.

Liberal democracy   a political system that combines popular sovereignty and majority rule with minority rights, rule of law, and separation of powers.

Misogyny   hatred of women.

Nativism   an ideology that holds that states should be inhabited exclusively by members of the native group (the nation) and that non-native (or "alien") elements, whether persons or ideas, are fundamentally threatening to the homogeneous nation-state.

Populism   a (thin) ideology that considers society to be ultimately separated into two homogeneous and antagonistic groups, the pure people and the corrupt elite, and which argues that politics should be an expression of the *volonté générale* (general will) of the people.

Racism   the belief that people are divided into biological groups (races) which are hierarchically ordered.

Radical right   ideologies that believe that inequalities between people are natural and positive and that accept the essence of democracy but oppose fundamental elements of *liberal* democracy.

Toxic masculinity   defines manhood by violence, sex, status, and aggression.

Further Reading

The far right is among the most discussed political topics, and this is reflected in the wealth of available academic and non-academic literature. However, most focuses on radical right parties in Western Europe, while other groups and regions are much less covered. Very few, if any, books cover the full far right across the globe, as this book tries to do. What follows is a selection of some of the more accessible and useful (English language) literature on the topic.

Two excellent academic introductions to the topic are Jens Rydgren (ed.), *The Oxford Handbook of the Radical Right* (Oxford University Press, 2018), and Cas Mudde (ed.), *The Populist Radical Right: A Reader* (Routledge, 2017).

Jean-Yves Camus and Nicolas Lebourg, *Far-Right Politics in Europe* (Harvard University Press, 2017), provides a very broad overview of the **history** of the postwar European far right, while Andrea Mammone, Emmanuel Godin, and Brian Jenkins (eds.), *Varieties of Right-Wing Extremism in Europe* (Routledge, 2012), has a broad ideological and organizational scope too. Chip Berlet and Matthew N. Lyons, *Right-Wing Populism in America: Too Close for Comfort* (The Guilford Press, 2000), is the slightly dated, but still definitive, text on the history of the US far right. More encyclopedic overviews of the splintered US far-right scene are Betty A. Dobratz and Stephanie L. Shanks-Meile, *The White Separatist Movement in the United States* (Johns Hopkins University Press, 2000), and Stephen E. Atkins (ed.), *Encyclopedia of Right-Wing Extremism in Modern American History* (ABC-CLIO, 2011). For good introductions to the far right in Eastern Europe, see Michael Minkenberg (ed.), *The Radical Right in Eastern Europe: Democracy under Siege?* (Palgrave Macmillan, 2017), and Vera Stojarova, *The Far Right in the Balkans* (Manchester University Press, 2013).

An excellent introduction to the **ideology and issues** of the far right is Ruth Wodak, *The Politics of Fear: What Right-Wing Populist Discourses Mean* (Sage, 2015), which analyzes their discursive strategies. A broad-range analysis of far-right ideologies is provided by Gabriella Lazaridis, Giovanna Campani, and Annie Benveniste (eds.), *The Rise of the Far Right in Europe: Populist Shifts and "Othering"* (Palgrave Macmillan, 2016), while Sofia Vasilopoulou, *Far Right Parties and Euroskepticism: Patterns of Opposition* (Rowman & Littlefield, 2018), is the definitive study on far-right Euroscepticism. For the US, George Hawley, *Right-Wing Critics of American Conservatism* (Kansas University Press, 2016), is an encyclopedic intellectual history of the US radical right, while Mark Sedgwick (ed.), *Key Thinkers of the Radical Right: Behind the New Threat to Liberal Democracy* (Oxford University Press, 2019), highlights some of the key thinkers of the historical and contemporary far right.

The key texts on the **organization** of radical right parties are David Art, *Inside the Radical Right: The Development of Anti-Immigrant Parties in Western Europe* (Cambridge University Press, 2011), and Reinhard Heinisch and Oscar Mazzoleni (eds.),

Understanding Populist Party Organization: The Radical Right in Western Europe (Palgrave Macmillan, 2016). Duncan McDonnell and Annika Werner, *International Populism: The Radical Right in the European Parliament* (Hurst, 2019), analyzes the complex collaborations of far-right parties in the European Parliament, while Martin Durham and Margaret Power, *New Perspectives on the Transnational Right* (Palgrave, 2010), discusses a broad range of collaborations between European and North American far-right groups since the early twentieth century. The key book on CasaPound Italy is Caterina Froio, Pietro Castelli Gattinara, Giorgia Bulli, and Matteo Albanese, *The Hybrid Politics of CasaPound Italia* (Routledge, 2019).

Bert Klandersmans and Nonna Mayer (eds.), *Extreme Right Activists in Europe: Through the Magnifying Glass* (Routledge, 2009), provides great insights into the key **people** in West European far-right groups.

Most studies of far-right **mobilization** focus exclusively on (West) European **political parties**. The classic study is Hans-Georg Betz, *Radical Right-Wing Populism in Western Europe* (Macmillan, 2004). On far-right **movements**, see Donatella della Porta, Manuela Caiani, and Claudius Wagemann (eds.), *Mobilizing on the Extreme Right: Germany, Italy and the United States* (Oxford University Press, 2012), and Lawrence Rosenthal and Christine Trost (eds.), *Steep: The Precipitous Rise of the Tea Party* (University of California Press, 2012). Outside of Europe and the US, Naoto Higuchi, *Japan's Ultra-Right* (Trans Pacific Press, 2014), and Christophe Jalffrelot (ed.), *The Sangh Parivar: A Reader* (Oxford University Press, 2005), cover Japan and India, respectively. Max Taylor, P.M. Currie, and Donald Holbrook (eds.), *Extreme Right-Wing Political Violence and Terrorism* (Bloomsbury, 2013), provides a comprehensive overview of far-right *political violence and terrorism* in Europe and the US, while

José Pedro Zúquete, *The Identitarians: The Movement Against Globalism and Islam in Europe* (University of Notre Dame Press, 2018), is the definitive book on the Identitarian movement.

With regard to *subcultures*, George Hawley, *Making Sense of the Alt-Right* (Columbia University Press, 2017), Gary Armstrong, *Football Hooligans: Knowing the Score* (Berg, 2003), and Kevin Borgeson and Robin Valeri, *Skinhead History, Identity and Culture* (Routledge, 2017), are key texts on the "alt-right," hooligans, and skinheads, respectively. Cynthia Miller-Idriss, *The Extreme Gone Mainstream: Commercialization and Far Right Youth Culture in Germany* (Princeton University Press, 2017), is excellent on the importance of fashion in the mainstreaming of far-right culture, while Kirsten Dyck, *Reichsrock: The International Web of White-Power and Neo-Nazi Hate Music* (Rutgers University Press, 2017), covers the importance of white power music.

The key theories of the **causes** of the rise of radical right parties are concisely discussed and presented, within the British context, in Robert Ford and Matthew Goodwin, *Revolt on the Right: Explaining Support for the Radical Right in Britain* (Routledge, 2014). Other important theories are advanced in Mabel Berezin, *Illiberal Politics in Neoliberal Times: Culture, Security and Populism in the New Europe* (Cambridge University Press, 2009), and Jens Rydgren (ed.), *Class Politics and the Radical Right* (Routledge, 2013). For the US, the books by Kathleen Belew, *Bring the War Home: The White Power Movement and Paramilitary America* (Harvard University Press, 2018), and Christopher S. Parker and Matt A. Barreto, *Change They Can Believe In: The Tea Party and Reactionary Politics in America* (Princeton University Press, 2013), provide original explanations. On the role of the media, see Antonis A. Ellinas, *The Media and the Far Right in Western Europe:*

Playing the Nationalist Card (Cambridge University Press, 2010), and Nicole Hemmer, *Messengers of the Right: Conservative Media and the Transformation of American Politics* (University of Pennsylvania Press, 2016).

The study of the **consequences** of the far right is relatively recent. Some studies focus exclusively on specific policy effects of radical right parties, notably with regard to immigration, such as João Carvalho, *Impact of Extreme Right Parties on Immigration Policy: Comparing Britain, France and Italy* (Routledge, 2014). Other studies focus on the mainstreaming of European radical right parties, most notably Tjitske Akkerman, Sarah L. de Lange, and Matthijs Rooduijn (eds.), *Radical Right-Wing Populist Parties in Europe: Into the Mainstream?* (Routledge, 2015), as well as their impact on party systems, like Steven Wolinetz and Andrej Zaslove (eds.), *Absorbing the Blow: Populist Parties and Their Impact on Parties and Party Systems* (ECPR Press, 2018). Specifically on Eastern Europe, see Michael Minkenberg (ed.), *Transforming the Transformation? The East European Radical Right in the Political Process* (Routledge, 2015).

There are a growing number of studies of the **responses** to far-right politics, including William Downs, *Political Extremism in Democracies: Combating Intolerance* (Palgrave Macmillan, 2012), Erich Bleich, *The Freedom To Be Racist? How the United States and Europe Struggle to Preserve Freedom and Combat Racism* (Oxford University Press, 2011), and Bertelmans Stiftung (ed.), *Strategies for Combating Right-Wing Extremism in Europe* (Bertelmans Stiftung, 2010). An older text is Roger Eatwell and Cas Mudde (eds.), *Western Democracies and the New Extreme Right Challenge* (Routledge, 2003).

On the importance of **gender** within far-right groups, see the classic study by Kathleen Blee, *Inside Organized*

Racism: Women in the Hate Movement (University of California Press, 2002), and the more recent edited volume by Cynthia Miller-Idriss and Hillary Pilkington (eds.), *Gender and the Radical and Extreme Right: Mechanisms of Transmission and the Role of Educational Interventions* (Routledge, 2019), which also addresses the issue of sexuality. Finally, Michael Kimmel, *Healing from Hate: How Young Men Get Into – and Out of – Violent Extremism* (University of California Press, 2018), focuses specifically on masculinity.

For the best **journalistic accounts** of the far right, read Sasha Polakow-Suransky, *Go Back to Where You Came From: The Backlash Against Immigration and the Fate of Western Democracy* (Nation Books, 2017), and (the somewhat dated) Nick Ryan, *Homeland: Into a World of Hate* (Mainstream, 2003). Among the tsunami of new books on the US contemporary radical right, David Niewert, *Alt-America: The Rise of the Radical Right in the Age of Trump* (Verso, 2018), stands out for its depth and scope.

Some interesting **autobiographies** of former far-right activists include Christian Picciolini, *White American Youth: My Descent into America's Most Violent Hate Movement – and How I Got Out* (Hachette, 2017), Frank Meeink and Jody M. Roy, *Autobiography of a Recovering Skinhead* (Hawthorne, 2010), and Ingo Hasselbach, *Führer-Ex: Memoirs of a Former Neo-Nazi* (Random House, 1996).

Finally, there are several **academic and non-governmental organizations** that provide up-to-date information on far-right events, groups, and individuals, including:

Anti-Defamation League (ADL): *www.adl.org*
Center for Research on Extremism (C-REX): *www. sv.uio.no/c-rex/english*
Center for Right-Wing Studies (CRWS): *crws.berkeley. edu*

Hope not Hate (HnH): *www.hopenothate.org.uk*
Political Research Associates: *www.politicalresearch.
org*
Southern Poverty Law Center (SPLC): *www.splcenter.
org*

Index

Abhinav Bharat 91
Åkesson, Jimmie 72–3, 154
Alliance for Peace and
    Freedom (APF) 66
Alliance of Young
    Democrats–Hungarian
    Civic Alliance (Fidesz)
    21–3, 38, 40–1, 67–8,
    79, 83, 115–16, 125–8,
    135, 164; *see also* Orbán,
    Viktor
Alternative for Germany
    (AfD) 75, 79, 110, 118,
    134, 136, 146, 153–4
"alt-right" 60–1, 78, 111,
    141, 151, 158, 160
Alves, Damares 157
ambivalent sexism 151, 172
American Independent Party
    see Wallace, George
anti-fascism 142, 145
antisemitism 28
Austrian Freedom Party
    (FPÖ) 3, 5, 17, 21–2, 42,
    47–8, 67–8, 74, 79, 83–4,
    104–5, 111, 125, 137–8,
    146, 171
authoritarianism 28–30

Azov Battalion 87, 92

Baudet, Thiery 27, 85, 150
benevolent sexism 149–50,
    160
Bennett, Naftali 74
Berlusconi, Silvio 137
"black bloc" 142; *see also*
    anti-fascism
Bloc Against Islam (Czech
    Republic) 88
Bolsonaro, Jair 23
    background 72
    foreign policy 41
    government 116
    homophobia 153, 157
    immigration 33
    media 109
    rallies 88
    religion 42
    security 35
Brexit 125
Brexit Party 23, 67–8

Cameron, David 122
CasaPound Italy (CPI) 68, 111
Center Democrats
    (Netherlands) 77

Center Party (Netherlands) 2, 17, 98
cordon sanitaire 134, 140, 144
corruption 36–8
Croatian Party of Rights 17
cultural backlash 101

Daily Express 109
Danish People's Party (DF) 22, 42, 67, 75, 117, 154, 168
Department of Homeland Security 132

economic anxiety 101
English Defence League (EDL) 58, 66, 75, 87, 141, 153, 155
Estonian Conservative People's Party (EKRE) 27, 41
ethnocracy 28, 115
ethnopluralism 27
Euronat 67
Europe of Nations and Freedom (ENF) 67
European Alliance for Freedom (EAF) 67
European Social Movement (ESM) 13–14
European Union (EU) 39–41
extreme right 7, 30–1, 106–7, 119–20

familialism 148, 172
far right 7
    paramilitary groups/militias 91–3
    terrorism 36, 82, 89, 90–1, 132–3, 143
Farage, Nigel 68
Fascism 25–6, 41, 104, 107

feminism 151
femonationalism 152, 172–3
First Amendment of the US Constitution 130
Flemish Bloc (VB) 17, 41, 55, 115, 134, 143
Flemish Interest (VB) *see* Flemish Bloc (VB)
Fortuyn, Pim 75
Forum for Democracy (FvD) *see* Baudet, Thiery
"Fourteen Words" 149
Fox News 108–9, 112

globalization 101–2
Golden Dawn (XA) 21, 66–7, 72, 89, 102, 135, 164, 175
Great Recession 20
Greater Romania Party 17
Groenewald, Petrus 74
Group of the European Right 66–7

Haider, Jörg 105
Hanson, Pauline 20, 75, 160
Hindutva 23, 44, 50, 88, 93, 115; *see also* Indian People's Party (BJP); National Volunteer Organization (RSS)
Hofer, Norbert 74, 84
homonationalism 153
homophobia 152–3, 157
homosexuality 153
hooliganism 62–3
hostile sexism 150, 158

Identitarian movement 54, 86, 94–6, 111
immigration 31–3
Indian People's Party (BJP) 2, 20, 23, 30, 33, 37,

44, 50–1, 74, 83, 93, 115–16, 123, 164, 169, 178; *see also* Modi, Narendra
irredentism 38
Islam 45
Islamophobia 28, 33, 36, 42, 47, 52, 54, 56, 58, 63, 66, 75, 87, 95, 109, 115, 123, 135, 152–3, 155, 173
issue ownership 110
issue salience 121
Italian Social Movement (MSI) 13–14, 17, 66

Japan Conference (Nippon Kaigi) 58

Kach party *see* Kahanism
Kahanism 19, 45, 89–90
Kast, Antonio 74
Kjærsgaard, Pia 75
Ku Klux Klan (KKK) 16, 42, 46, 56–7
Kühnen, Michael 75

Law and Justice (PiS) 21–2, 40–2, 55, 83, 87, 115, 12, 153, 156
Le Pen, Jean-Marie 15, 67, 71–2, 84
Le Pen, Marine 36, 40, 41, 67, 74–5, 84, 152, 162
League/Northern League (LN) 5, 18, 22, 37, 47–8, 67–8, 73, 77, 91, 111, 137, 148; *see also* Salvini, Matteo
left 6–7
liberal democracy 30, 114, 143, 146, 168, 177–9
Likud 23, 74, 84, 116

Maréchal-Le Pen, Marion 15, 55
Merkel, Angela 39, 104, 110, 122, 136
Michaloliakos, Nikolaos 72
misogyny 150
Modi, Narendra 23, 30, 35, 41, 74
Movement for a Better Hungary (Jobbik) 23, 92, 116, 128, 135, 154
Mutual Aid Association of Former Waffen-SS Soldiers 12

National Action 91
National Democratic Party of Germany (NPD) 15–16, 131–2, 135
National European Social Movement (Netherlands) 13
National Front (FN – France) 17, 37, 41, 55, 66, 79, 115, 140, 171; *see also* Le Pen, Jean-Marie; Le Pen, Marine; Maréchal-Le Pen, Marion
National Front (NF – UK) 16, 63
National Policy Institute 54, 60
National Rally (RN) *see* National Front (FN)
National Socialist Underground 91, 156
National Union Attack 22
National Volunteer Organization (RSS) 23, 44, 74, 93, 140
Nationalist Action Party (MHP) 45, 89
nativism 27–8

Nazism 26
Nemzeti Rock 59
Netanyahu, Benjamin *see* Likud
Netto Uyoku 77–8
Nordic Resistance Movement (NMR) 65–6, 86
"normal pathology thesis" 106
nouvelle droite 27, 43, 53–4

Okamura, Tomio 76
One Nation Party (Australia) *see* Hanson, Pauline
Operational Forces Action 91
Orbán, Viktor 32, 40, 57, 122, 124, 126–8, 156–7

Palin, Sarah 160
Party for Freedom (PVV) 22, 35, 51–2, 79; *see also* Wilders, Geert
pathological normalcy 107
Patriotic Europeans Against the Islamization of the Occident (PEGIDA) 58, 66, 87, 141–2
People's Party – Our Slovakia (L'SNS) 21, 66, 88, 103
populism 7–8, 30, 36
populist radical right 7, 30–1, 106–8, 120
Poujadism 14–15
Progress Party (Denmark) 15
Progress Party (Norway) 15
Proud Boys 76, 86
Putin, Vladimir 41, 68

racism 26–7
radical right *see* populist radical right
"refugee crisis" 4, 20, 87–8, 122, 167

Reich Citizens' Movement 93
religion 41–5
right 6–7
Republican Party (United States) 19–20, 116
The Republicans (Germany) 17
Research and Study Group for European Civilization (GRECE) 54–5

Saint-Martin Fund 12
Salvini, Matteo 5, 47, 67, 73, 111
Sarkozy, Nicolas 122
September 11, 2001, 9/11 terrorist attacks 20, 34, 82, 132
skinheads 63–4, 105, 108, 162
Skokie Affair 130–1
Slovak National Party (SNS) 17
social media 110-2
Socialist Reich Party (SRP) 13, 131
Soros, George 32, 161
sovereign citizens 93, 146
Spencer, Richard 54, 60, 111, 145, 154
Strache, Heinz-Christian 111
Stuart Donaldson, Ian 63–4
Sweden Democrats (SD) 17, 42
Swiss People's Party (SVP) 17, 21–2, 35, 77, 79, 83, 85, 154, 164

Tea Party 23
toxic masculinity 150
Trump, Donald 23
  background 72
  corruption 37

crime 34, 35
demonstrations 88–9
electorate 78, 79, 101
foreign policy 38, 41,
  125–6
government 123, 124
media 109, 111–12
radical right 61, 68

United Kingdom
  Independence Party
  (UKIP) 23, 36, 153
United Nations (UN) 38–9
Uyoku dantai 59

Van Grieken, Tom 72–3, 154,
  173

Vox 40, 41, 174

Wall Street Journal 109
Wallace, George 16
wehrhafte Demokratie
  (militant democracy) 131
Weidel, Alice 75, 153
welfare chauvinism 101
Wilders, Geert 35, 40, 51–2,
  111
Willkommenspolitik
  ("Welcome Politics")
  122

Zaitokukai 58–9, 88
Zeman, Miloš 88
Zhirinovsky, Vladimir 39